Kirby Manga Mania

VOLUME 5

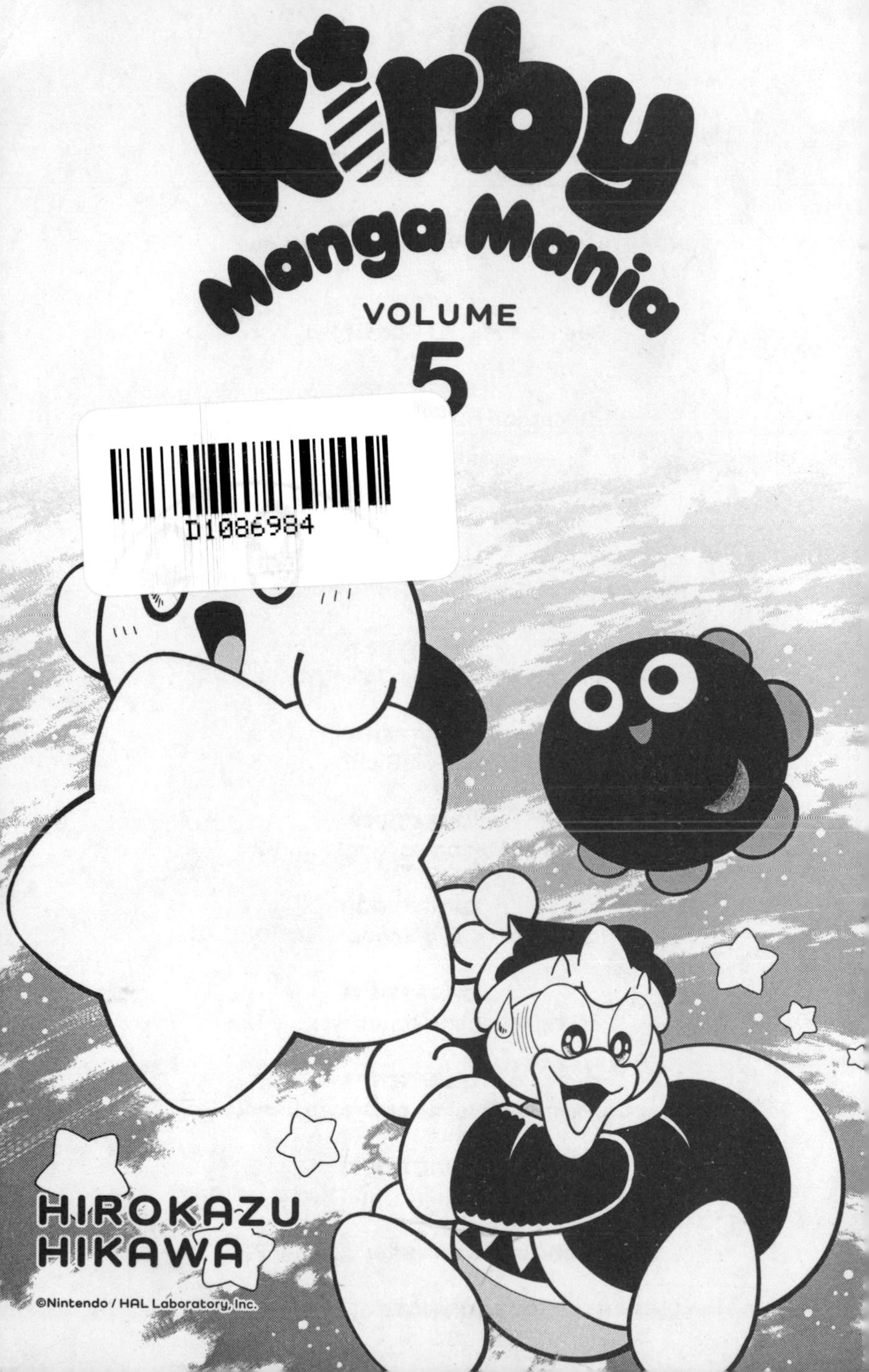

HIROKAZU HIKAWA

CONTENTS

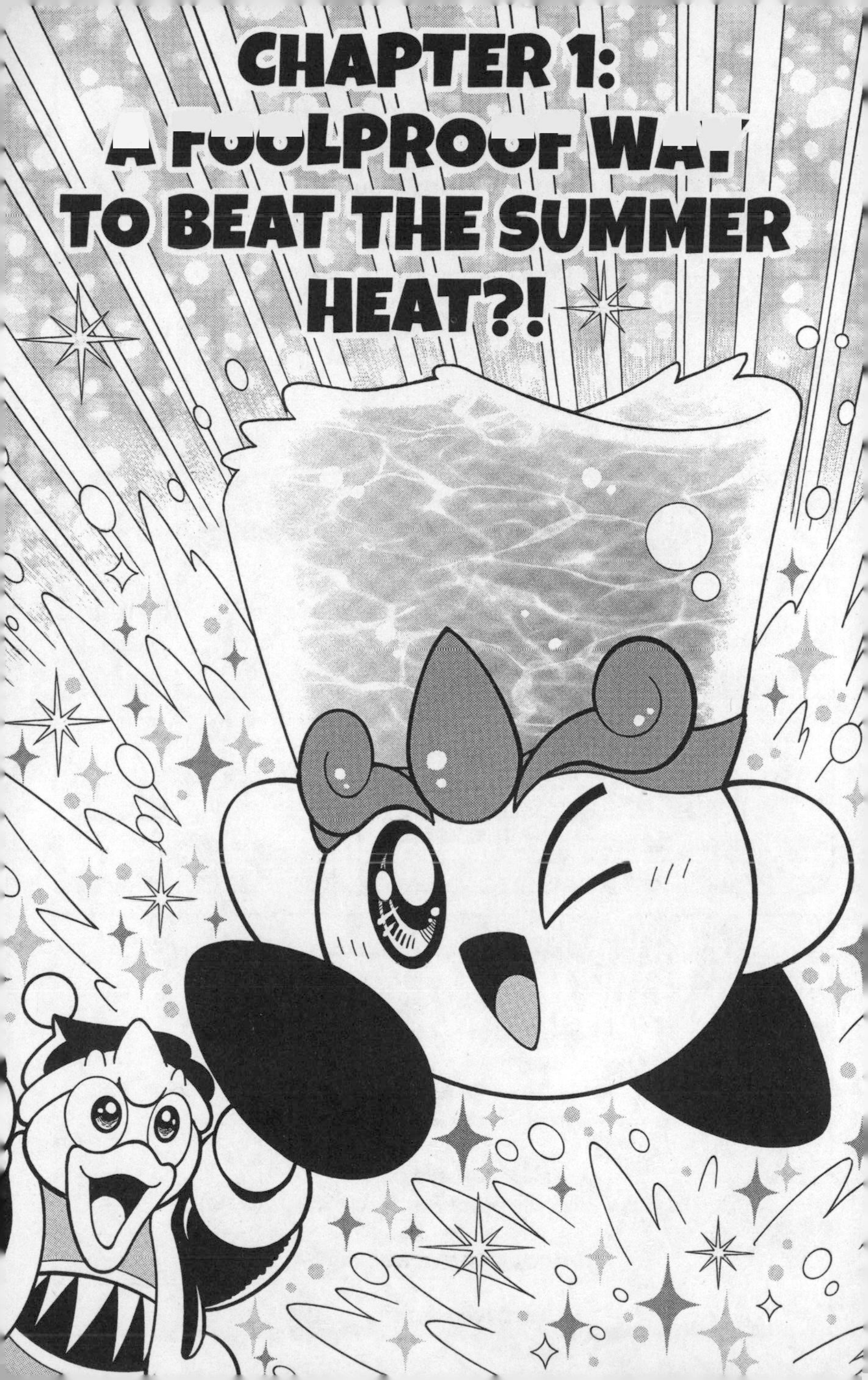
CHAPTER 1:
A FOOLPROOF WAY
TO BEAT THE SUMMER
HEAT?!

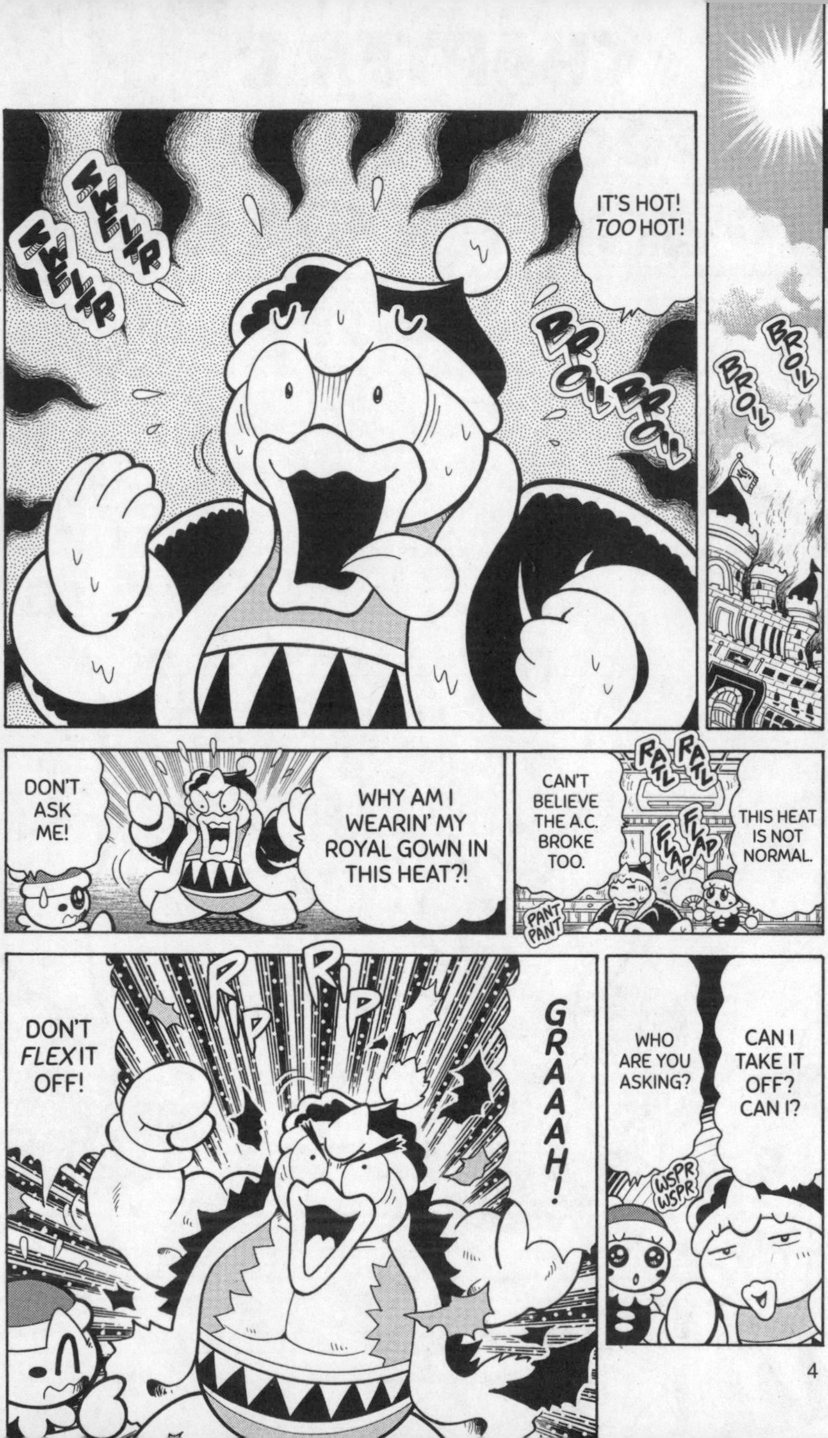
BROIL
BROIL
IT'S HOT! *TOO* HOT!
BROIL BROIL
SWELTR
SWELTR
THIS HEAT IS NOT NORMAL.
RATL RATL
CAN'T BELIEVE THE A.C. BROKE TOO.
FLAP FLAP
PANT PANT
WHY AM I WEARIN' MY ROYAL GOWN IN THIS HEAT?!
DON'T ASK ME!
CAN I TAKE IT OFF? CAN I?
WHO ARE YOU ASKING?
WSPR WSPR
GRAAAAH!
RIP RIP
DON'T *FLEX* IT OFF!

AUTHOR'S COMMENT

DRAWING WATER KIRBY FEELS GREAT! HE HAS A REALLY REFRESHING FEEL IN THE VIDEO GAMES TOO. BUT IT'S HARD TO DRAW WATER! I USED SCREENTONES TO TRY TO EVOKE IT BETTER.

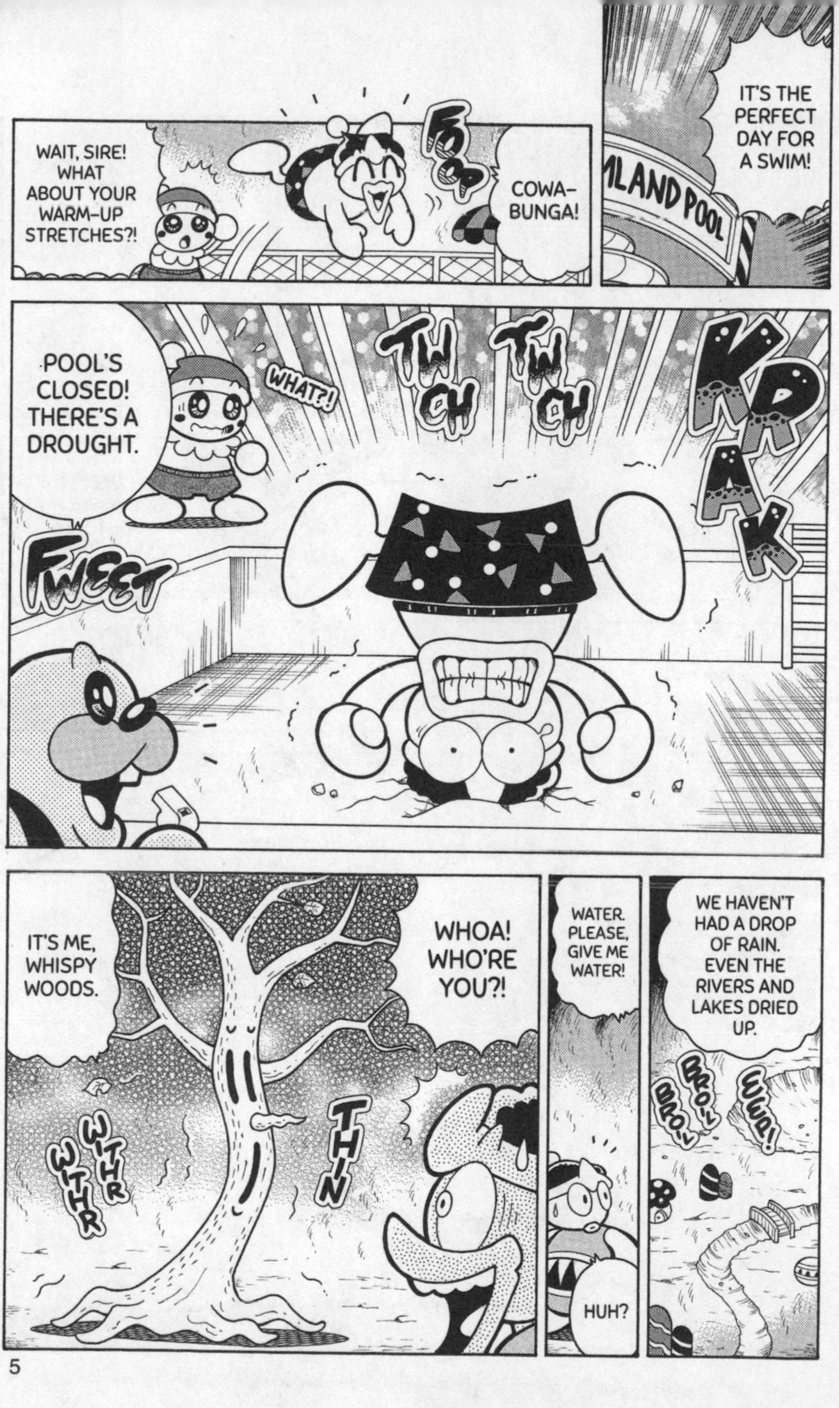
IT'S THE PERFECT DAY FOR A SWIM!
MLAND POOL
COWA-BUNGA!
FOOP
WAIT, SIRE! WHAT ABOUT YOUR WARM-UP STRETCHES?!
KRAK
TWITCH
TWITCH
WHAT?!
POOL'S CLOSED! THERE'S A DROUGHT.
FWEET
WE HAVEN'T HAD A DROP OF RAIN. EVEN THE RIVERS AND LAKES DRIED UP.
WATER. PLEASE, GIVE ME WATER!
HUH?
WHOA! WHO'RE YOU?!
THIN
IT'S ME, WHISPY WOODS.
WITHR
WITHR

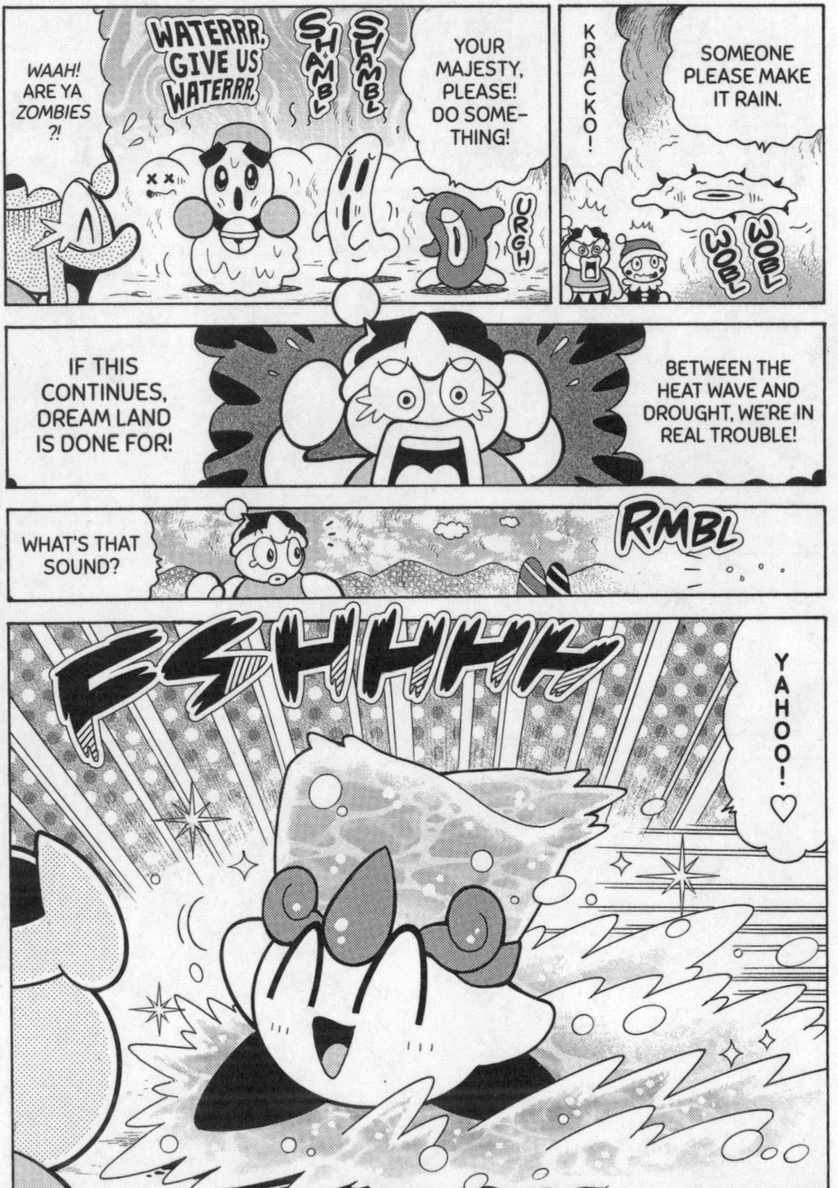
SOMEONE PLEASE MAKE IT RAIN.
KRACKO!
WOBL
WOBL
YOUR MAJESTY, PLEASE! DO SOME-THING!
SHAMBL
SHAMBL
WATERRR, GIVE US WATERRR,
WAAH! ARE YA ZOMBIES?!
URGH
BETWEEN THE HEAT WAVE AND DROUGHT, WE'RE IN REAL TROUBLE!
IF THIS CONTINUES, DREAM LAND IS DONE FOR!
RMBL
WHAT'S THAT SOUND?
YAHOO! ♡
FSHHHH

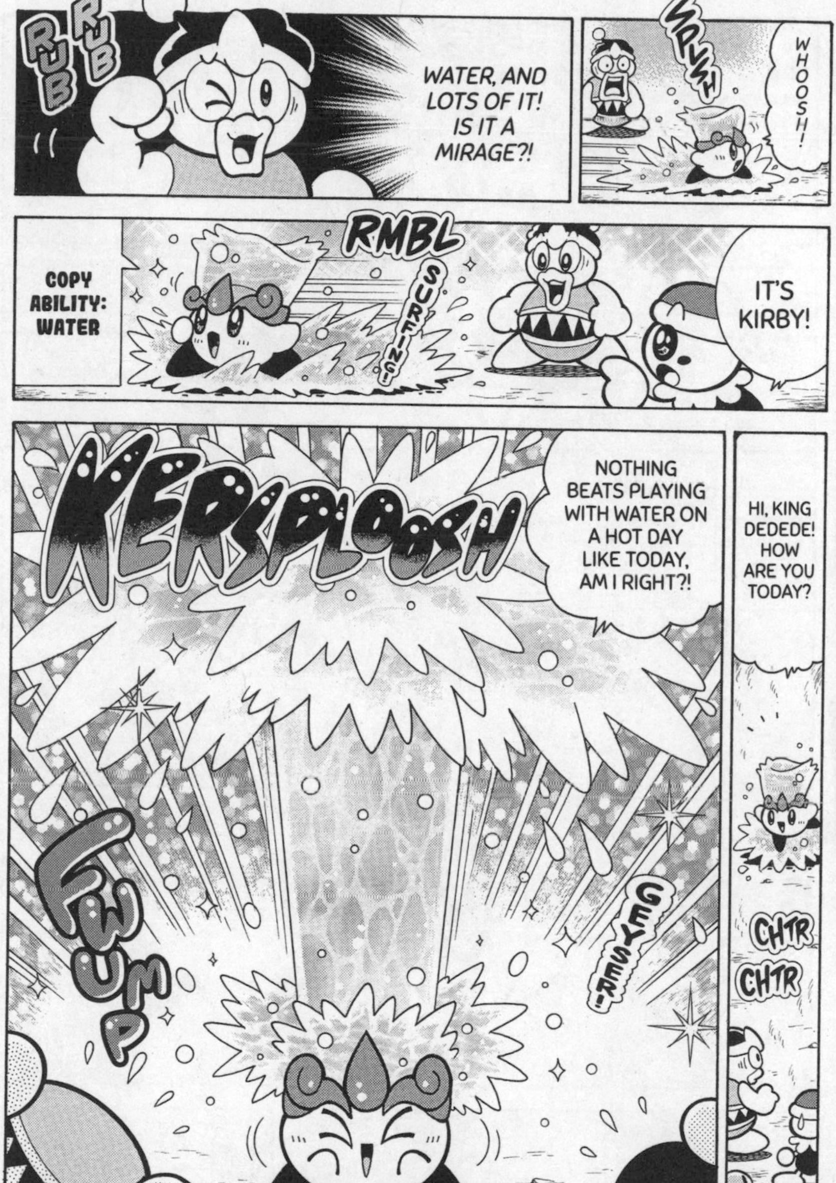
WHOOSH!
SPLASH
RUB RUB
WATER, AND LOTS OF IT! IS IT A MIRAGE?!
IT'S KIRBY!
RMBL
SURFING!
COPY ABILITY: WATER
HI, KING DEDEDE! HOW ARE YOU TODAY?
CHTR CHTR
NOTHING BEATS PLAYING WITH WATER ON A HOT DAY LIKE TODAY, AM I RIGHT?!
KERSPLOOSH
GEYSER!
FWUMP

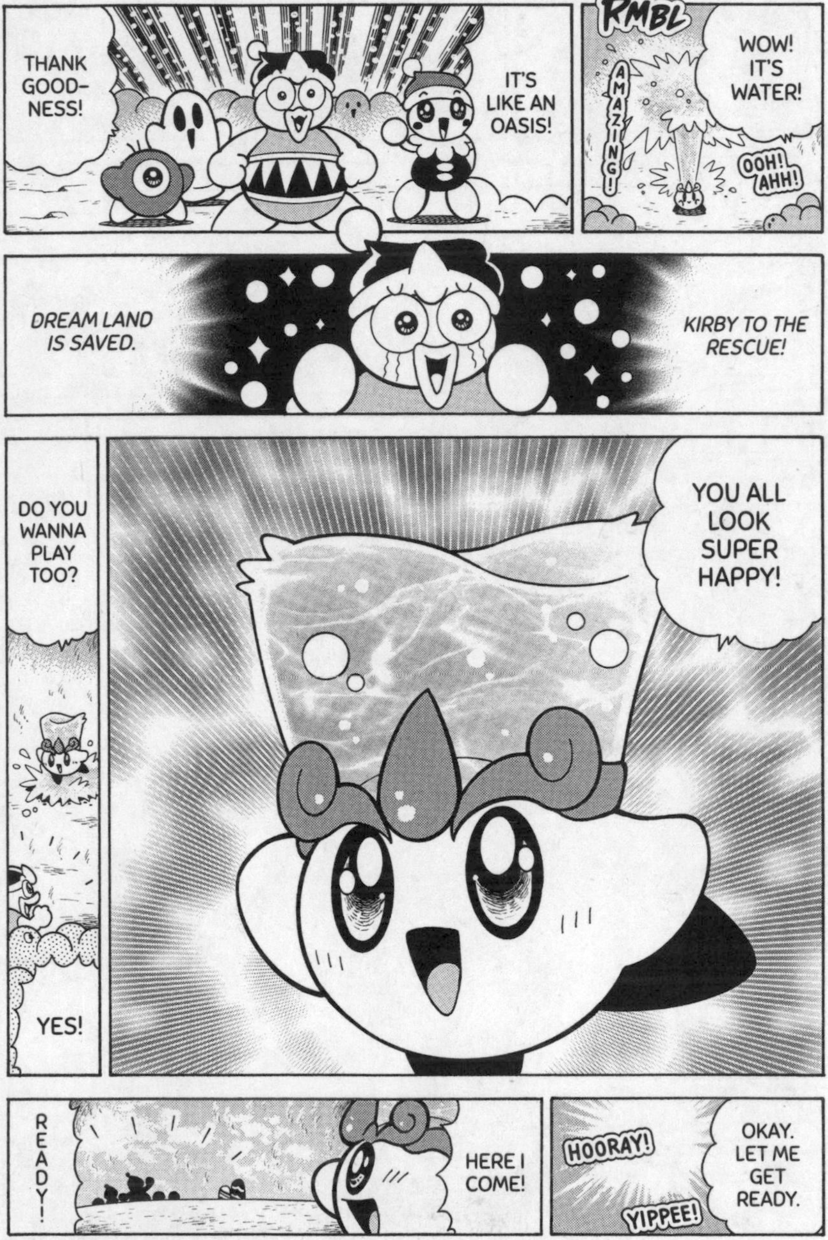
RMBL
WOW! IT'S WATER!
AMAZING!
OOH! AHH!
IT'S LIKE AN OASIS!
THANK GOODNESS!
KIRBY TO THE RESCUE!
DREAM LAND IS SAVED.
YOU ALL LOOK SUPER HAPPY!
DO YOU WANNA PLAY TOO?
YES!
OKAY. LET ME GET READY.
HOORAY!
YIPPEE!
HERE I COME!
READY!

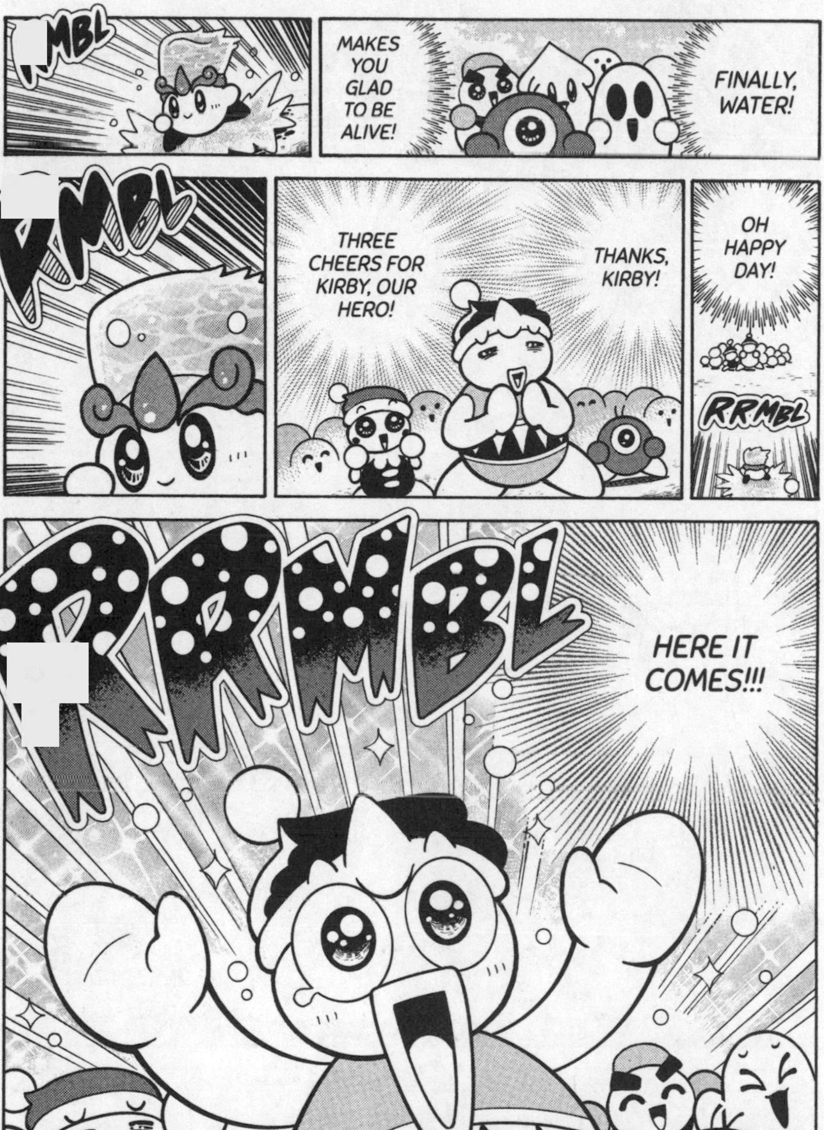
FINALLY, WATER!
MAKES YOU GLAD TO BE ALIVE!
OH HAPPY DAY!
RRMBL
THANKS, KIRBY!
THREE CHEERS FOR KIRBY, OUR HERO!
RRMBL
HERE IT COMES!!!

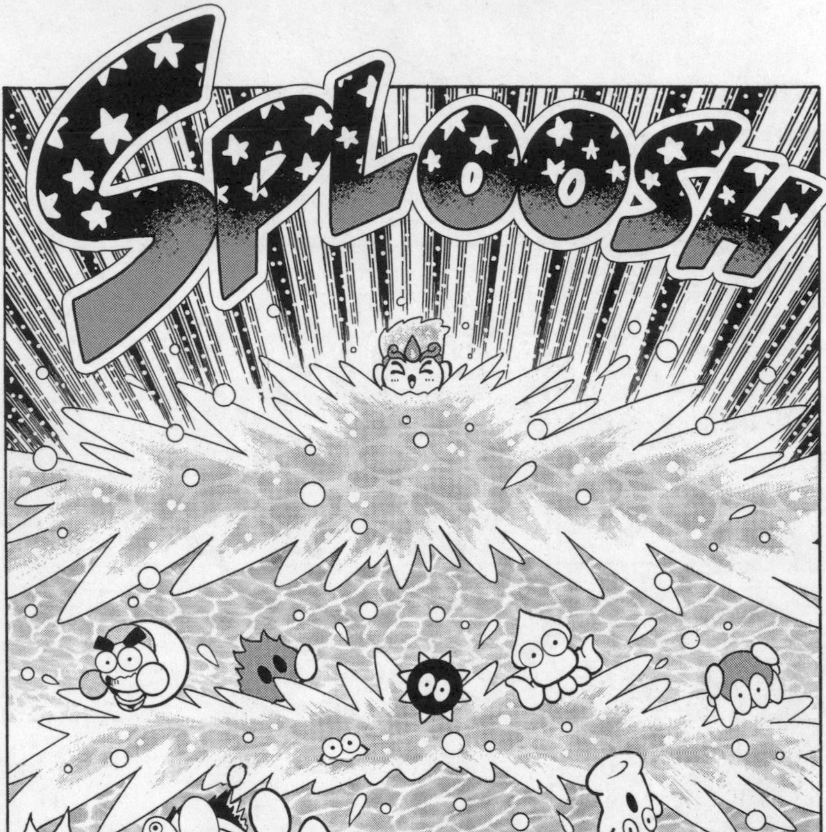
SPLOOSH!!
YER KIDDIN'!
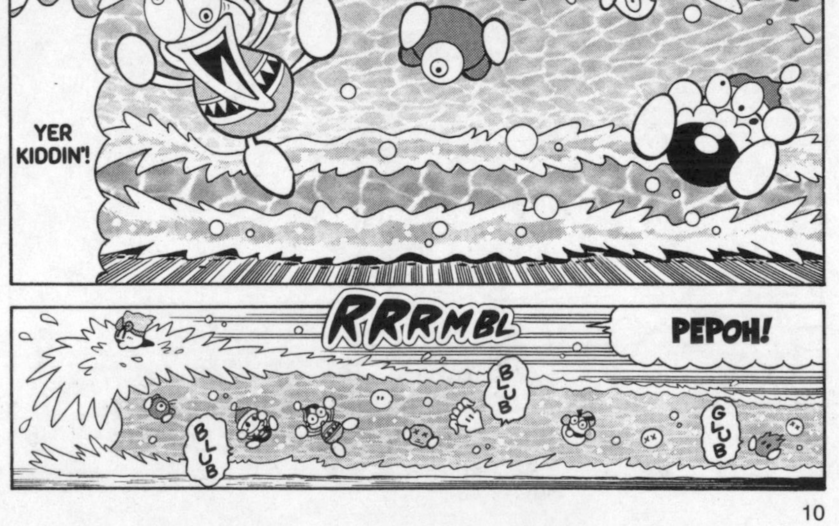
PEPOH!
RRRMBL
GLUB
BLUB
BLUB

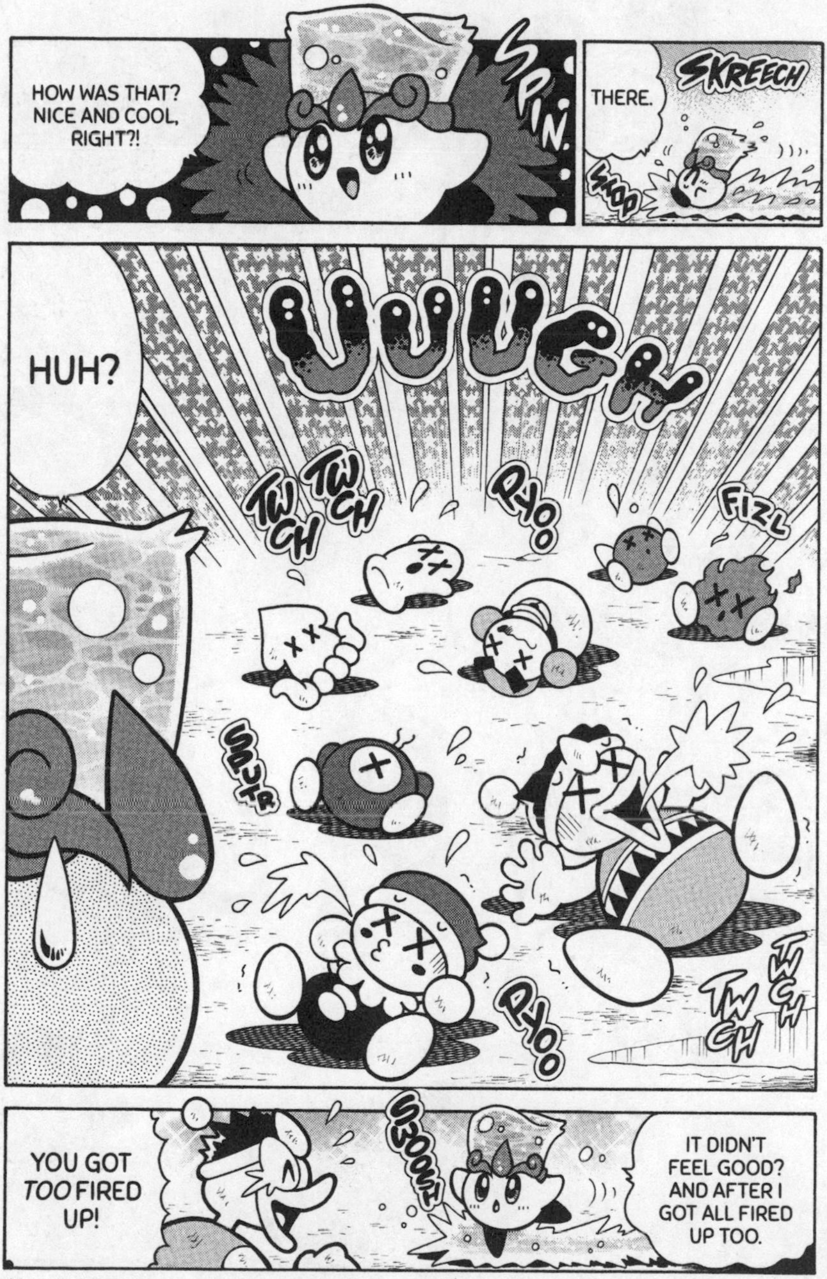
THERE.
SKREECH
SKID
SPIN
HOW WAS THAT? NICE AND COOL, RIGHT?!
UUUGH
HUH?
FIZL
P-YOO
TWCH TWCH
SPUTR
TWCH TWCH
P-YOO
IT DIDN'T FEEL GOOD? AND AFTER I GOT ALL FIRED UP TOO.
SWOOSH
YOU GOT *TOO* FIRED UP!

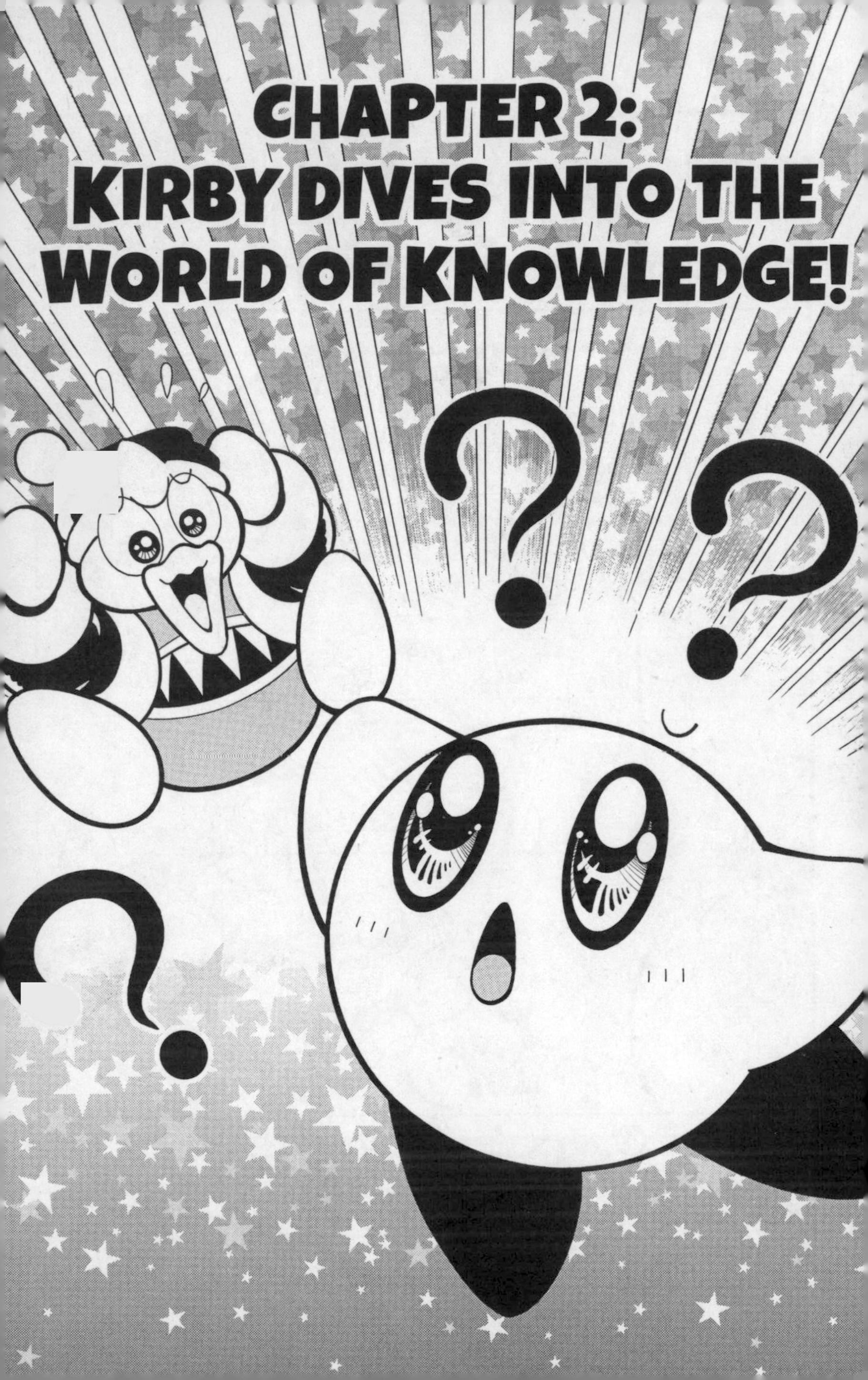
CHAPTER 2:
KIRBY DIVES INTO THE WORLD OF KNOWLEDGE!

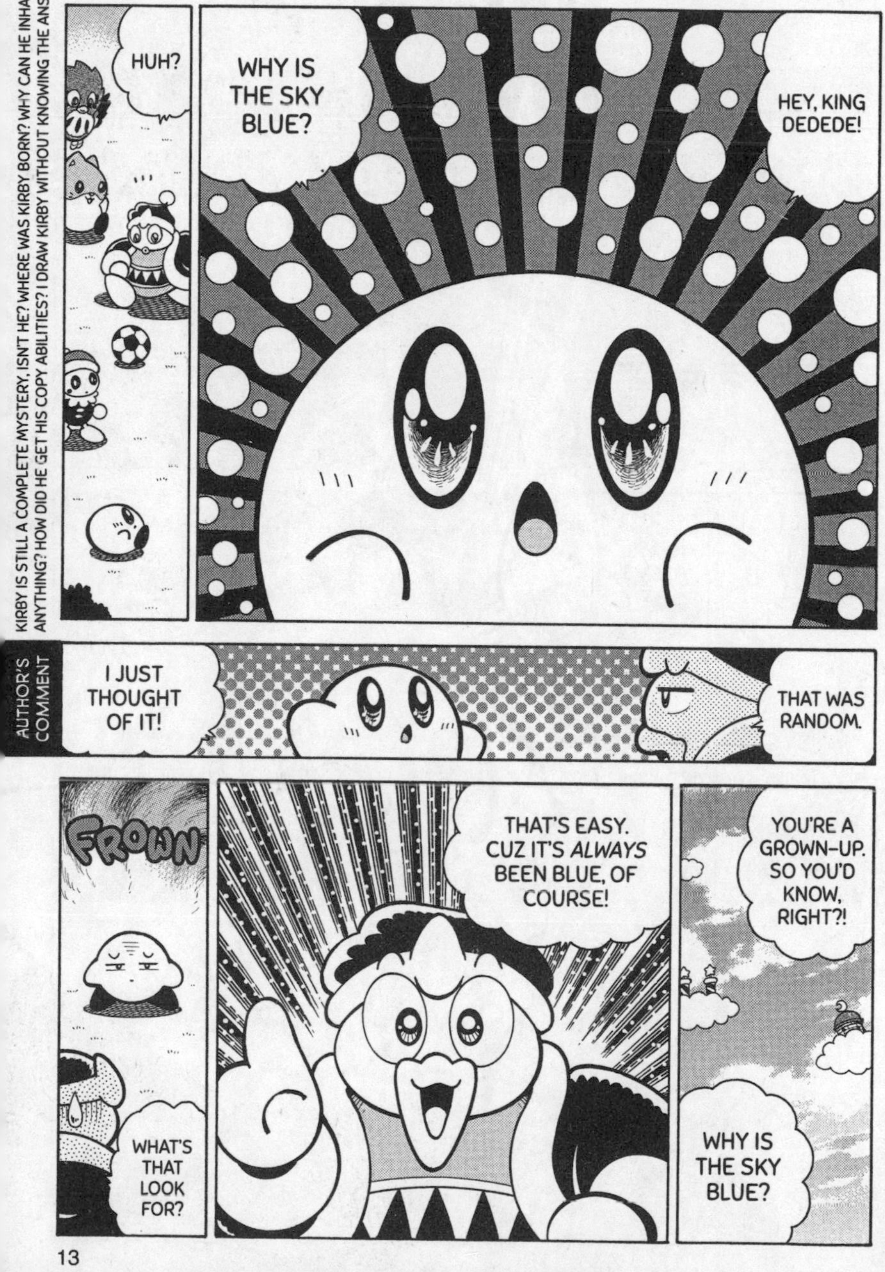
HEY, KING DEDEDE!
WHY IS THE SKY BLUE?
HUH?
THAT WAS RANDOM.
I JUST THOUGHT OF IT!
YOU'RE A GROWN-UP. SO YOU'D KNOW, RIGHT?!
WHY IS THE SKY BLUE?
THAT'S EASY. CUZ IT'S *ALWAYS* BEEN BLUE, OF COURSE!
FROWN
WHAT'S THAT LOOK FOR?

AUTHOR'S COMMENT

KIRBY IS STILL A COMPLETE MYSTERY, ISN'T HE? WHERE WAS KIRBY BORN? WHY CAN HE INHALE ANYTHING? HOW DID HE GET HIS COPY ABILITIES? I DRAW KIRBY WITHOUT KNOWING THE ANSWERS.

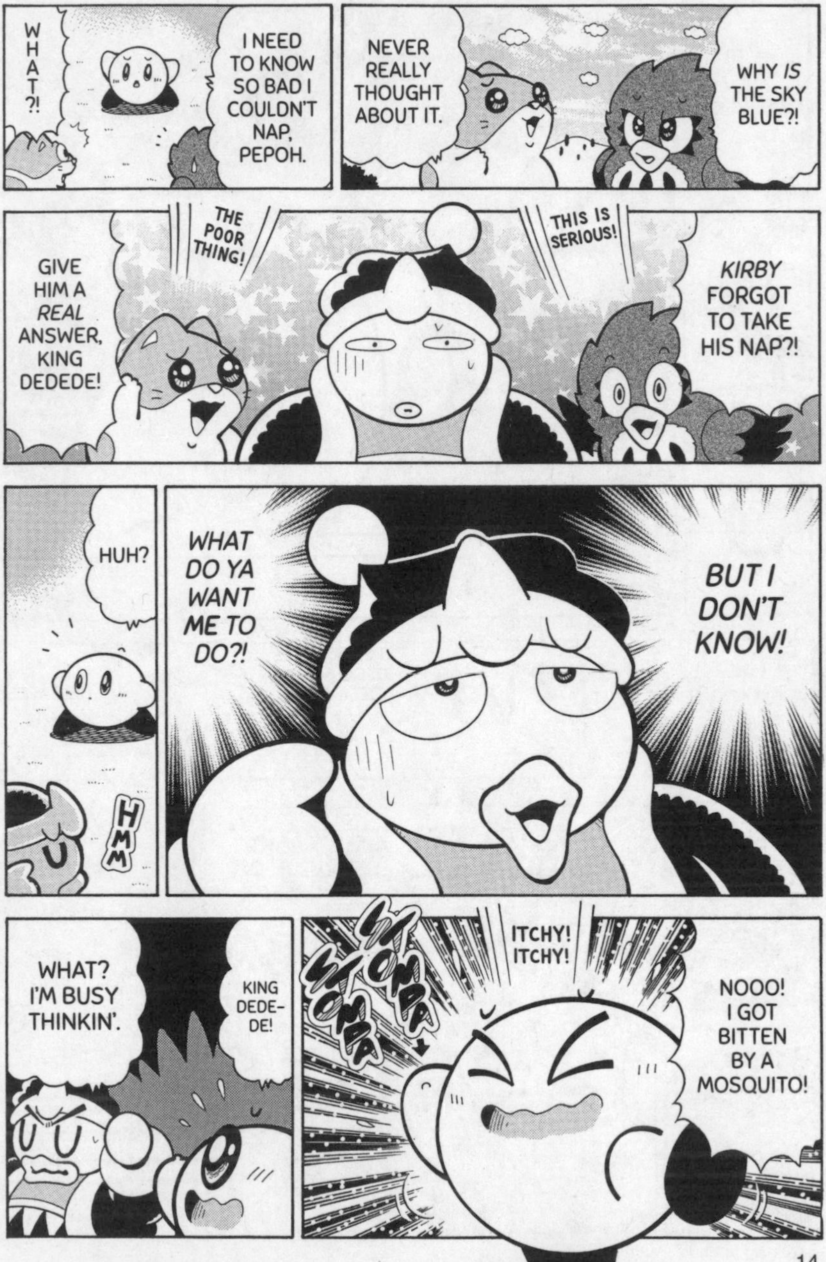
WHY IS THE SKY BLUE?!
NEVER REALLY THOUGHT ABOUT IT.
I NEED TO KNOW SO BAD I COULDN'T NAP, PEPOH.
WHAT?!
KIRBY FORGOT TO TAKE HIS NAP?!
THIS IS SERIOUS!
THE POOR THING!
GIVE HIM A REAL ANSWER, KING DEDEDE!
BUT I DON'T KNOW!
WHAT DO YA WANT ME TO DO?!
HUH?
HMM
NOOO! I GOT BITTEN BY A MOSQUITO!
ITCHY! ITCHY!
KING DEDE-DE!
WHAT? I'M BUSY THINKIN'.

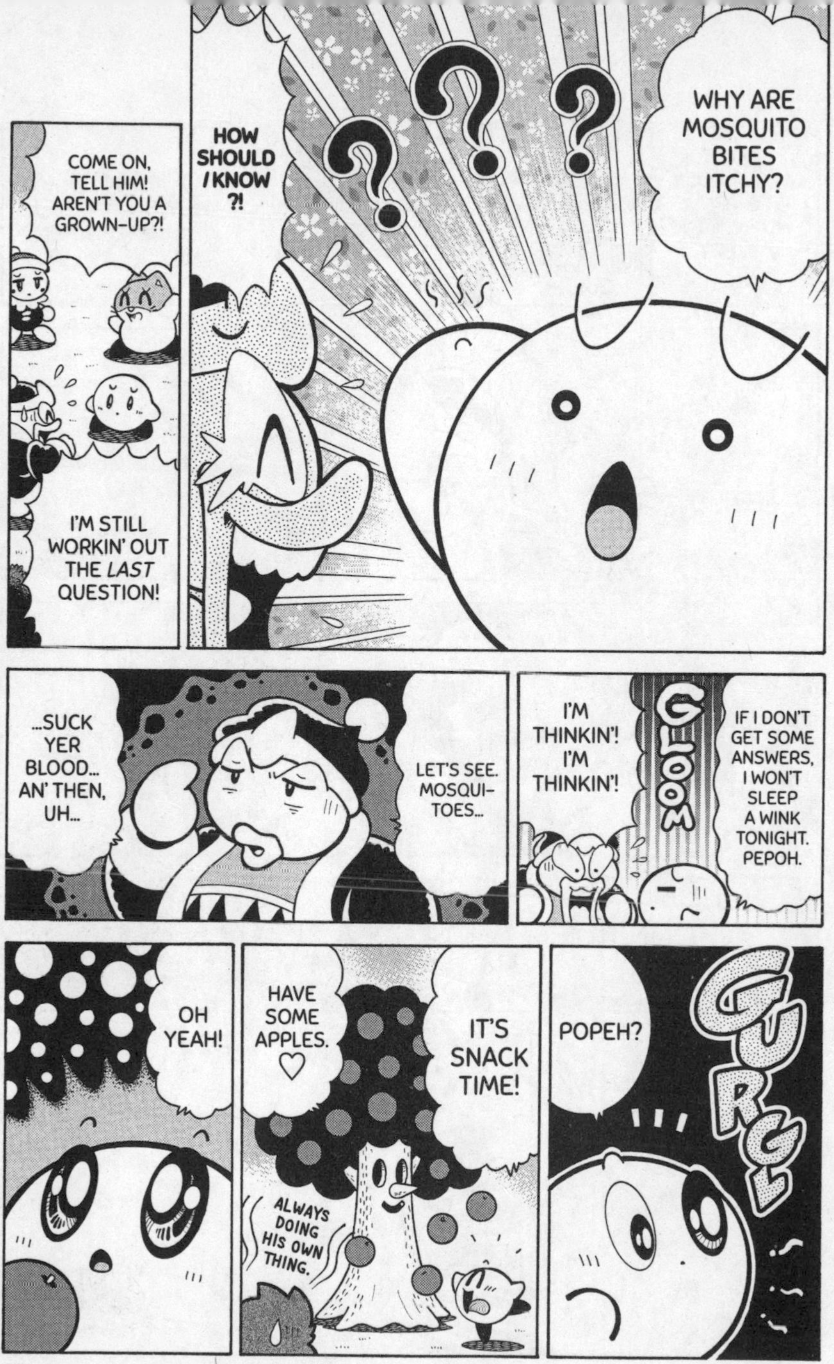
WHY ARE MOSQUITO BITES ITCHY?
HOW SHOULD I KNOW?!
COME ON, TELL HIM! AREN'T YOU A GROWN-UP?!
I'M STILL WORKIN' OUT THE *LAST* QUESTION!
IF I DON'T GET SOME ANSWERS, I WON'T SLEEP A WINK TONIGHT. PEPOH.
GLOOM
I'M THINKIN'! I'M THINKIN'!
LET'S SEE. MOSQUI-TOES...
...SUCK YER BLOOD... AN' THEN, UH...
GURGL
POPEH?
IT'S SNACK TIME!
HAVE SOME APPLES. ♡
ALWAYS DOING HIS OWN THING.
OH YEAH!

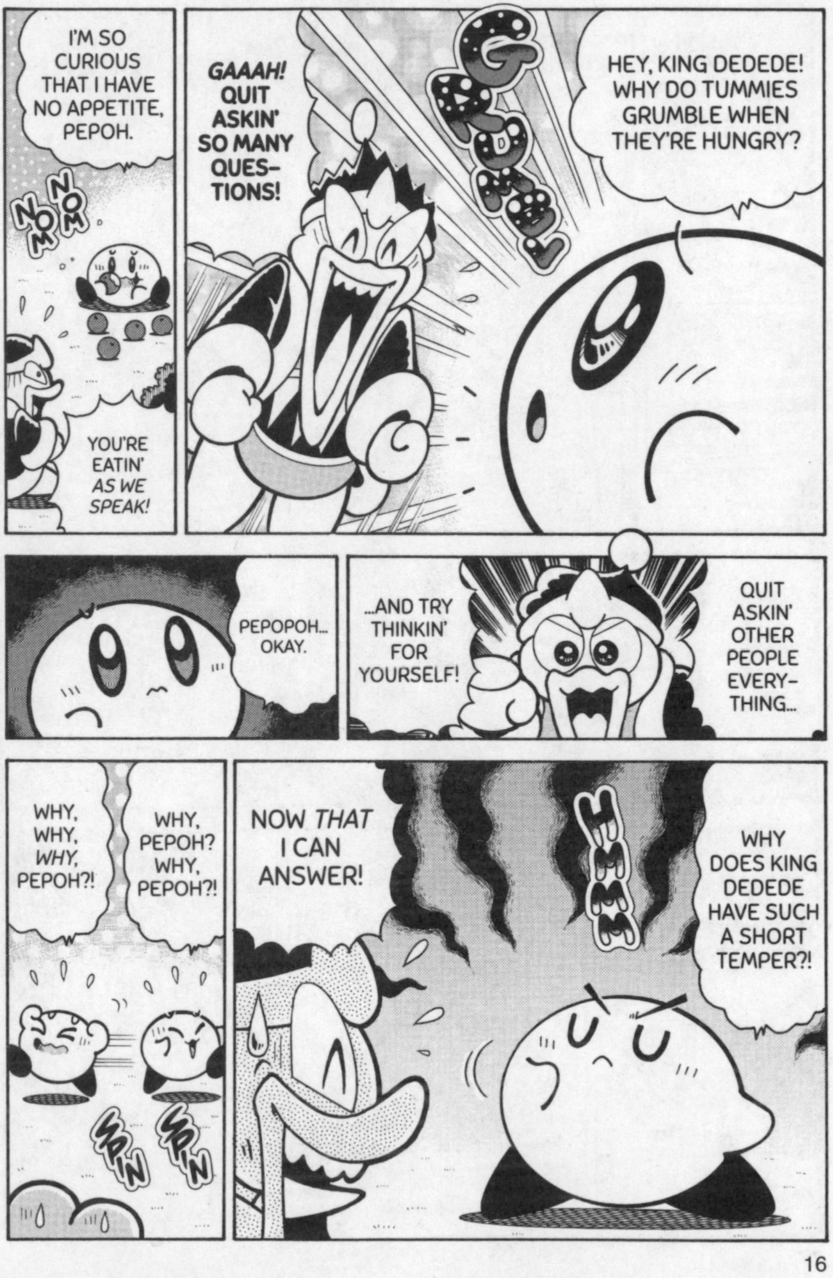
HEY, KING DEDEDE! WHY DO TUMMIES GRUMBLE WHEN THEY'RE HUNGRY?
GAAAH! QUIT ASKIN' SO MANY QUES-TIONS!
I'M SO CURIOUS THAT I HAVE NO APPETITE, PEPOH.
NOM NOM
YOU'RE EATIN' *AS WE SPEAK!*
QUIT ASKIN' OTHER PEOPLE EVERY-THING...
...AND TRY THINKIN' FOR YOURSELF!
PEPOPOH... OKAY.
WHY DOES KING DEDEDE HAVE SUCH A SHORT TEMPER?!
NOW *THAT* I CAN ANSWER!
WHY, PEPOH? WHY, PEPOH?!
WHY, WHY, *WHY,* PEPOH?!
SPIN
SPIN

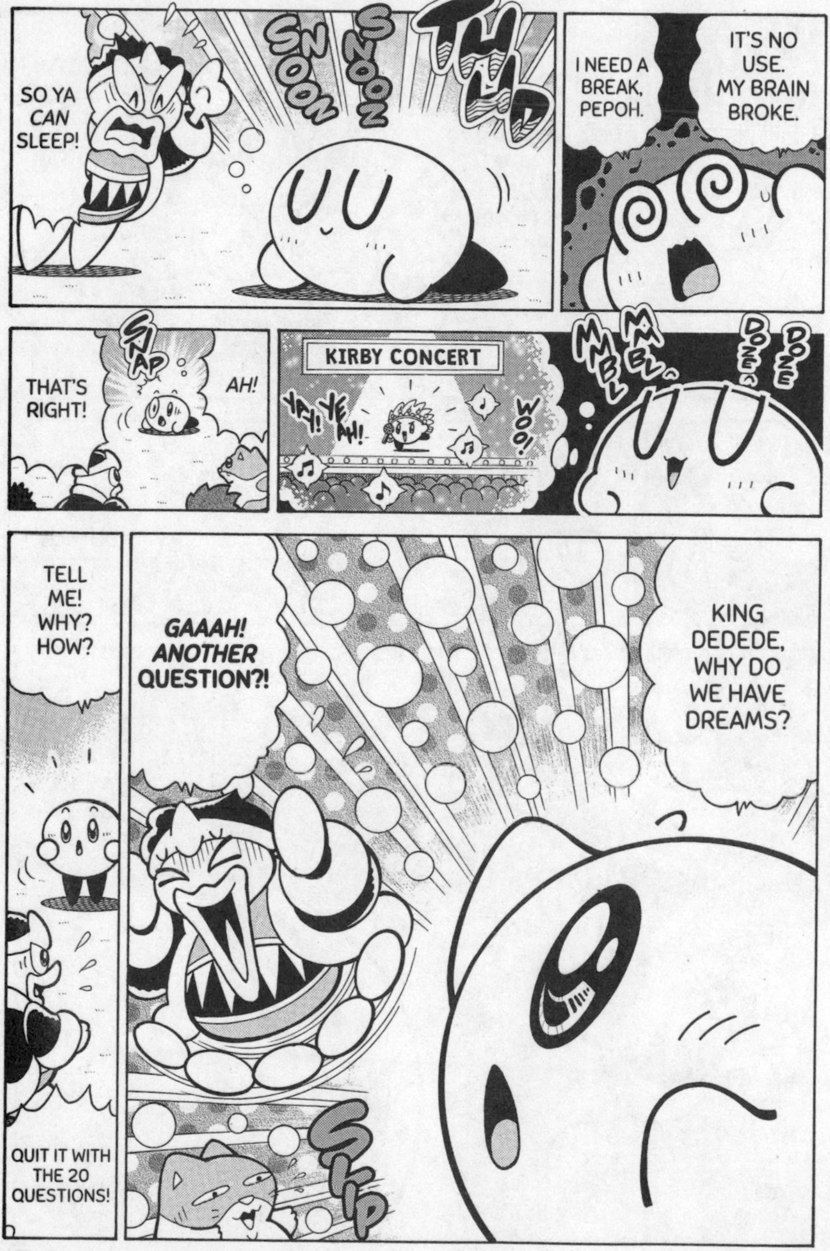
IT'S NO USE. MY BRAIN BROKE.
I NEED A BREAK, PEPOH.
THUD
SNOOZ
SNOOZ
SO YA *CAN* SLEEP!
DOZE
DOZE
MMBL
MMBL
KIRBY CONCERT
WOO!
YEAH!
YAY!
AH!
SNAP
THAT'S RIGHT!
KING DEDEDE, WHY DO WE HAVE DREAMS?
GAAAH! ANOTHER **QUESTION?!**
SKIP
TELL ME! WHY? HOW?
QUIT IT WITH THE 20 QUESTIONS!

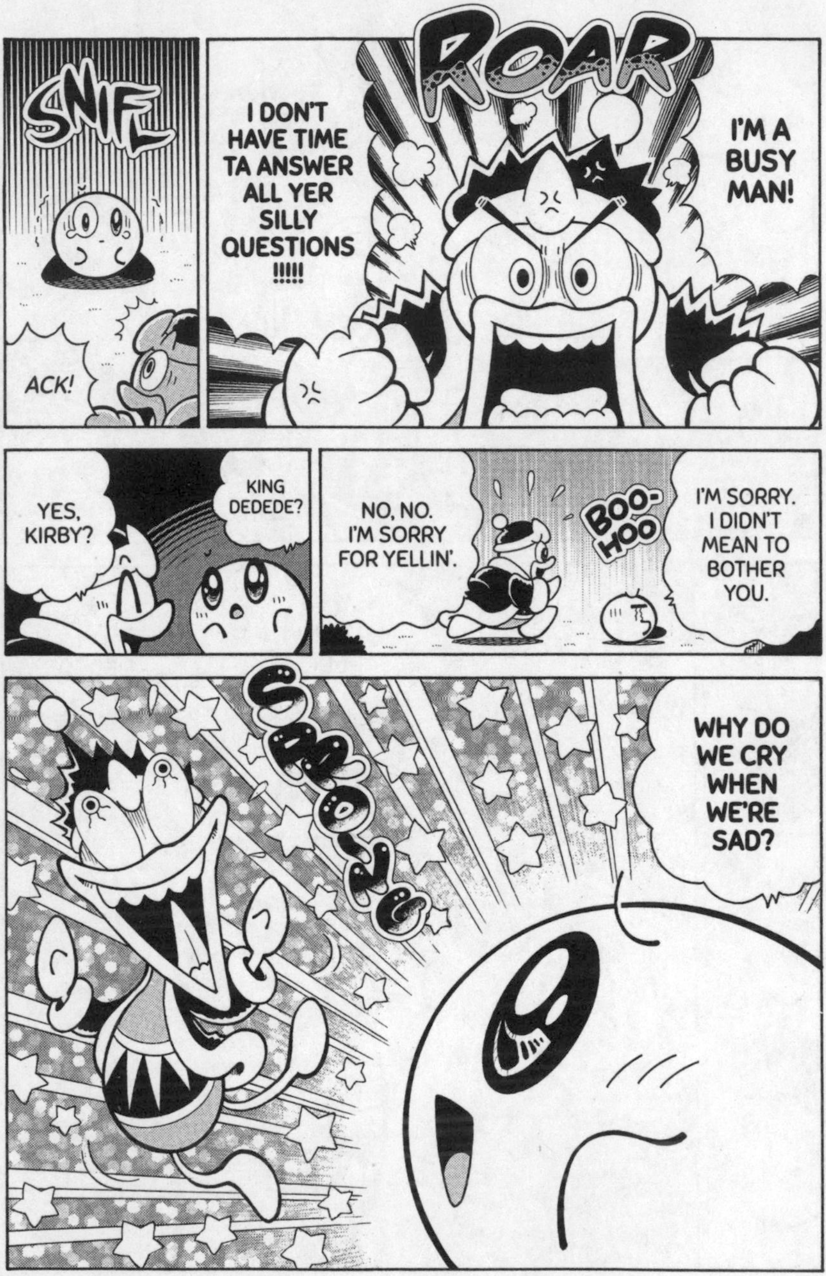
ROAR
I'M A BUSY MAN!
I DON'T HAVE TIME TA ANSWER ALL YER SILLY QUESTIONS !!!!!
SNIFL
ACK!
I'M SORRY. I DIDN'T MEAN TO BOTHER YOU.
BOO-HOO
NO, NO. I'M SORRY FOR YELLIN'.
KING DEDEDE?
YES, KIRBY?
WHY DO WE CRY WHEN WE'RE SAD?
SPROING

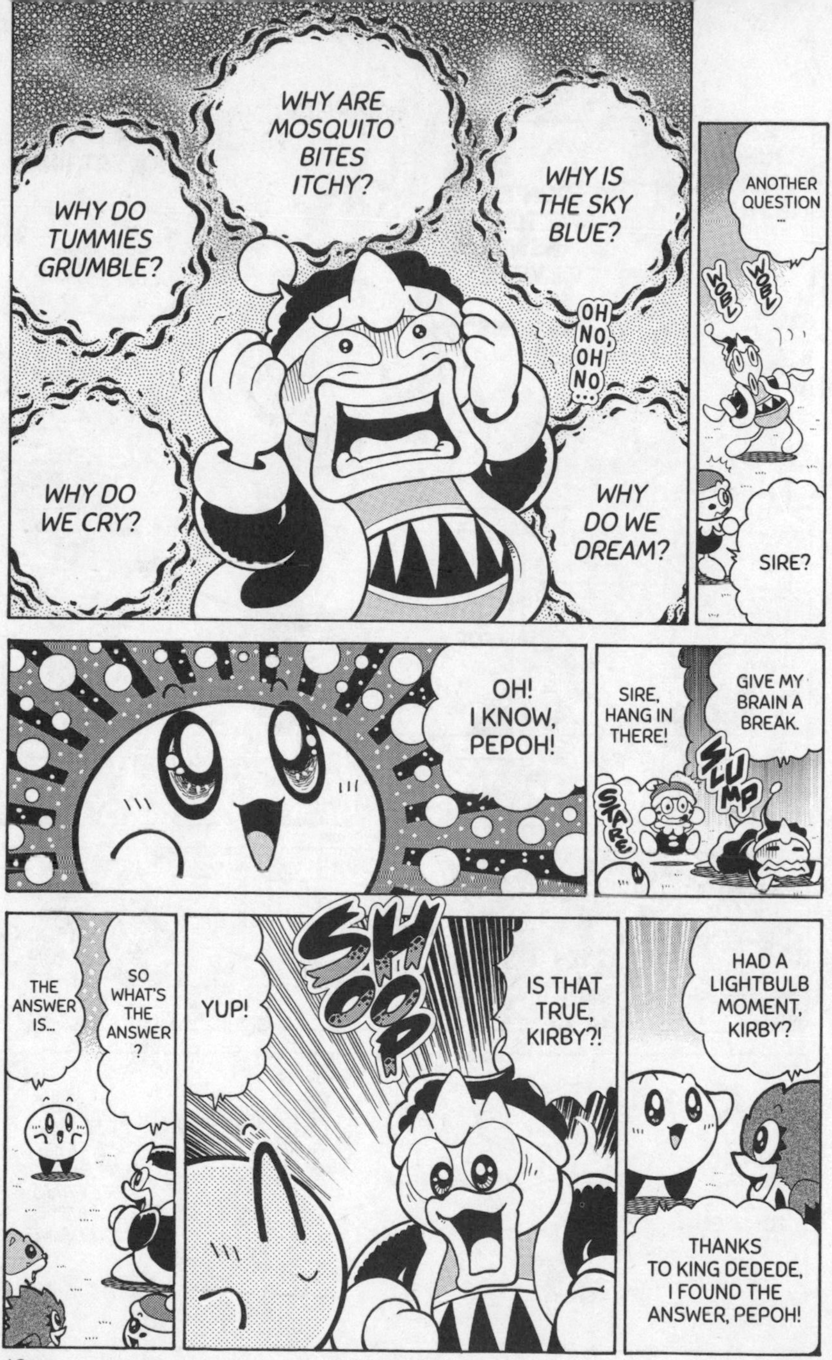

ANOTHER QUESTION ...
WOBL
WOBL
SIRE?
WHY ARE MOSQUITO BITES ITCHY?
WHY IS THE SKY BLUE?
WHY DO TUMMIES GRUMBLE?
OH NO, OH NO...
WHY DO WE DREAM?
WHY DO WE CRY?
GIVE MY BRAIN A BREAK.
SIRE, HANG IN THERE!
SLUMP
STARE
OH! I KNOW, PEPOH!
HAD A LIGHTBULB MOMENT, KIRBY?
THANKS TO KING DEDEDE, I FOUND THE ANSWER, PEPOH!
IS THAT TRUE, KIRBY?!
SWOOP
YUP!
SO WHAT'S THE ANSWER?
THE ANSWER IS...

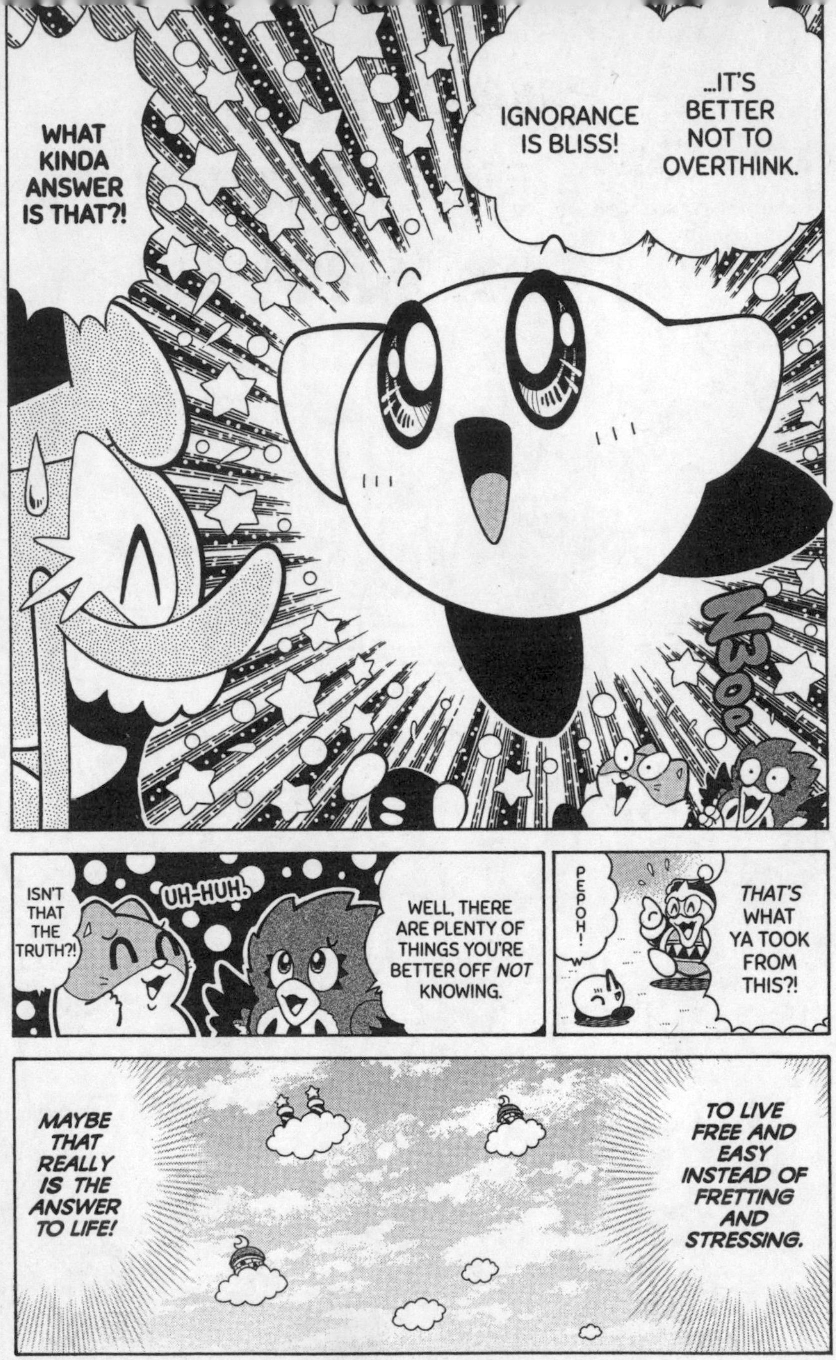
...IT'S BETTER NOT TO OVERTHINK.
IGNORANCE IS BLISS!
WHAT KINDA ANSWER IS THAT?!
THAT'S WHAT YA TOOK FROM THIS?!
PEPOH!
WELL, THERE ARE PLENTY OF THINGS YOU'RE BETTER OFF *NOT* KNOWING.
UH-HUH.
ISN'T THAT THE TRUTH?!
TO LIVE FREE AND EASY INSTEAD OF FRETTING AND STRESSING.
MAYBE THAT REALLY IS THE ANSWER TO LIFE!

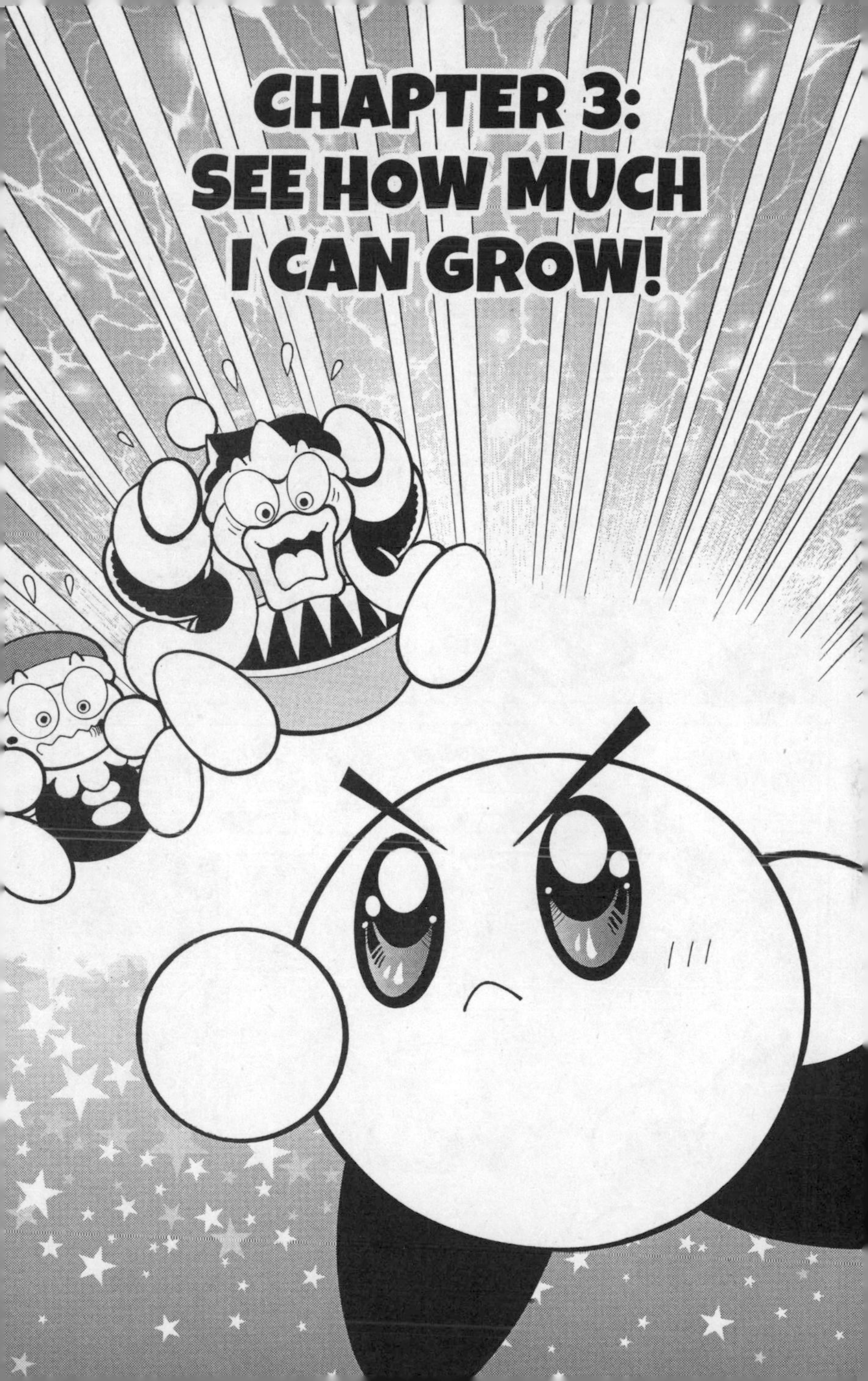
CHAPTER 3:
SEE HOW MUCH
I CAN GROW!

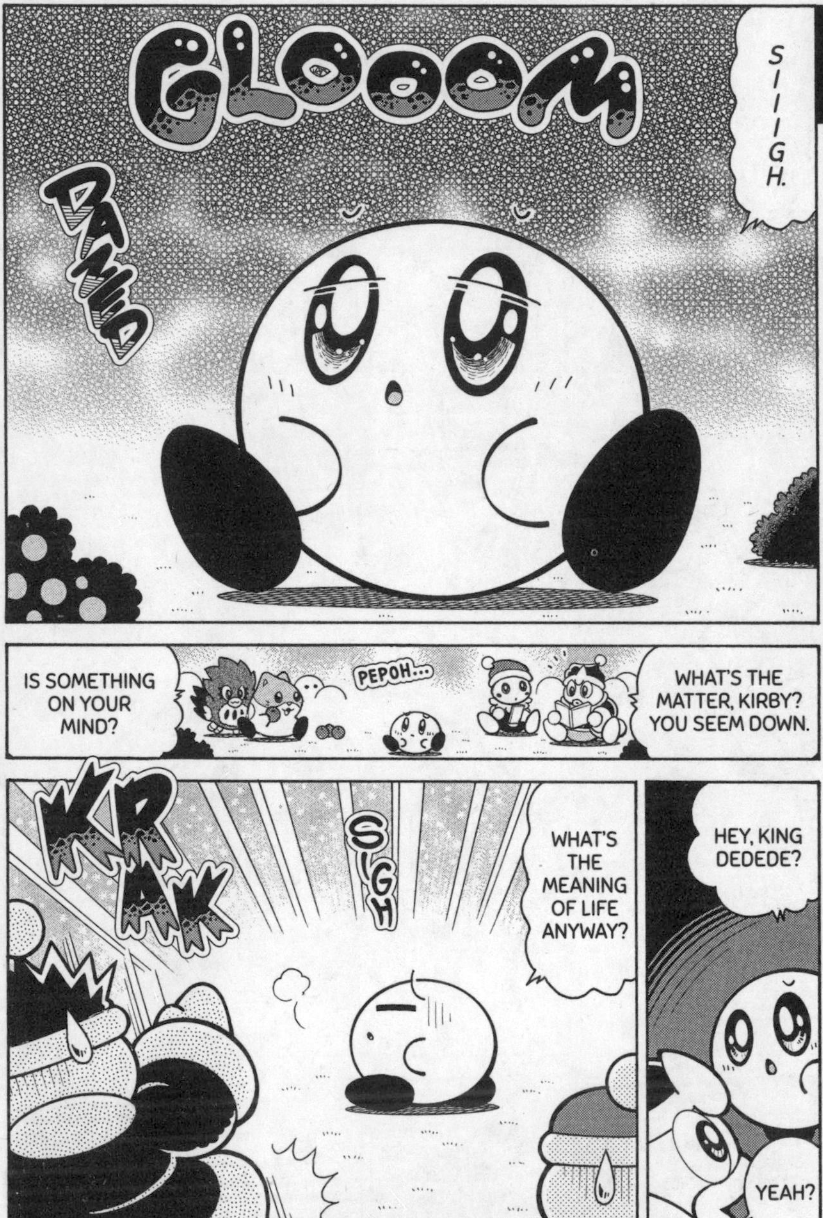
SIIIGH.
GLOOOM
DAMED
WHAT'S THE MATTER, KIRBY? YOU SEEM DOWN.
PEPOH...
IS SOMETHING ON YOUR MIND?
HEY, KING DEDEDE?
YEAH?
WHAT'S THE MEANING OF LIFE ANYWAY?
SIGH
KRAK

AUTHOR'S COMMENT

I'LL BE 55 THIS YEAR, BUT I HAVEN'T MATURED AT ALL. I PUT OFF THE THINGS I DON'T WANT TO DO. I RUN FROM UNPLEASANT THINGS. I'VE BECOME AN OVERGROWN BOY... OOPS.

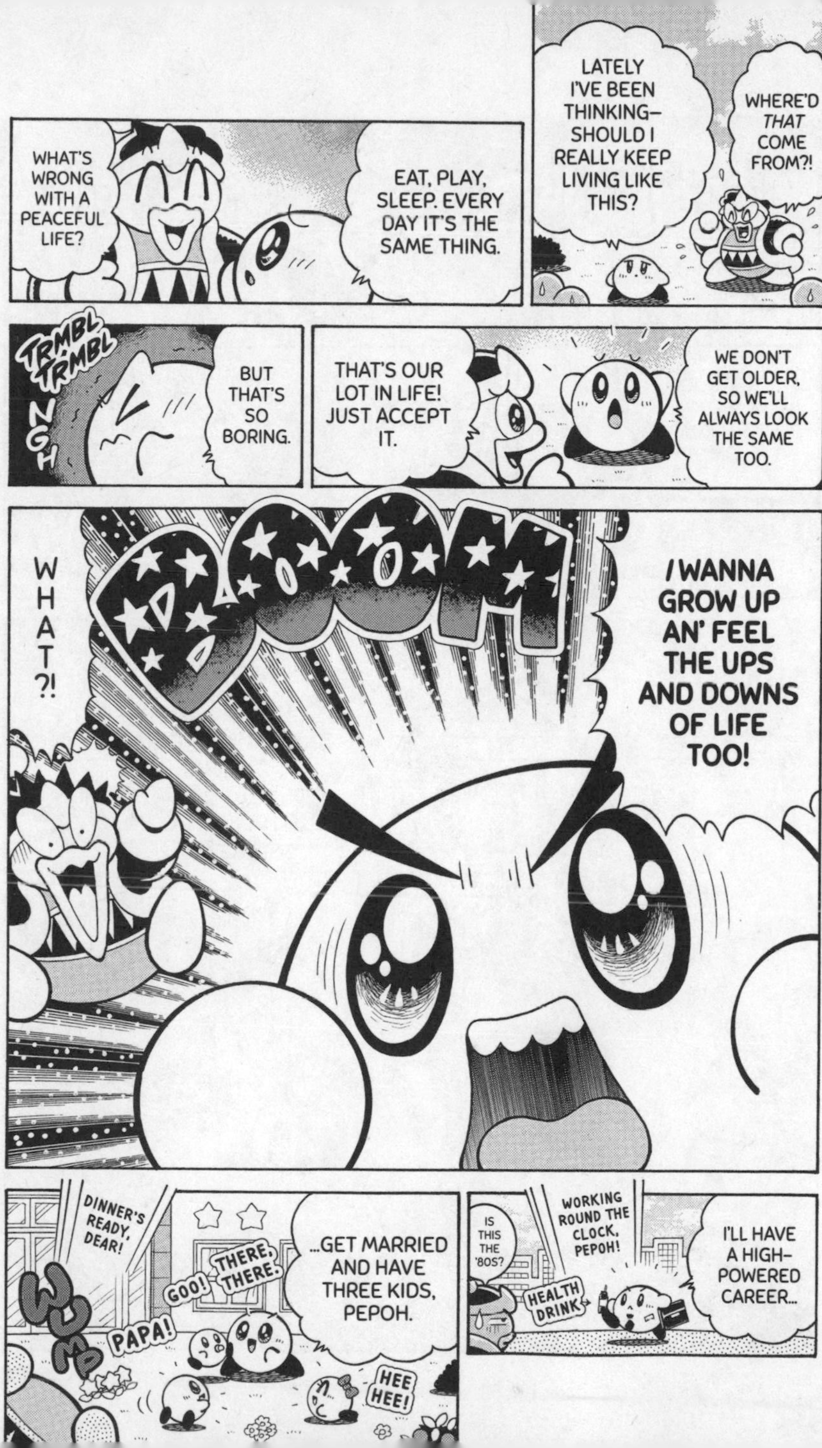

LATELY I'VE BEEN THINKING— SHOULD I REALLY KEEP LIVING LIKE THIS?
WHERE'D *THAT* COME FROM?!
EAT, PLAY, SLEEP. EVERY DAY IT'S THE SAME THING.
WHAT'S WRONG WITH A PEACEFUL LIFE?
WE DON'T GET OLDER, SO WE'LL ALWAYS LOOK THE SAME TOO.
THAT'S OUR LOT IN LIFE! JUST ACCEPT IT.
BUT THAT'S SO BORING.
TRMBL TRMBL
NGH
I WANNA GROW UP AN' FEEL THE UPS AND DOWNS OF LIFE TOO!
BOOM
WHAT?!
I'LL HAVE A HIGH-POWERED CAREER...
WORKING ROUND THE CLOCK, PEPOH!
IS THIS THE '80S?
HEALTH DRINK
...GET MARRIED AND HAVE THREE KIDS, PEPOH.
THERE, THERE.
GOO!
DINNER'S READY, DEAR!
PAPA!
WUMP
HEE HEE!

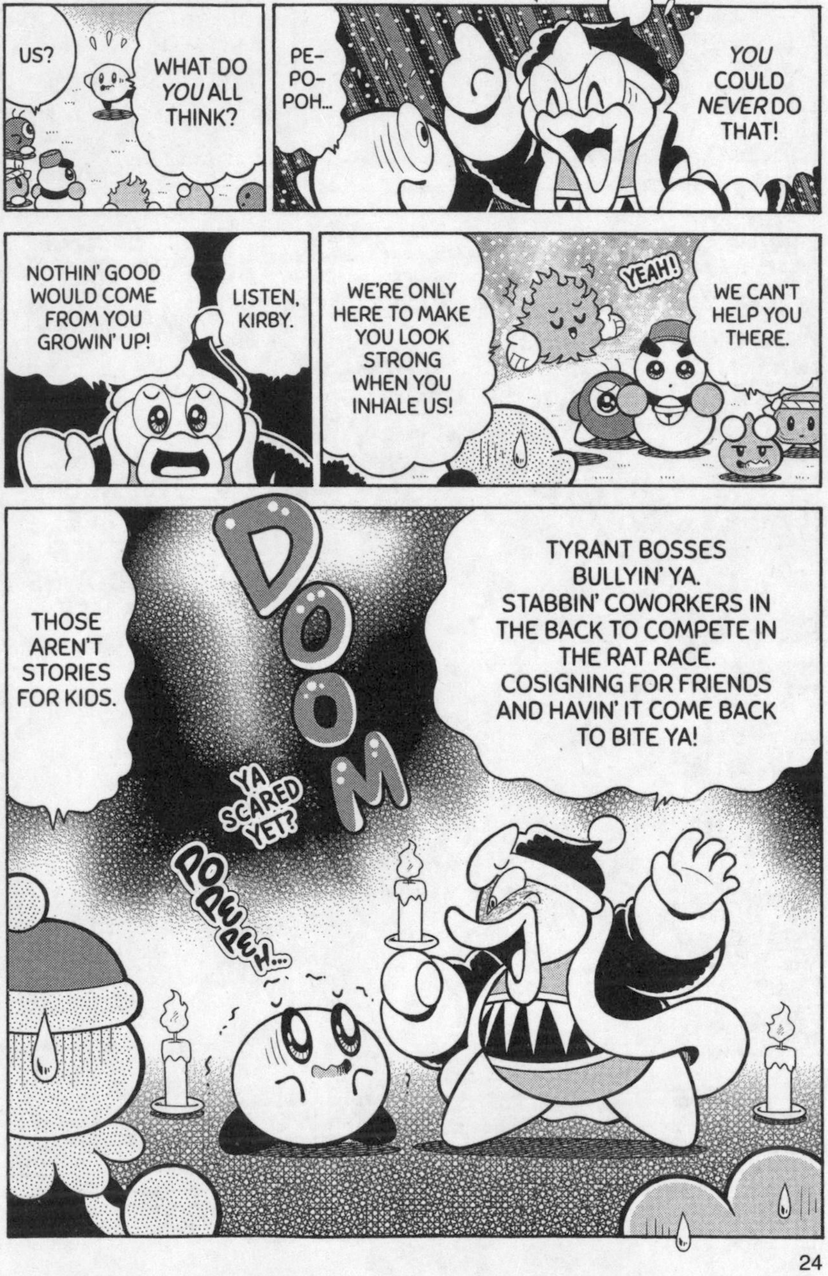
YOU COULD NEVER DO THAT!
PE-PO-POH...
WHAT DO YOU ALL THINK?
US?
WE CAN'T HELP YOU THERE.
YEAH!
WE'RE ONLY HERE TO MAKE YOU LOOK STRONG WHEN YOU INHALE US!
LISTEN, KIRBY.
NOTHIN' GOOD WOULD COME FROM YOU GROWIN' UP!
TYRANT BOSSES BULLYIN' YA. STABBIN' COWORKERS IN THE BACK TO COMPETE IN THE RAT RACE. COSIGNING FOR FRIENDS AND HAVIN' IT COME BACK TO BITE YA!
DOOM
THOSE AREN'T STORIES FOR KIDS.
YA SCARED YET?
POPEPEH...

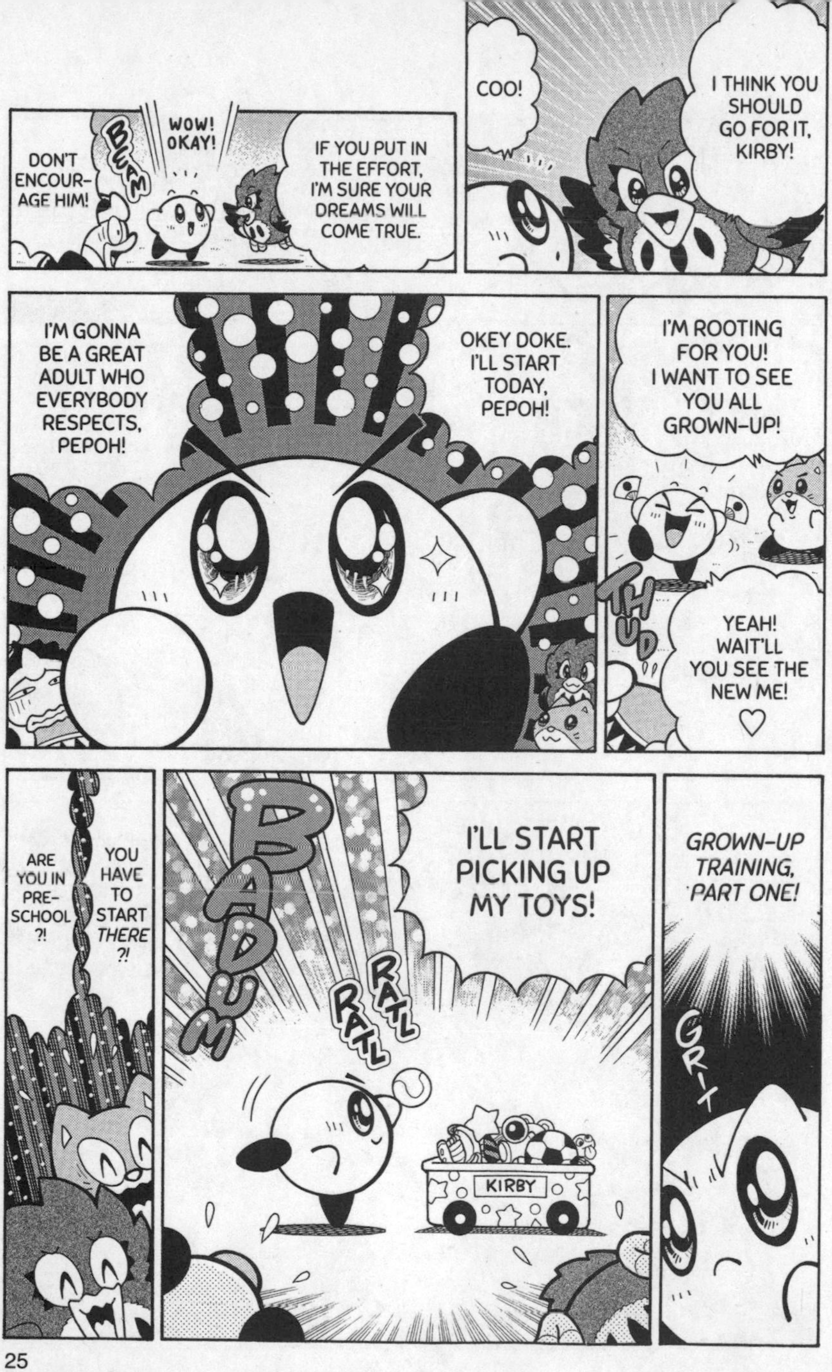
I THINK YOU SHOULD GO FOR IT, KIRBY!
COO!
IF YOU PUT IN THE EFFORT, I'M SURE YOUR DREAMS WILL COME TRUE.
WOW! OKAY!
BEAM
DON'T ENCOURAGE HIM!
I'M ROOTING FOR YOU! I WANT TO SEE YOU ALL GROWN-UP!
YEAH! WAIT'LL YOU SEE THE NEW ME! ♡
THUD
OKEY DOKE. I'LL START TODAY, PEPOH!
I'M GONNA BE A GREAT ADULT WHO EVERYBODY RESPECTS, PEPOH!
GROWN-UP TRAINING, PART ONE!
GRIT
I'LL START PICKING UP MY TOYS!
BADUM
RATL RATL
KIRBY
YOU HAVE TO START *THERE* ?!
ARE YOU IN PRE-SCHOOL ?!

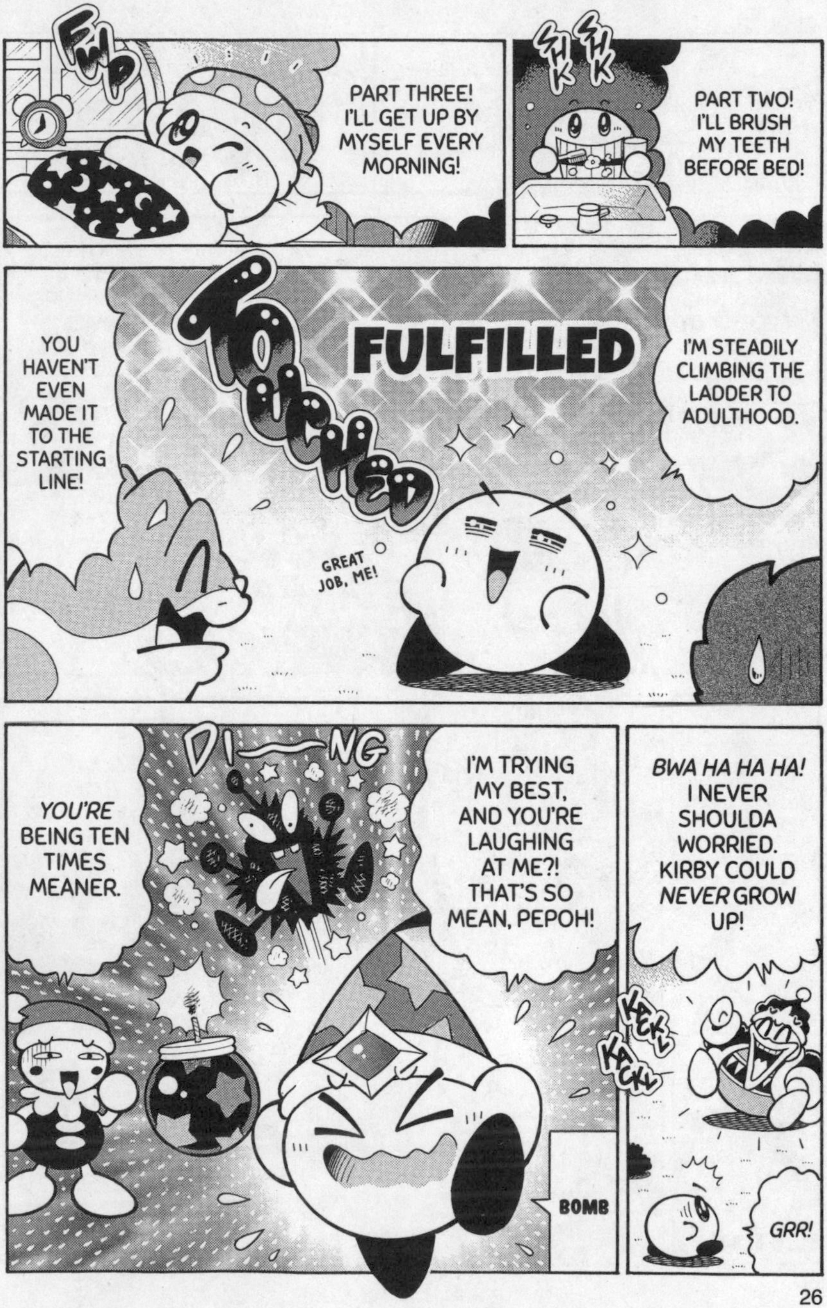

SHK SHK
PART TWO! I'LL BRUSH MY TEETH BEFORE BED!
FWP
PART THREE! I'LL GET UP BY MYSELF EVERY MORNING!
I'M STEADILY CLIMBING THE LADDER TO ADULTHOOD.
FULFILLED
TOUCHED
GREAT JOB, ME!
YOU HAVEN'T EVEN MADE IT TO THE STARTING LINE!
BWA HA HA HA! I NEVER SHOULDA WORRIED. KIRBY COULD *NEVER* GROW UP!
KACK KACK
GRR!
I'M TRYING MY BEST, AND YOU'RE LAUGHING AT ME?! THAT'S SO MEAN, PEPOH!
DI—NG
YOU'RE BEING TEN TIMES MEANER.
BOMB

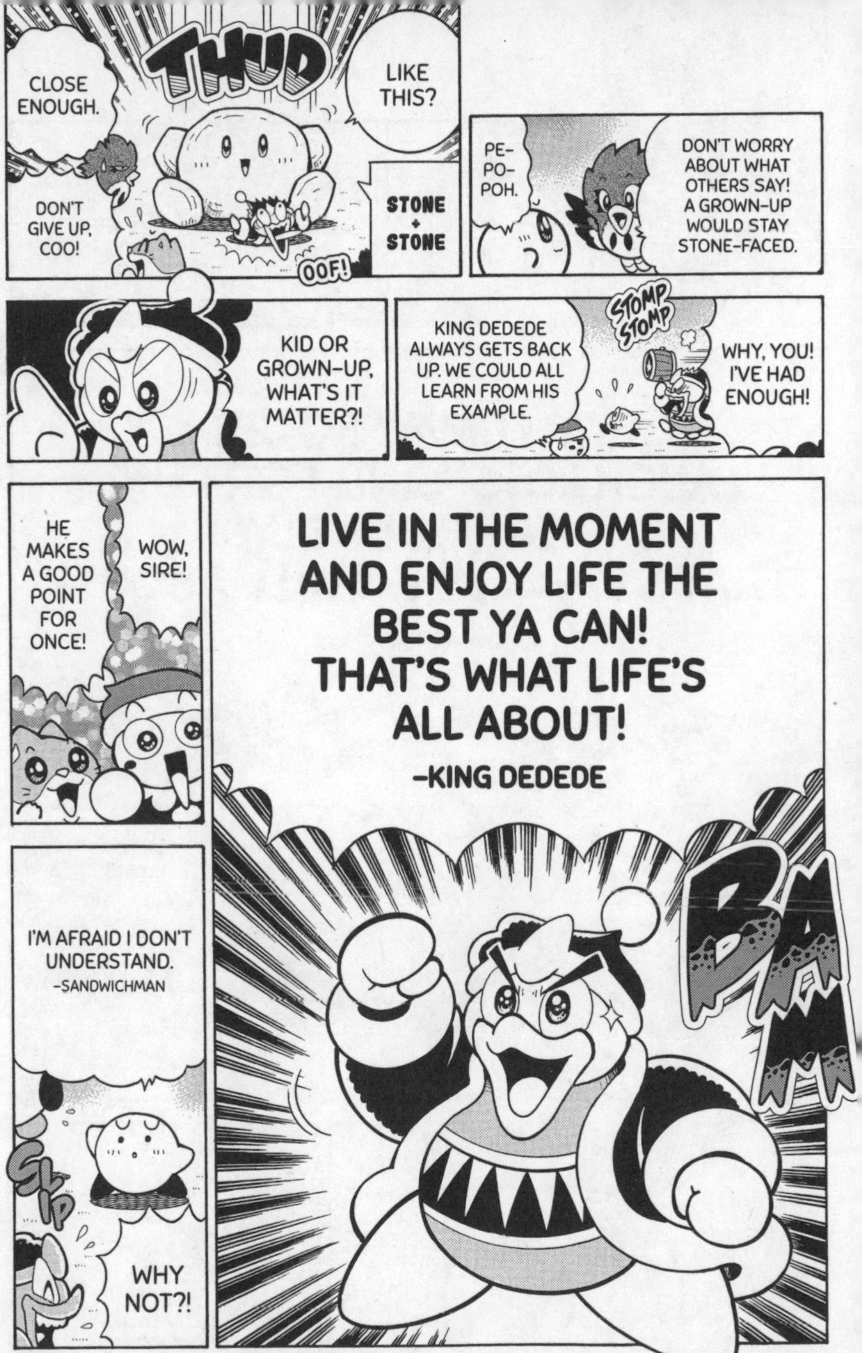
DON'T WORRY ABOUT WHAT OTHERS SAY! A GROWN-UP WOULD STAY STONE-FACED.
PE-PO-POH.
LIKE THIS?
THUD
CLOSE ENOUGH.
STONE + STONE
DON'T GIVE UP, COO!
OOF!
STOMP STOMP
WHY, YOU! I'VE HAD ENOUGH!
KING DEDEDE ALWAYS GETS BACK UP. WE COULD ALL LEARN FROM HIS EXAMPLE.
KID OR GROWN-UP, WHAT'S IT MATTER?!
LIVE IN THE MOMENT AND ENJOY LIFE THE BEST YA CAN! THAT'S WHAT LIFE'S ALL ABOUT!
-KING DEDEDE
BAM
WOW, SIRE!
HE MAKES A GOOD POINT FOR ONCE!
I'M AFRAID I DON'T UNDERSTAND.
-SANDWICHMAN
SLIP
WHY NOT?!

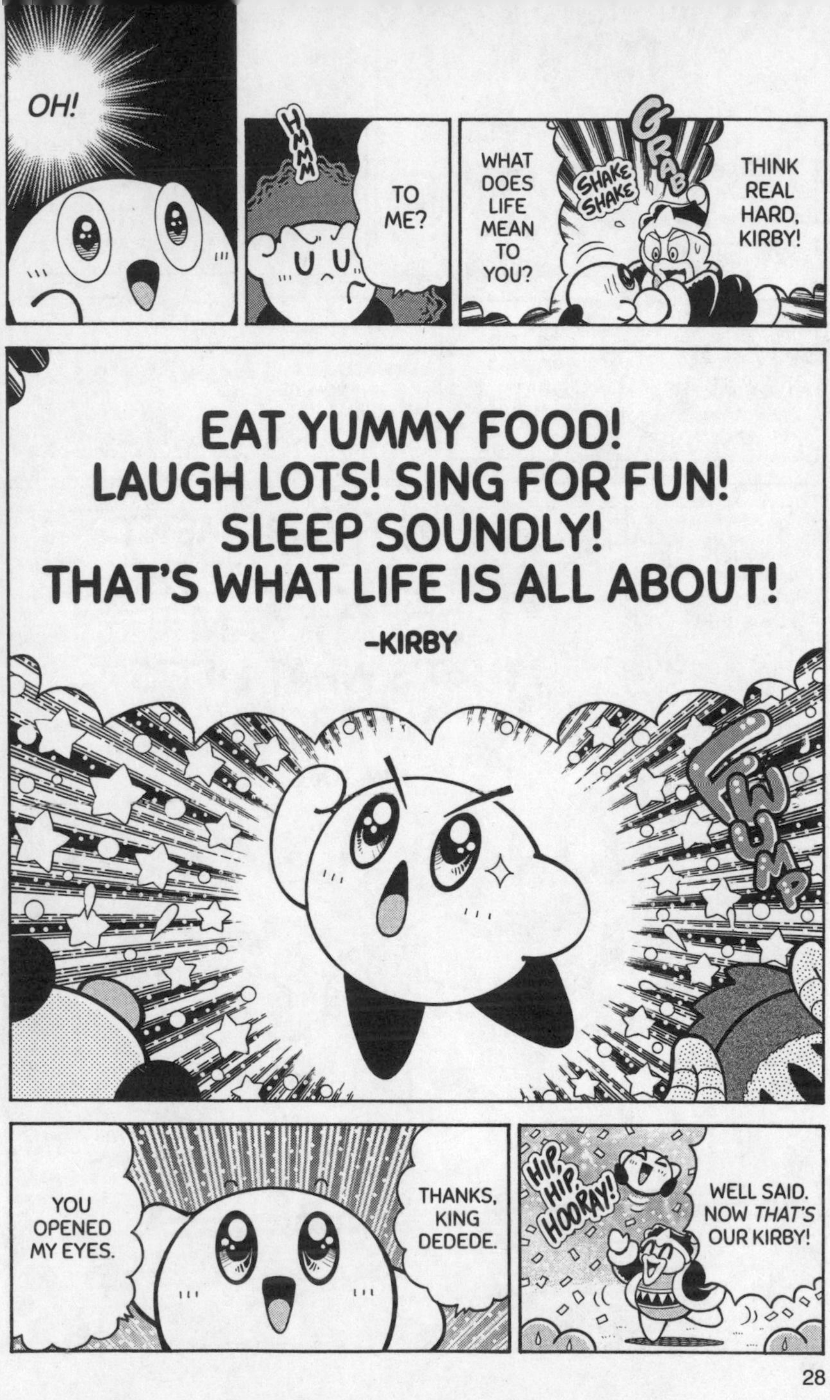
THINK REAL HARD, KIRBY!
GRAB
SHAKE SHAKE
WHAT DOES LIFE MEAN TO YOU?
HMMM
TO ME?
OH!
EAT YUMMY FOOD! LAUGH LOTS! SING FOR FUN! SLEEP SOUNDLY! THAT'S WHAT LIFE IS ALL ABOUT!
-KIRBY
FWUMP
WELL SAID. NOW *THAT'S* OUR KIRBY!
HIP, HIP, HOORAY!
THANKS, KING DEDEDE.
YOU OPENED MY EYES.

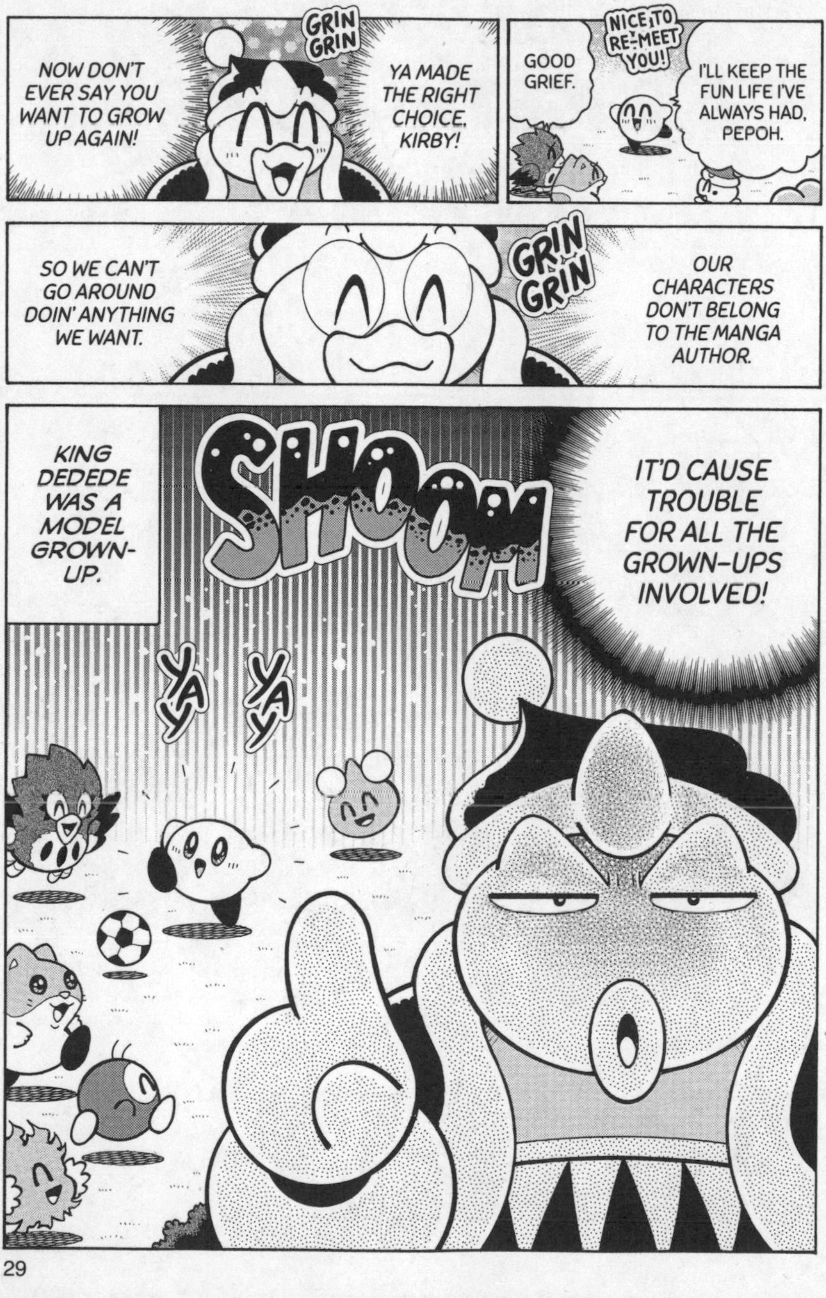
I'LL KEEP THE FUN LIFE I'VE ALWAYS HAD, PEPOH.
NICE TO RE-MEET YOU!
GOOD GRIEF.
YA MADE THE RIGHT CHOICE, KIRBY!
GRIN GRIN
NOW DON'T EVER SAY YOU WANT TO GROW UP AGAIN!
OUR CHARACTERS DON'T BELONG TO THE MANGA AUTHOR.
GRIN GRIN
SO WE CAN'T GO AROUND DOIN' ANYTHING WE WANT.
IT'D CAUSE TROUBLE FOR ALL THE GROWN-UPS INVOLVED!
SHOOM
KING DEDEDE WAS A MODEL GROWN-UP.
YAY
YAY

CHAPTER 4: A METHOD FOR MAKING UP!

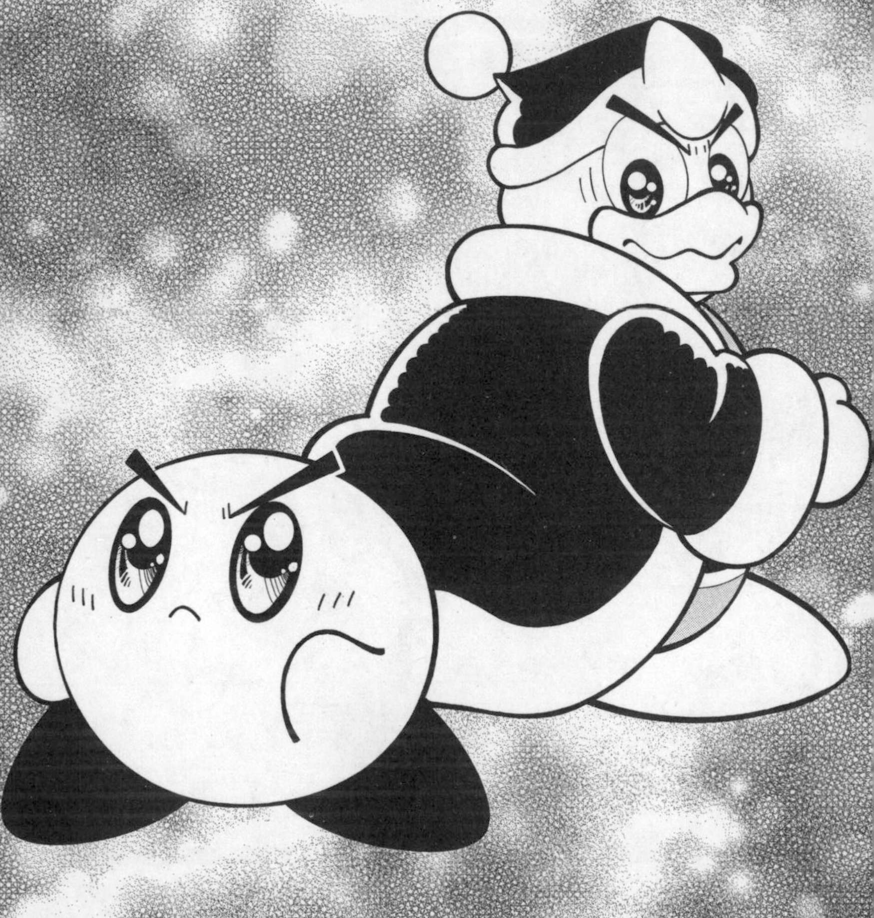

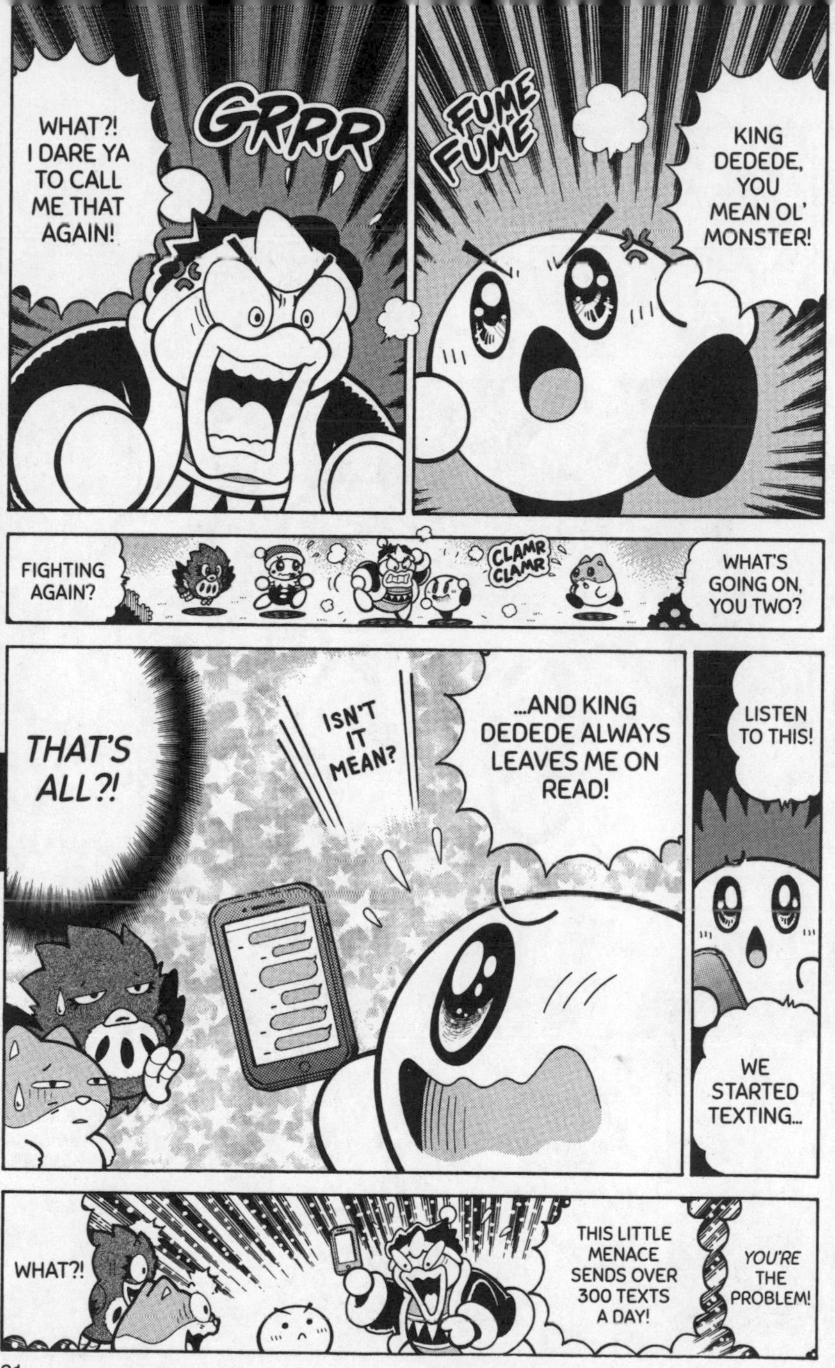
FUME FUME
KING DEDEDE, YOU MEAN OL' MONSTER!
GRRR
WHAT?! I DARE YA TO CALL ME THAT AGAIN!
WHAT'S GOING ON, YOU TWO?
CLAMR CLAMR
FIGHTING AGAIN?
LISTEN TO THIS!
WE STARTED TEXTING...
...AND KING DEDEDE ALWAYS LEAVES ME ON READ!
ISN'T IT MEAN?
THAT'S ALL?!
YOU'RE THE PROBLEM!
THIS LITTLE MENACE SENDS OVER 300 TEXTS A DAY!
WHAT?!

AUTHOR'S COMMENT

I HAVE BARELY ANY APPS ON MY CELL PHONE. I WORRY THEY'LL HARVEST MY DATA. I DON'T WANT TOO MANY PHOTOS TAKEN OF ME EITHER. I WORRY IT'LL HARVEST MY SOUL... (WHAT YEAR AM I LIVING IN?)

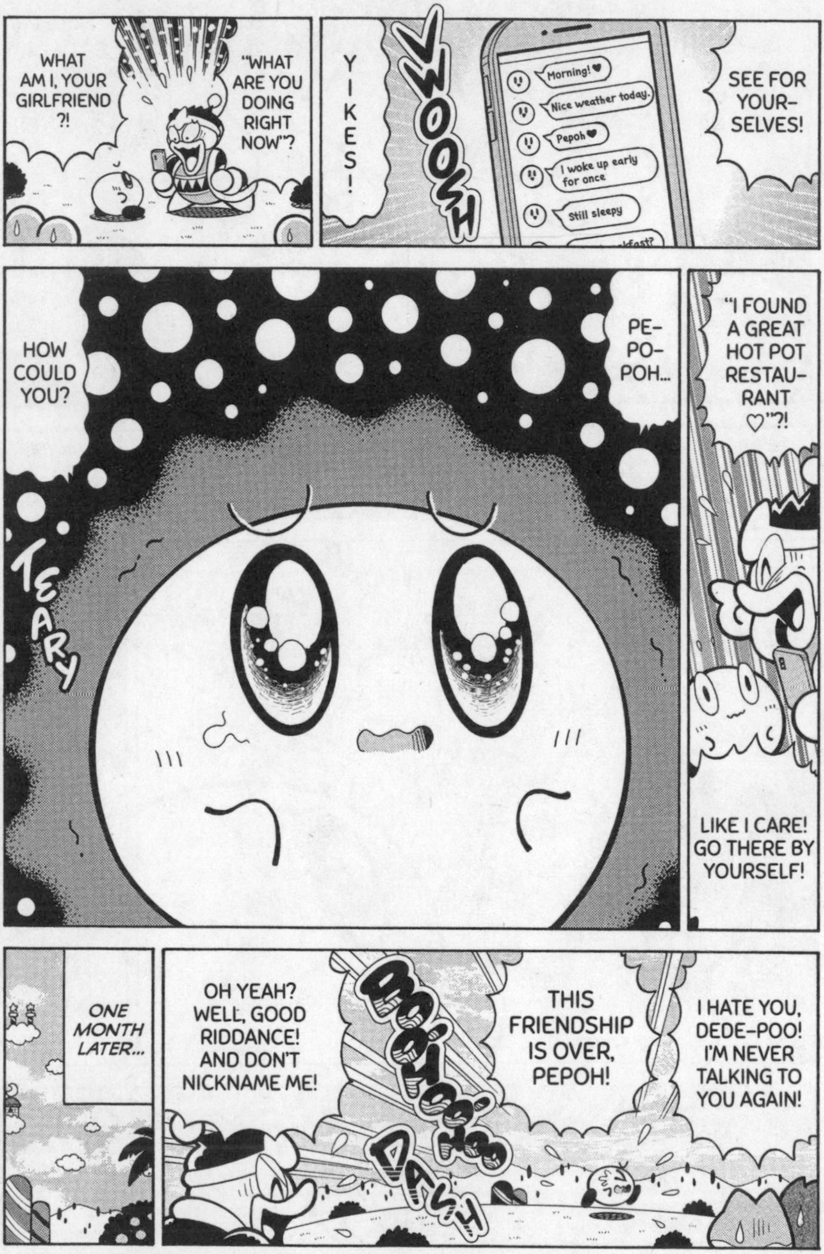
SEE FOR YOURSELVES!
Morning!♥
Nice weather today.
Pepoh♥
I woke up early for once
Still sleepy
WHOOSH
YIKES!
"WHAT ARE YOU DOING RIGHT NOW"?
WHAT AM I, YOUR GIRLFRIEND?!
"I FOUND A GREAT HOT POT RESTAURANT ♡"?!
LIKE I CARE! GO THERE BY YOURSELF!
PE-PO-POH...
HOW COULD YOU?
TEARY
I HATE YOU, DEDE-POO! I'M NEVER TALKING TO YOU AGAIN!
THIS FRIENDSHIP IS OVER, PEPOH!
DASH
OH YEAH? WELL, GOOD RIDDANCE! AND DON'T NICKNAME ME!
ONE MONTH LATER...

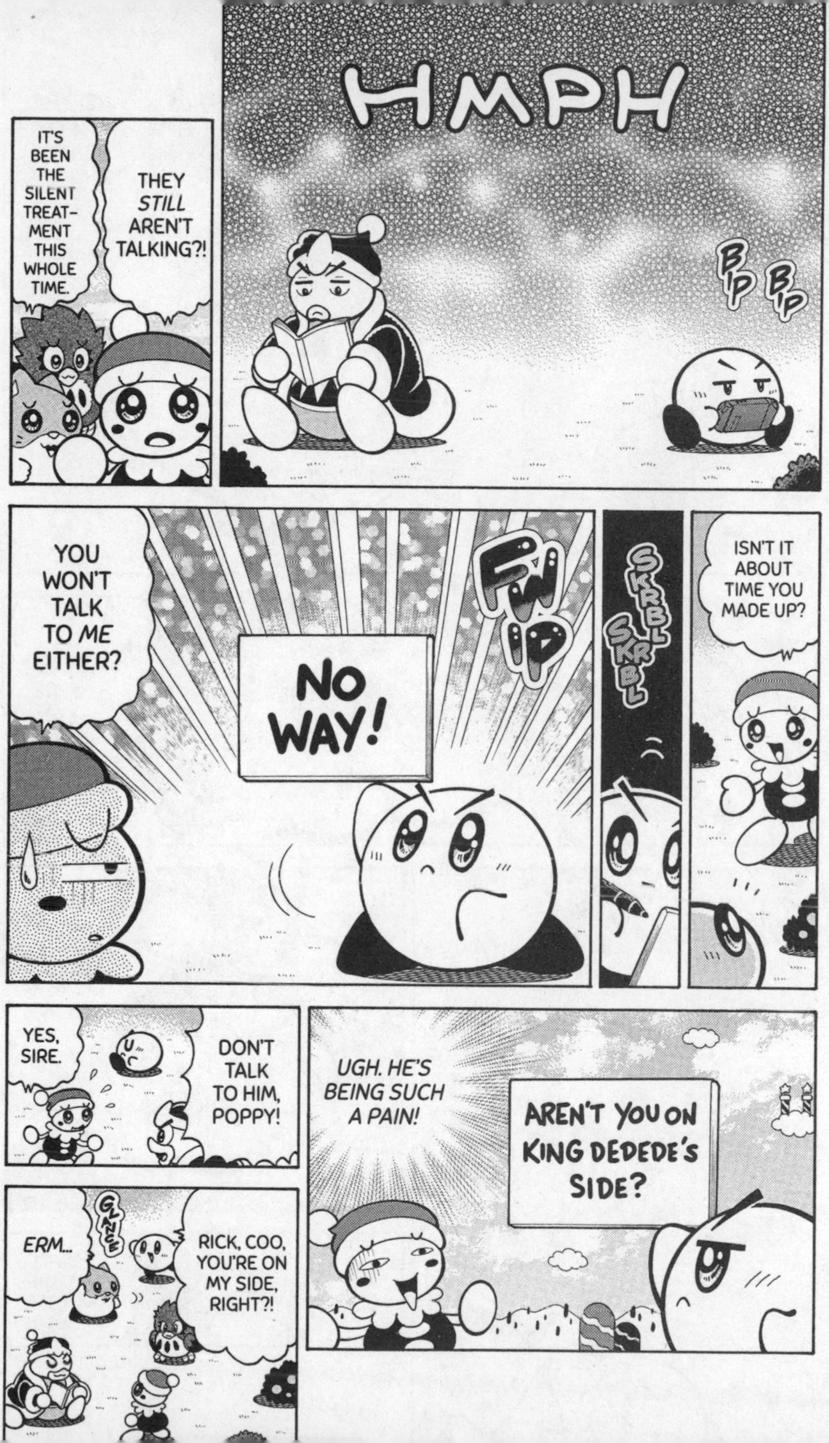
HMPH
BIP BIP
THEY STILL AREN'T TALKING?!
IT'S BEEN THE SILENT TREATMENT THIS WHOLE TIME.
ISN'T IT ABOUT TIME YOU MADE UP?
SKRBL SKRBL
FWIP
NO WAY!
YOU WON'T TALK TO ME EITHER?
AREN'T YOU ON KING DEDEDE'S SIDE?
UGH. HE'S BEING SUCH A PAIN!
DON'T TALK TO HIM, POPPY!
YES, SIRE.
RICK, COO, YOU'RE ON MY SIDE, RIGHT?!
GLANCE
ERM...

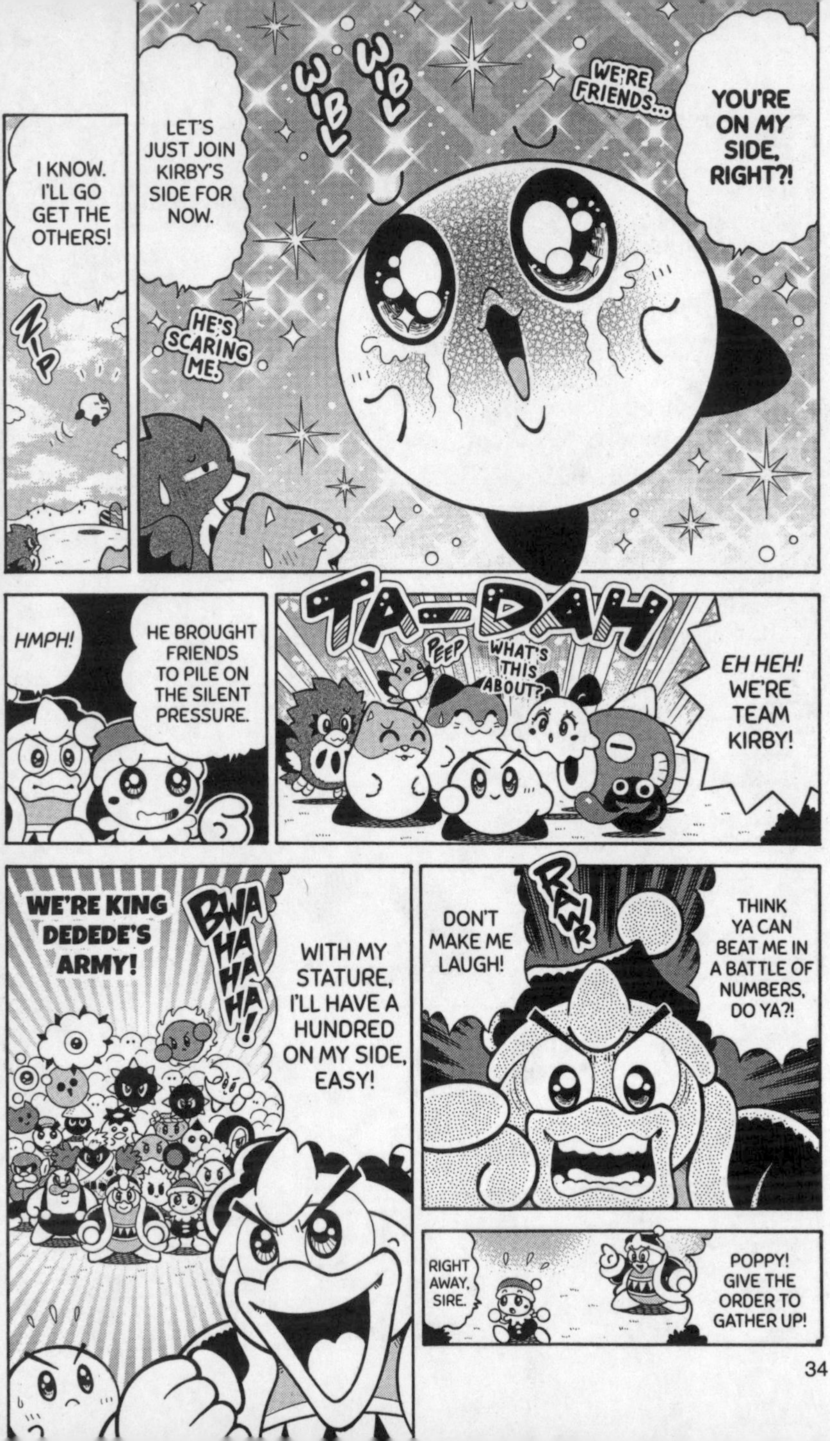
YOU'RE ON MY SIDE, RIGHT?!
WE'RE FRIENDS...
WIBL WIBL
LET'S JUST JOIN KIRBY'S SIDE FOR NOW.
HE'S SCARING ME.
I KNOW. I'LL GO GET THE OTHERS!
ZIP
TA-DAH
EH HEH! WE'RE TEAM KIRBY!
WHAT'S THIS ABOUT?
PEEP
HE BROUGHT FRIENDS TO PILE ON THE SILENT PRESSURE.
HMPH!
THINK YA CAN BEAT ME IN A BATTLE OF NUMBERS, DO YA?!
RAWR
DON'T MAKE ME LAUGH!
POPPY! GIVE THE ORDER TO GATHER UP!
RIGHT AWAY, SIRE.
WITH MY STATURE, I'LL HAVE A HUNDRED ON MY SIDE, EASY!
BWA HA HA HA HA!
WE'RE KING DEDEDE'S ARMY!

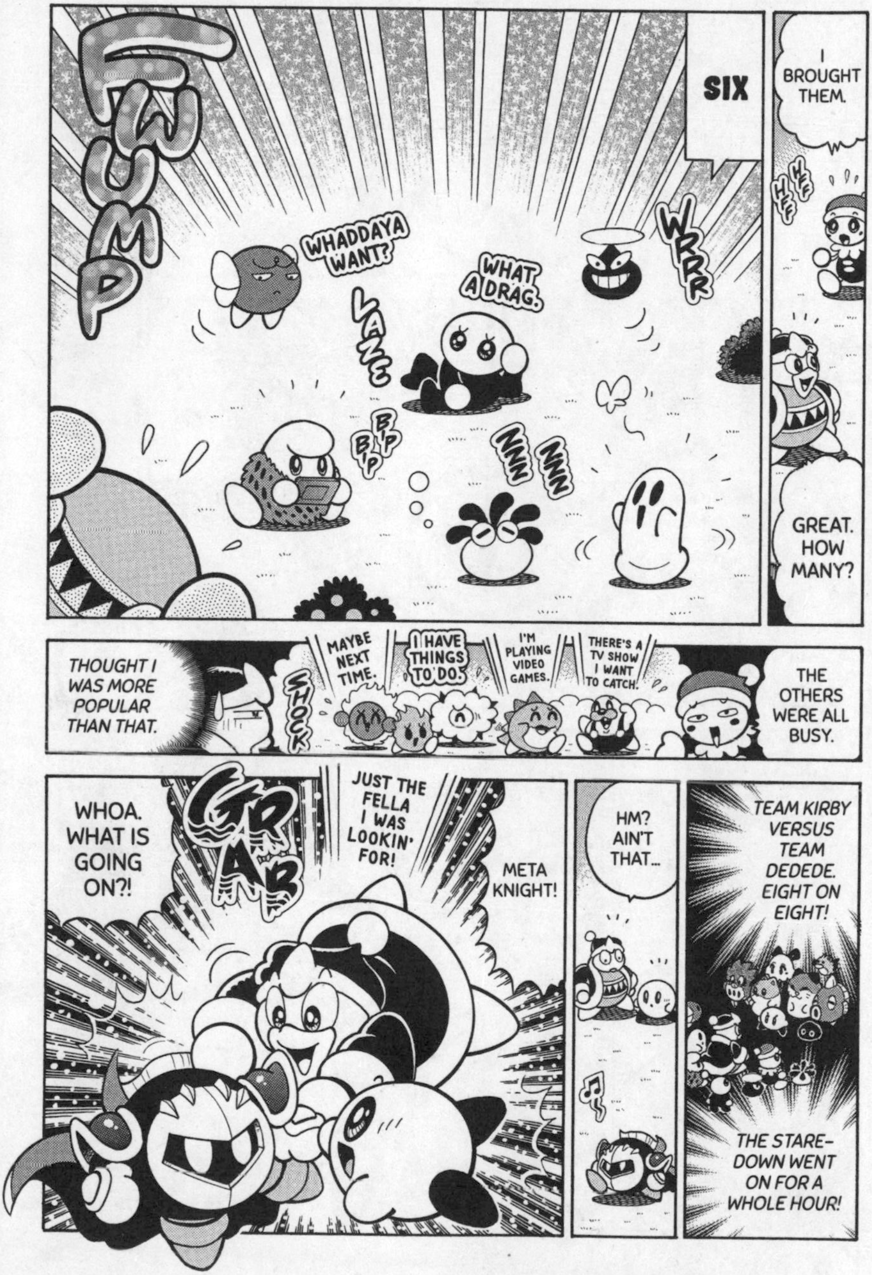
I BROUGHT THEM.
HEF HEF
GREAT. HOW MANY?
SIX
FWUMP
WRRR
WHAT A DRAG.
WHADDAYA WANT?
LAZE
BIP BIP
ZZZ ZZZ
THE OTHERS WERE ALL BUSY.
THERE'S A TV SHOW I WANT TO CATCH.
I'M PLAYING VIDEO GAMES.
I HAVE THINGS TO DO.
MAYBE NEXT TIME.
SHOCK
THOUGHT I WAS MORE POPULAR THAN THAT.
TEAM KIRBY VERSUS TEAM DEDEDE. EIGHT ON EIGHT!
THE STARE-DOWN WENT ON FOR A WHOLE HOUR!
HM? AIN'T THAT...
META KNIGHT!
JUST THE FELLA I WAS LOOKIN' FOR!
GRAB
WHOA. WHAT IS GOING ON?!

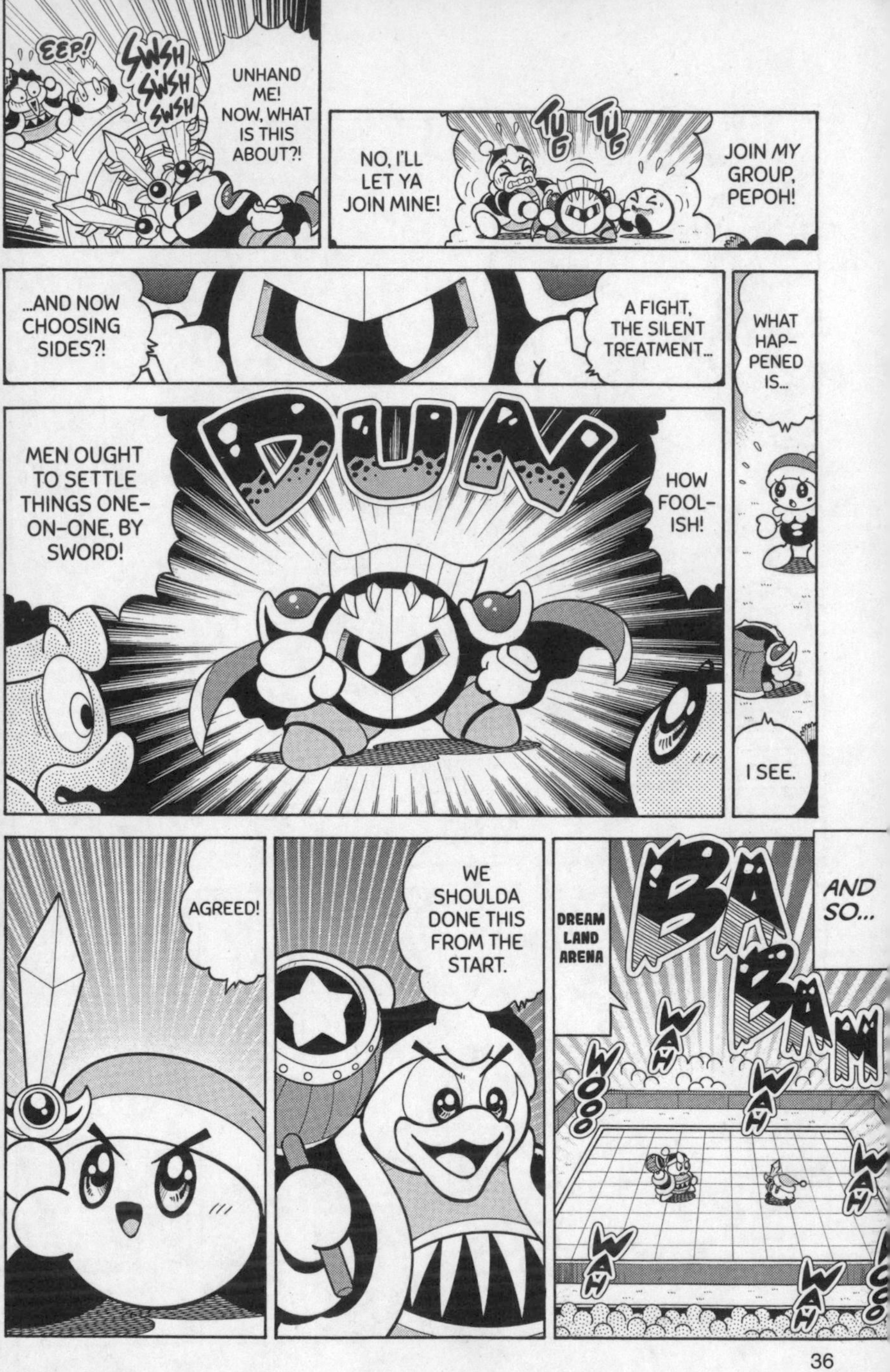
JOIN MY GROUP, PEPOH!
TUG TUG
NO, I'LL LET YA JOIN MINE!
UNHAND ME! NOW, WHAT IS THIS ABOUT?!
SWSH SWSH SWSH
EEP!
WHAT HAP-PENED IS...
I SEE.
A FIGHT, THE SILENT TREATMENT...
...AND NOW CHOOSING SIDES?!
HOW FOOL-ISH!
DUN
MEN OUGHT TO SETTLE THINGS ONE-ON-ONE, BY SWORD!
AND SO...
BA BAM
DREAM LAND ARENA
WAH WAH
WOOO
WAH WAH
WE SHOULDA DONE THIS FROM THE START.
AGREED!

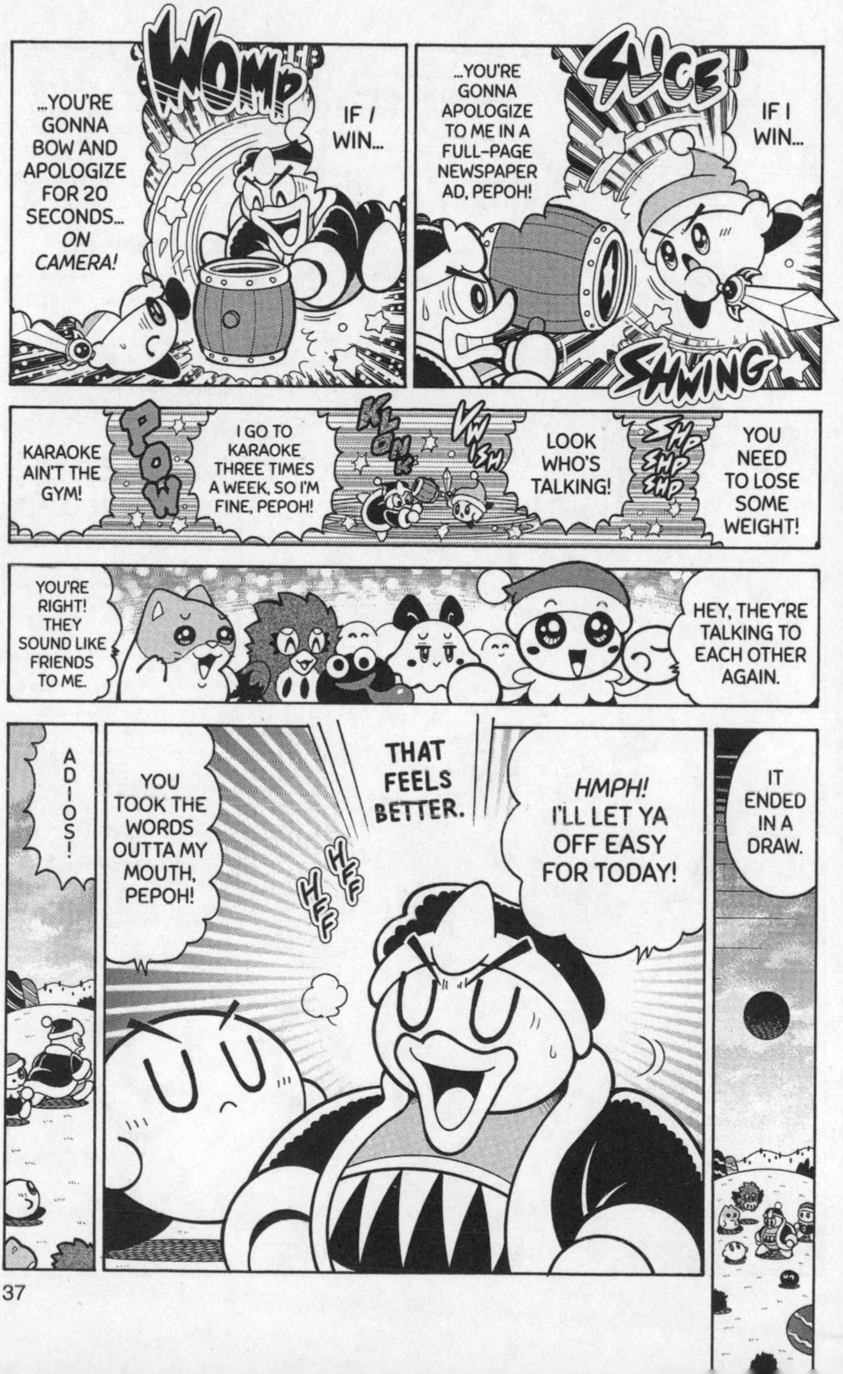
SLICE
IF I WIN...
...YOU'RE GONNA APOLOGIZE TO ME IN A FULL-PAGE NEWSPAPER AD, PEPOH!
SHWING
WOMP
IF I WIN...
...YOU'RE GONNA BOW AND APOLOGIZE FOR 20 SECONDS... *ON CAMERA!*
YOU NEED TO LOSE SOME WEIGHT!
SHP SHP SHP
LOOK WHO'S TALKING!
VWISH
KLONK
I GO TO KARAOKE THREE TIMES A WEEK, SO I'M FINE, PEPOH!
POW
KARAOKE AIN'T THE GYM!
HEY, THEY'RE TALKING TO EACH OTHER AGAIN.
YOU'RE RIGHT! THEY SOUND LIKE FRIENDS TO ME.
IT ENDED IN A DRAW.
HMPH! I'LL LET YA OFF EASY FOR TODAY!
THAT FEELS BETTER.
HFF HFF
YOU TOOK THE WORDS OUTTA MY MOUTH, PEPOH!
ADIOS!

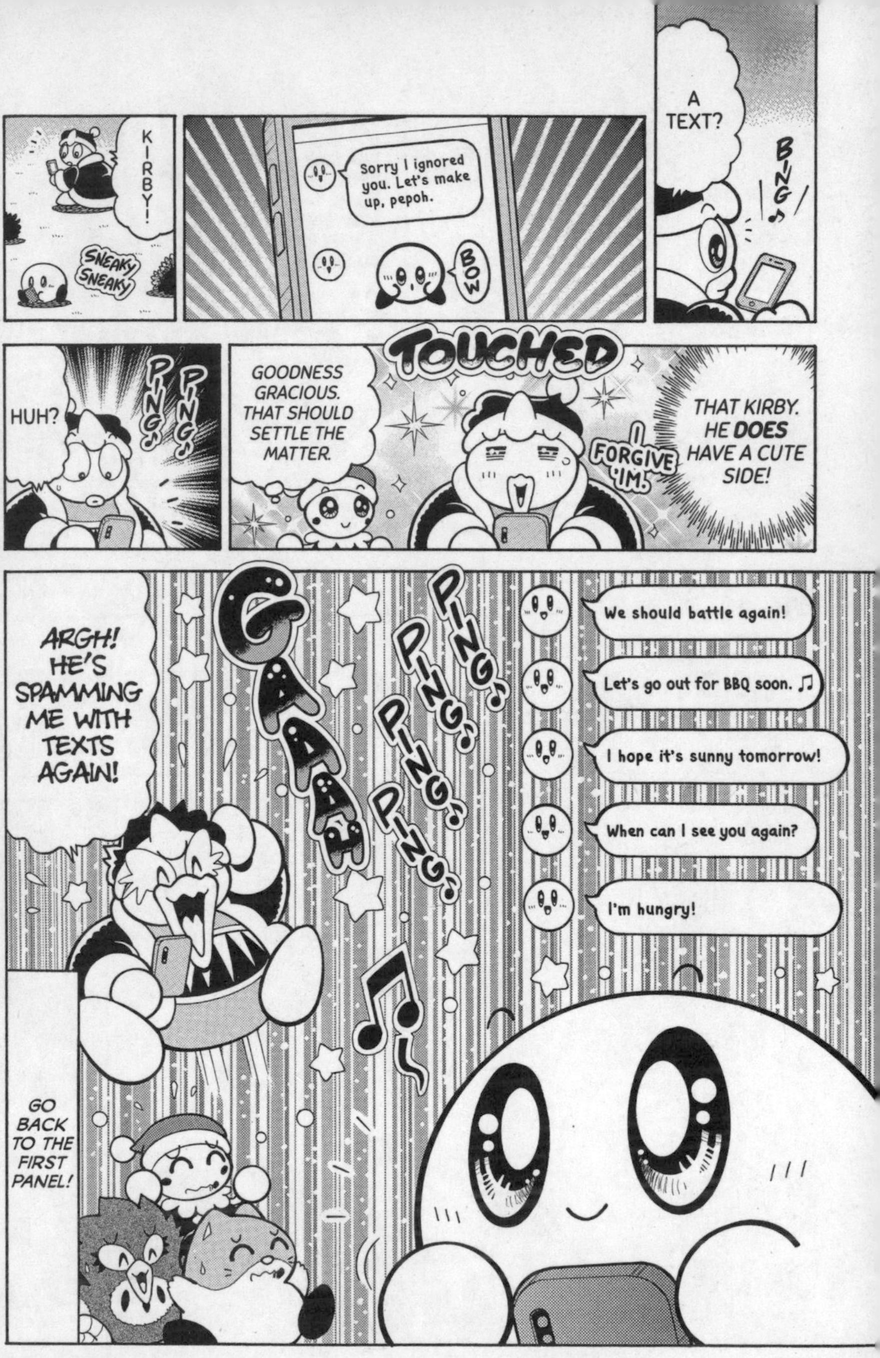
A TEXT?
BING♪
Sorry I ignored you. Let's make up, pepoh.
BOW
KIRBY!
SNEAKY SNEAKY
TOUCHED
THAT KIRBY. HE **DOES** HAVE A CUTE SIDE!
I FORGIVE 'IM.
GOODNESS GRACIOUS. THAT SHOULD SETTLE THE MATTER.
PING♪ PING♪
HUH?
We should battle again!
Let's go out for BBQ soon. ♫
I hope it's sunny tomorrow!
When can I see you again?
I'm hungry!
PING♪ PING♪ PING♪ PING♪
GAAAAH
ARGH! HE'S SPAMMING ME WITH TEXTS AGAIN!
GO BACK TO THE FIRST PANEL!

CHAPTER 5: KIRBY'S SONG CHANGES THE WORLD!

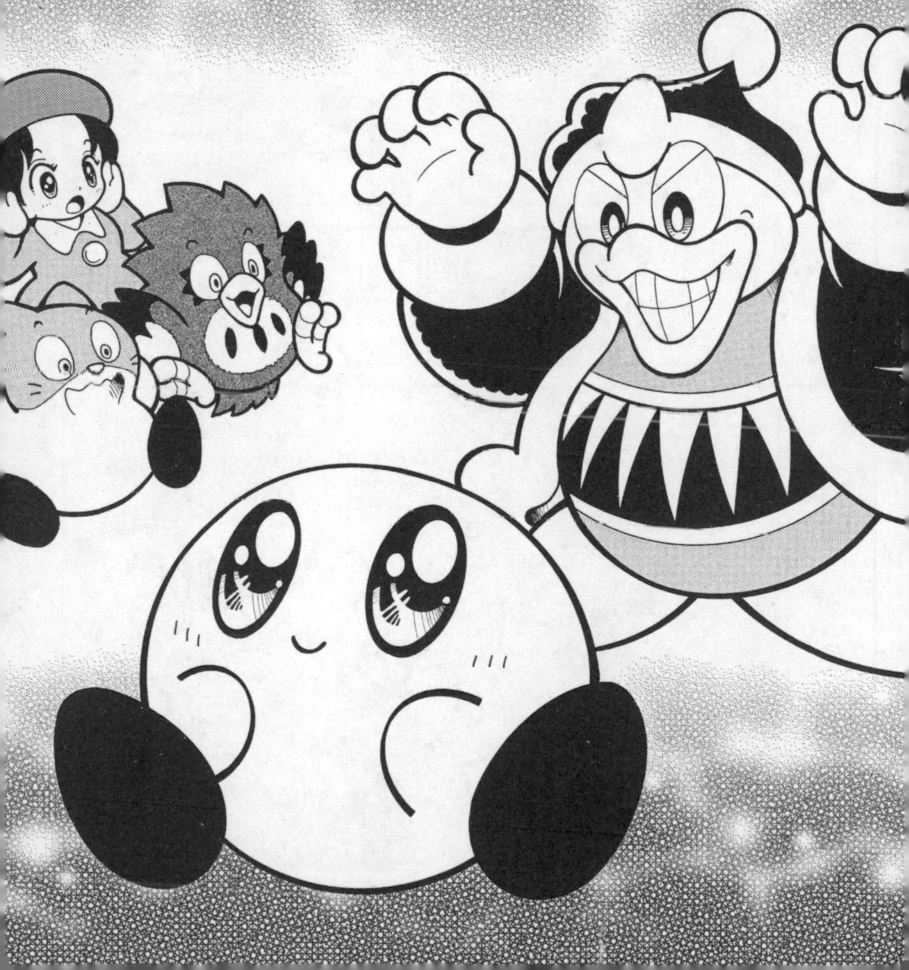

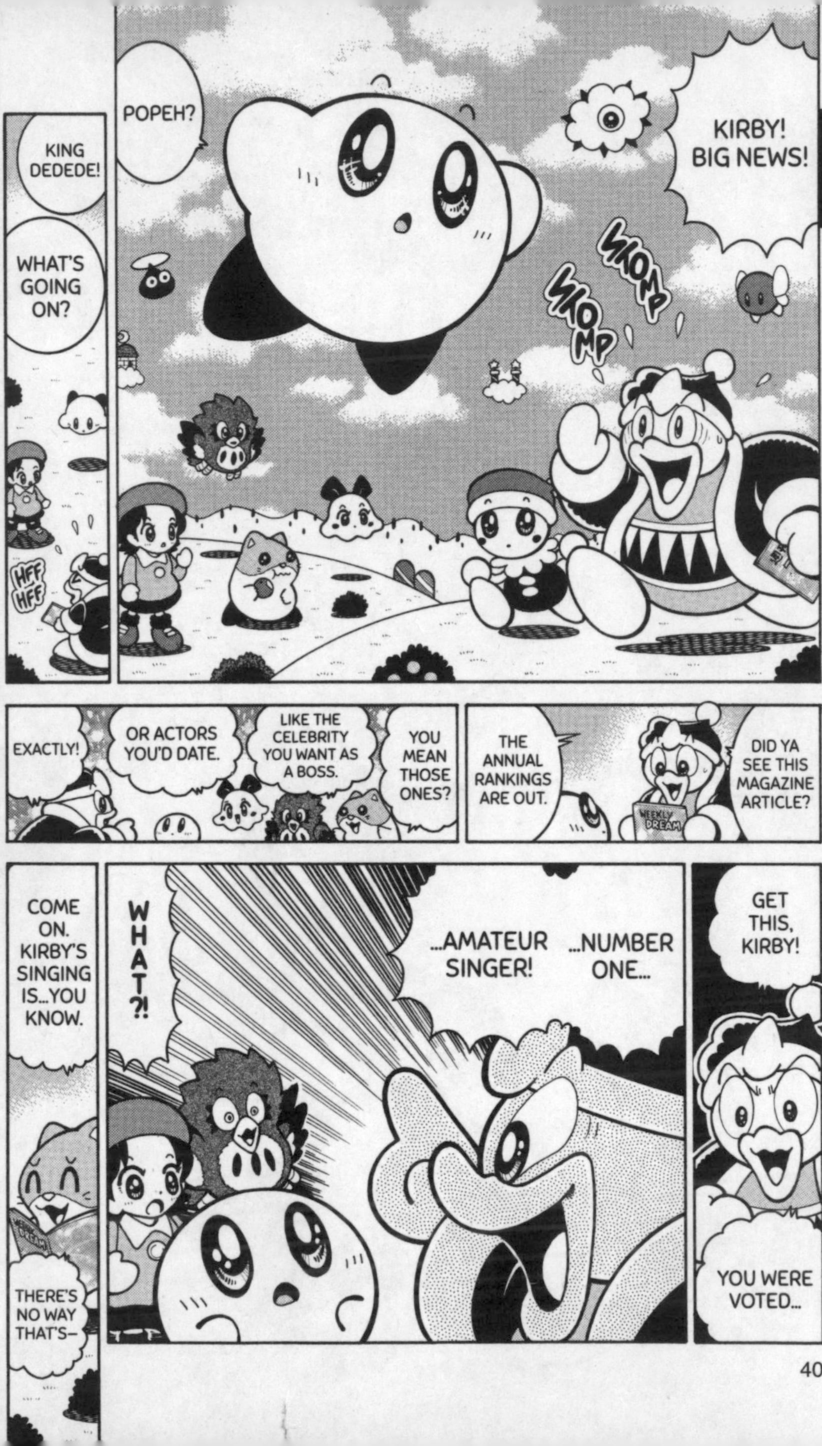
KIRBY! BIG NEWS!
SKOMP
SKOMP
SKOMP
POPEH?
KING DEDEDE!
WHAT'S GOING ON?
HFF HFF
DID YA SEE THIS MAGAZINE ARTICLE?
WEEKLY DREAM
THE ANNUAL RANKINGS ARE OUT.
YOU MEAN THOSE ONES?
LIKE THE CELEBRITY YOU WANT AS A BOSS.
OR ACTORS YOU'D DATE.
EXACTLY!
GET THIS, KIRBY!
YOU WERE VOTED...
...NUMBER ONE...
...AMATEUR SINGER!
WHAT?!
COME ON. KIRBY'S SINGING IS...YOU KNOW.
THERE'S NO WAY THAT'S—

AUTHOR'S COMMENT

BACK IN THE DAY, HAMBURGERS WERE TOO BIG TO HOLD IN ONE HAND. YOU COULD EAT AND EAT POTATO CHIPS AND NOT MAKE A DENT IN THE BAG. MANGA VOLUMES WERE THICK AND WORTH READING. HEY, ISN'T THIS BOOK PRETTY THIN FOR THE PRICE? *UWAAAH.*

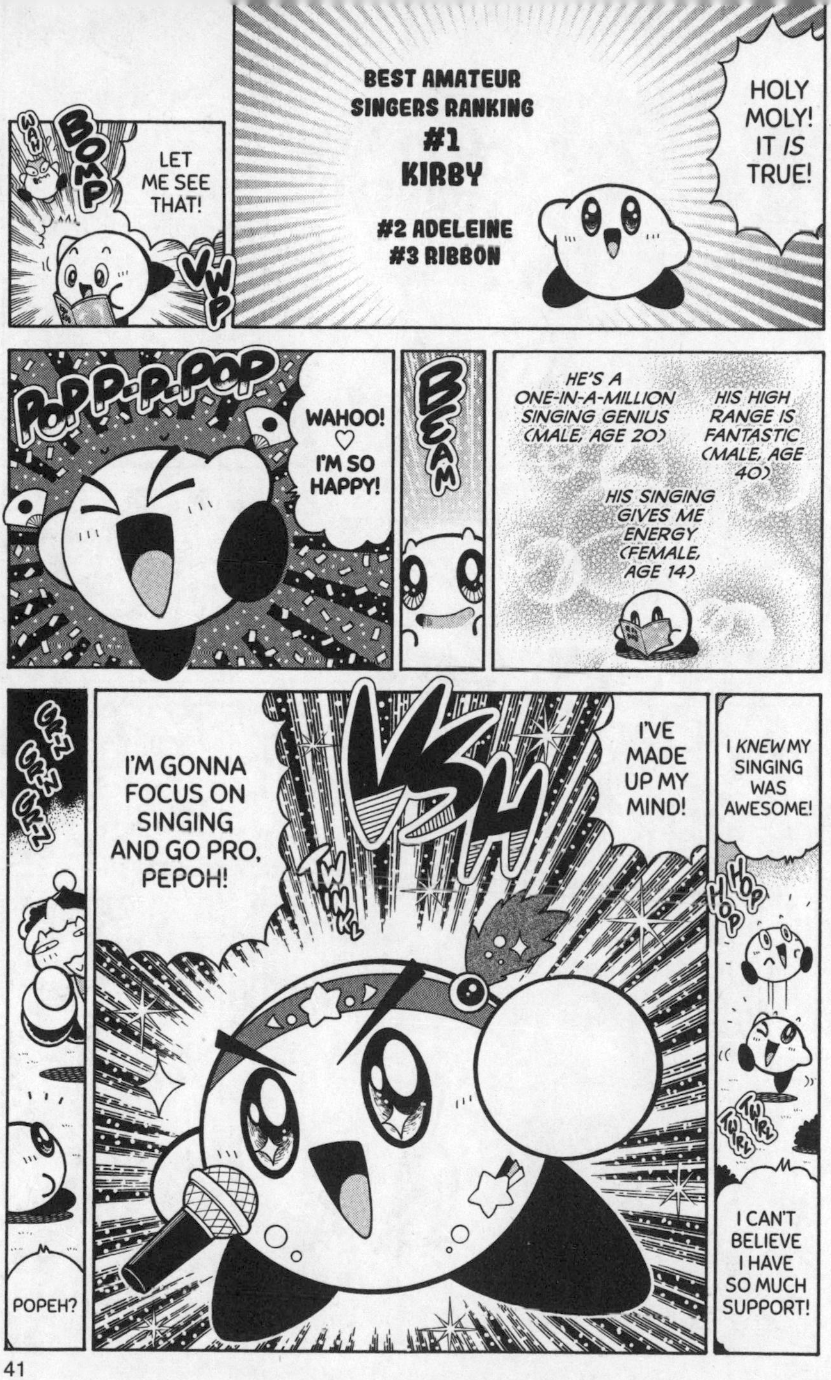
HOLY MOLY! IT *IS* TRUE!
BEST AMATEUR SINGERS RANKING
#1 KIRBY
#2 ADELEINE
#3 RIBBON
WAH
BOMP
LET ME SEE THAT!
VWP
HIS HIGH RANGE IS FANTASTIC (MALE, AGE 40)
HE'S A ONE-IN-A-MILLION SINGING GENIUS (MALE, AGE 20)
HIS SINGING GIVES ME ENERGY (FEMALE, AGE 14)
BEAM
WAHOO! ♡ I'M SO HAPPY!
POP P-P-POP
I KNEW MY SINGING WAS AWESOME!
HOP HOP
TWIRL TWIRL
I CAN'T BELIEVE I HAVE SO MUCH SUPPORT!
I'VE MADE UP MY MIND!
VSH
I'M GONNA FOCUS ON SINGING AND GO PRO, PEPOH!
TWINKL
GR-N GR-N GR-N
POPEH?

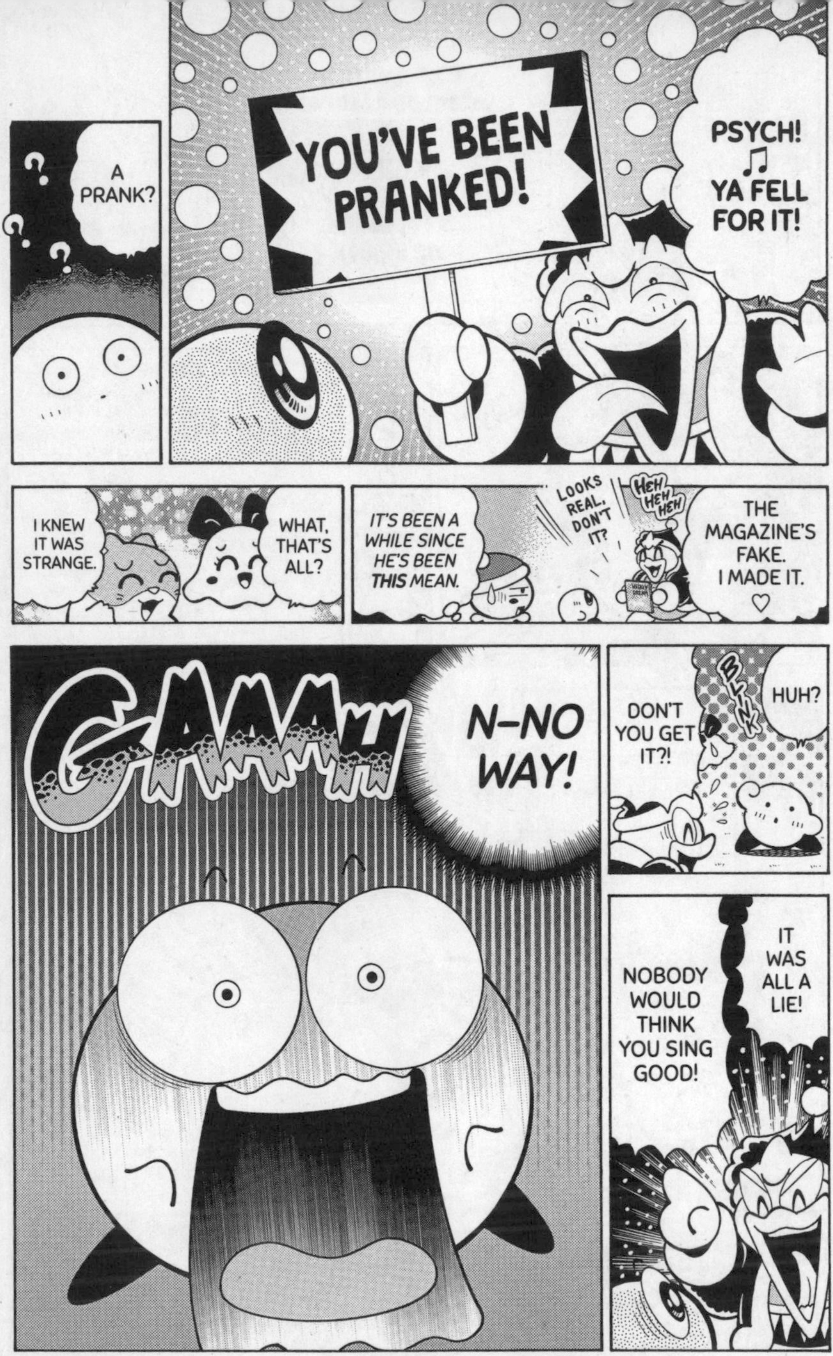
PSYCH! ♫ YA FELL FOR IT!
YOU'VE BEEN PRANKED!
A PRANK?
THE MAGAZINE'S FAKE. I MADE IT. ♡
HEH HEH HEH
LOOKS REAL, DON'T IT?
IT'S BEEN A WHILE SINCE HE'S BEEN THIS MEAN.
WHAT, THAT'S ALL?
I KNEW IT WAS STRANGE.
HUH?
BLINK
DON'T YOU GET IT?!
IT WAS ALL A LIE!
NOBODY WOULD THINK YOU SING GOOD!
N-NO WAY!
GAAAH

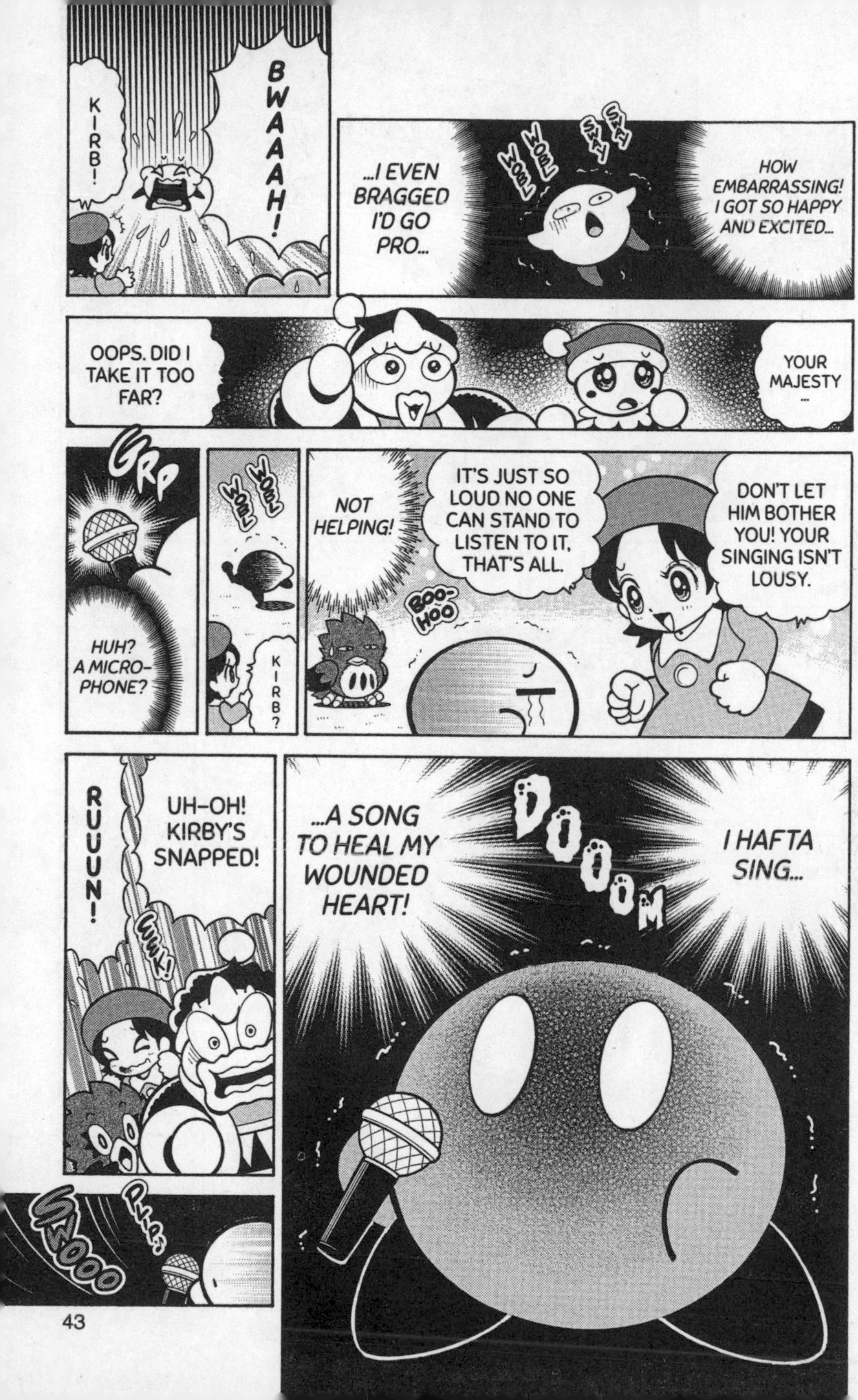
HOW EMBARRASSING! I GOT SO HAPPY AND EXCITED...
...I EVEN BRAGGED I'D GO PRO...
WOBL WOBL
BWAAAAH!
KIRBI!
YOUR MAJESTY...
OOPS. DID I TAKE IT TOO FAR?
DON'T LET HIM BOTHER YOU! YOUR SINGING ISN'T LOUSY.
IT'S JUST SO LOUD NO ONE CAN STAND TO LISTEN TO IT, THAT'S ALL.
NOT HELPING!
BOO-HOO
WOBL WOBL
KIRB?
GRP
HUH? A MICROPHONE?
I HAFTA SING...
...A SONG TO HEAL MY WOUNDED HEART!
DOOOOM
UH-OH! KIRBY'S SNAPPED!
RUUUUN!
SWOOO

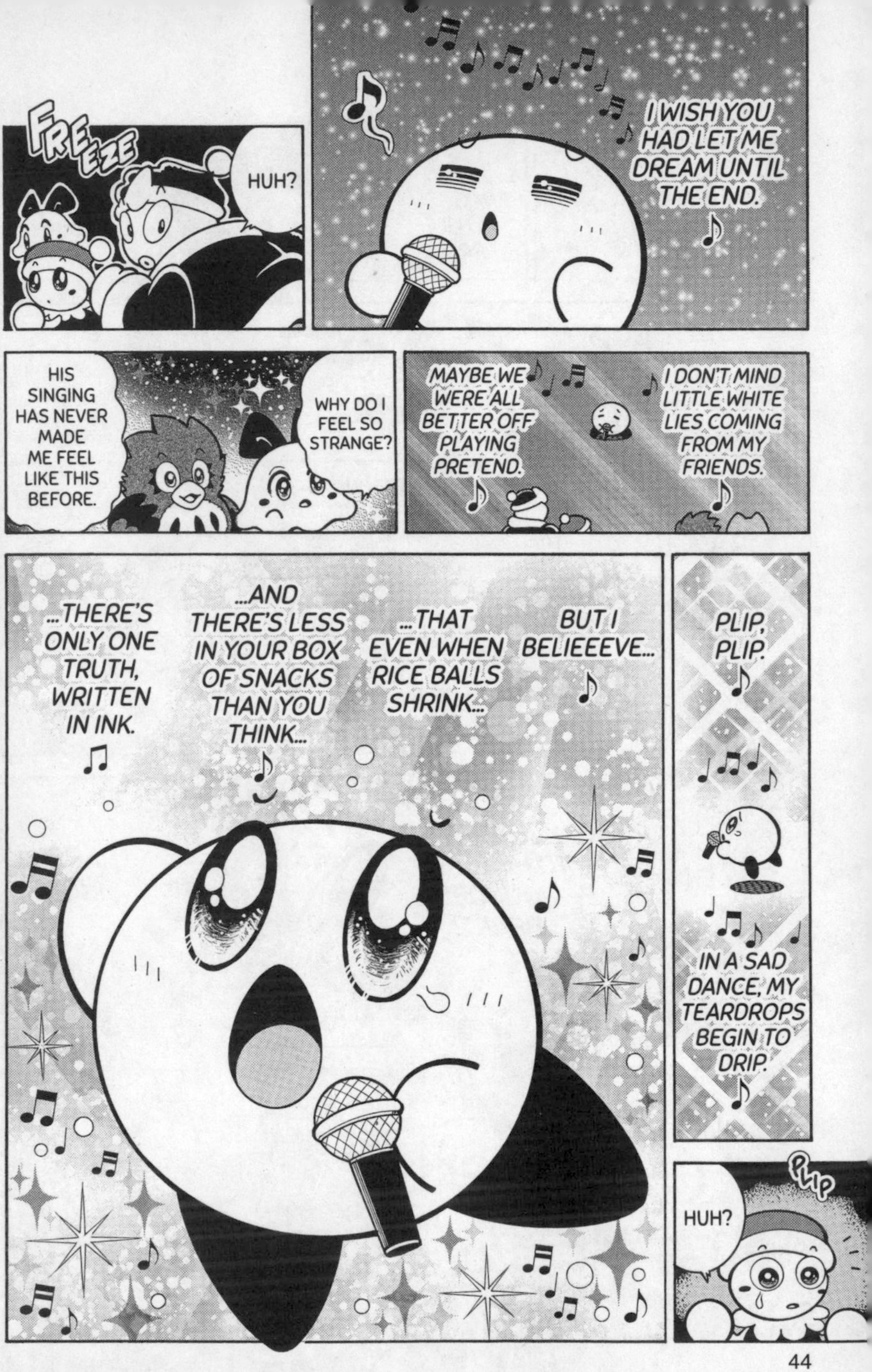

I WISH YOU HAD LET ME DREAM UNTIL THE END.
FREEZE
HUH?
I DON'T MIND LITTLE WHITE LIES COMING FROM MY FRIENDS.
MAYBE WE WERE ALL BETTER OFF PLAYING PRETEND.
WHY DO I FEEL SO STRANGE?
HIS SINGING HAS NEVER MADE ME FEEL LIKE THIS BEFORE.
PLIP, PLIP.
IN A SAD DANCE, MY TEARDROPS BEGIN TO DRIP.
PLIP
HUH?
BUT I BELIEEEVE...
...THAT EVEN WHEN RICE BALLS SHRINK...
...AND THERE'S LESS IN YOUR BOX OF SNACKS THAN YOU THINK...
...THERE'S ONLY ONE TRUTH, WRITTEN IN INK.

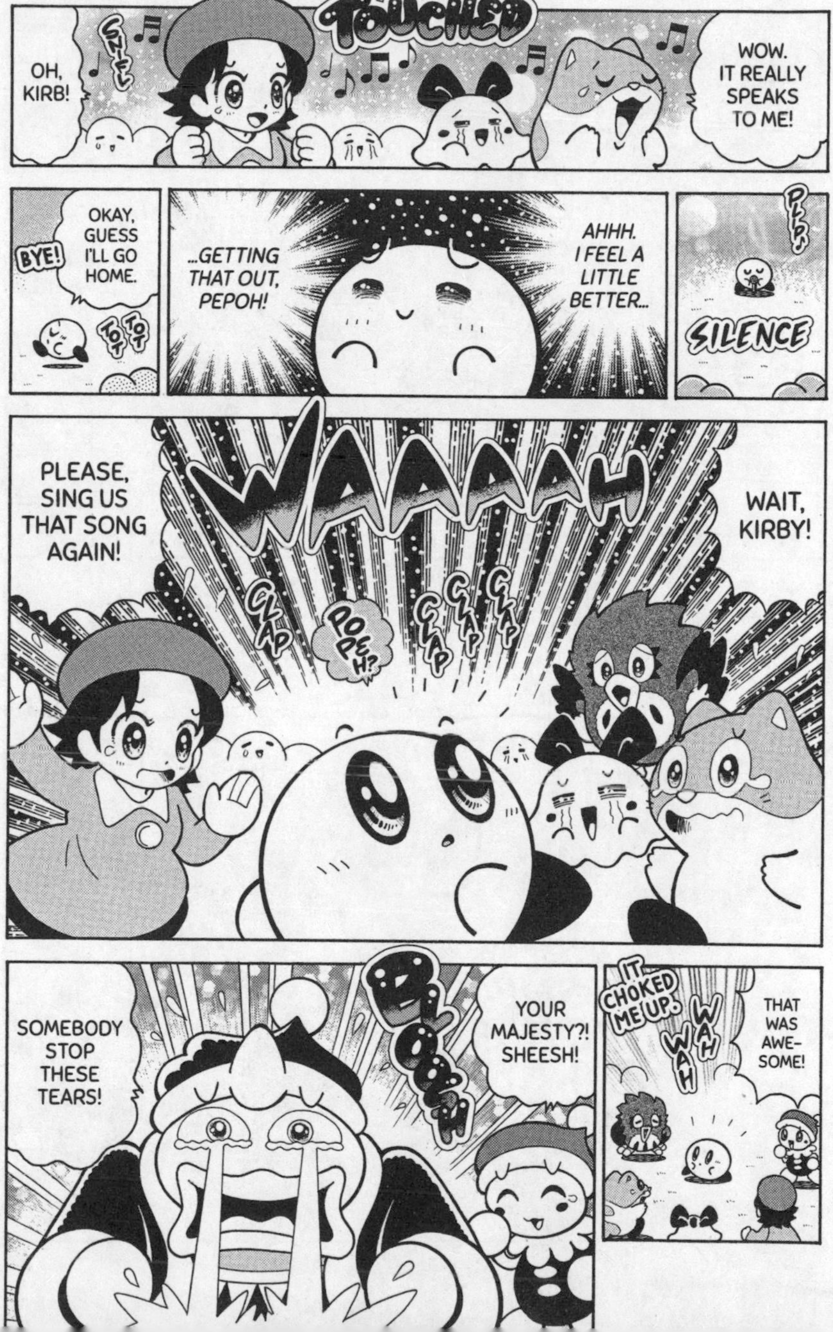

WOW. IT REALLY SPEAKS TO ME!
TOUCHED
SNIFF
OH, KIRB!
PLIP♪
SILENCE
AHHH. I FEEL A LITTLE BETTER...
...GETTING THAT OUT, PEPOH!
OKAY, GUESS I'LL GO HOME.
BYE!
TOT TOT
WAIT, KIRBY!
WAAAAAH
CLAP CLAP CLAP CLAP
POPEH?
PLEASE, SING US THAT SONG AGAIN!
THAT WAS AWE-SOME!
WAH WAH
IT CHOKED ME UP.
YOUR MAJESTY?! SHEESH!
BLOOOH
SOMEBODY STOP THESE TEARS!

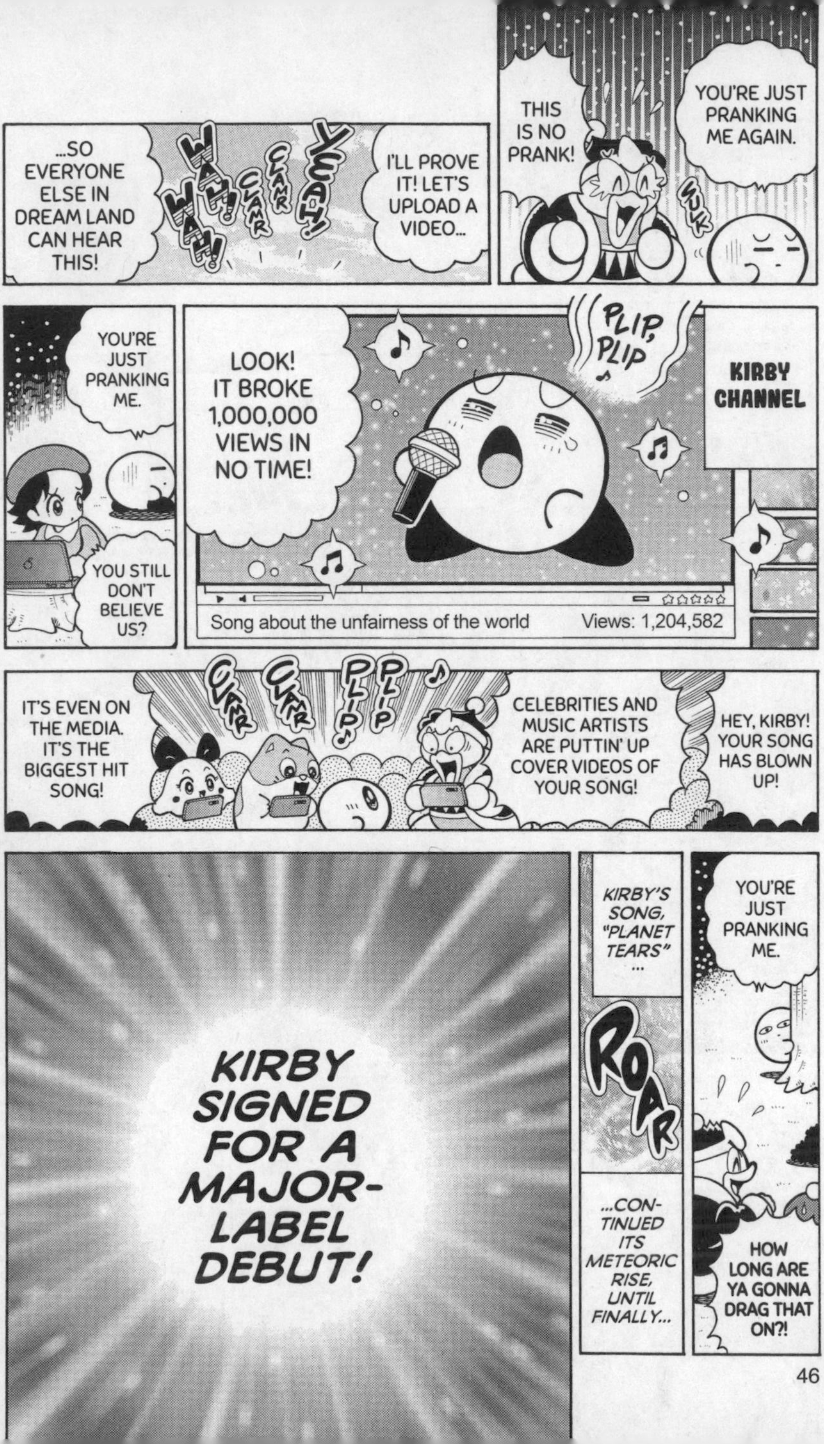

YOU'RE JUST PRANKING ME AGAIN.
THIS IS NO PRANK!
SULK
I'LL PROVE IT! LET'S UPLOAD A VIDEO...
YEAH!
CLAMR CLAMR
WAH WAH!
...SO EVERYONE ELSE IN DREAM LAND CAN HEAR THIS!
KIRBY CHANNEL
PLIP, PLIP
LOOK! IT BROKE 1,000,000 VIEWS IN NO TIME!
Song about the unfairness of the world
Views: 1,204,582
YOU'RE JUST PRANKING ME.
YOU STILL DON'T BELIEVE US?
HEY, KIRBY! YOUR SONG HAS BLOWN UP!
CELEBRITIES AND MUSIC ARTISTS ARE PUTTIN' UP COVER VIDEOS OF YOUR SONG!
PLIP PLIP
CLAMR CLAMR
IT'S EVEN ON THE MEDIA. IT'S THE BIGGEST HIT SONG!
YOU'RE JUST PRANKING ME.
HOW LONG ARE YA GONNA DRAG THAT ON?!
KIRBY'S SONG, "PLANET TEARS"...
ROAR
...CONTINUED ITS METEORIC RISE, UNTIL FINALLY...
KIRBY SIGNED FOR A MAJOR-LABEL DEBUT!

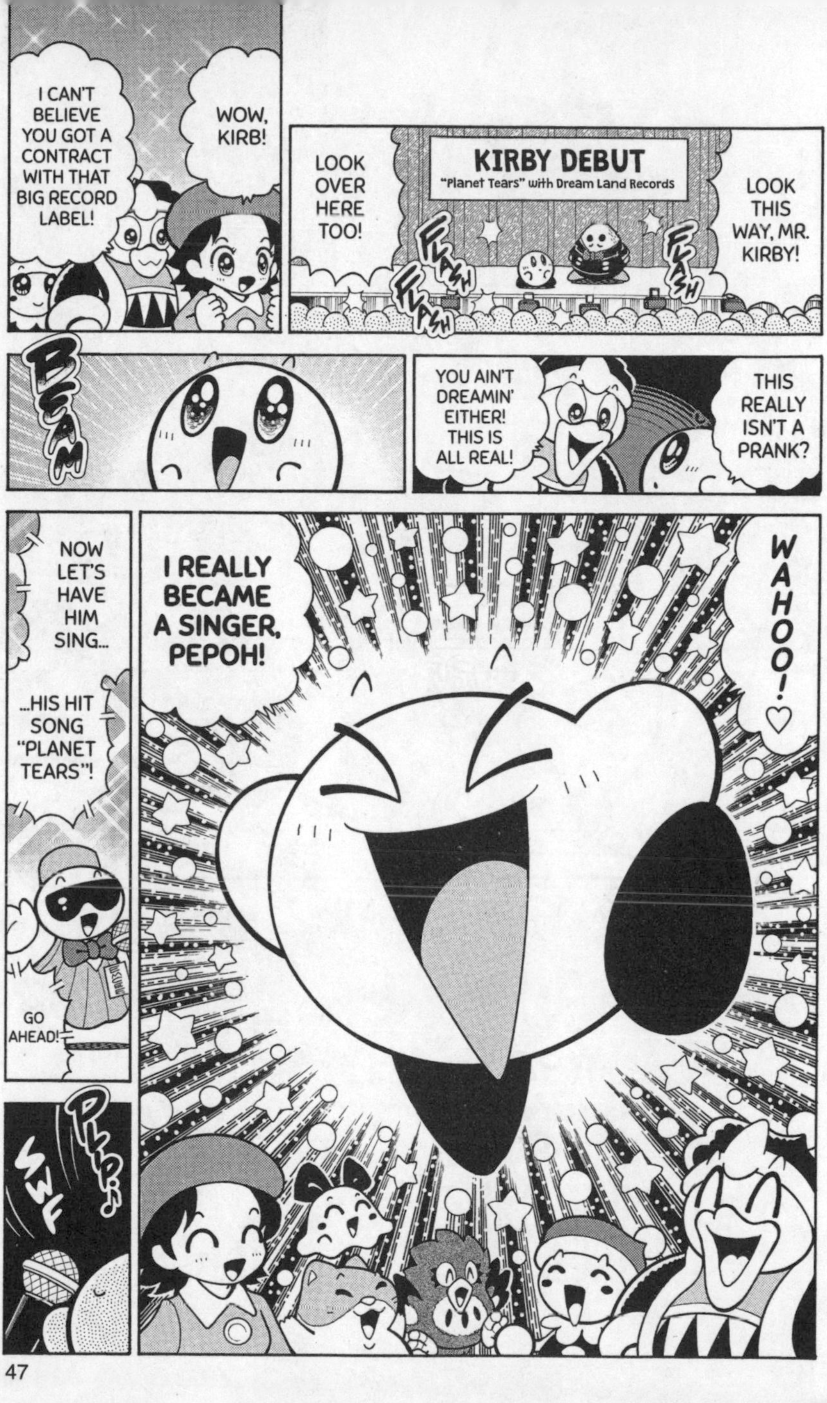
KIRBY DEBUT
"Planet Tears" with Dream Land Records
LOOK THIS WAY, MR. KIRBY!
FLASH
FLASH
FLASH
LOOK OVER HERE TOO!
WOW, KIRB!
I CAN'T BELIEVE YOU GOT A CONTRACT WITH THAT BIG RECORD LABEL!
THIS REALLY ISN'T A PRANK?
YOU AIN'T DREAMIN' EITHER! THIS IS ALL REAL!
BEAM
WAHOO!♡
I REALLY BECAME A SINGER, PEPOH!
NOW LET'S HAVE HIM SING...
...HIS HIT SONG "PLANET TEARS"!
GO AHEAD!
PLIP
SWF

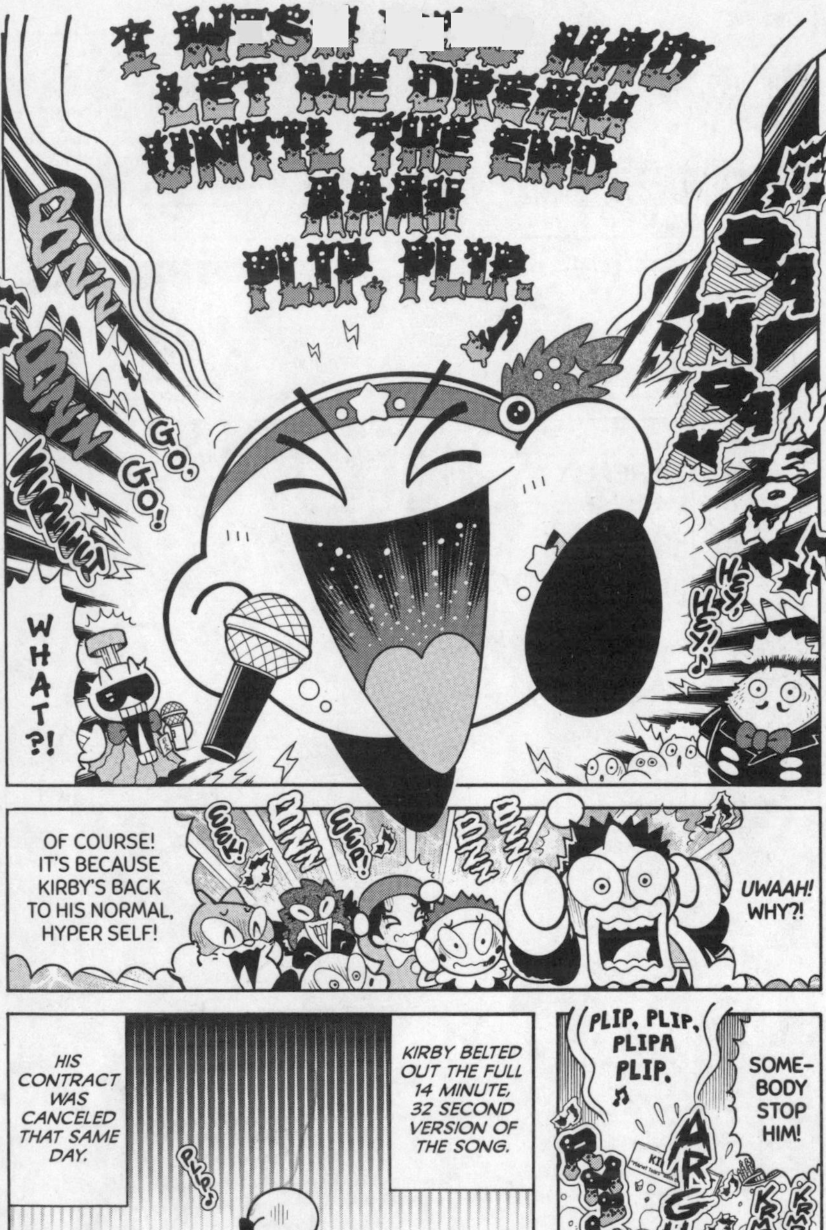
HAD
LET ME DREAM
UNTIL THE END.
AAAH
PLIP, PLIP.
HEY, HEY!
GO, GO!
WHAT?!
UWAAH! WHY?!
OF COURSE! IT'S BECAUSE KIRBY'S BACK TO HIS NORMAL, HYPER SELF!
PLIP, PLIP, PLIPA PLIP.
SOME-BODY STOP HIM!
ARGH
KRMBL
KRMBL
KIRBY BELTED OUT THE FULL 14 MINUTE, 32 SECOND VERSION OF THE SONG.
HIS CONTRACT WAS CANCELED THAT SAME DAY.

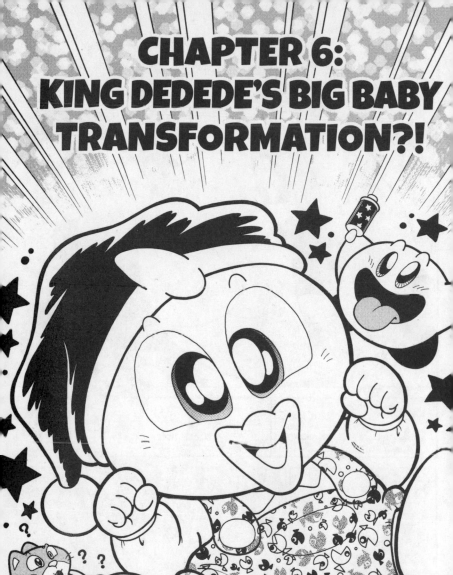

CHAPTER 6: KING DEDEDE'S BIG BABY TRANSFORMATION?!

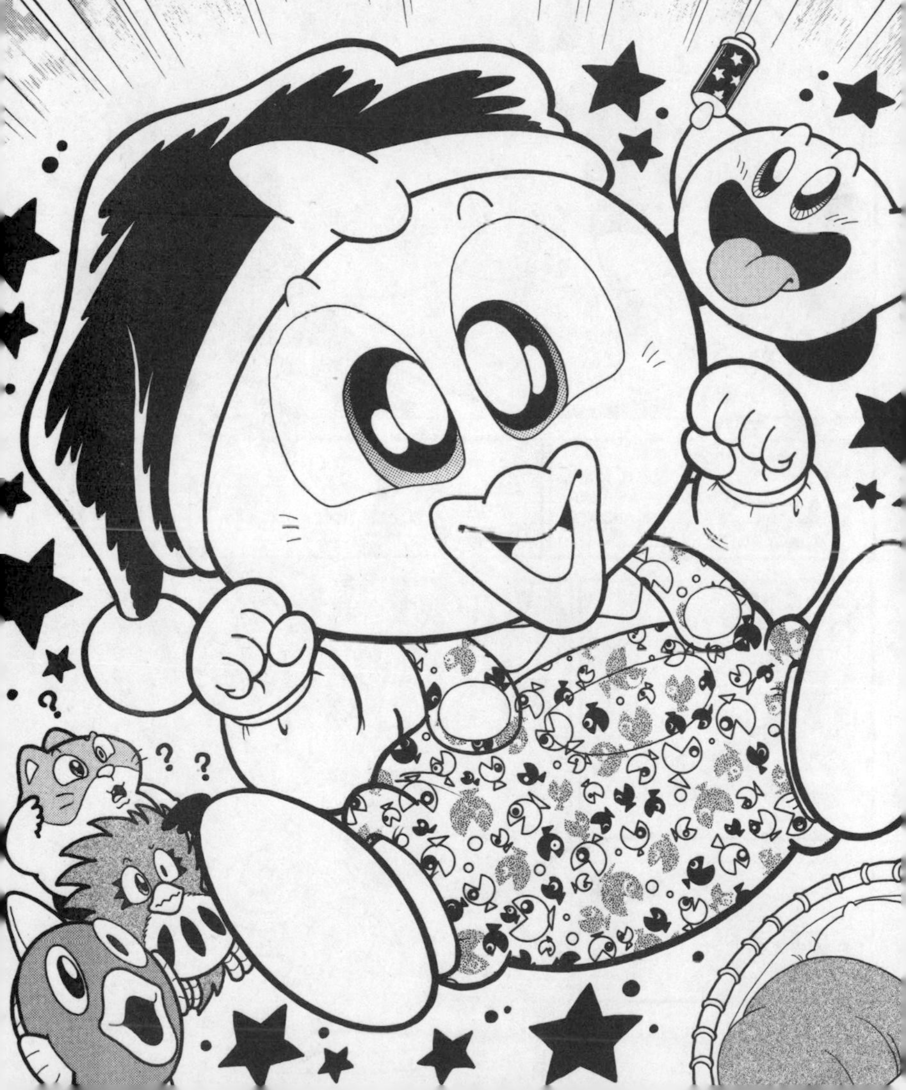

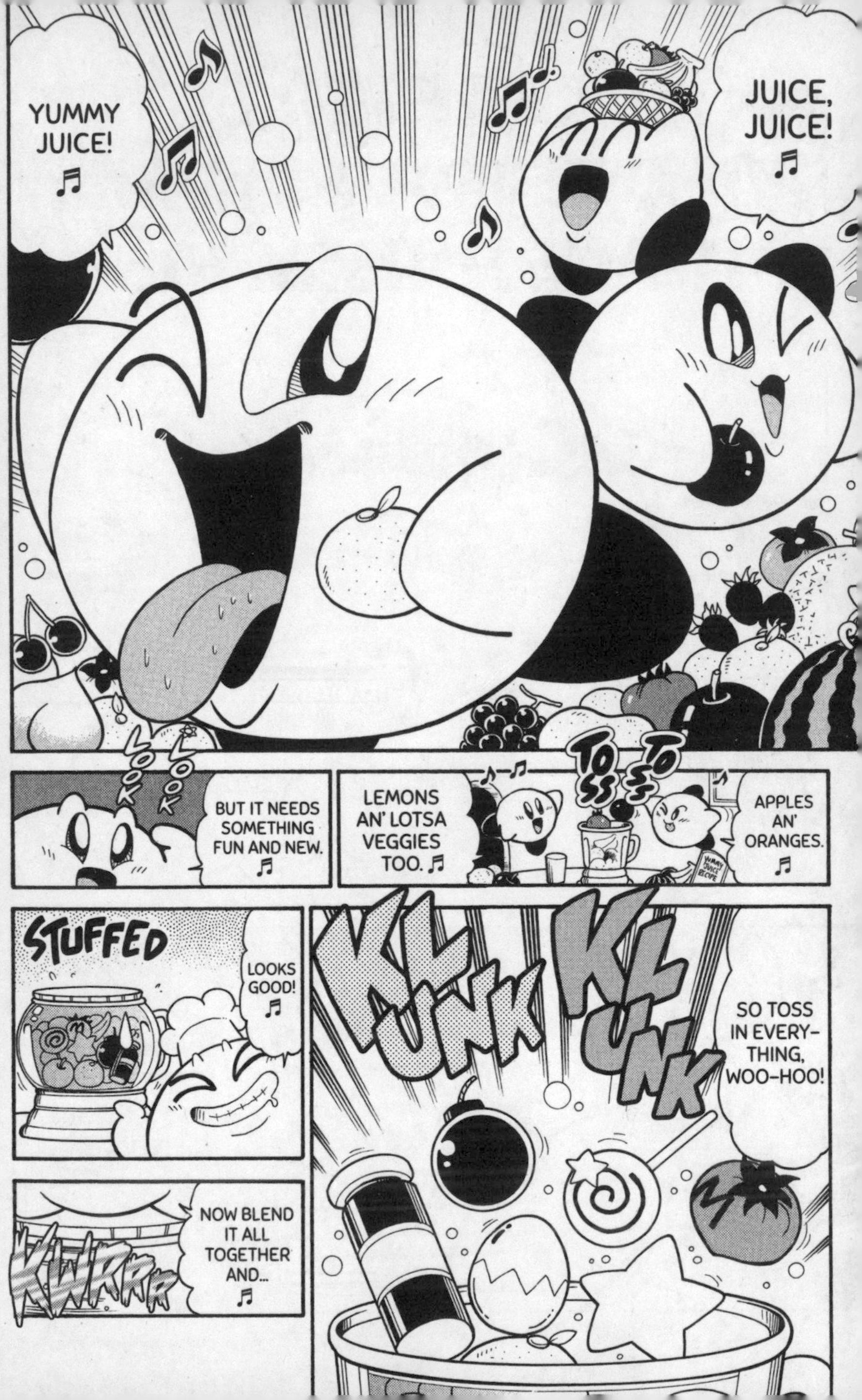
JUICE, JUICE! ♬
YUMMY JUICE! ♬
APPLES AN' ORANGES. ♬
TOSS
TOSS
LEMONS AN' LOTSA VEGGIES TOO. ♬
BUT IT NEEDS SOMETHING FUN AND NEW. ♬
LOOK
LOOK
SO TOSS IN EVERY-THING, WOO-HOO!
KLUNK
KLUNK
STUFFED
LOOKS GOOD! ♬
NOW BLEND IT ALL TOGETHER AND... ♬
KWRRR

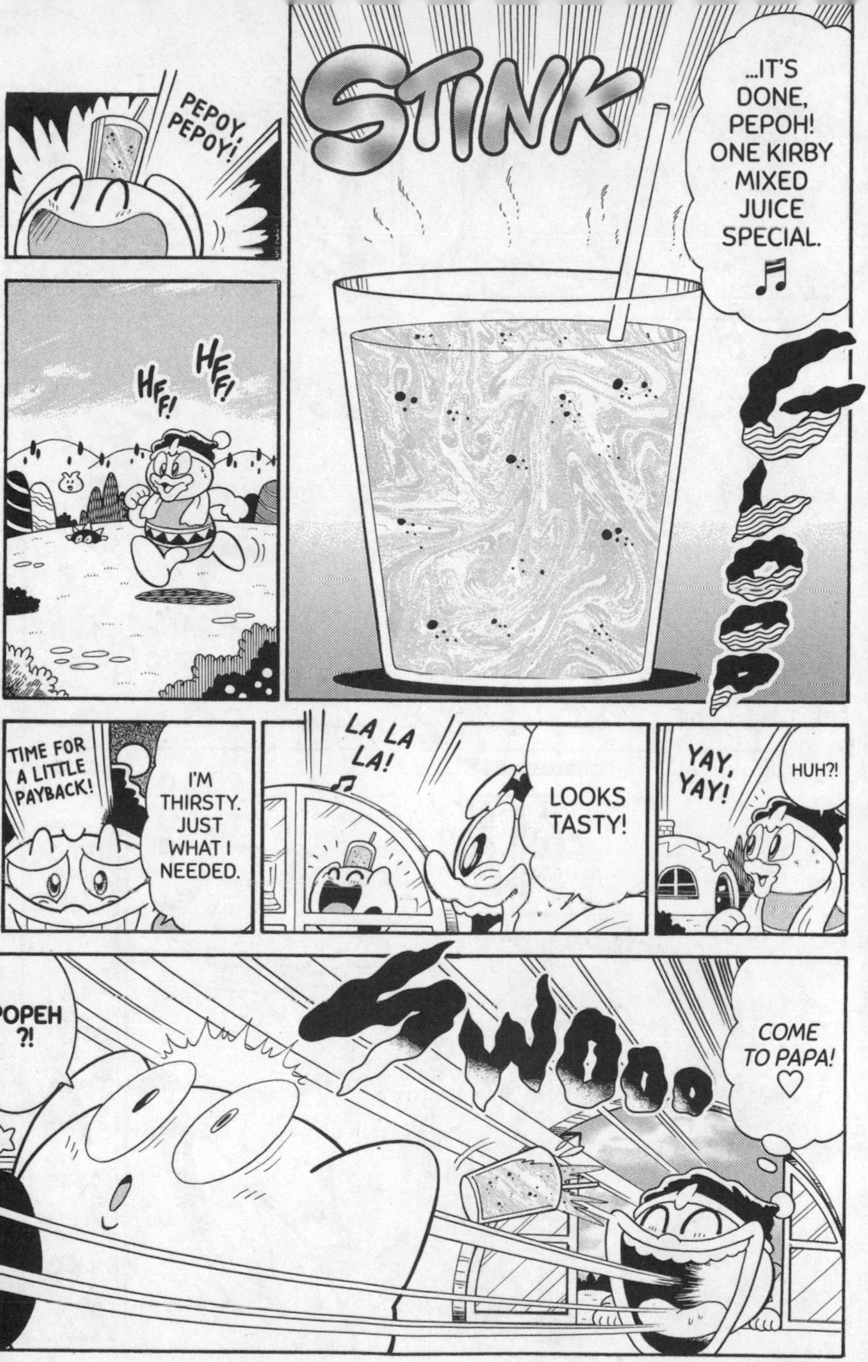
STINK
...IT'S DONE, PEPOH! ONE KIRBY MIXED JUICE SPECIAL. ♬
GLOOP
PEPOY, PEPOY!
HEFF! HEFF!
YAY, YAY!
HUH?!
LA LA LA! ♪
LOOKS TASTY!
TIME FOR A LITTLE PAYBACK!
I'M THIRSTY. JUST WHAT I NEEDED.
COME TO PAPA! ♡
GWOOO
POPEH ?!

AUTHOR'S COMMENT

I'D WANT TO RAISE A BABY KIRBY! THE NAME PANCHO CAME FROM KAZUO "PANCHO" ITO. KNOWN FOR MODERATING JAPAN'S PROFESSIONAL BASEBALL DRAFT CONFERENCE.

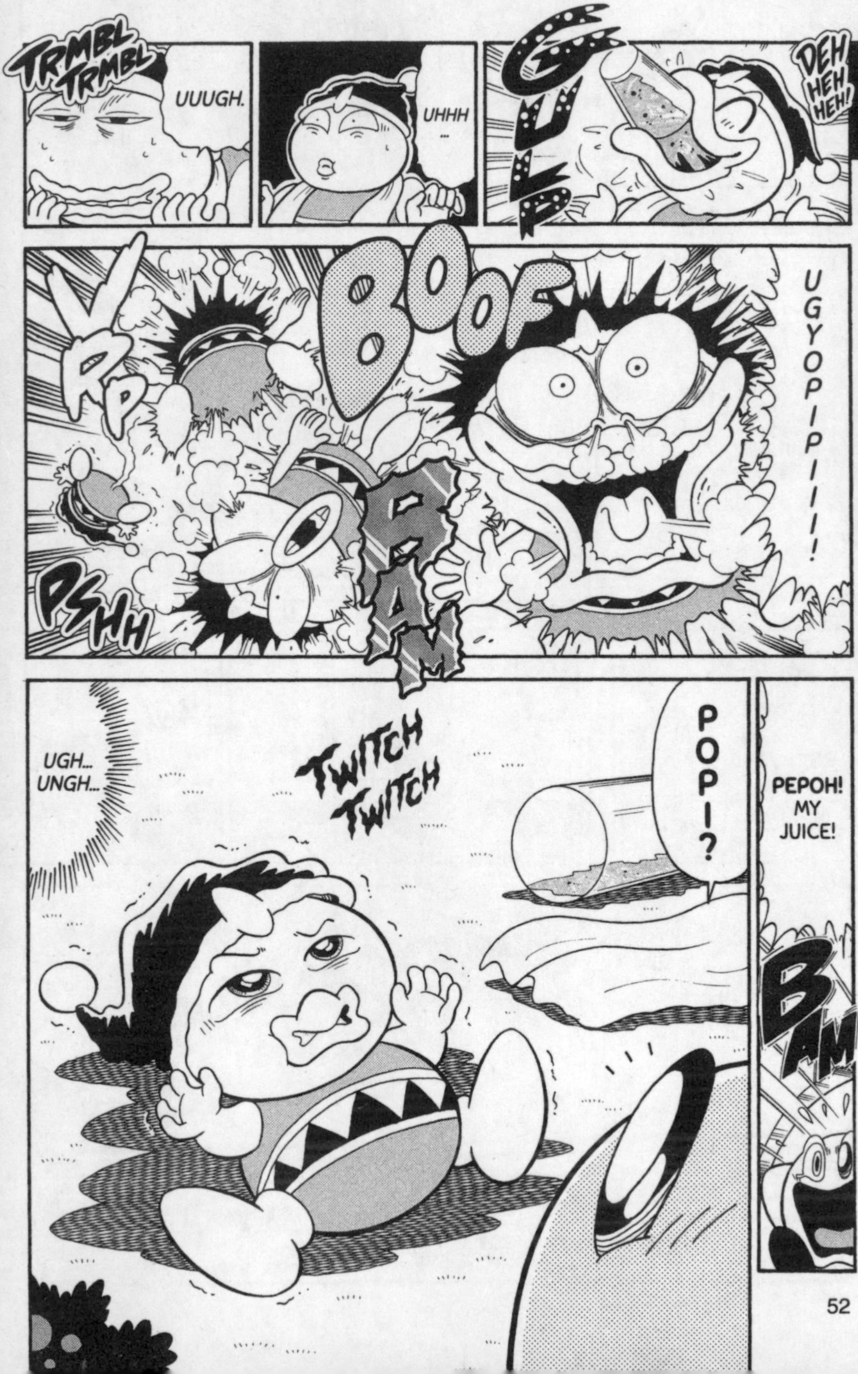
GULP
DEH HEH HEH!
UHHH...
TRMBL TRMBL
UUUGH.
UGYOPIPI!!!!
BOOF
BAM
RP
PSHH
PEPOH! MY JUICE!
BAM
POPI?
TWITCH TWITCH
UGH... UNGH...

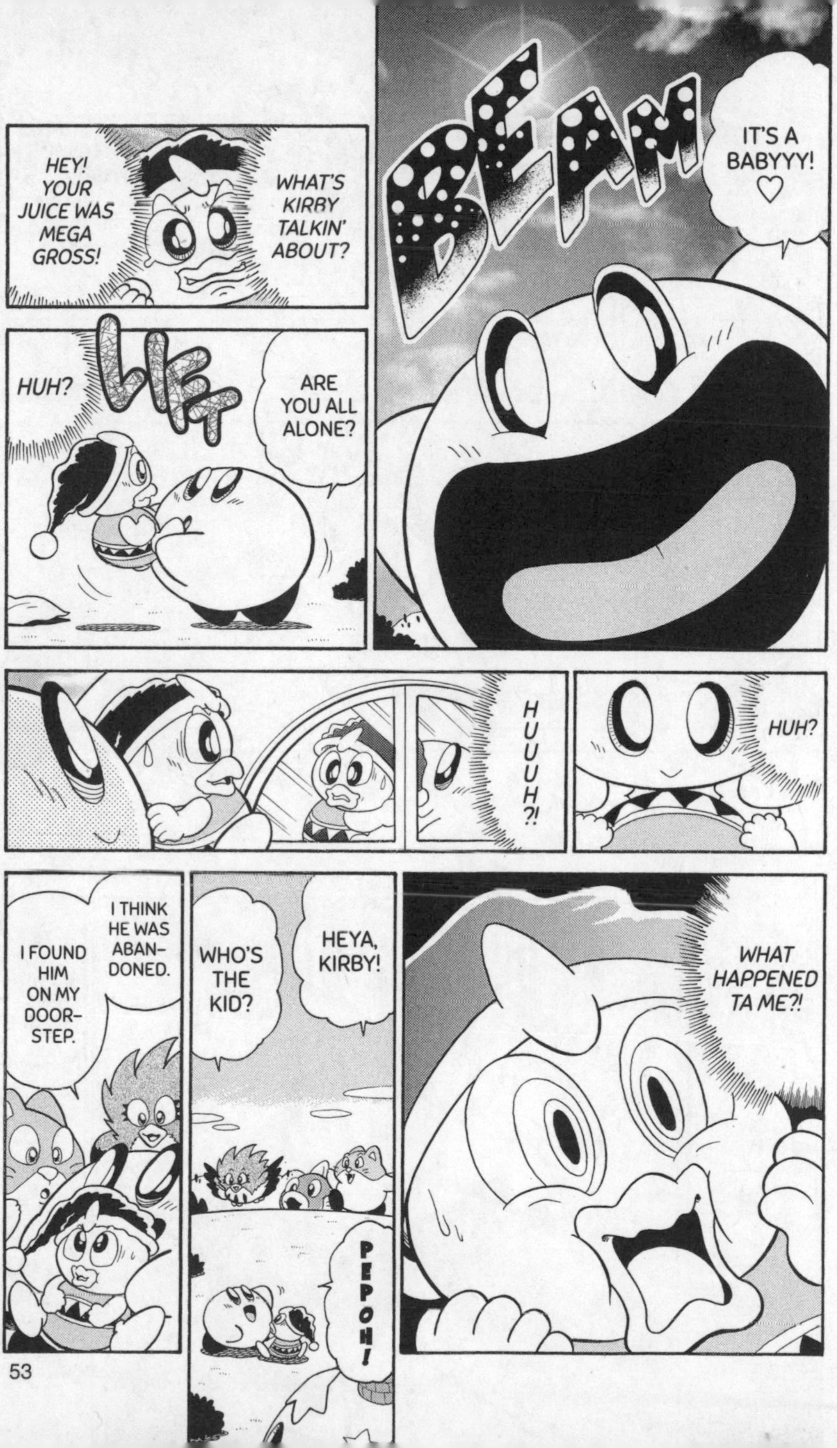
BEAM
IT'S A BABYYY! ♡
WHAT'S KIRBY TALKIN' ABOUT?
HEY! YOUR JUICE WAS MEGA GROSS!
ARE YOU ALL ALONE?
LIFT
HUH?
HUH?
HUUUUH?!
WHAT HAPPENED TA ME?!
HEYA, KIRBY!
WHO'S THE KID?
PEPOH!
I THINK HE WAS ABAN-DONED.
I FOUND HIM ON MY DOOR-STEP.

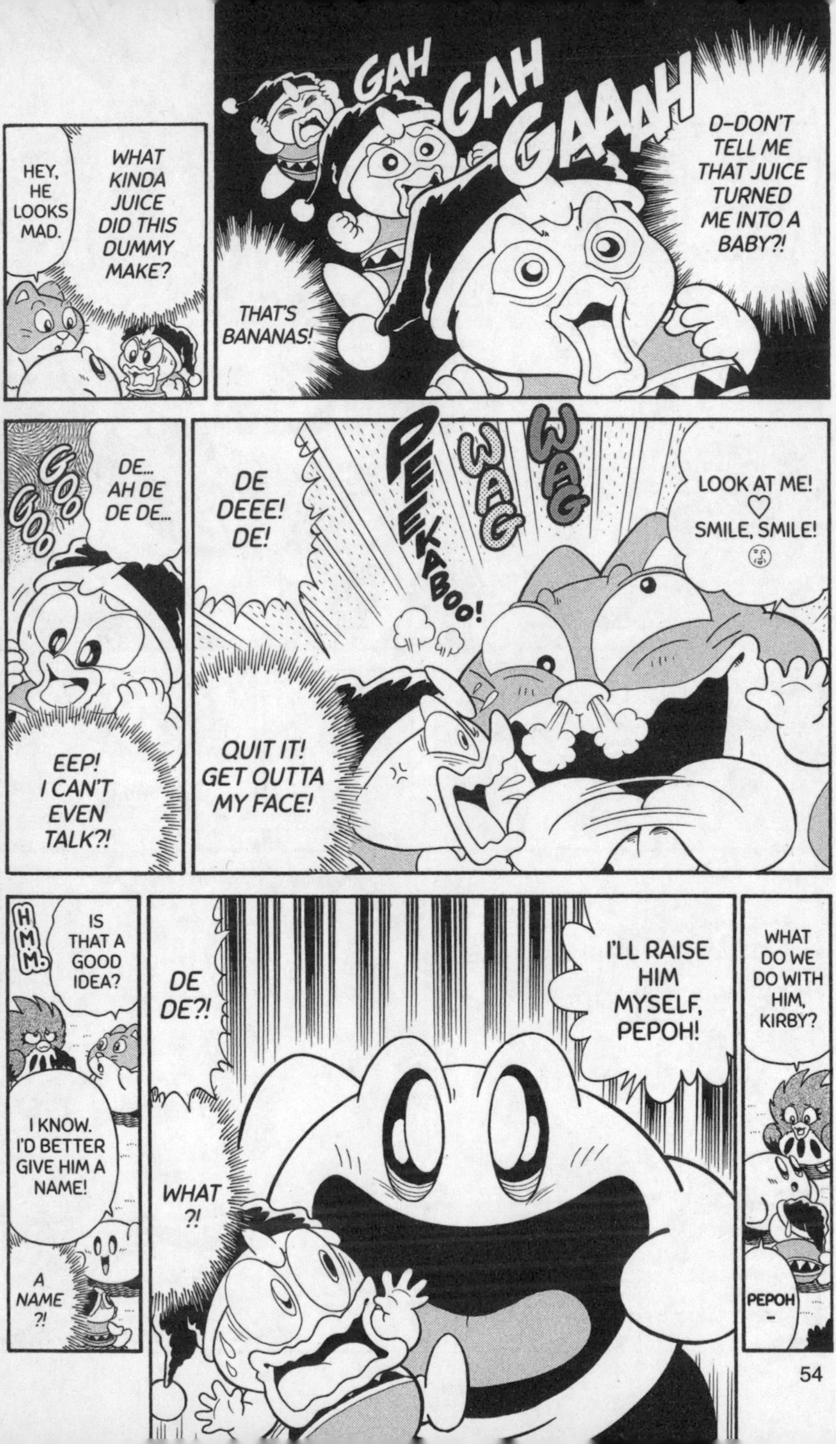
GAH
GAH
GAAAH
D-DON'T TELL ME THAT JUICE TURNED ME INTO A BABY?!
THAT'S BANANAS!
WHAT KINDA JUICE DID THIS DUMMY MAKE?
HEY, HE LOOKS MAD.
LOOK AT ME! ♡ SMILE, SMILE!
WAG
WAG
PEEKABOO!
DE DEEE! DE!
QUIT IT! GET OUTTA MY FACE!
DE... AH DE DE DE...
GOO
GOO
EEP! I CAN'T EVEN TALK?!
WHAT DO WE DO WITH HIM, KIRBY?
PEPOH...
I'LL RAISE HIM MYSELF, PEPOH!
DE DE?!
WHAT?!
IS THAT A GOOD IDEA?
HMMM.
I KNOW. I'D BETTER GIVE HIM A NAME!
A NAME?!

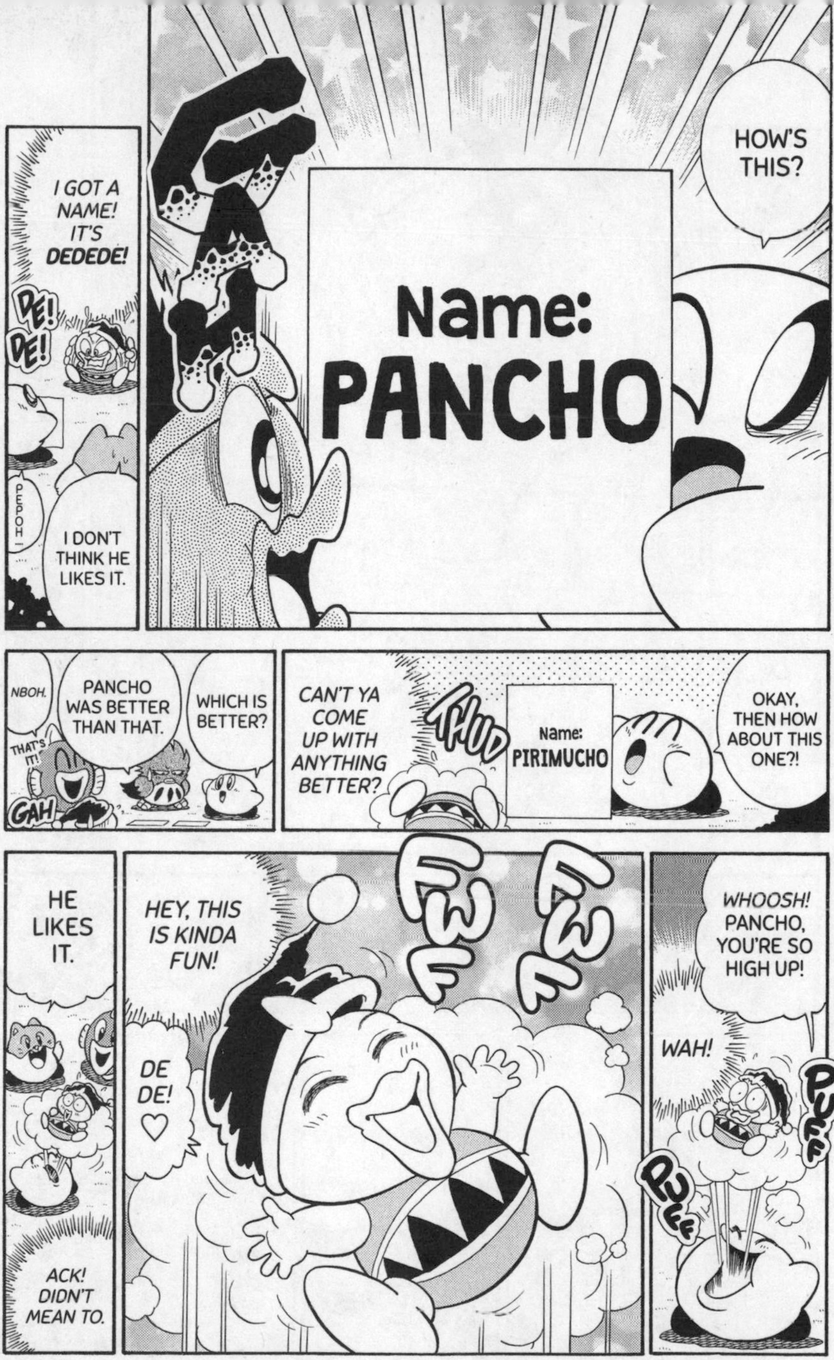
HOW'S THIS?
Name: PANCHO
I GOT A NAME! IT'S DEDEDE!
DE! DE!
PEPOH....
I DON'T THINK HE LIKES IT.
OKAY, THEN HOW ABOUT THIS ONE?!
Name: PIRIMUCHO
THUD
CAN'T YA COME UP WITH ANYTHING BETTER?
WHICH IS BETTER?
PANCHO WAS BETTER THAN THAT.
NBOH.
THAT'S IT!
GAH
WHOOSH! PANCHO, YOU'RE SO HIGH UP!
WAH!
PUFF
PUFF
FWF
FWF
HEY, THIS IS KINDA FUN!
DE DE! ♡
HE LIKES IT.
ACK! DIDN'T MEAN TO.

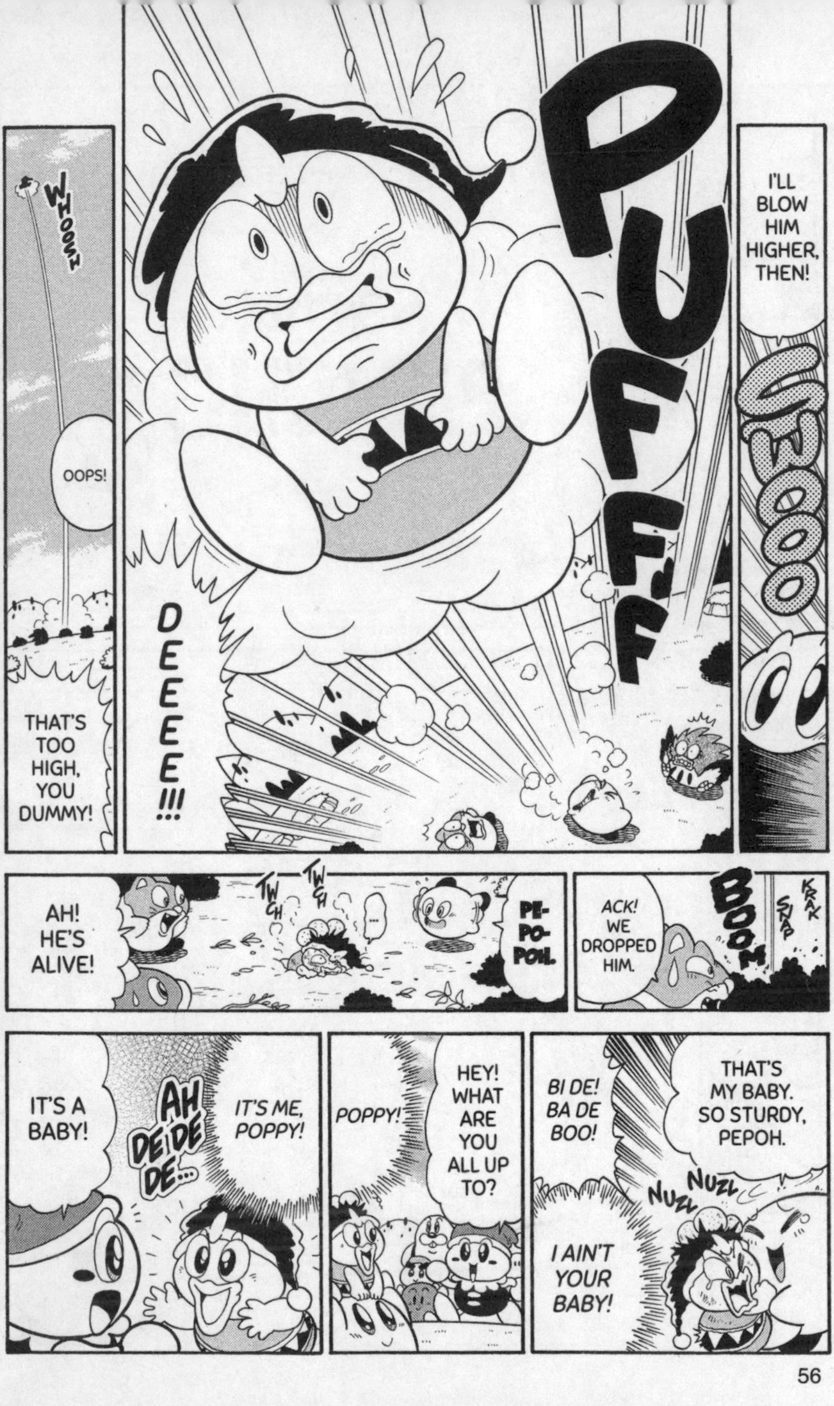
I'LL BLOW HIM HIGHER, THEN!
SWOOOO
PUFFFFF
DEEEEE!!!
WHOOSH
OOPS!
THAT'S TOO HIGH, YOU DUMMY!
ACK! WE DROPPED HIM.
BOOOM
KRAK
SNAP
PE-PO-POH.
...
TWCH
TWCH
AH! HE'S ALIVE!
THAT'S MY BABY. SO STURDY, PEPOH.
NUZL
NUZL
BI DE! BA DE BOO!
I AIN'T YOUR BABY!
HEY! WHAT ARE YOU ALL UP TO?
POPPY!
IT'S ME, POPPY!
AH DE DE DE...
IT'S A BABY!

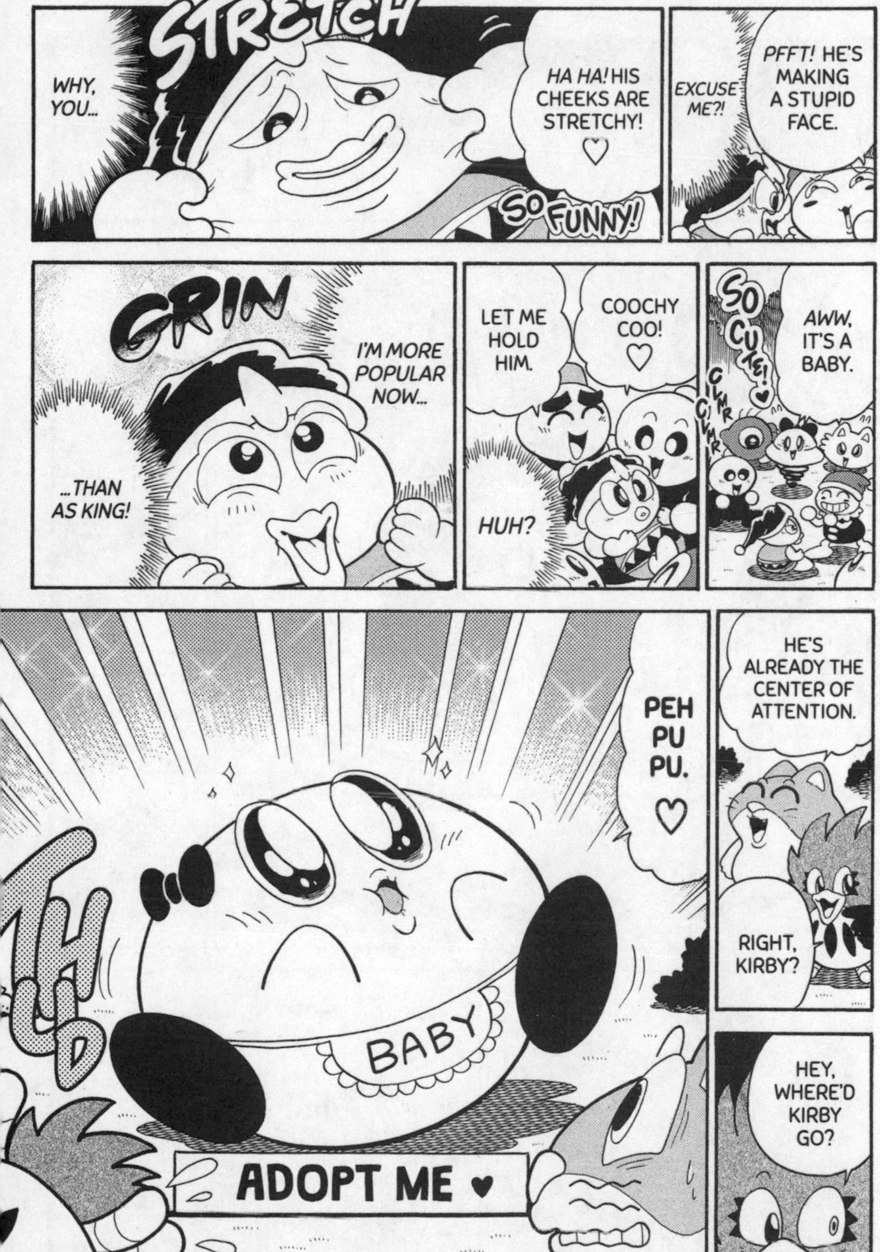
PFFT! HE'S MAKING A STUPID FACE.
EXCUSE ME?!
STRETCH
HA HA! HIS CHEEKS ARE STRETCHY! ♡
WHY, YOU...
SO FUNNY!
AWW, IT'S A BABY.
SO CUTE! ♡
COOCHY COO! ♡
LET ME HOLD HIM.
HUH?
GRIN
I'M MORE POPULAR NOW...
...THAN AS KING!
HE'S ALREADY THE CENTER OF ATTENTION.
RIGHT, KIRBY?
HEY, WHERE'D KIRBY GO?
PEH PU PU. ♡
THUD
BABY
ADOPT ME ♡

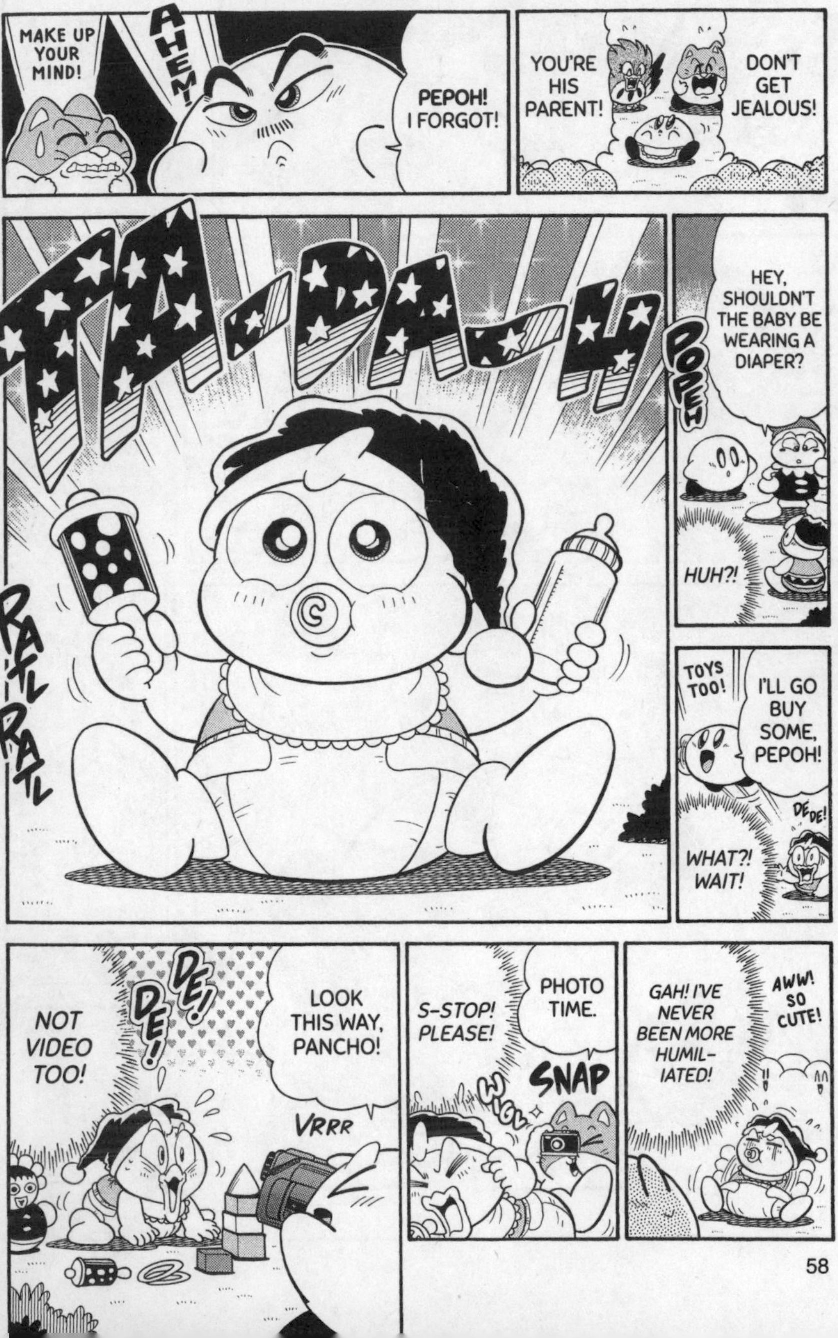
DON'T GET JEALOUS!
YOU'RE HIS PARENT!
PEPOH! I FORGOT!
AHEM!
MAKE UP YOUR MIND!
HEY, SHOULDN'T THE BABY BE WEARING A DIAPER?
POPEH
HUH?!
I'LL GO BUY SOME, PEPOH!
TOYS TOO!
DE DE!
WHAT?! WAIT!
TA-DA-H
RATL RATL
AWW! SO CUTE!
GAH! I'VE NEVER BEEN MORE HUMIL-IATED!
PHOTO TIME.
S-STOP! PLEASE!
SNAP
LOOK THIS WAY, PANCHO!
DE DE!
NOT VIDEO TOO!
VRRR

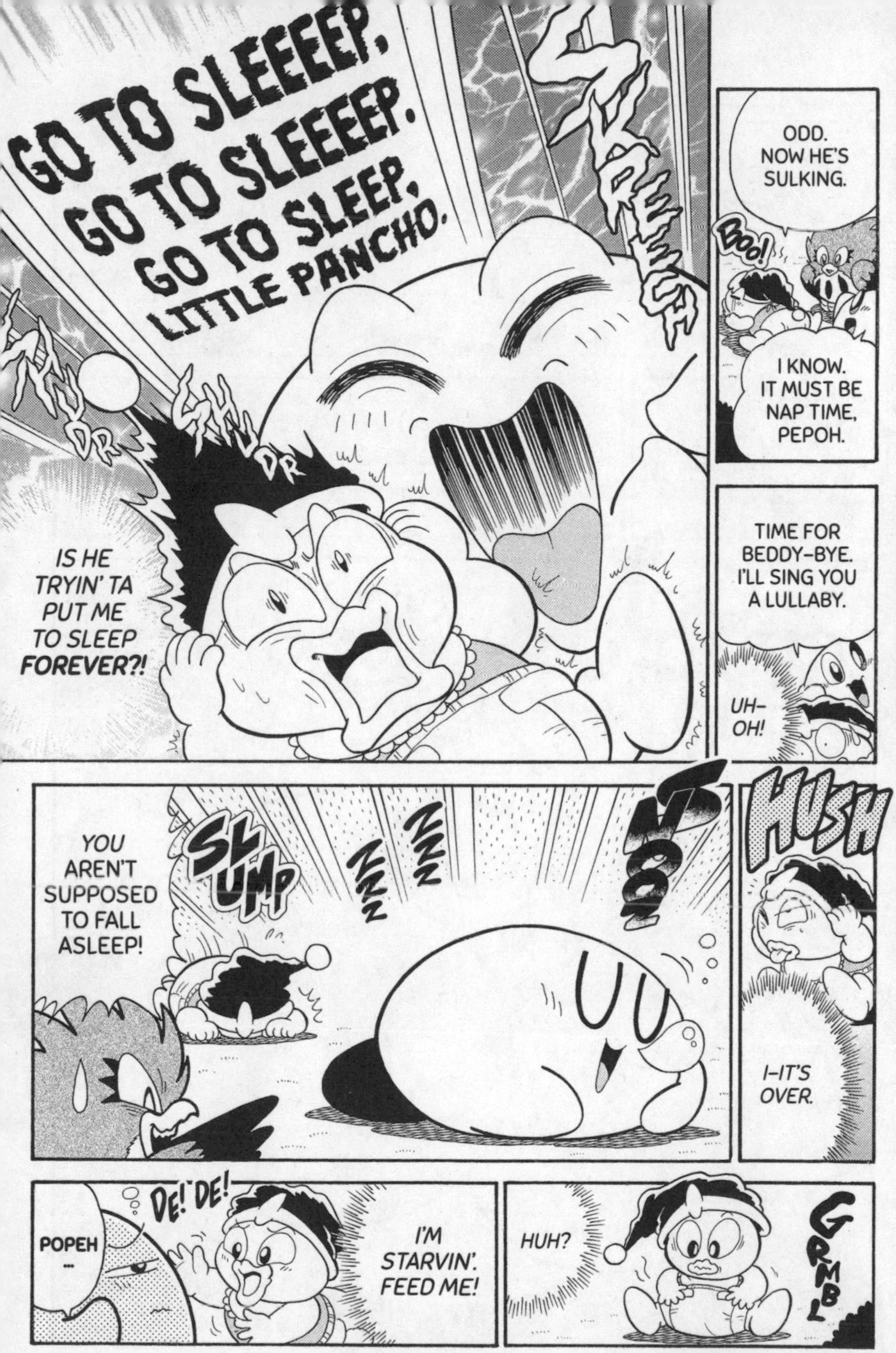
ODD. NOW HE'S SULKING.
BOO!
I KNOW. IT MUST BE NAP TIME, PEPOH.
TIME FOR BEDDY-BYE. I'LL SING YOU A LULLABY.
UH-OH!
GO TO SLEEEEP, GO TO SLEEEEP. GO TO SLEEP, LITTLE PANCHO.
IS HE TRYIN' TA PUT ME TO SLEEP FOREVER?!
HUSH
I-IT'S OVER.
ZZZ
ZZZ
SLUMP
YOU AREN'T SUPPOSED TO FALL ASLEEP!
GRMBL
HUH?
I'M STARVIN'. FEED ME!
DE! DE!
POPEH ...

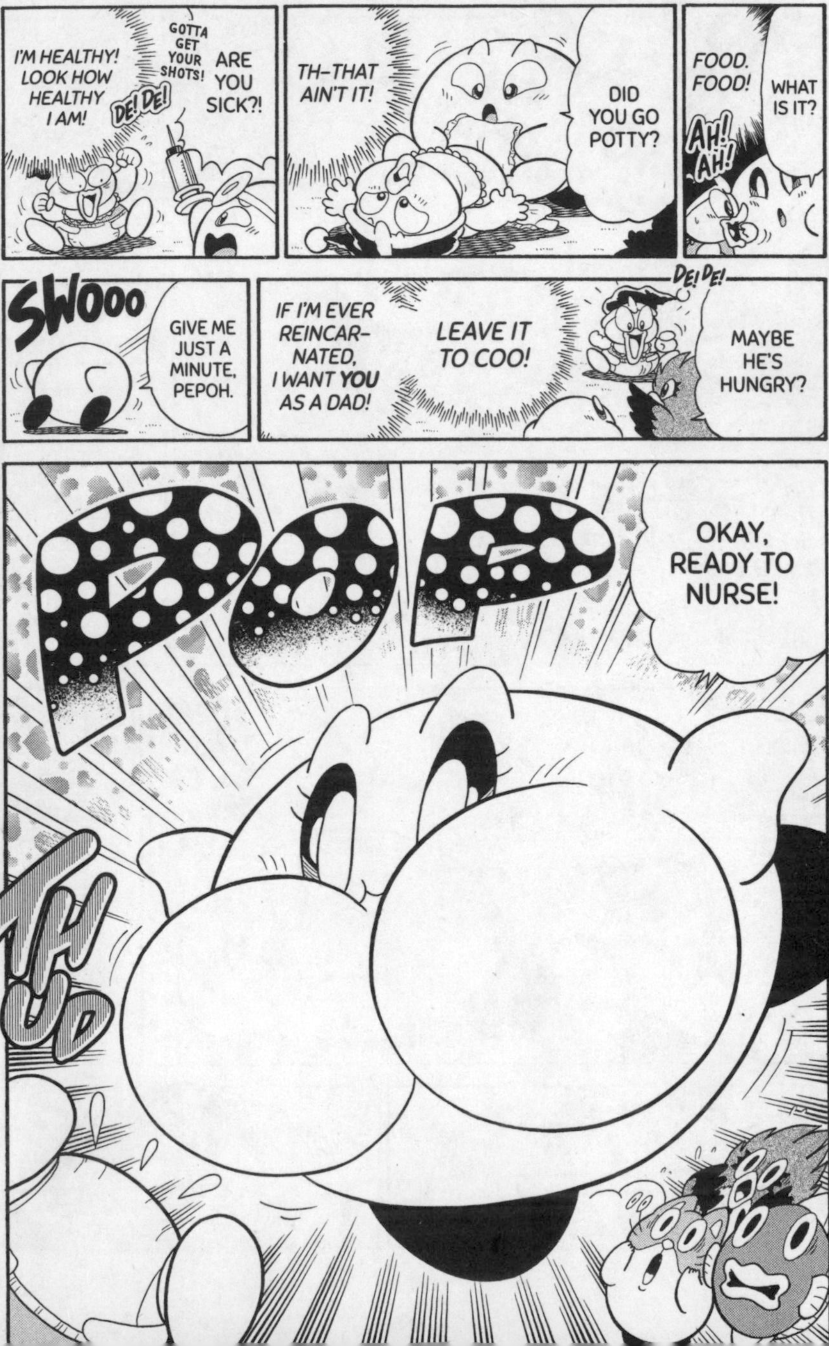
WHAT IS IT?
FOOD. FOOD!
AH! AH!
DID YOU GO POTTY?
TH-THAT AIN'T IT!
ARE YOU SICK?!
GOTTA GET YOUR SHOTS!
I'M HEALTHY! LOOK HOW HEALTHY I AM!
DE! DE!
DE! DE!
MAYBE HE'S HUNGRY?
LEAVE IT TO COO!
IF I'M EVER REINCARNATED, I WANT **YOU** AS A DAD!
GIVE ME JUST A MINUTE, PEPOH.
SWOOO
OKAY, READY TO NURSE!
POP
THUD

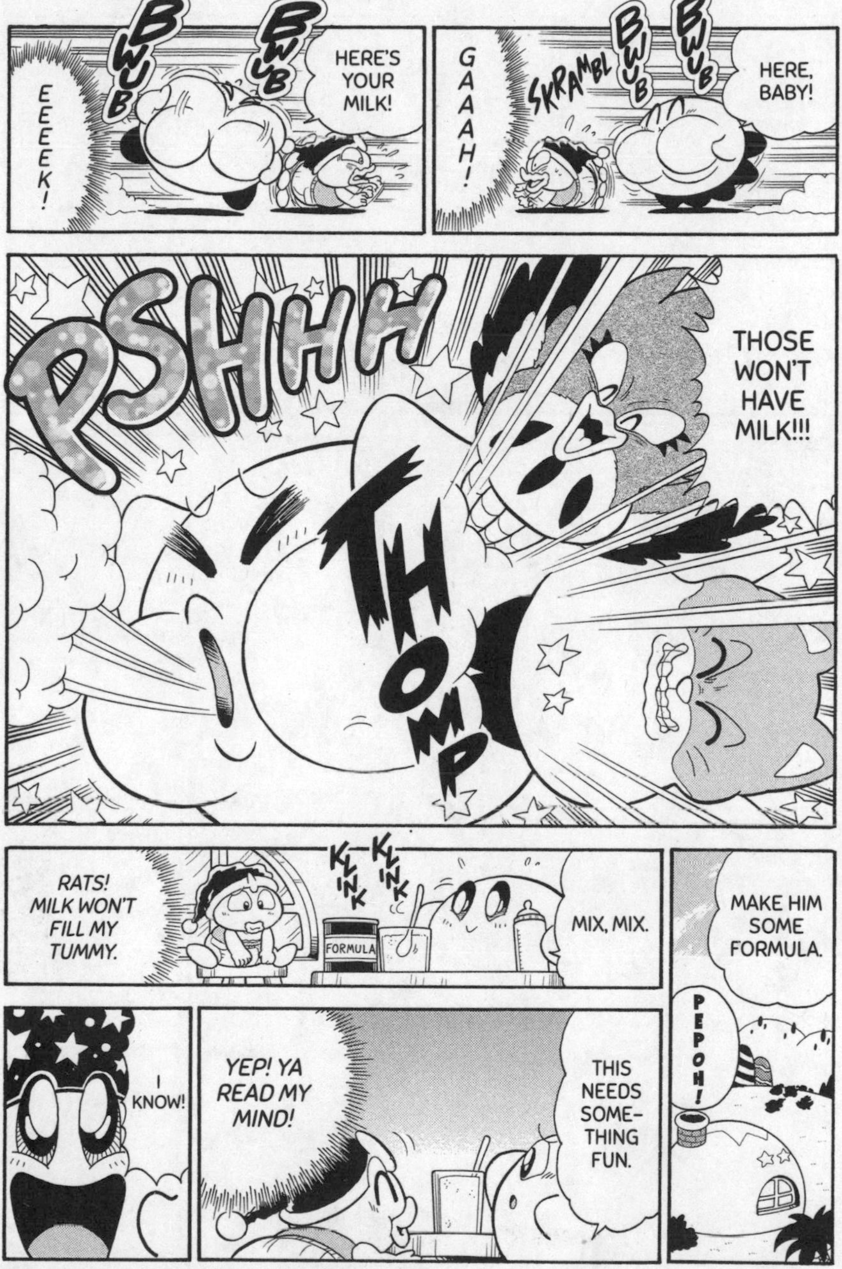
HERE, BABY!
BWUB
BWUB
SKRAMBL
GAAAH!
HERE'S YOUR MILK!
BWUB
BWUB
EEEEEK!
THOSE WON'T HAVE MILK!!!
THOMP
PSHHH
MAKE HIM SOME FORMULA.
PEPOH!
MIX, MIX.
KLINK
KLINK
FORMULA
RATS! MILK WON'T FILL MY TUMMY.
THIS NEEDS SOME-THING FUN.
YEP! YA READ MY MIND!
I KNOW!

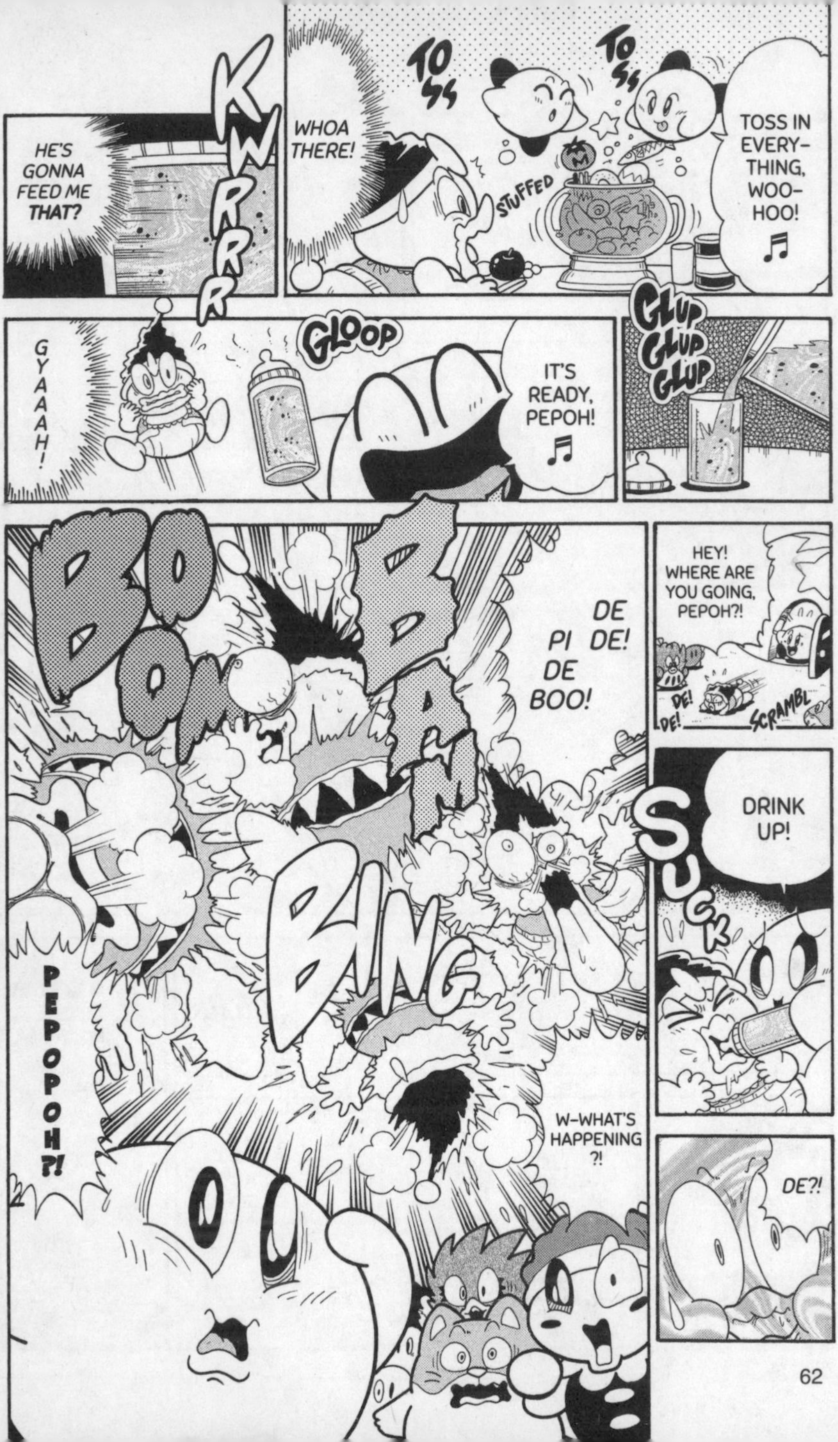
TOSS
TOSS
TOSS IN EVERY-THING, WOO-HOO! ♬
WHOA THERE!
STUFFED
KWRRRR
HE'S GONNA FEED ME THAT?
GLUP GLUP GLUP
IT'S READY, PEPOH! ♬
GLOOP
GYAAAAH!
HEY! WHERE ARE YOU GOING, PEPOH?!
DE!
DE!
SCRAMBL
DRINK UP!
SUCK
DE?!
BOOM
BAM
DE
PI DE!
DE
BOO!
BING
W-WHAT'S HAPPENING?!
PEPOPOH?!

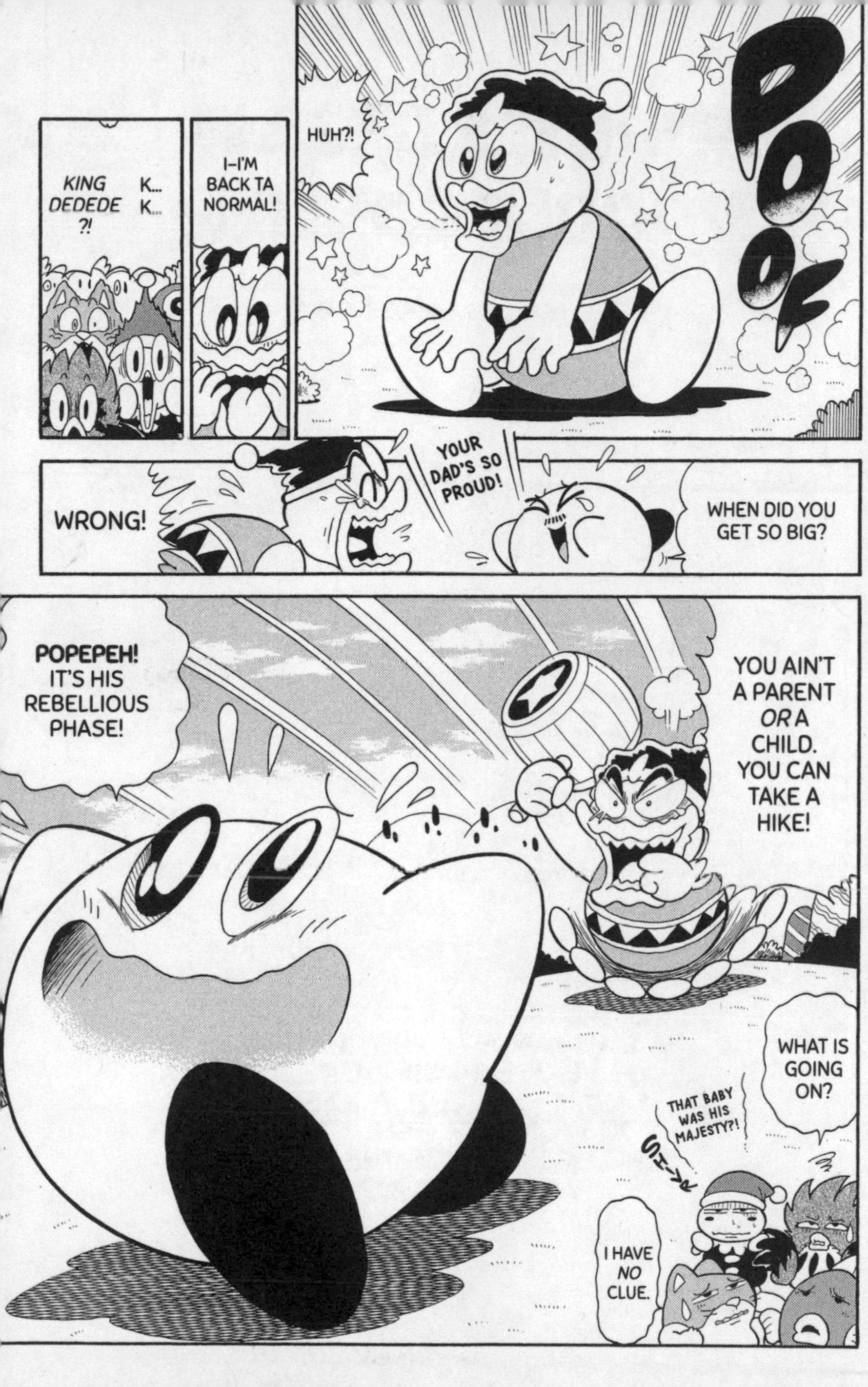
POOF
HUH?!
I-I'M BACK TA NORMAL!
K... K...
KING DEDEDE ?!
WHEN DID YOU GET SO BIG?
YOUR DAD'S SO PROUD!
WRONG!
YOU AIN'T A PARENT *OR* A CHILD. YOU CAN TAKE A HIKE!
POPEPEH! IT'S HIS REBELLIOUS PHASE!
WHAT IS GOING ON?
THAT BABY WAS HIS MAJESTY?!
I HAVE *NO* CLUE.

KIRBY'S DREAM DOODLE CORNER

KIRBY FACES PRACTICE 1

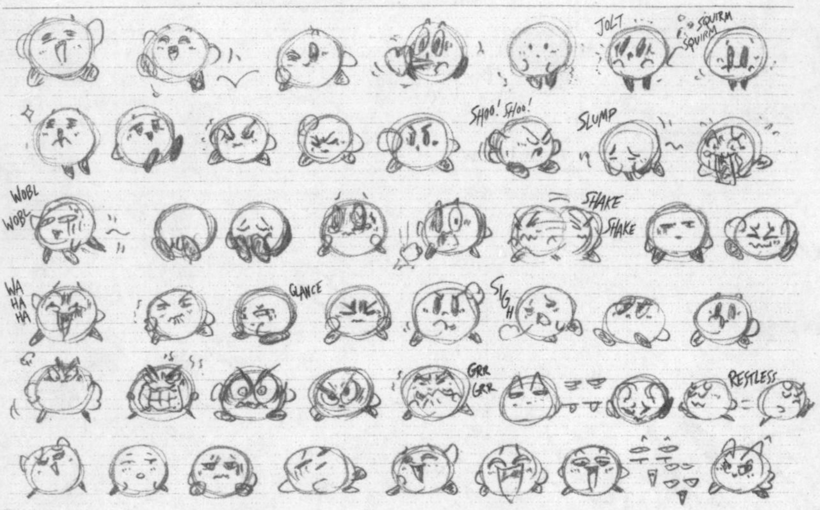
SQUIRM
SQUIRM
JOLT
SLUMP
SHOO! SHOO!
SHAKE
SHAKE
WOBL
WOBL
SIGH
GLANCE
WA
HA
HA
RESTLESS
GRR
GRR

AS THE MAIN CHARACTER OF A GAG MANGA, KIRBY HAS TO BE VERY EXPRESSIVE. THAT SAID, IF I TAKE IT *TOO* FAR, YOU WON'T BE ABLE TO TELL WHO HE IS. THAT'S THE TOUGH PART ABOUT KIRBY.

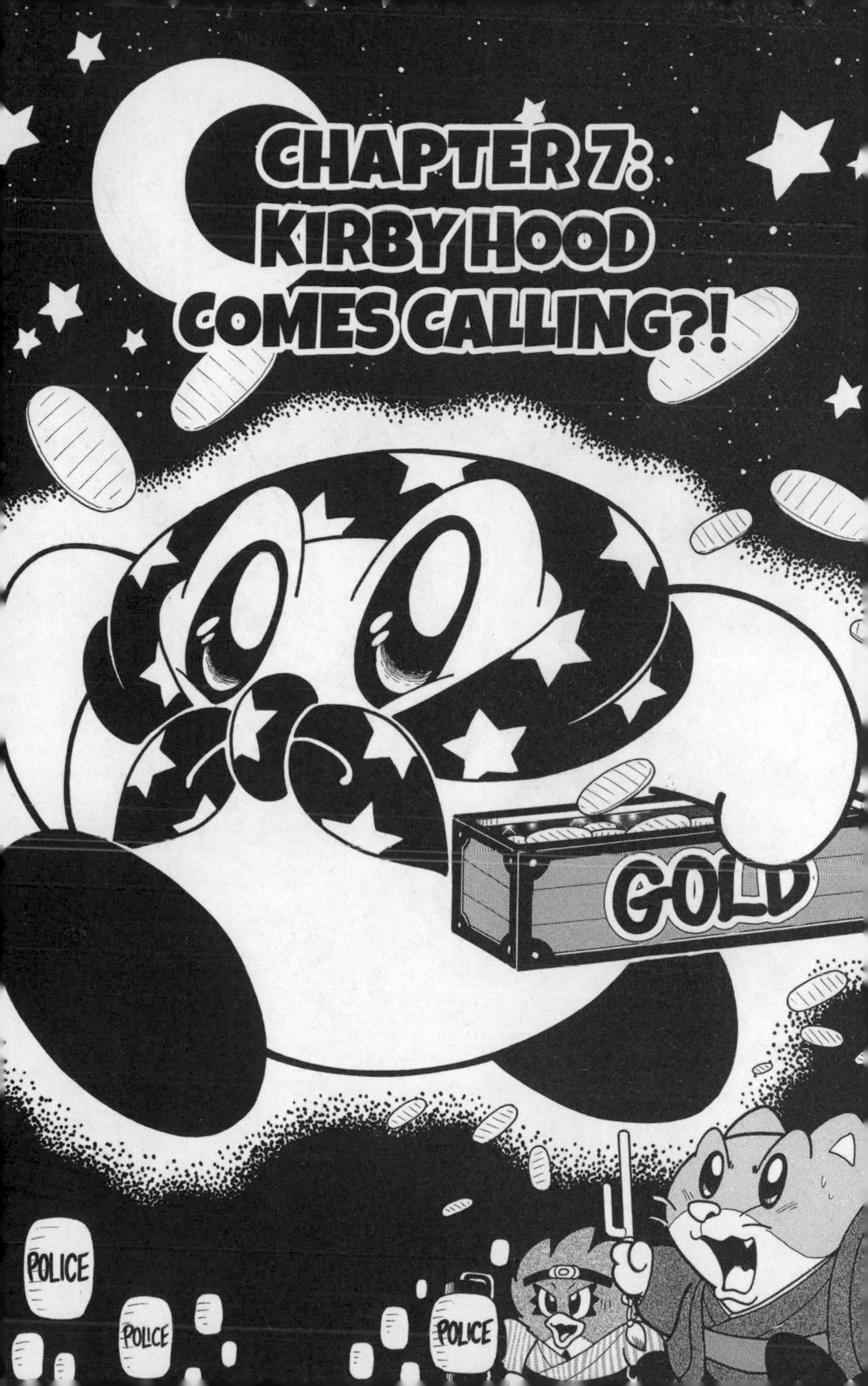
CHAPTER 7: KIRBY HOOD COMES CALLING?!
GOLD
POLICE
POLICE
POLICE

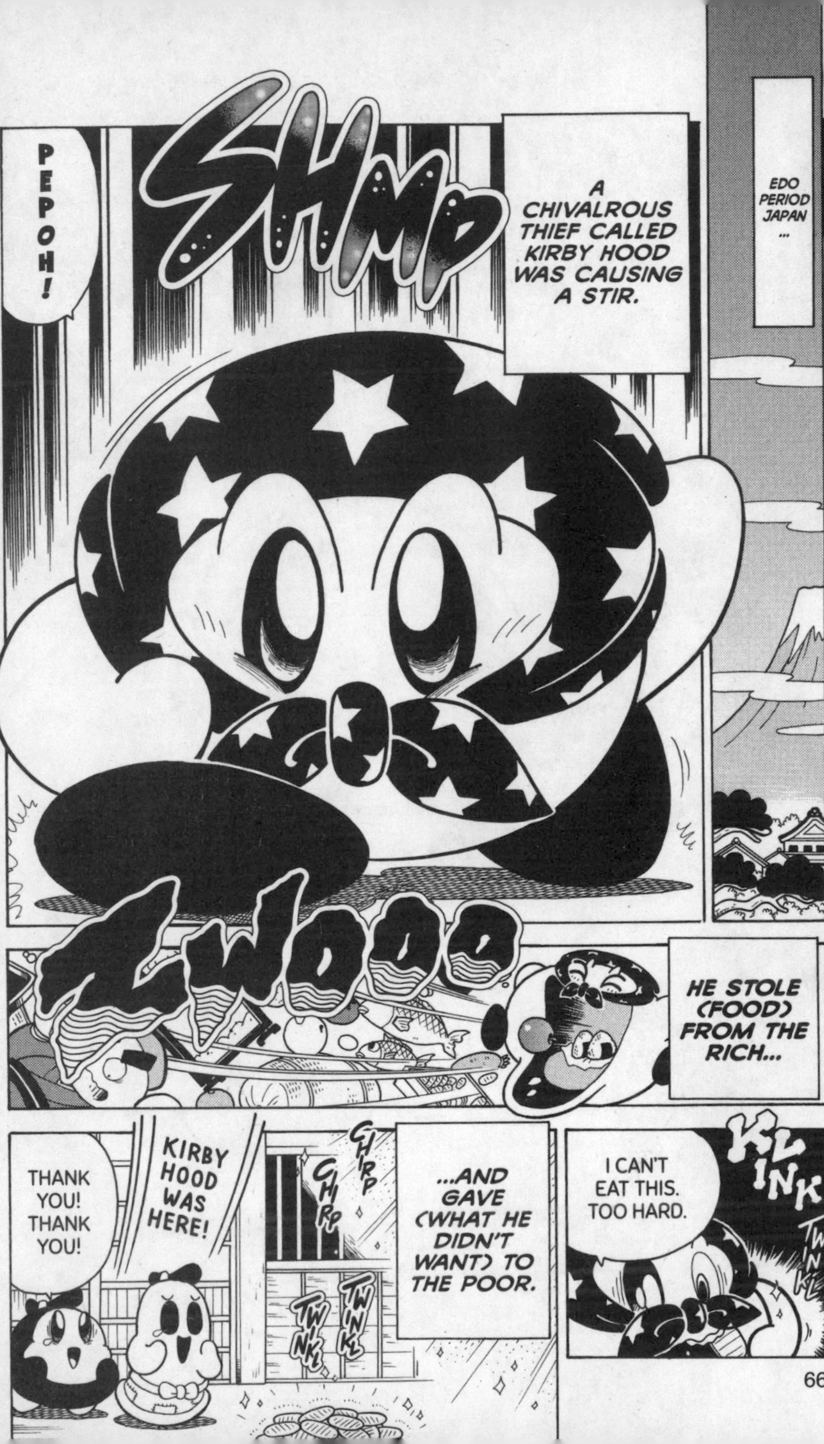
EDO PERIOD JAPAN ...
A CHIVALROUS THIEF CALLED KIRBY HOOD WAS CAUSING A STIR.
SHMP
PEPOH!
HE STOLE (FOOD) FROM THE RICH...
ZWOOO
KLINK
TWNKL
I CAN'T EAT THIS. TOO HARD.
...AND GAVE (WHAT HE DIDN'T WANT) TO THE POOR.
CHIRP
CHIRP
TWINKL
TWINKL
KIRBY HOOD WAS HERE!
THANK YOU! THANK YOU!

AUTHOR'S COMMENT

I LOVE HISTORICAL STORIES, SO I PUT ONE IN AGAIN. WHILE THE FINAL SCENE AND PUNCHLINE ARE PRETTY TYPICAL, IT LEAVES YOU WITH A GOOD FEELING.

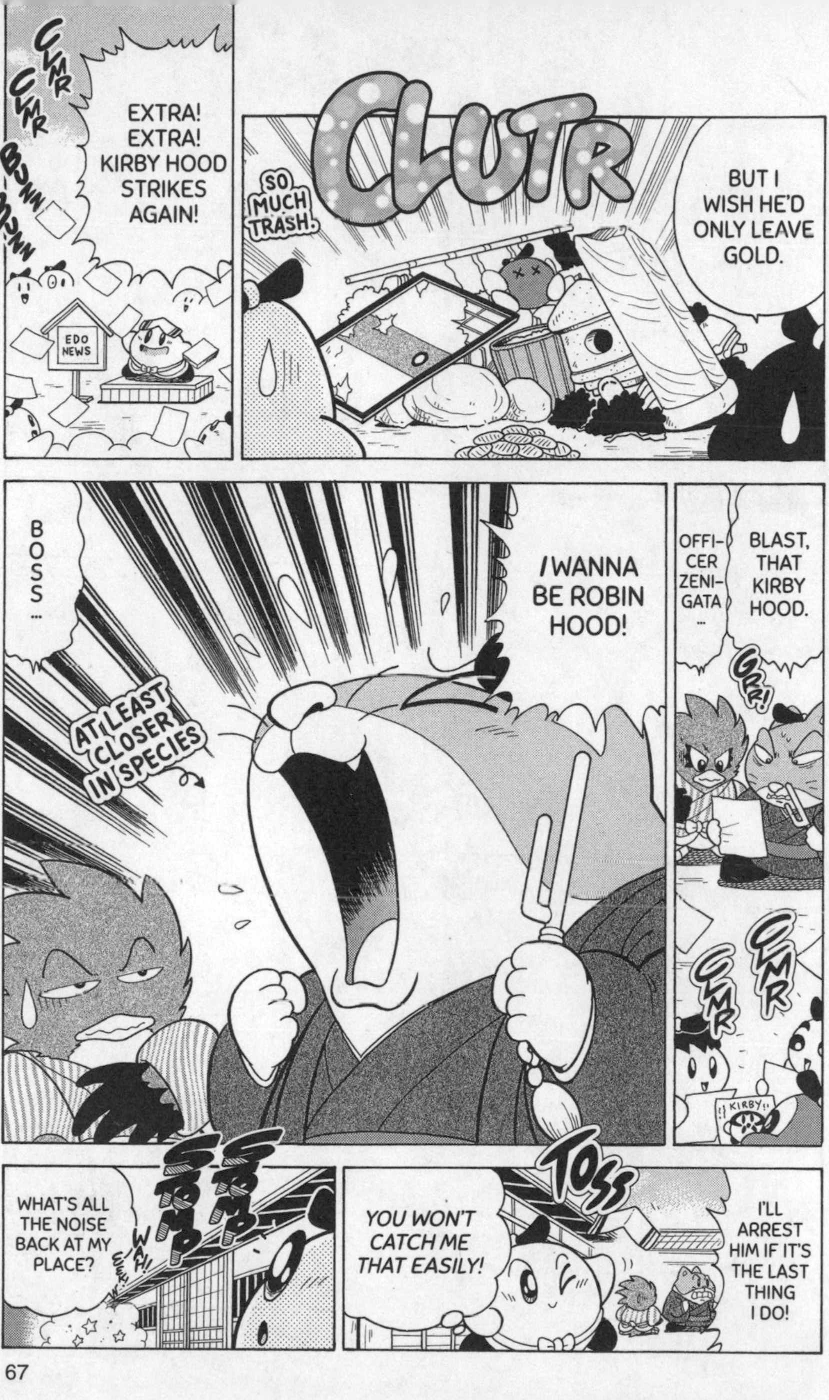
CLUTR
BUT I WISH HE'D ONLY LEAVE GOLD.
SO MUCH TRASH.
CLMR CLMR
EXTRA! EXTRA! KIRBY HOOD STRIKES AGAIN!
BUNN BUNN
EDO NEWS
BLAST, THAT KIRBY HOOD.
OFFICER ZENIGATA...
GRR!
CLMR CLMR
KIRBY
I WANNA BE ROBIN HOOD!
BOSS...
AT LEAST CLOSER IN SPECIES
TOSS
I'LL ARREST HIM IF IT'S THE LAST THING I DO!
YOU WON'T CATCH ME THAT EASILY!
STOMP STOMP
WAH!
WAH!
WHAT'S ALL THE NOISE BACK AT MY PLACE?

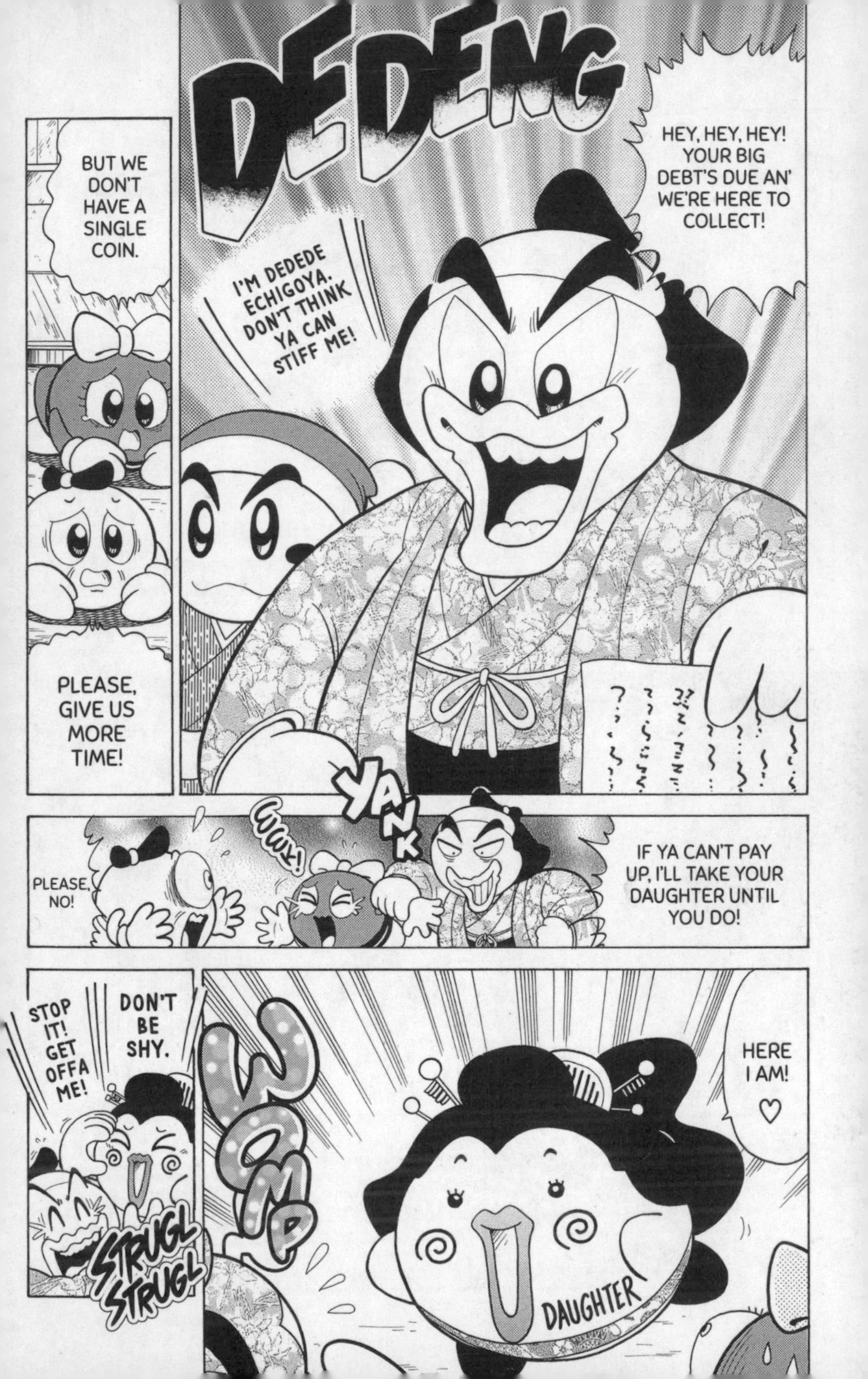
DEDENG
HEY, HEY, HEY! YOUR BIG DEBT'S DUE AN' WE'RE HERE TO COLLECT!
I'M DEDEDE ECHIGOYA. DON'T THINK YA CAN STIFF ME!
BUT WE DON'T HAVE A SINGLE COIN.
PLEASE, GIVE US MORE TIME!
IF YA CAN'T PAY UP, I'LL TAKE YOUR DAUGHTER UNTIL YOU DO!
YANK
PLEASE, NO!
HERE I AM! ♡
WOMP
DAUGHTER
DON'T BE SHY.
STOP IT! GET OFFA ME!
STRUGL STRUGL

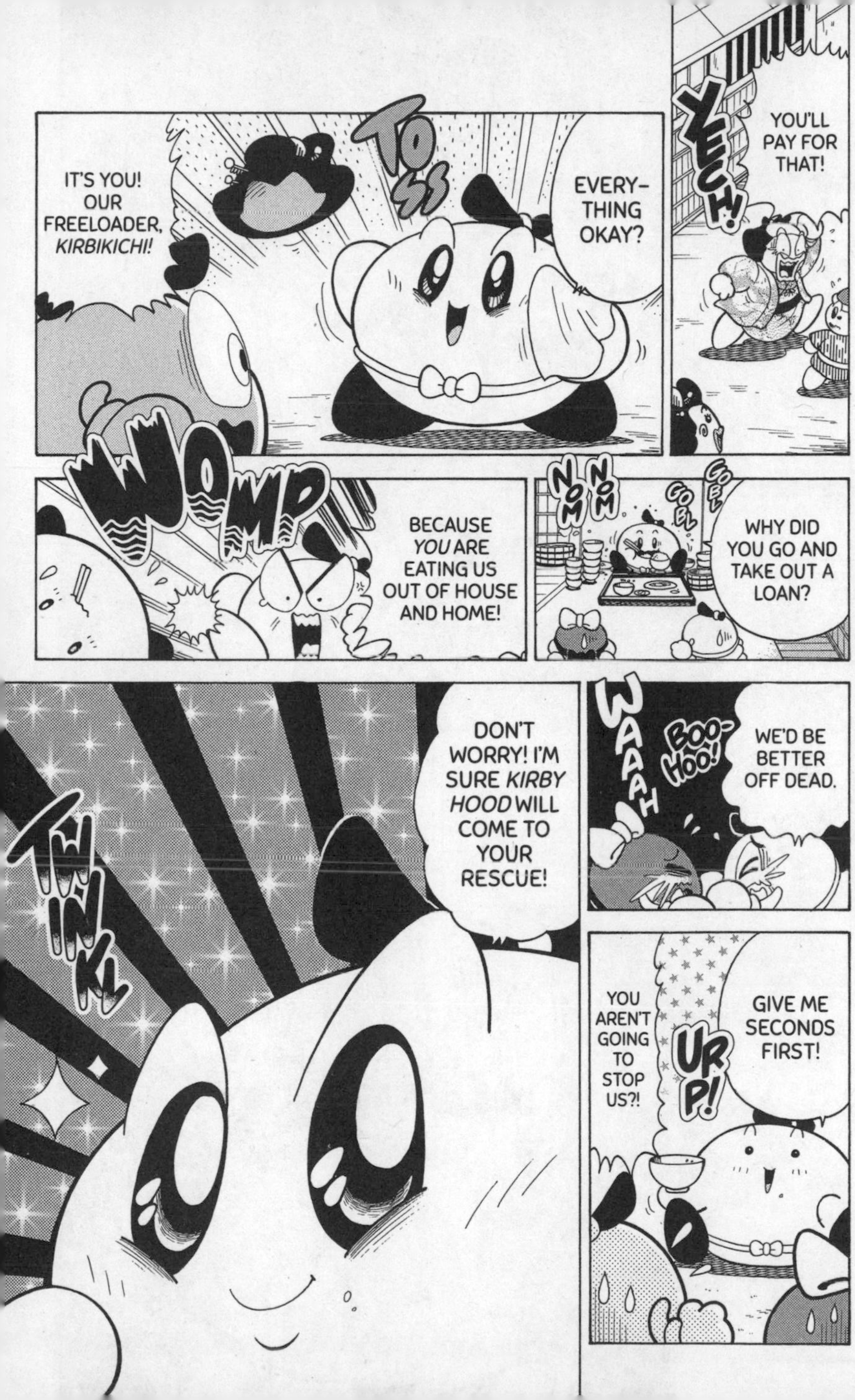
YOU'LL PAY FOR THAT!
YECH!
EVERY-THING OKAY?
TOSS
IT'S YOU! OUR FREELOADER, *KIRBIKICHI!*
WHY DID YOU GO AND TAKE OUT A LOAN?
GOBL
GOBL
NOM
NOM
BECAUSE *YOU* ARE EATING US OUT OF HOUSE AND HOME!
WOMP
WE'D BE BETTER OFF DEAD.
BOO-HOO!
WAAAH
GIVE ME SECONDS FIRST!
URP!
YOU AREN'T GOING TO STOP US?!
DON'T WORRY! I'M SURE *KIRBY HOOD* WILL COME TO YOUR RESCUE!
TWINKL

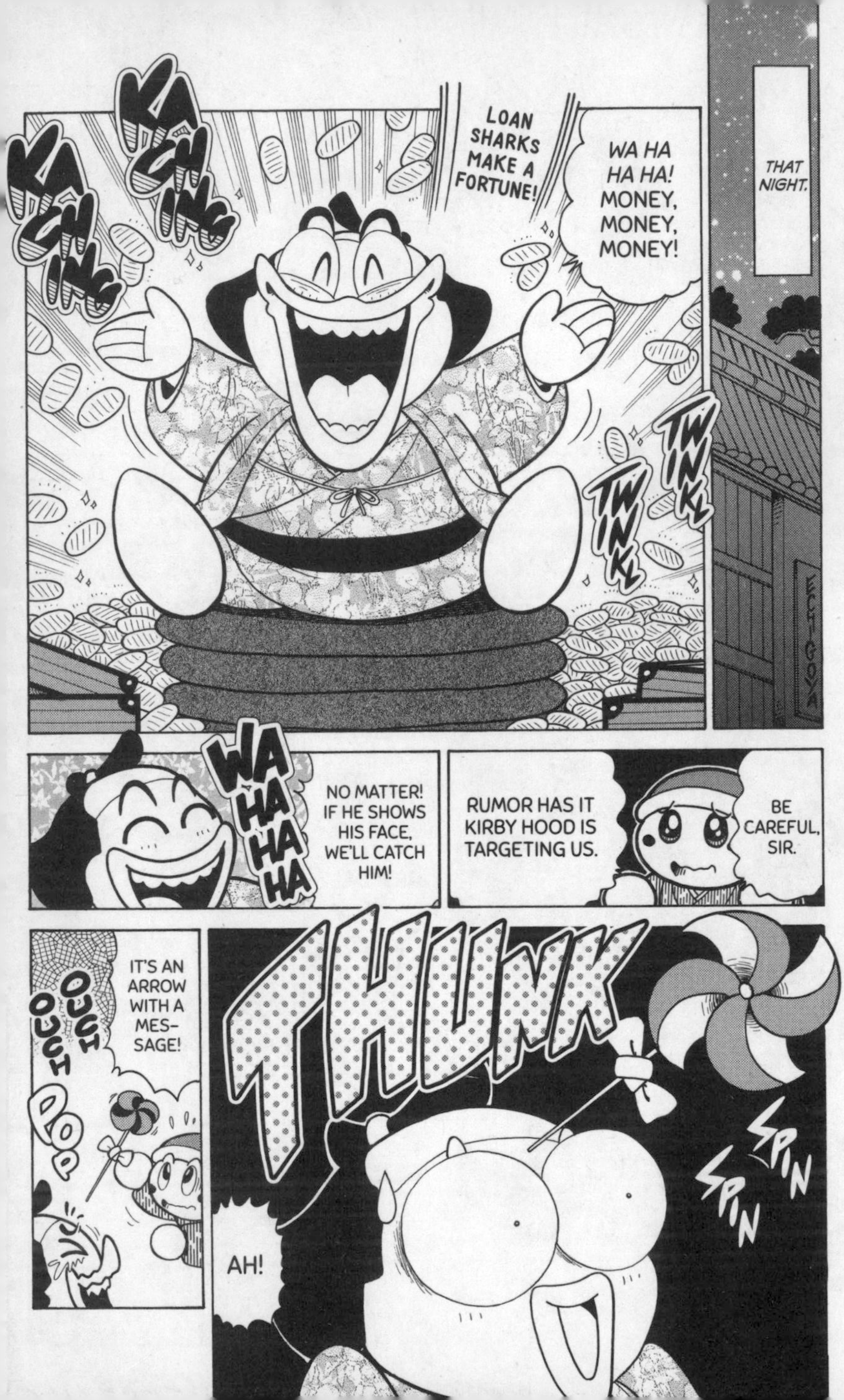
THAT NIGHT.
ECHIGOYA
WA HA HA HA! MONEY, MONEY, MONEY!
LOAN SHARKS MAKE A FORTUNE!
TWINK TWINK
KA-CHING KA-CHING
BE CAREFUL, SIR.
RUMOR HAS IT KIRBY HOOD IS TARGETING US.
NO MATTER! IF HE SHOWS HIS FACE, WE'LL CATCH HIM!
WA HA HA HA HA
THUNK
SPIN SPIN
AH!
IT'S AN ARROW WITH A MES-SAGE!
OUCH OUCH
POP

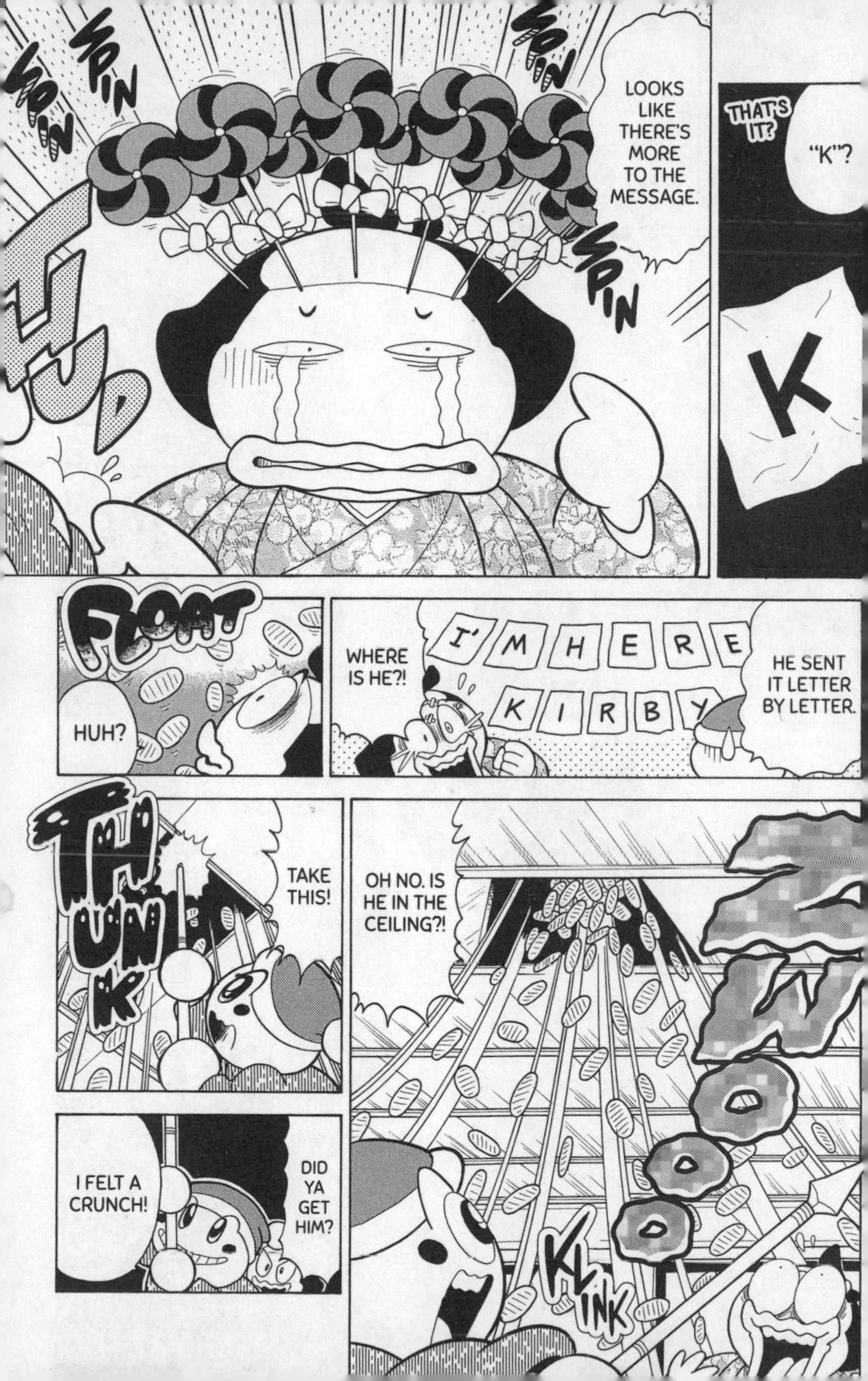
THAT'S IT?
"K"?
K
LOOKS LIKE THERE'S MORE TO THE MESSAGE.
SPIN SPIN
SPIN
SPIN
THUD
HE SENT IT LETTER BY LETTER.
I'M HERE KIRBY
WHERE IS HE?!
FLOAT
HUH?
OH NO. IS HE IN THE CEILING?!
KLINK
TAKE THIS!
THUNK
DID YA GET HIM?
I FELT A CRUNCH!

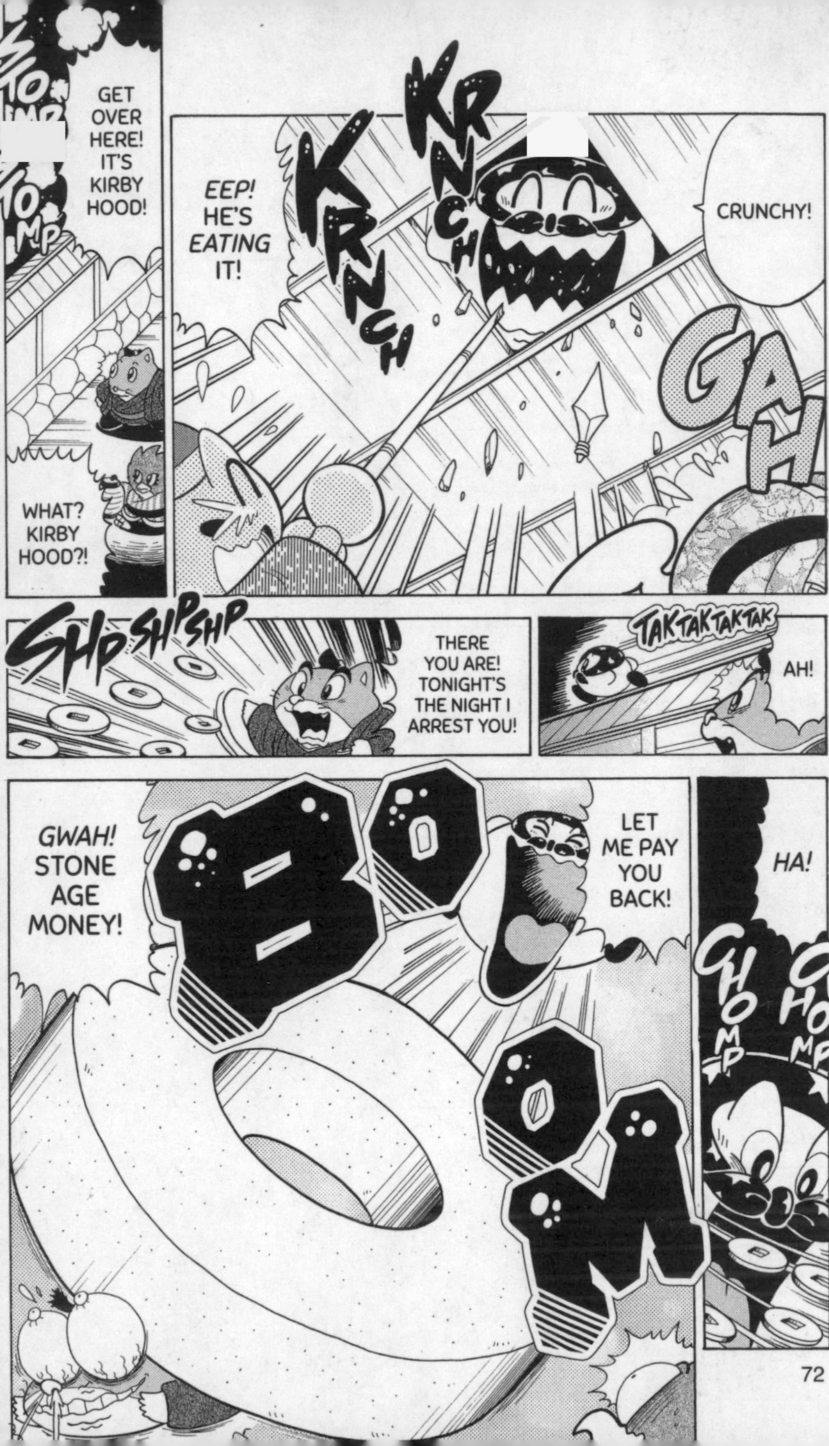
CRUNCHY!
KRNCH KRNCH
EEP! HE'S EATING IT!
GAH
GET OVER HERE! IT'S KIRBY HOOD!
WHAT? KIRBY HOOD?!
TAKTAKTAKTAK
AH!
SHP SHP SHP
THERE YOU ARE! TONIGHT'S THE NIGHT I ARREST YOU!
HA!
CHOMP CHOMP
LET ME PAY YOU BACK!
BOOM
GWAH! STONE AGE MONEY!

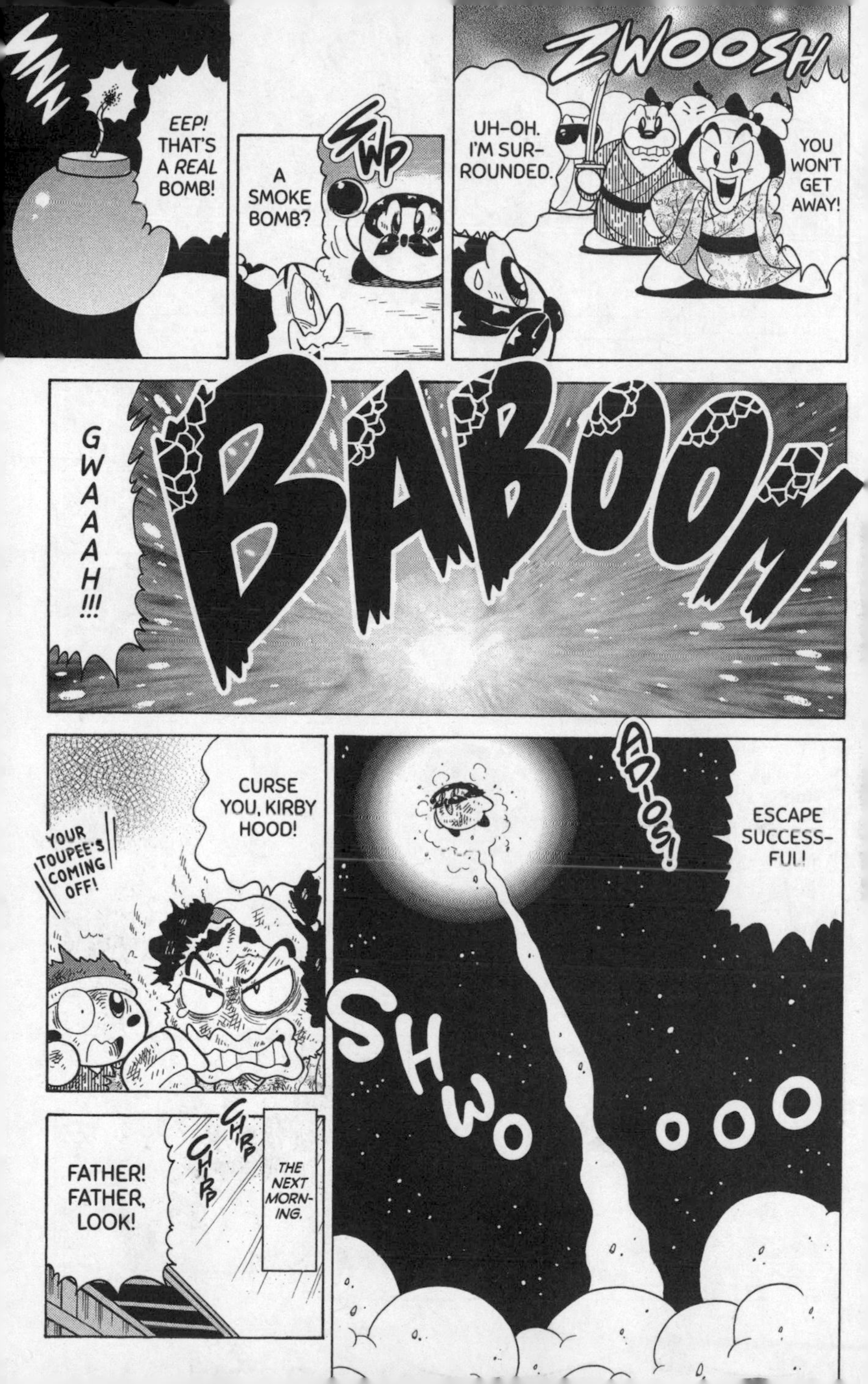
ZWOOSH
YOU WON'T GET AWAY!
UH-OH. I'M SUR-ROUNDED.
SWP
A SMOKE BOMB?
EEP! THAT'S A *REAL* BOMB!
BABOOM
GWAAAAH!!!
AD-IOS!
ESCAPE SUCCESS-FUL!
SHWOOOOO
CURSE YOU, KIRBY HOOD!
YOUR TOUPEE'S COMING OFF!
THE NEXT MORN-ING.
CHIRP
CHIRP
FATHER! FATHER, LOOK!

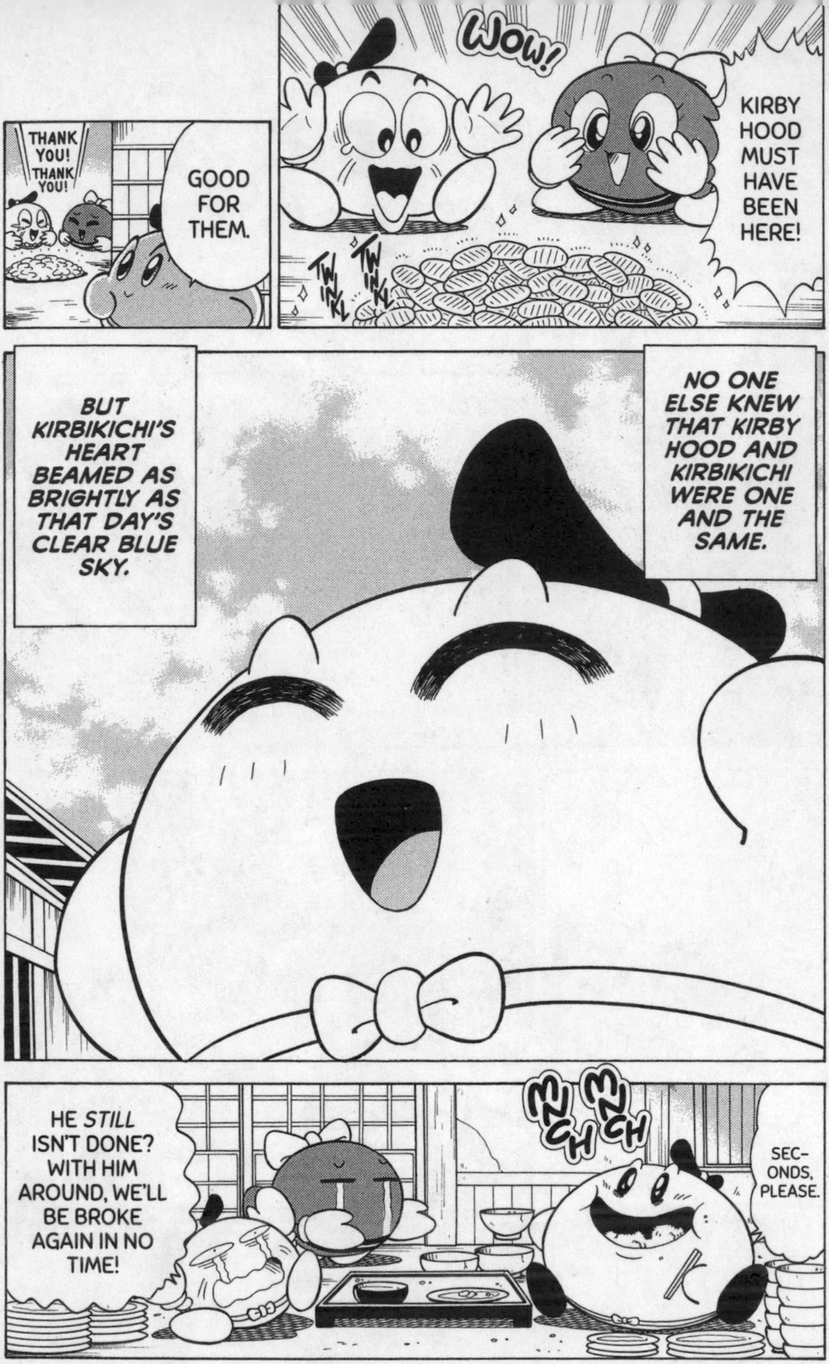
WOW!
KIRBY HOOD MUST HAVE BEEN HERE!
TWINKL TWINKL
THANK YOU! THANK YOU!
GOOD FOR THEM.
NO ONE ELSE KNEW THAT KIRBY HOOD AND KIRBIKICHI WERE ONE AND THE SAME.
BUT KIRBIKICHI'S HEART BEAMED AS BRIGHTLY AS THAT DAY'S CLEAR BLUE SKY.
SEC-ONDS, PLEASE.
MNCH MNCH
HE STILL ISN'T DONE? WITH HIM AROUND, WE'LL BE BROKE AGAIN IN NO TIME!

KIRBY'S DREAM DOODLE CORNER

KIRBY FACES PRACTICE 2

HEH!
HIC HIC
ACK!
CHTR CHTR
NNGH!
SIGH
VWP
DEFLATE
GA HA HA

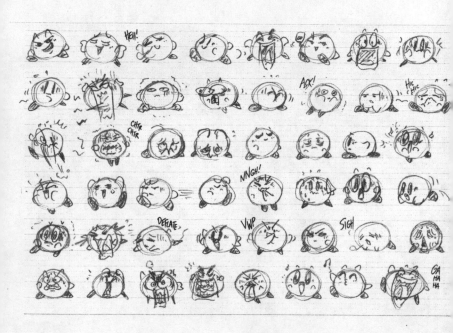

BUT WHEN YOU DRAW KIRBY, HE'S CUTE WITH *ANY* EXPRESSION. KIRBY'S MOVEMENTS AND FACES IN THE VIDEO GAMES ARE SUPER CUTE. I HOPE I MANAGE TO BRING THAT OUT IN MY MANGA.

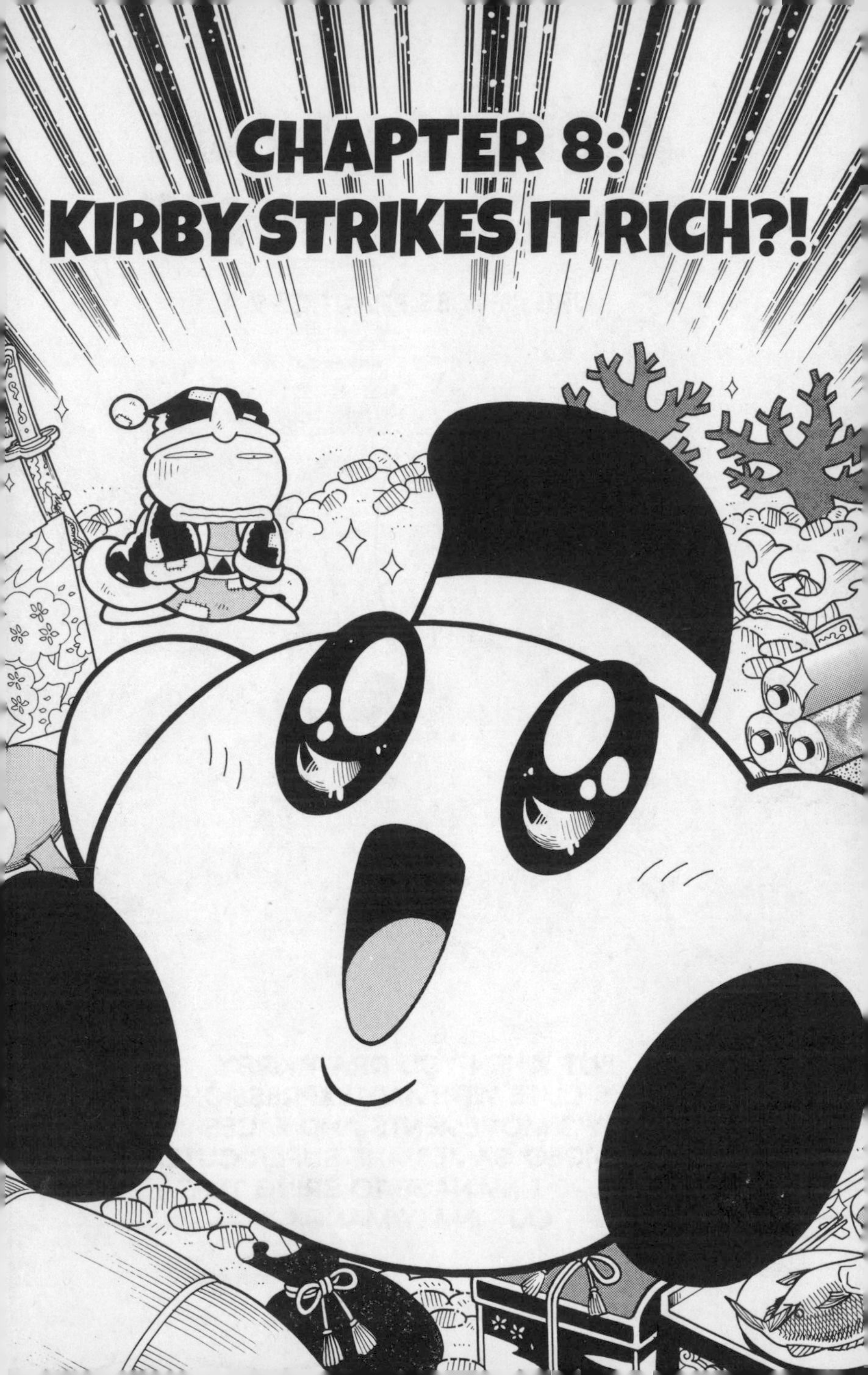
CHAPTER 8:
KIRBY STRIKES IT RICH?!

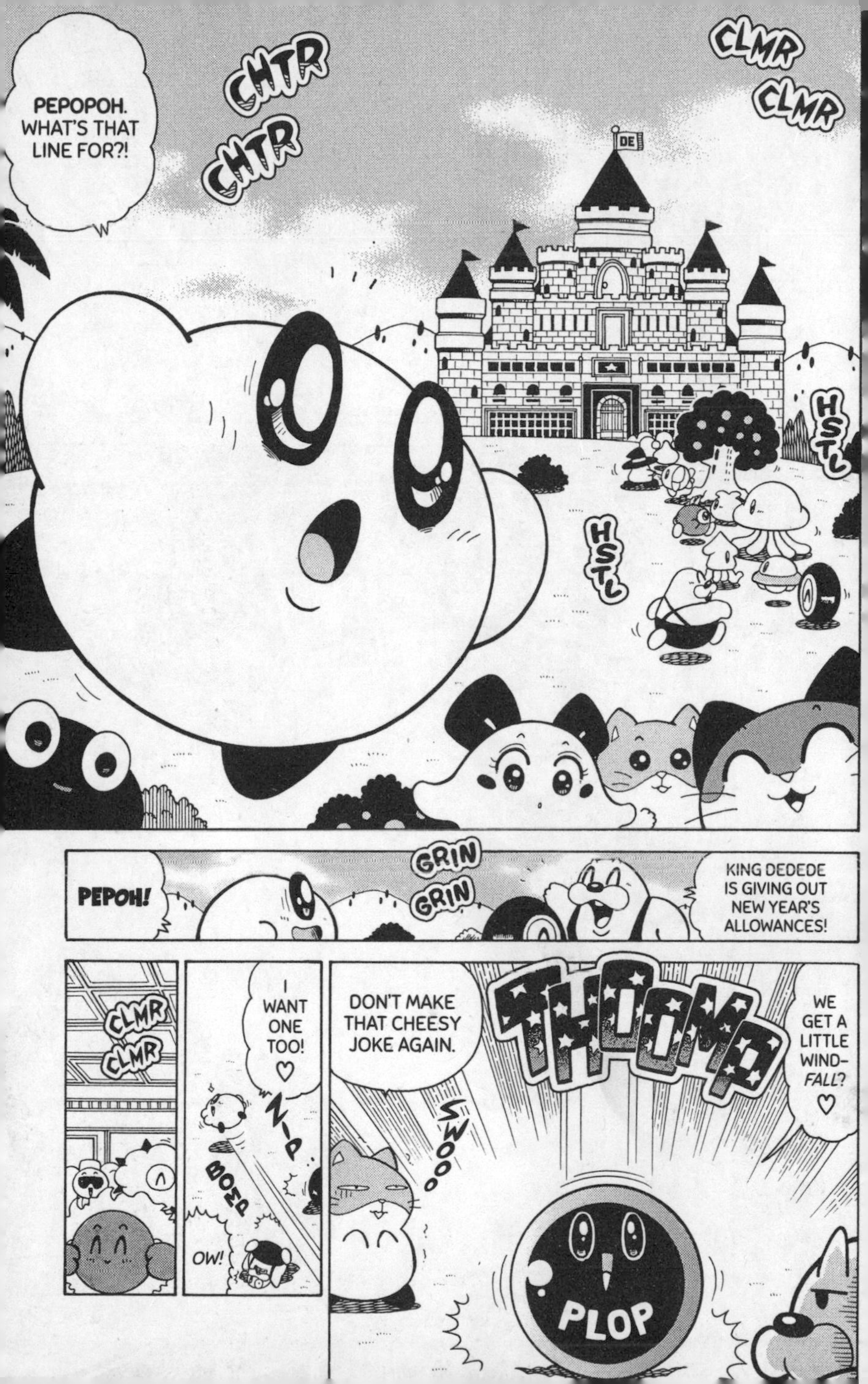
CLMR
CLMR
HSTL
HSTL
CHTR
CHTR
PEPOPOH. WHAT'S THAT LINE FOR?!
KING DEDEDE IS GIVING OUT NEW YEAR'S ALLOWANCES!
GRIN
GRIN
PEPOH!
WE GET A LITTLE WIND-FALL? ♡
THOMP
PLOP
DON'T MAKE THAT CHEESY JOKE AGAIN.
SWOOOO
I WANT ONE TOO! ♡
ZIP
OW!
CLMR
CLMR

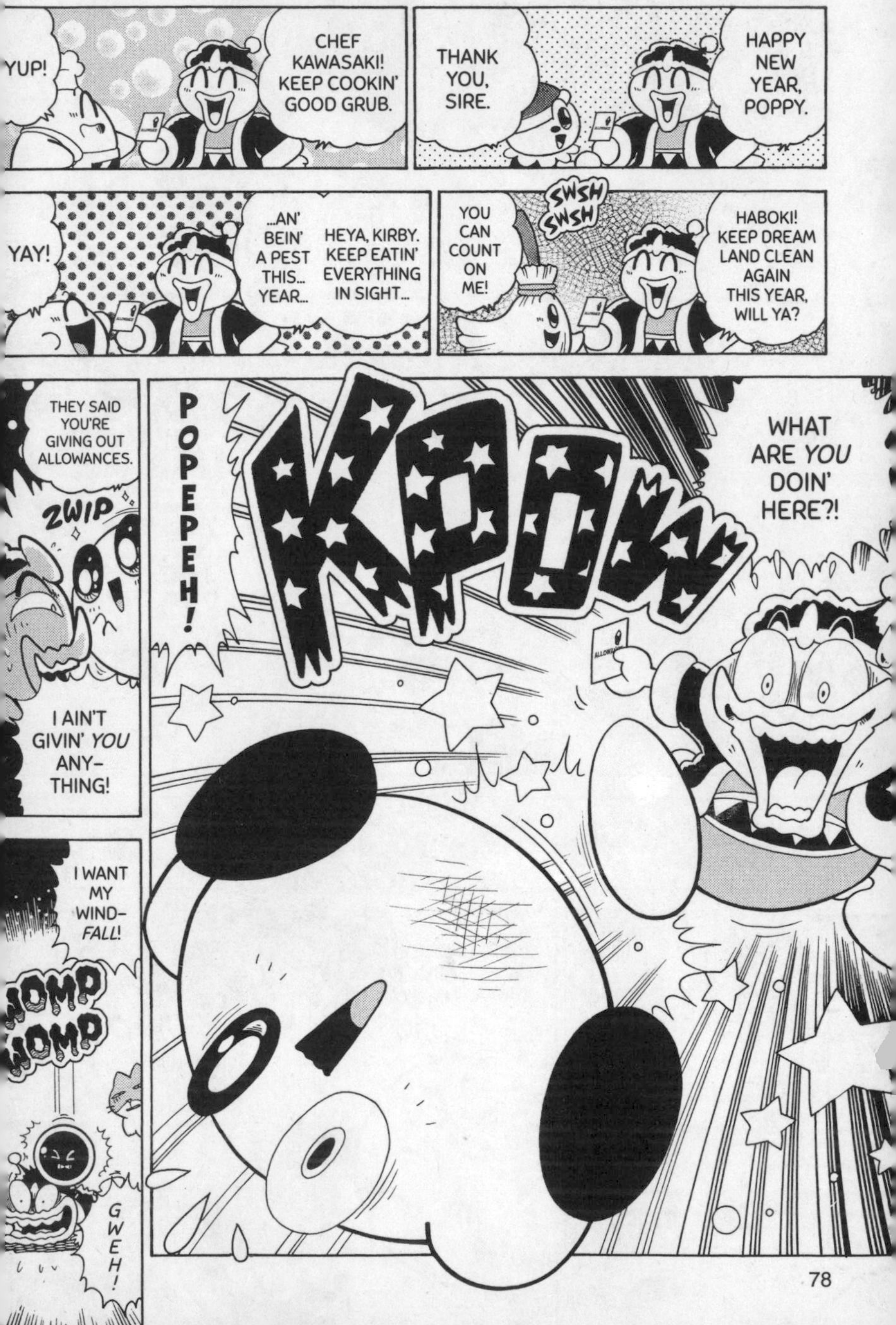
HAPPY NEW YEAR, POPPY.
THANK YOU, SIRE.
CHEF KAWASAKI! KEEP COOKIN' GOOD GRUB.
YUP!
HABOKI! KEEP DREAM LAND CLEAN AGAIN THIS YEAR, WILL YA?
SWSH SWSH
YOU CAN COUNT ON ME!
HEYA, KIRBY. KEEP EATIN' EVERYTHING IN SIGHT...
...AN' BEIN' A PEST THIS... YEAR...
YAY!
WHAT ARE *YOU* DOIN' HERE?!
KPOW
POPEPEH!
THEY SAID YOU'RE GIVING OUT ALLOWANCES.
ZWIP
I AIN'T GIVIN' *YOU* ANY-THING!
I WANT MY WIND-*FALL*!
OMP
OMP
GWEH!

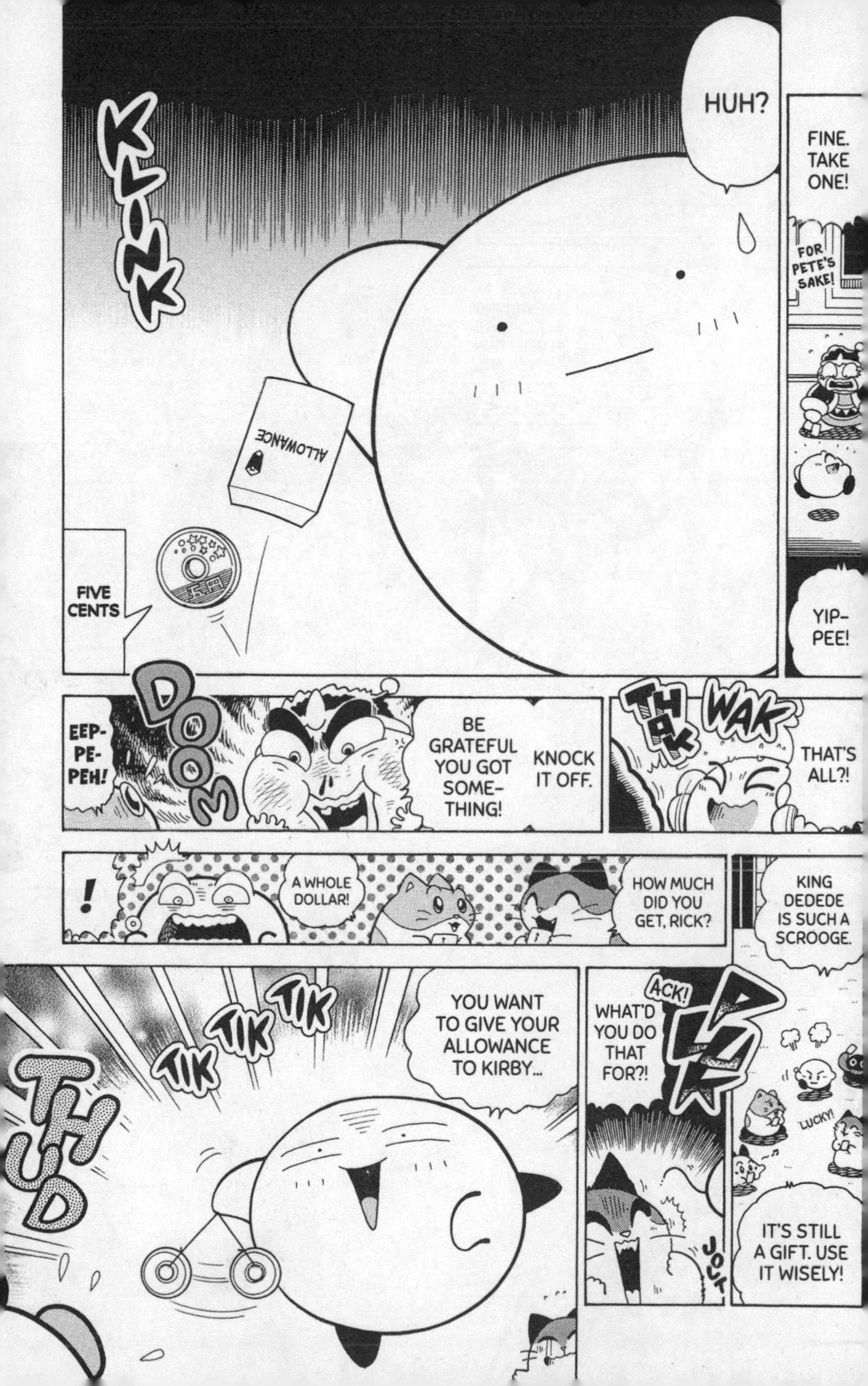
FINE. TAKE ONE!
FOR PETE'S SAKE!
YIP-PEE!
HUH?
KLUNK
ALLOWANCE
FIVE CENTS
THAT'S ALL?!
WAK
THAK
KNOCK IT OFF.
BE GRATEFUL YOU GOT SOME-THING!
DOOM
EEP-PE-PEH!
KING DEDEDE IS SUCH A SCROOGE.
HOW MUCH DID YOU GET, RICK?
A WHOLE DOLLAR!
!
LUCKY!
IT'S STILL A GIFT. USE IT WISELY!
ACK!
WHAT'D YOU DO THAT FOR?!
JOLT
YOU WANT TO GIVE YOUR ALLOWANCE TO KIRBY...
TIK
TIK
TIK
THUD

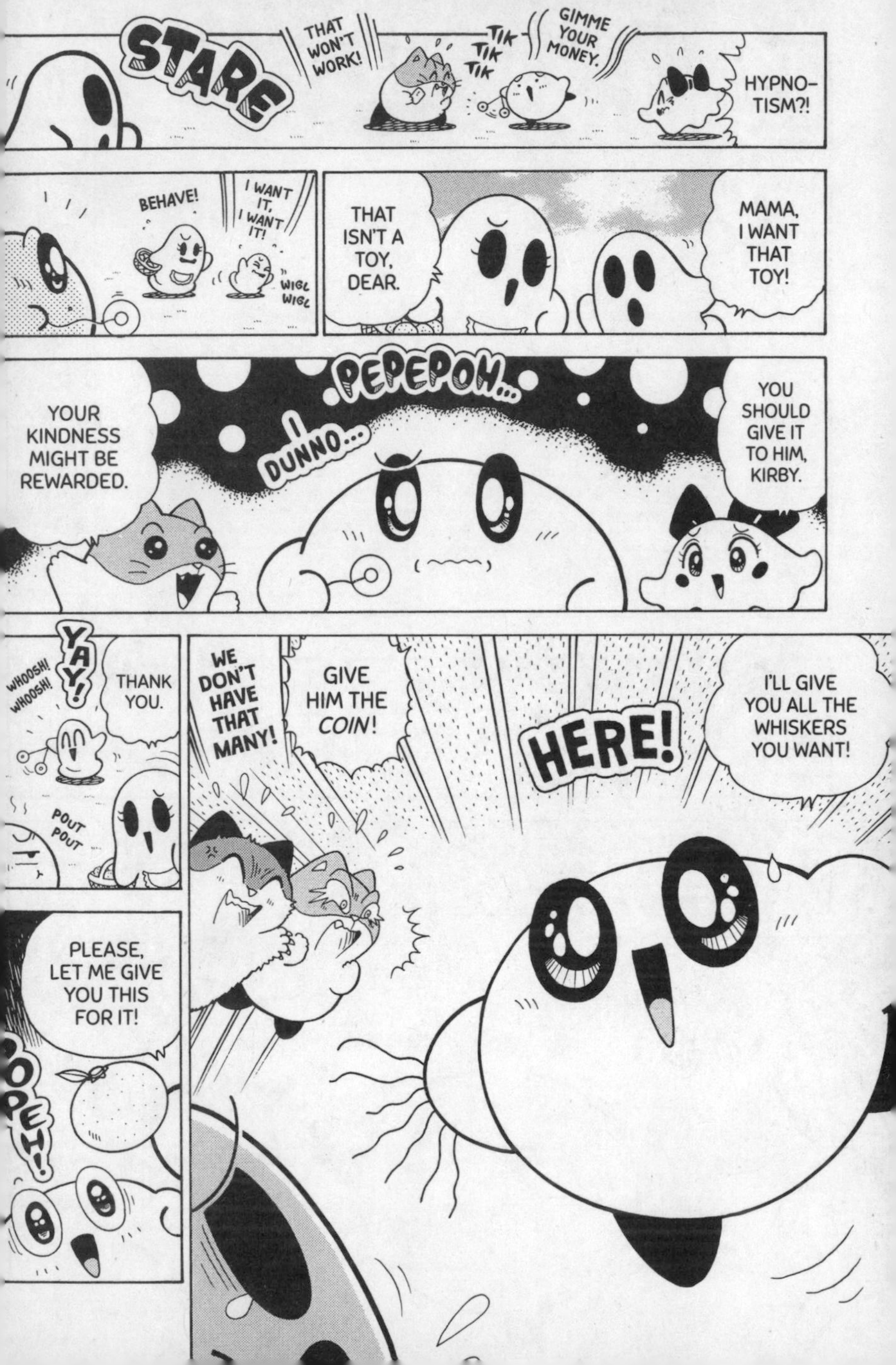
HYPNO-TISM?!
GIMME YOUR MONEY.
TIK TIK TIK
THAT WON'T WORK!
STARE
MAMA, I WANT THAT TOY!
THAT ISN'T A TOY, DEAR.
I WANT IT, I WANT IT!
BEHAVE!
WIGL WIGL
YOU SHOULD GIVE IT TO HIM, KIRBY.
PEPEPOH...
I DUNNO...
YOUR KINDNESS MIGHT BE REWARDED.
I'LL GIVE YOU ALL THE WHISKERS YOU WANT!
HERE!
GIVE HIM THE *COIN*!
WE DON'T HAVE THAT MANY!
THANK YOU.
YAY!
WHOOSH! WHOOSH!
POUT POUT
PLEASE, LET ME GIVE YOU THIS FOR IT!
OOPEH!

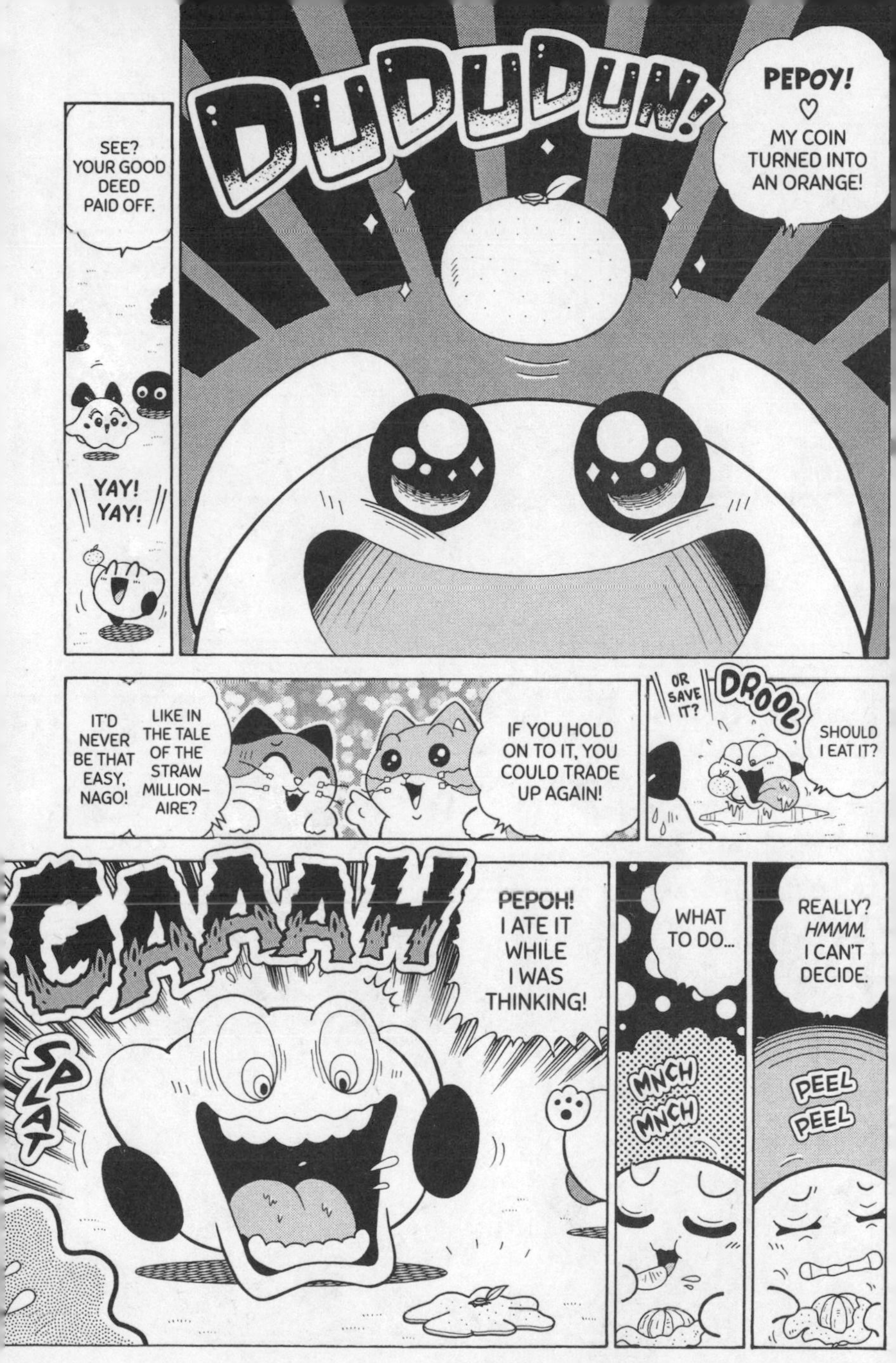

PEPOY! ♡ MY COIN TURNED INTO AN ORANGE!
DUDUDUN!
SEE? YOUR GOOD DEED PAID OFF.
YAY! YAY!
SHOULD I EAT IT?
DROOL
OR SAVE IT?
IF YOU HOLD ON TO IT, YOU COULD TRADE UP AGAIN!
LIKE IN THE TALE OF THE STRAW MILLION-AIRE?
IT'D NEVER BE THAT EASY, NAGO!
REALLY? *HMMM.* I CAN'T DECIDE.
PEEL PEEL
WHAT TO DO...
MNCH MNCH
PEPOH! I ATE IT WHILE I WAS THINKING!
GAAAH
SPLAT

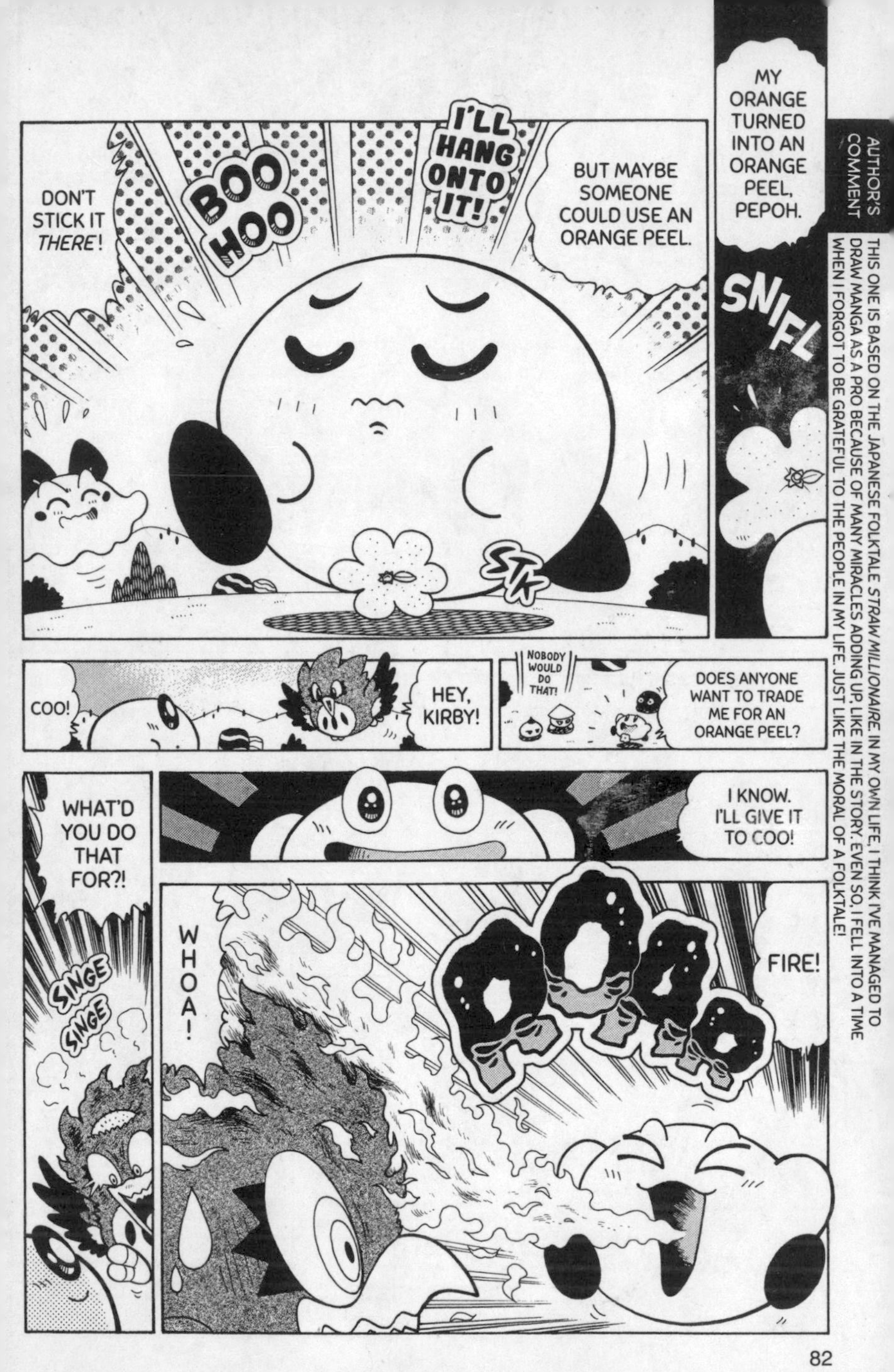
MY ORANGE TURNED INTO AN ORANGE PEEL, PEPOH.
SNIFL
BUT MAYBE SOMEONE COULD USE AN ORANGE PEEL.
I'LL HANG ONTO IT!
BOO HOO
DON'T STICK IT *THERE*!
STK
DOES ANYONE WANT TO TRADE ME FOR AN ORANGE PEEL?
NOBODY WOULD DO THAT!
HEY, KIRBY!
COO!
I KNOW. I'LL GIVE IT TO COO!
FIRE!
WHOA!
WHAT'D YOU DO THAT FOR?!
SINGE SINGE

AUTHOR'S COMMENT

THIS ONE IS BASED ON THE JAPANESE FOLKTALE *STRAW MILLIONAIRE*. IN MY OWN LIFE, I THINK I'VE MANAGED TO DRAW MANGA AS A PRO BECAUSE OF MANY MIRACLES ADDING UP, LIKE IN THE STORY. EVEN SO, I FELL INTO A TIME WHEN I FORGOT TO BE GRATEFUL TO THE PEOPLE IN MY LIFE. JUST LIKE THE MORAL OF A FOLKTALE!

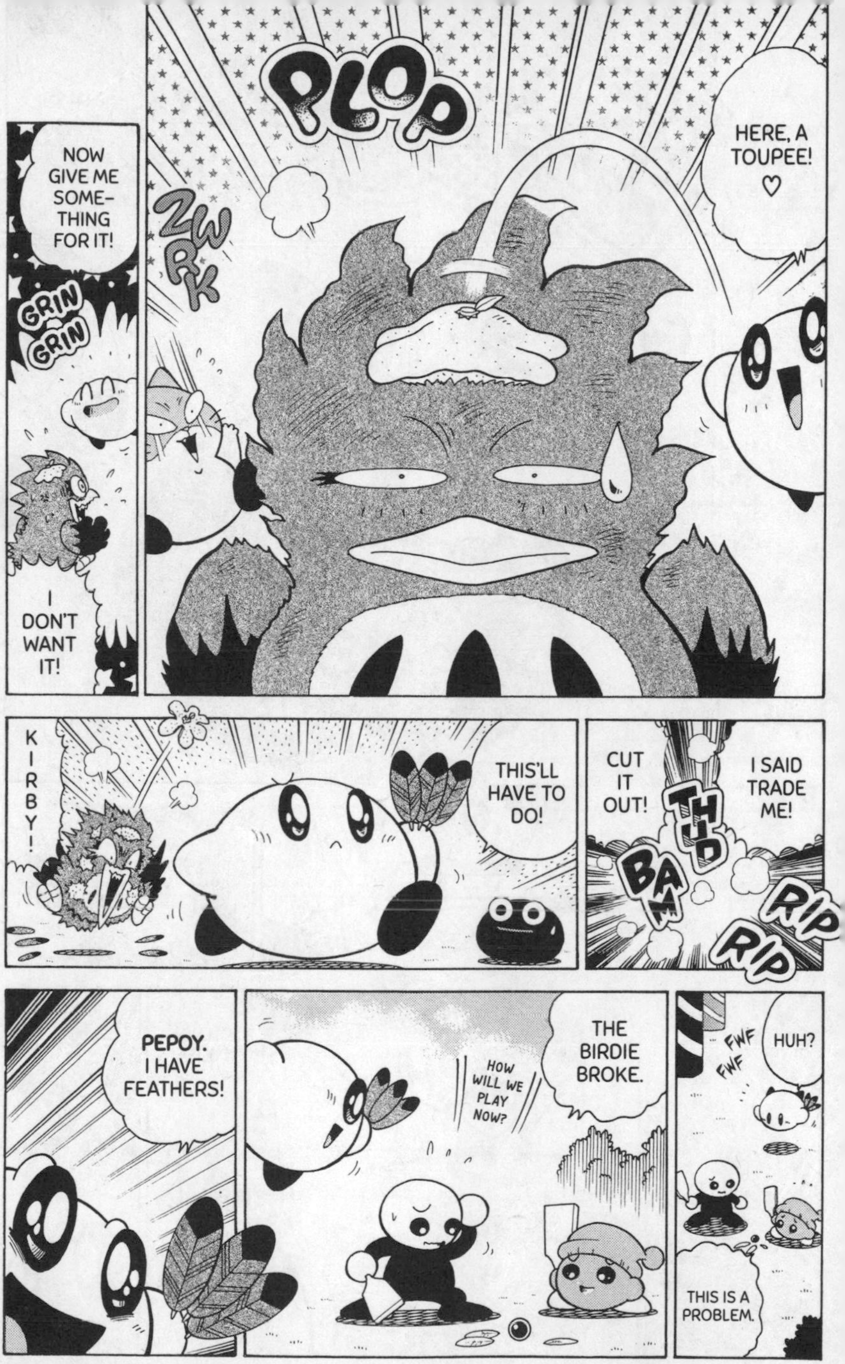
PLOP
HERE, A TOUPEE! ♡
ZWRK
NOW GIVE ME SOME-THING FOR IT!
GRIN GRIN
I DON'T WANT IT!
I SAID TRADE ME!
CUT IT OUT!
THUD
BAM
RIP RIP
THIS'LL HAVE TO DO!
KIRBY!
HUH?
FWF FWF
THIS IS A PROBLEM.
THE BIRDIE BROKE.
HOW WILL WE PLAY NOW?
PEPOY. I HAVE FEATHERS!

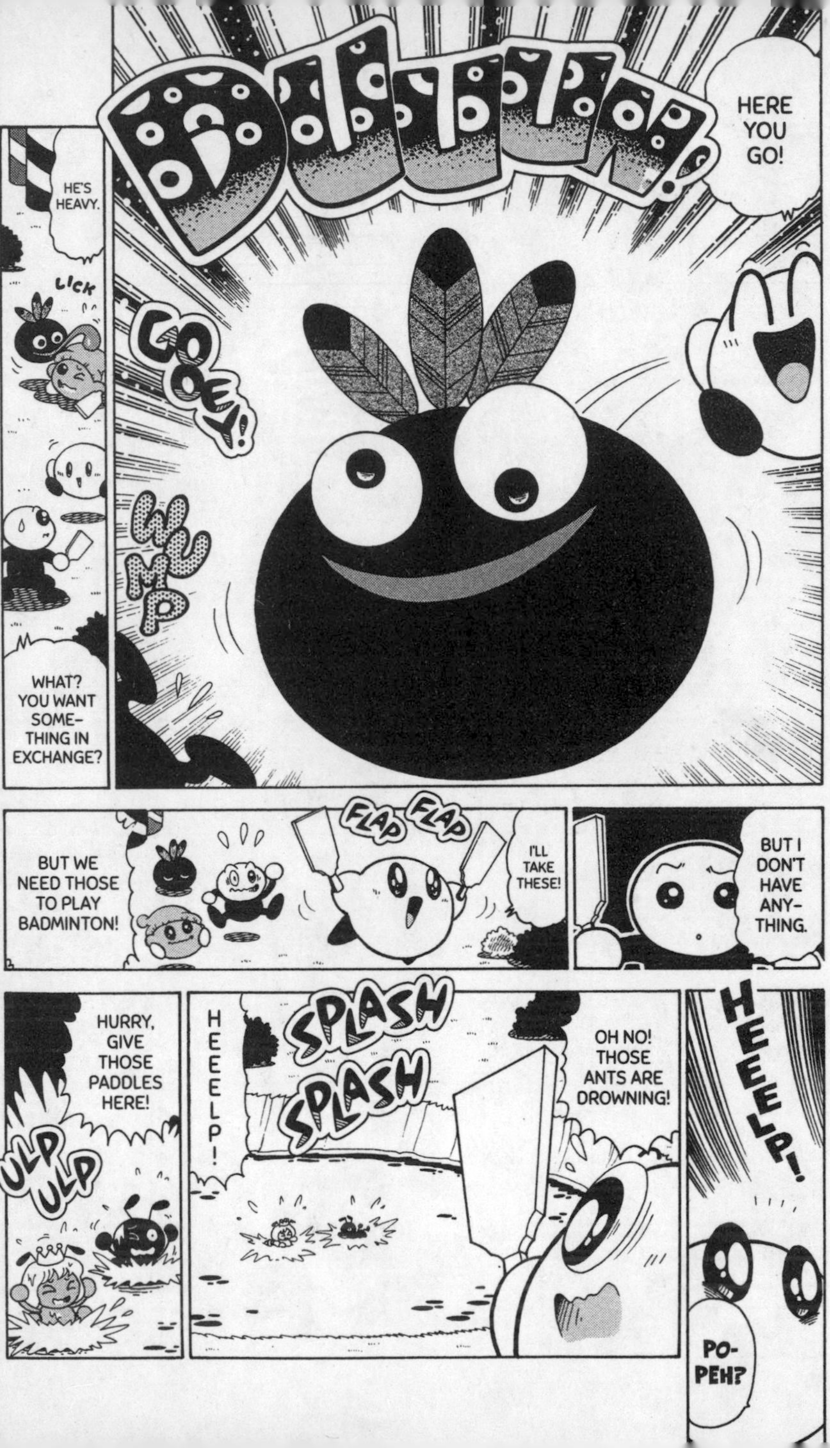
HERE YOU GO!
GOOEY!
WHUMP
HE'S HEAVY.
LICK
WHAT? YOU WANT SOME-THING IN EXCHANGE?
BUT I DON'T HAVE ANY-THING.
I'LL TAKE THESE!
FLAP FLAP
BUT WE NEED THOSE TO PLAY BADMINTON!
HEEELP!
PO-PEH?
OH NO! THOSE ANTS ARE DROWNING!
SPLASH
SPLASH
HEEELP!
HURRY, GIVE THOSE PADDLES HERE!
ULP ULP

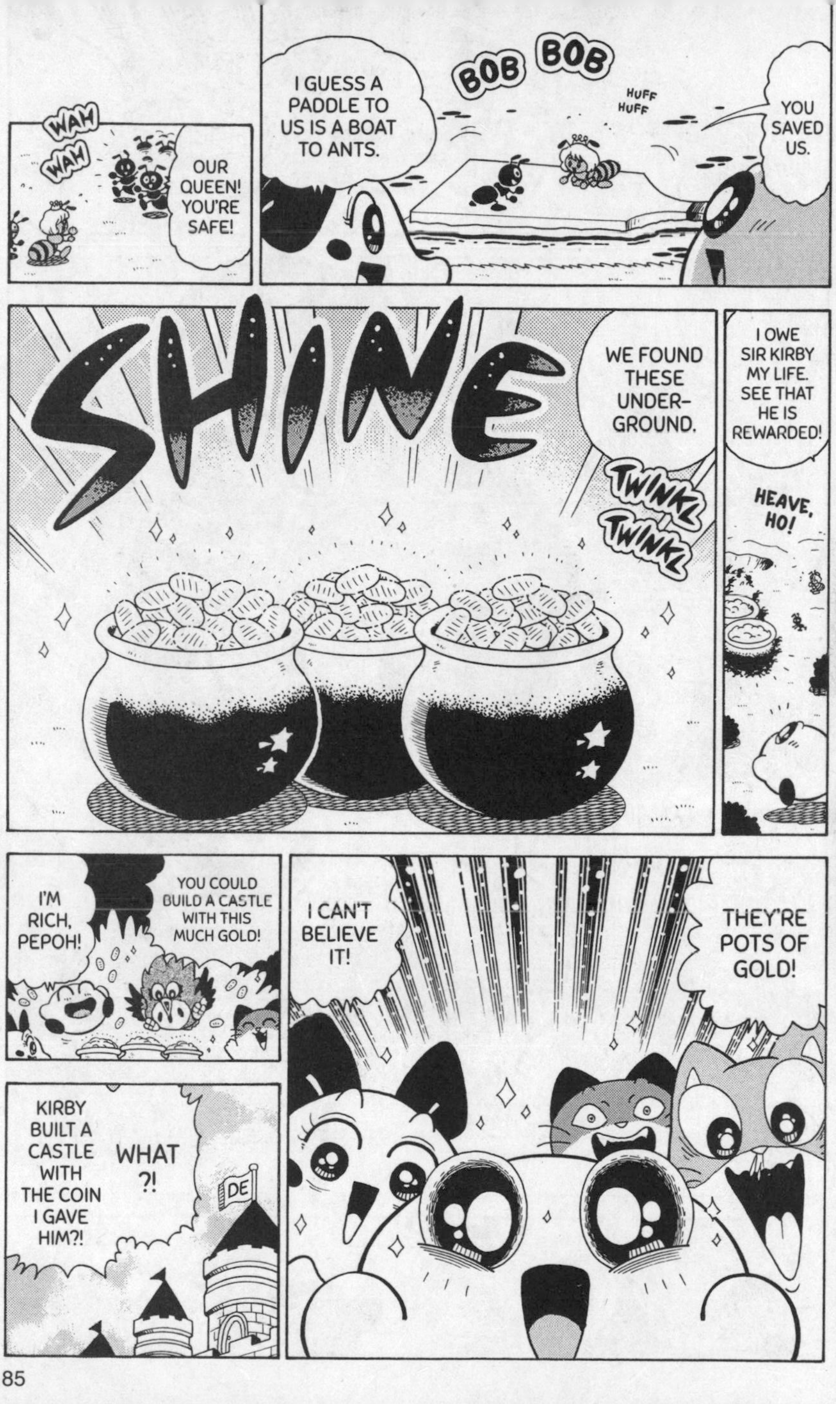
YOU SAVED US.
BOB BOB
HUFF HUFF
I GUESS A PADDLE TO US IS A BOAT TO ANTS.
OUR QUEEN! YOU'RE SAFE!
WAH WAH
I OWE SIR KIRBY MY LIFE. SEE THAT HE IS REWARDED!
HEAVE, HO!
WE FOUND THESE UNDER-GROUND.
TWINKL TWINKL
SHINE
THEY'RE POTS OF GOLD!
I CAN'T BELIEVE IT!
YOU COULD BUILD A CASTLE WITH THIS MUCH GOLD!
I'M RICH, PEPOH!
WHAT ?!
KIRBY BUILT A CASTLE WITH THE COIN I GAVE HIM?!
DE

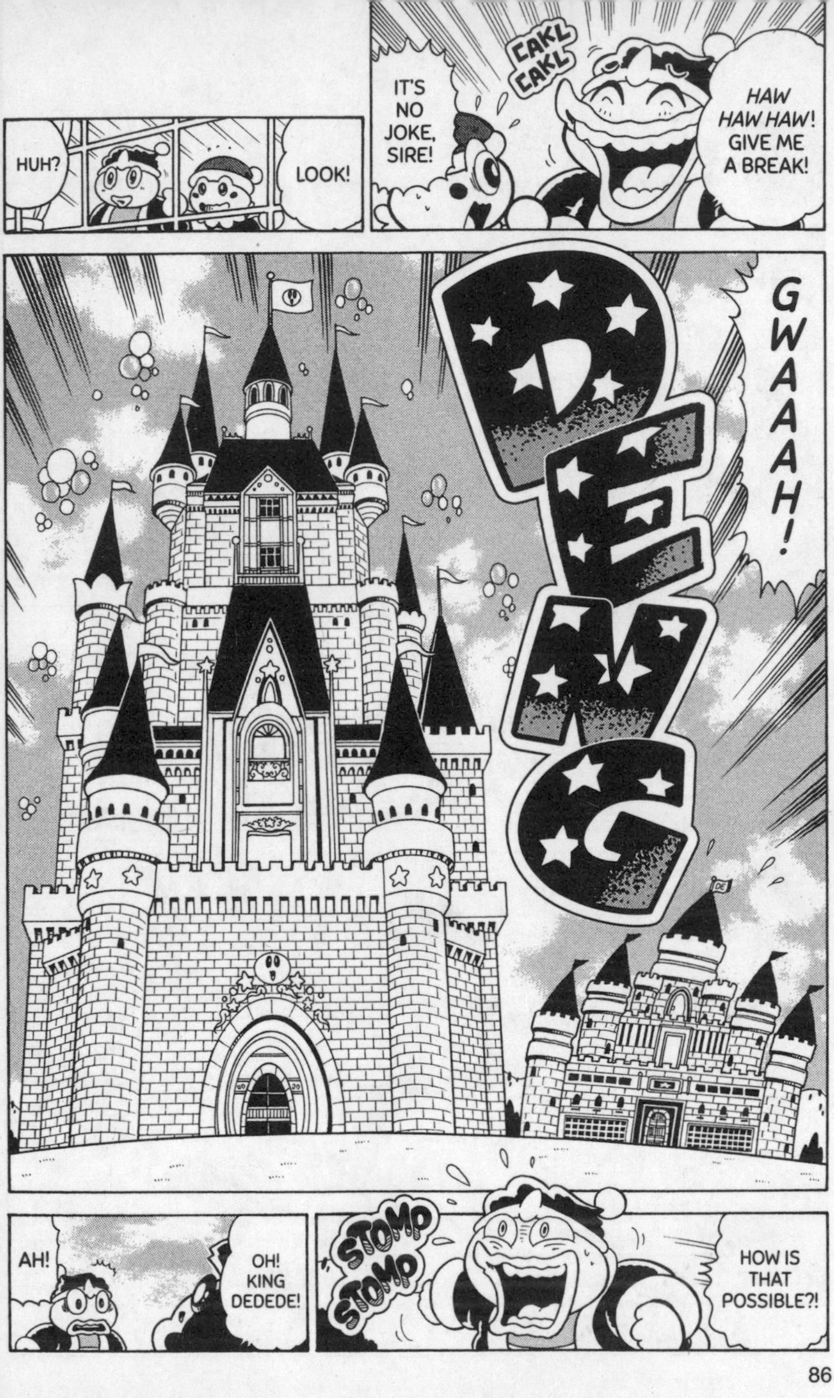
HAW HAW HAW! GIVE ME A BREAK!
CAKL CAKL
IT'S NO JOKE, SIRE!
LOOK!
HUH?
GWAAAAH!
DENG
HOW IS THAT POSSIBLE?!
STOMP STOMP
OH! KING DEDEDE!
AH!

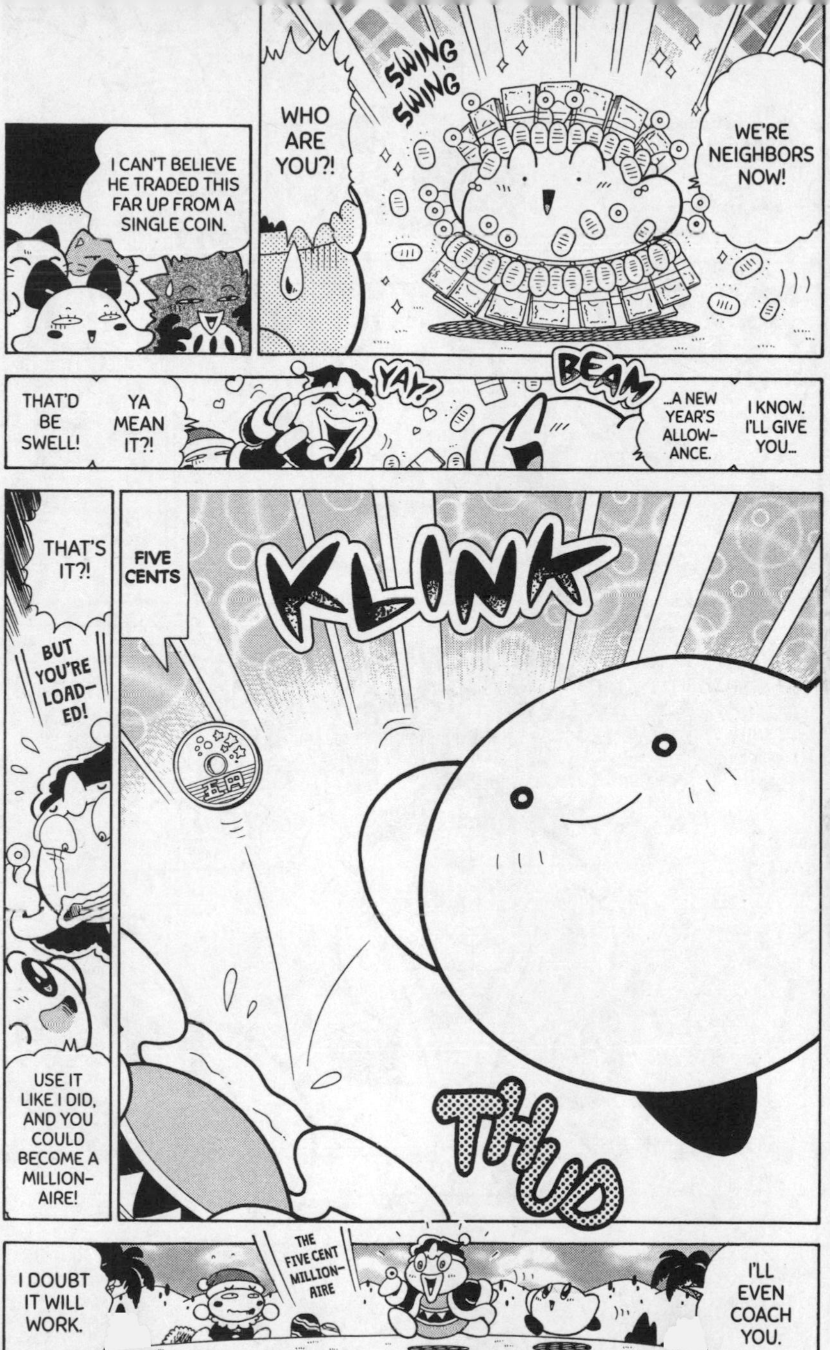
WE'RE NEIGHBORS NOW!
SWING SWING
WHO ARE YOU?!
I CAN'T BELIEVE HE TRADED THIS FAR UP FROM A SINGLE COIN.
I KNOW. I'LL GIVE YOU...
...A NEW YEAR'S ALLOW-ANCE.
BEAM
YAY!
YA MEAN IT?!
THAT'D BE SWELL!
KLINK
FIVE CENTS
THUD
THAT'S IT?!
BUT YOU'RE LOAD-ED!
USE IT LIKE I DID, AND YOU COULD BECOME A MILLION-AIRE!
I'LL EVEN COACH YOU.
THE FIVE CENT MILLION-AIRE
I DOUBT IT WILL WORK.

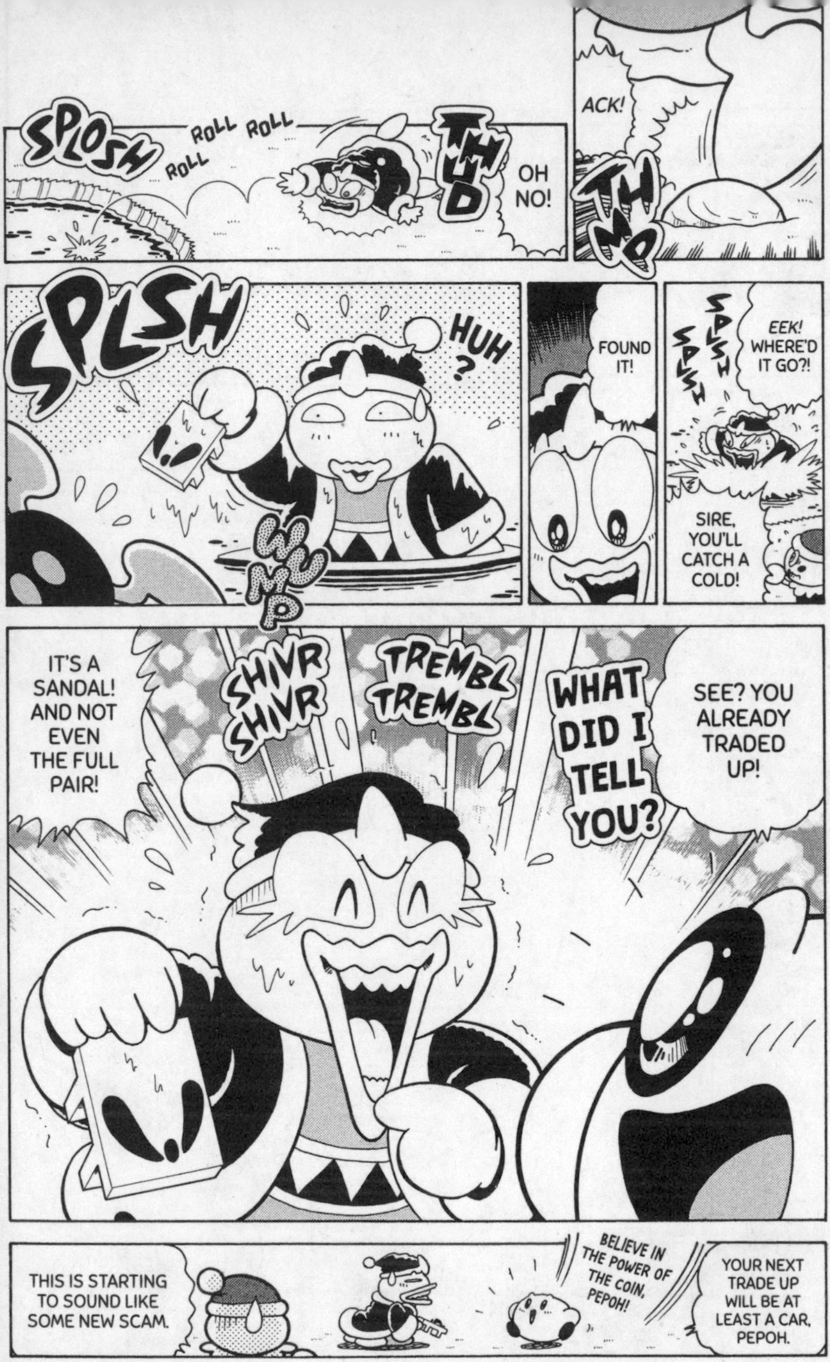
ACK!
THMP
OH NO!
THUD
ROLL ROLL
SPLOSH
ROLL
EEK! WHERE'D IT GO?!
SPLSH
SPLSH
SIRE, YOU'LL CATCH A COLD!
FOUND IT!
HUH?
SPLSH
WUMP
SEE? YOU ALREADY TRADED UP!
WHAT DID I TELL YOU?
TREMBL TREMBL
SHIVR SHIVR
IT'S A SANDAL! AND NOT EVEN THE FULL PAIR!
YOUR NEXT TRADE UP WILL BE AT LEAST A CAR, PEPOH.
BELIEVE IN THE POWER OF THE COIN, PEPOH!
THIS IS STARTING TO SOUND LIKE SOME NEW SCAM.

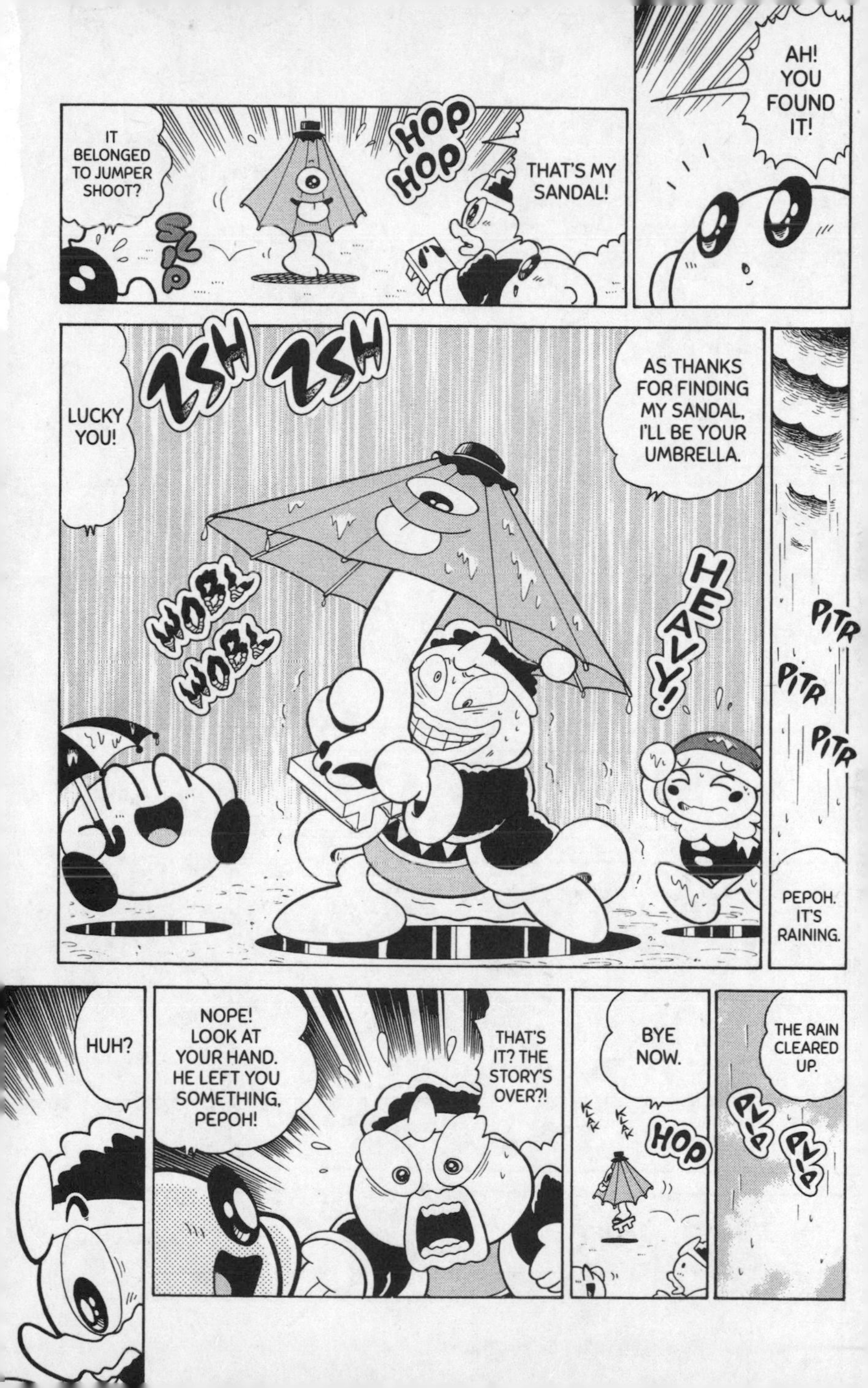
AH! YOU FOUND IT!
THAT'S MY SANDAL!
HOP HOP
IT BELONGED TO JUMPER SHOOT?
SLIP
PITR
PITR
PITR
PEPOH. IT'S RAINING.
AS THANKS FOR FINDING MY SANDAL, I'LL BE YOUR UMBRELLA.
HEAVY!
ZSH ZSH
LUCKY YOU!
WOBL WOBL
THE RAIN CLEARED UP.
BYE NOW.
HOP
KLAK KLAK
THAT'S IT? THE STORY'S OVER?!
NOPE! LOOK AT YOUR HAND. HE LEFT YOU SOMETHING, PEPOH!
HUH?

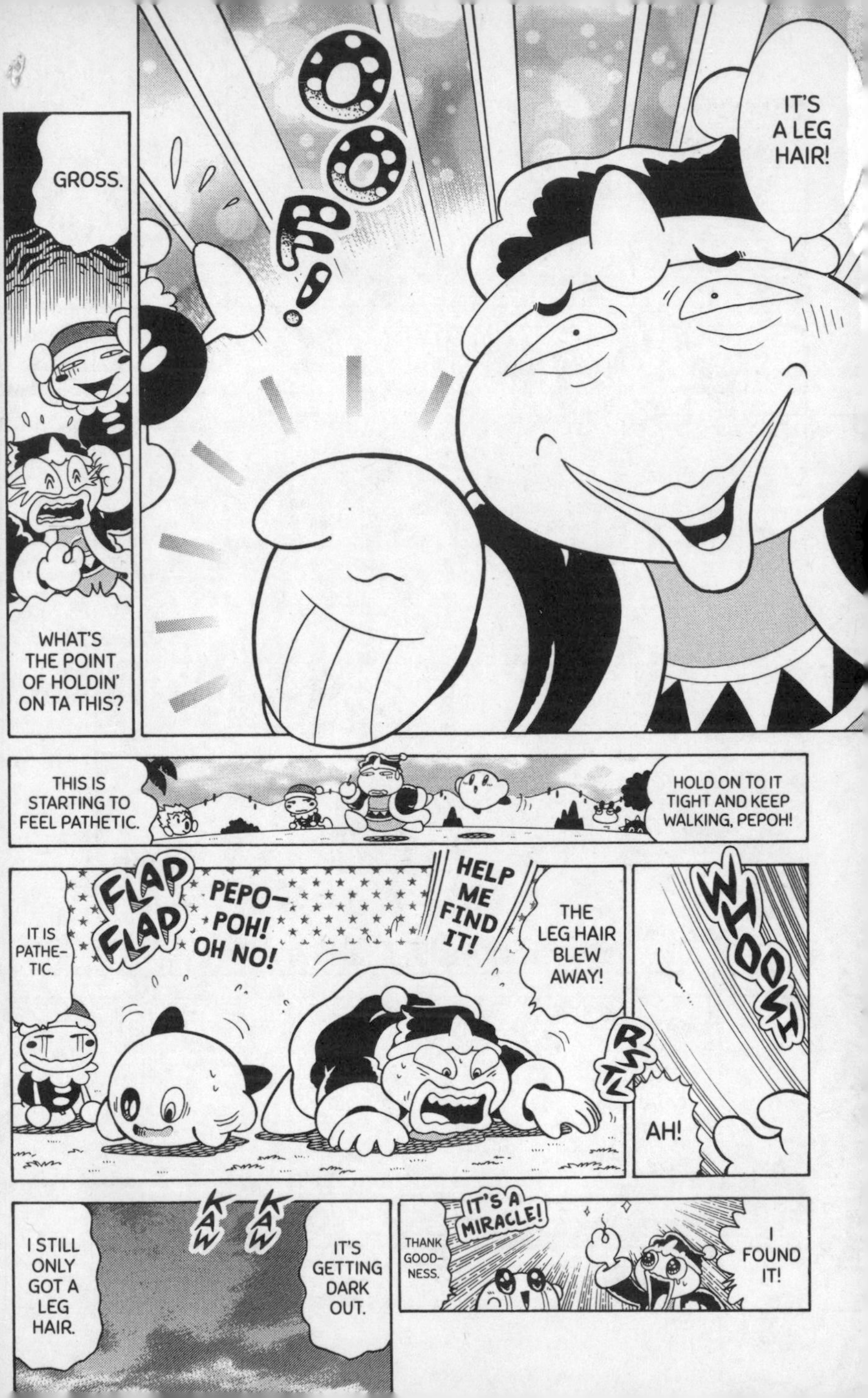
IT'S A LEG HAIR!
OOF!
GROSS.
WHAT'S THE POINT OF HOLDIN' ON TA THIS?
HOLD ON TO IT TIGHT AND KEEP WALKING, PEPOH!
THIS IS STARTING TO FEEL PATHETIC.
WHOOSH
RSTL
AH!
THE LEG HAIR BLEW AWAY!
HELP ME FIND IT!
PEPO-POH! OH NO!
FLAP FLAP
IT IS PATHE-TIC.
I FOUND IT!
IT'S A MIRACLE!
THANK GOOD-NESS.
KAW KAW
IT'S GETTING DARK OUT.
I STILL ONLY GOT A LEG HAIR.

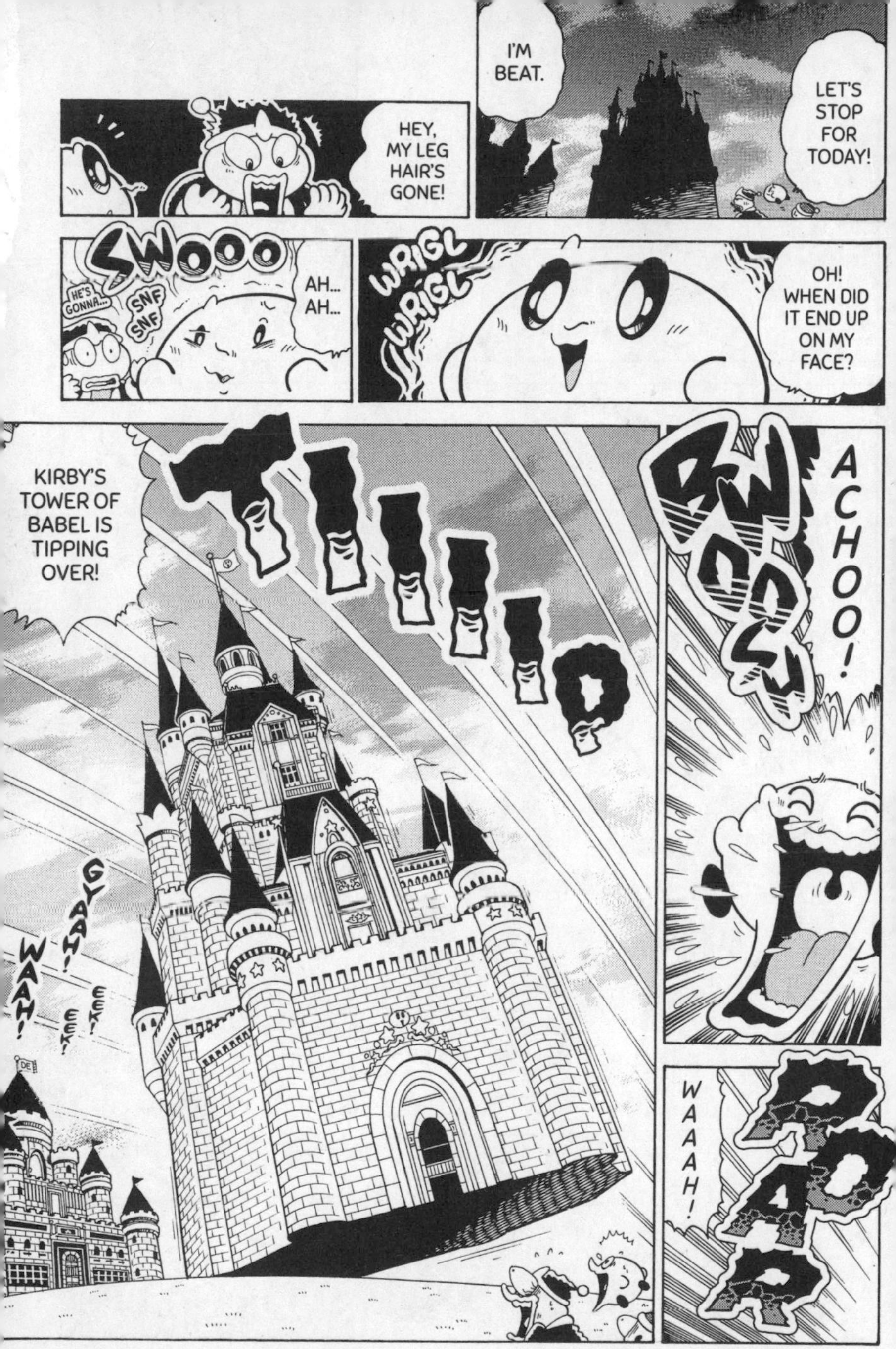
I'M BEAT.
LET'S STOP FOR TODAY!
HEY, MY LEG HAIR'S GONE!
OH! WHEN DID IT END UP ON MY FACE?
WRIGL WRIGL
AH... AH...
SWOOO
SNF SNF
HE'S GONNA...
ACHOO!
BWOOSH
WAAAAH!
KIRBY'S TOWER OF BABEL IS TIPPING OVER!
TIIIIP
GYAAAH!
EEK! EEK!
WAAH!

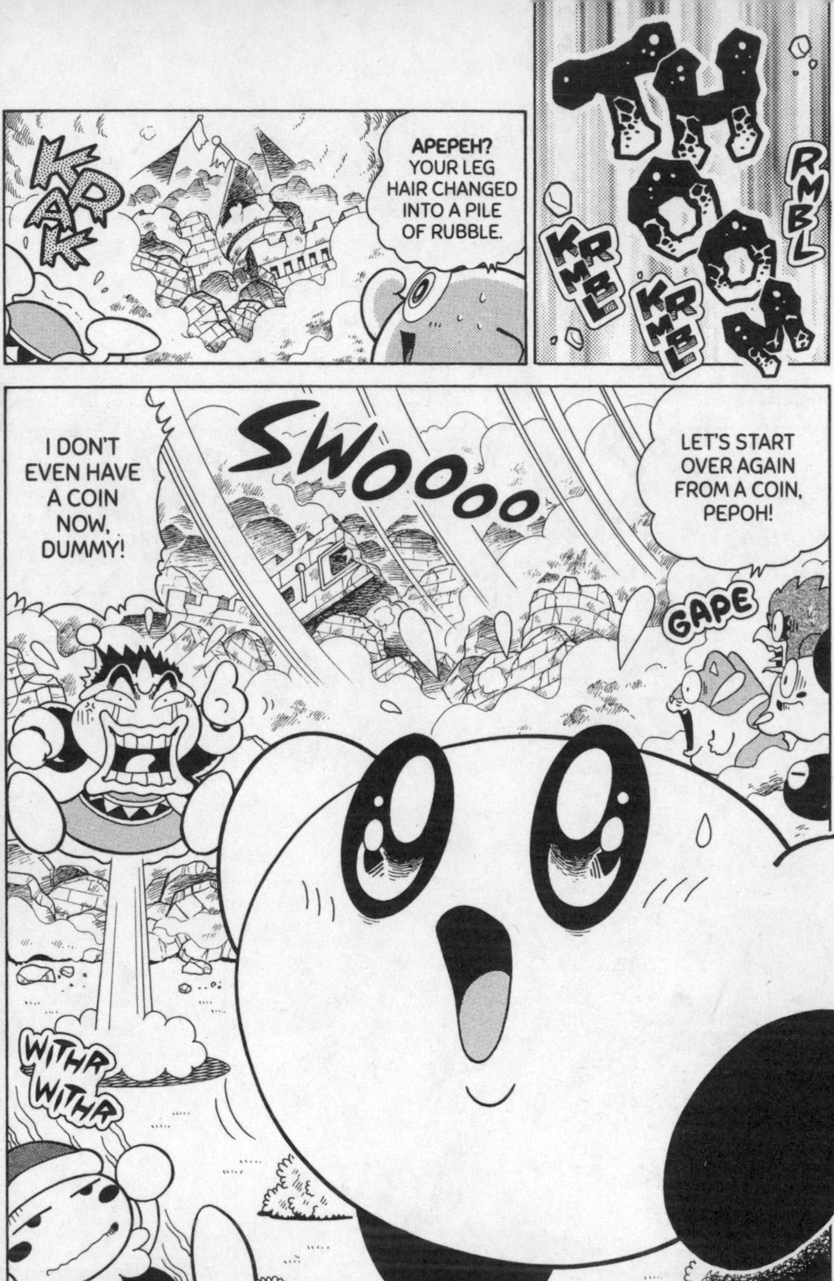
THOOOM
RMBL
KRMBL
KRMBL
KRAK
APEPEH? YOUR LEG HAIR CHANGED INTO A PILE OF RUBBLE.
LET'S START OVER AGAIN FROM A COIN, PEPOH!
SWOOOO
GAPE
I DON'T EVEN HAVE A COIN NOW, DUMMY!
WITHR WITHR

CHAPTER 9: KIRBY BECOMES KING!

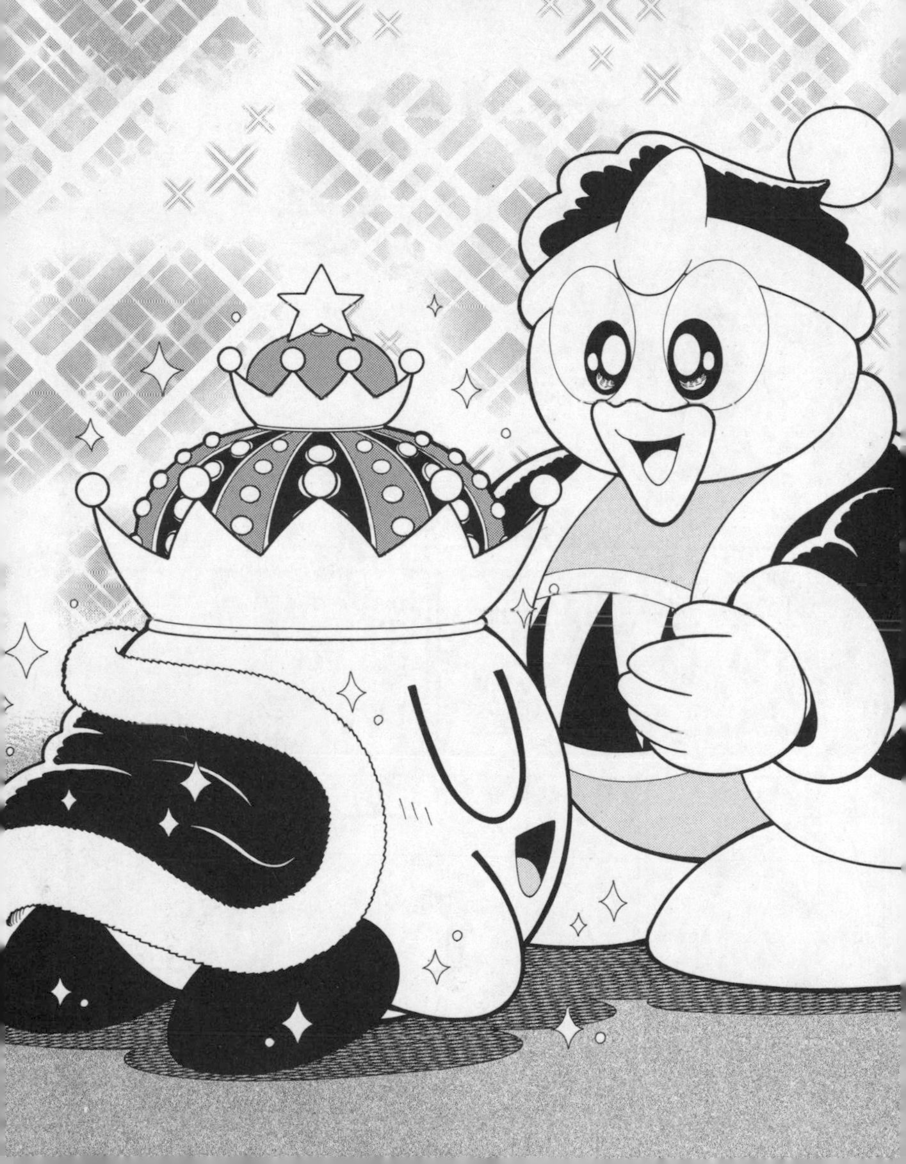

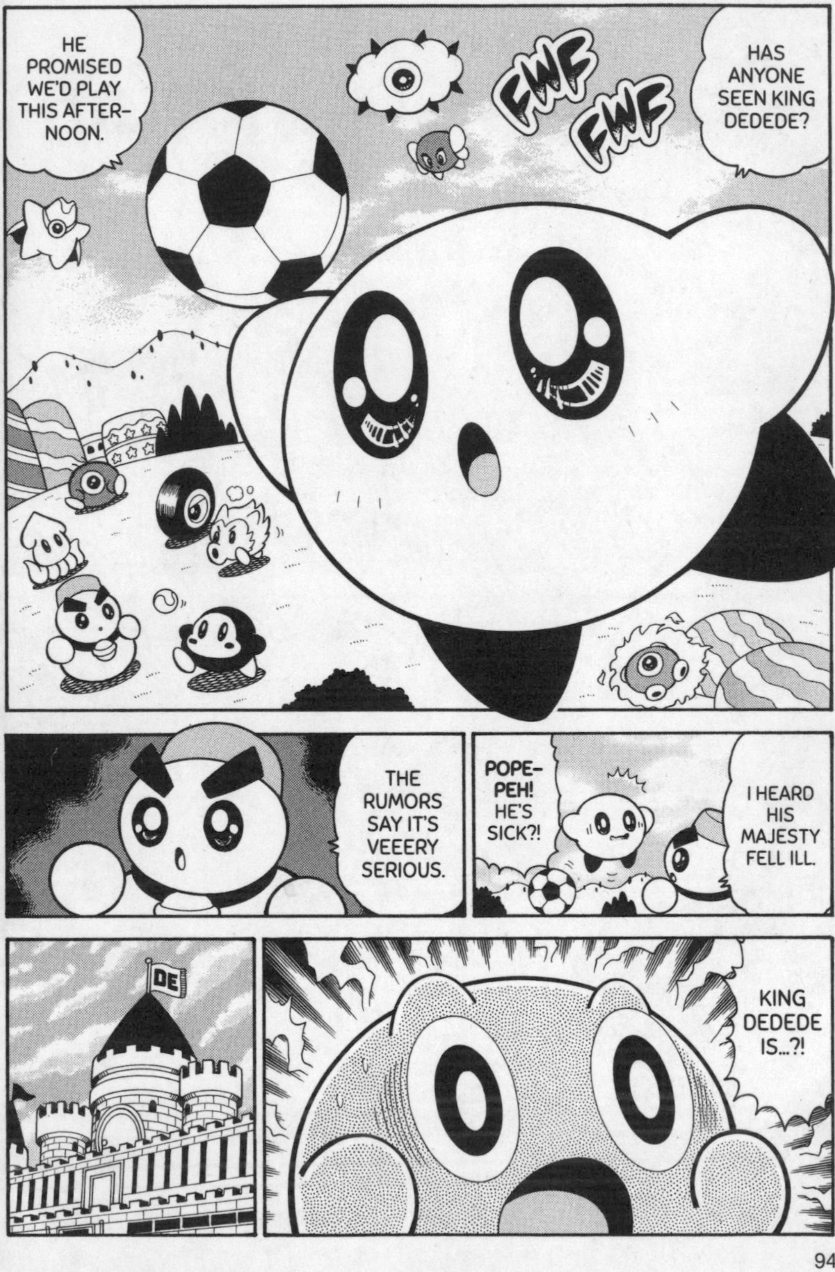
HAS ANYONE SEEN KING DEDEDE?
FWF FWF
HE PROMISED WE'D PLAY THIS AFTER-NOON.
I HEARD HIS MAJESTY FELL ILL.
POPE-PEH! HE'S SICK?!
THE RUMORS SAY IT'S VEEERY SERIOUS.
KING DEDEDE IS...?!
DE

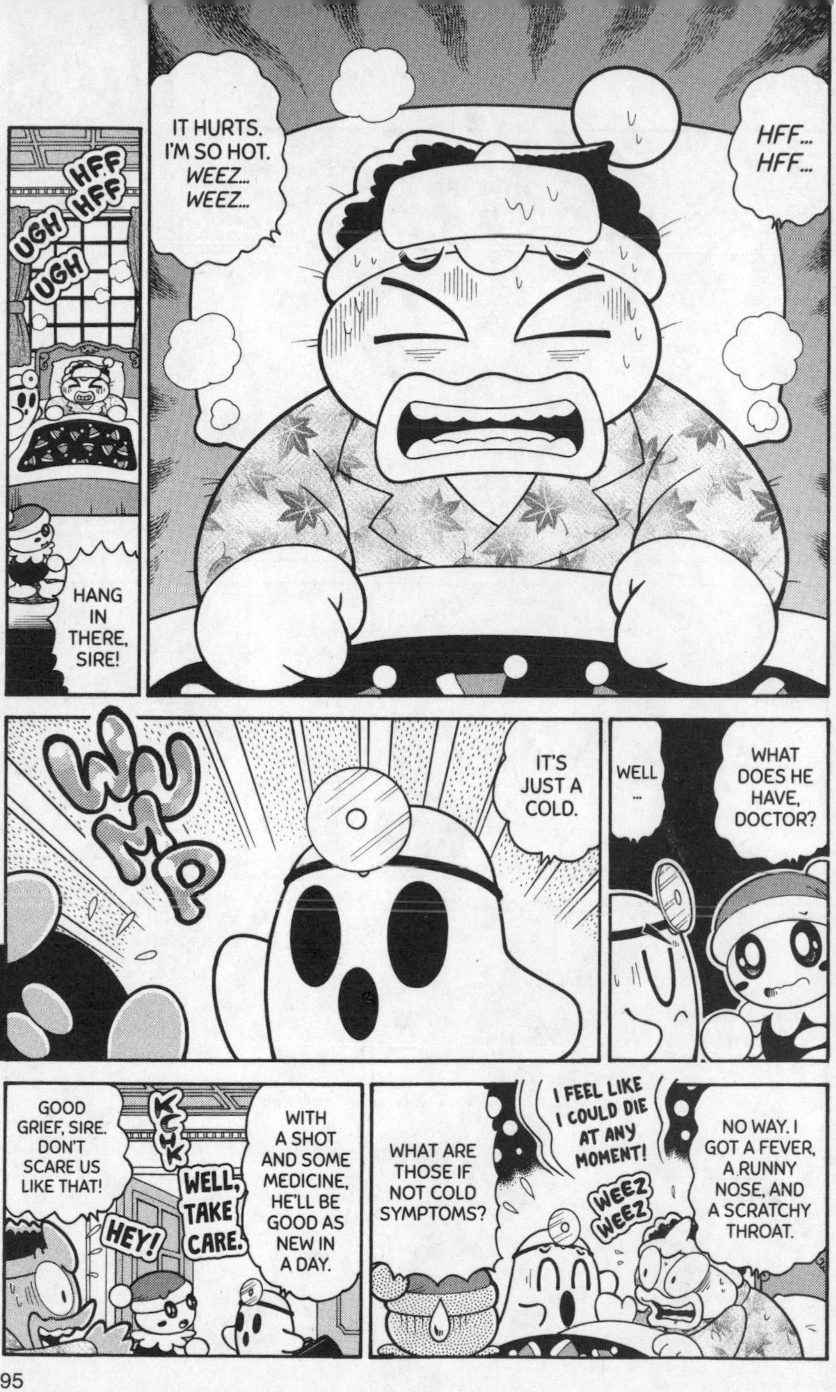
HFF... HFF...
IT HURTS. I'M SO HOT. WEEZ... WEEZ...
HFF HFF
UGH UGH
HANG IN THERE, SIRE!
WHAT DOES HE HAVE, DOCTOR?
WELL...
IT'S JUST A COLD.
WUMP
NO WAY. I GOT A FEVER, A RUNNY NOSE, AND A SCRATCHY THROAT.
I FEEL LIKE I COULD DIE AT ANY MOMENT!
WEEZ WEEZ
WHAT ARE THOSE IF NOT COLD SYMPTOMS?
WITH A SHOT AND SOME MEDICINE, HE'LL BE GOOD AS NEW IN A DAY.
KCHK
WELL, TAKE CARE.
HEY!
GOOD GRIEF, SIRE. DON'T SCARE US LIKE THAT!

AUTHOR'S COMMENT

I ALSO DREW KIRBY AS A KING ON THE COVER OF VOLUME 3 OF THE CLASSIC SERIES. HE MIGHT LOOK KINGLIER THAN KING DEDEDE. IF HE REALLY BECAME KING, THOUGH, DREAM LAND WOULD BE IN TROUBLE.

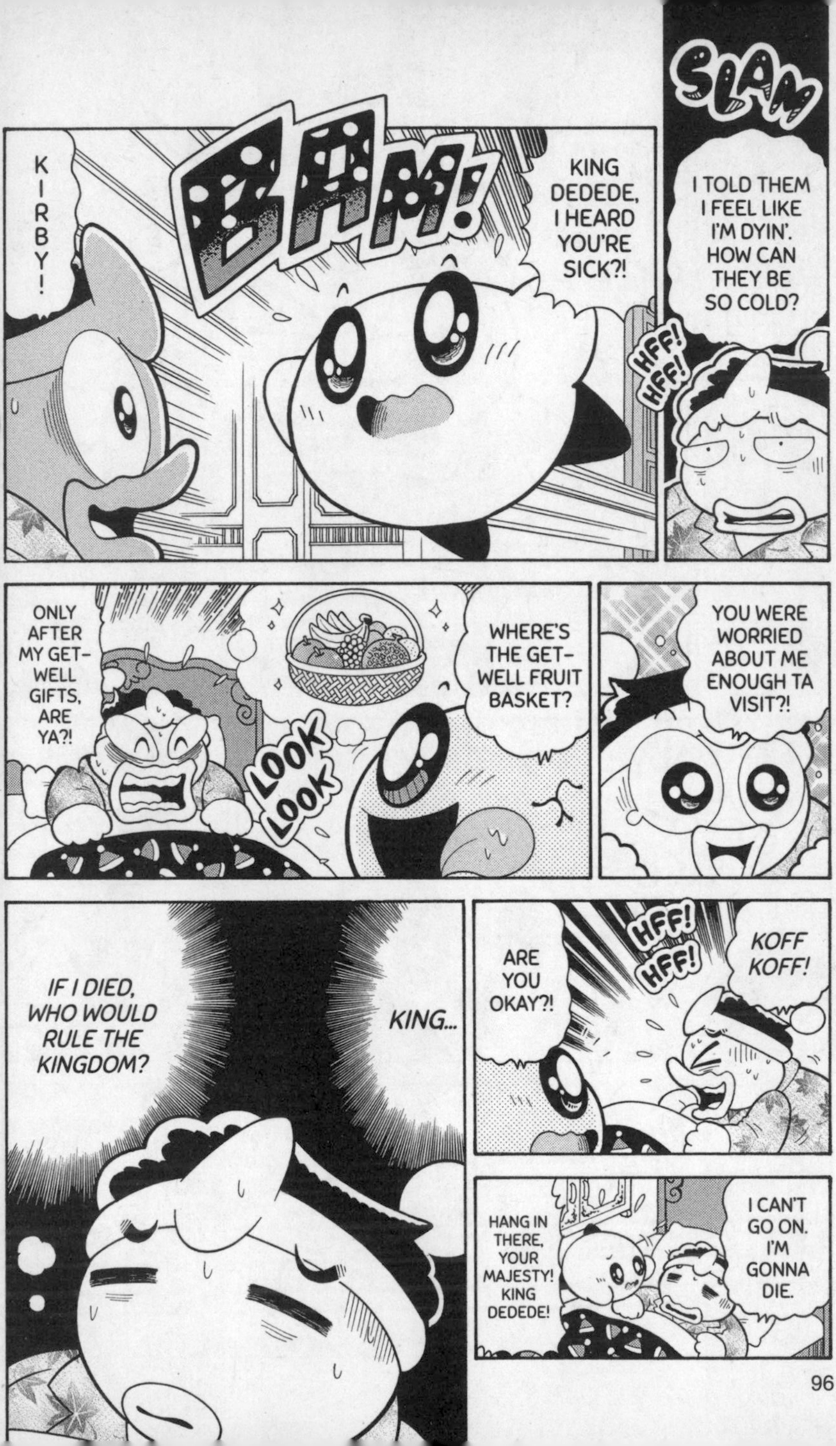
SLAM
I TOLD THEM I FEEL LIKE I'M DYIN'. HOW CAN THEY BE SO COLD?
HFF! HFF!
KING DEDEDE, I HEARD YOU'RE SICK?!
BAM!
KIRBY!
YOU WERE WORRIED ABOUT ME ENOUGH TA VISIT?!
WHERE'S THE GET-WELL FRUIT BASKET?
LOOK LOOK
ONLY AFTER MY GET-WELL GIFTS, ARE YA?!
KOFF KOFF!
HFF! HFF!
ARE YOU OKAY?!
I CAN'T GO ON. I'M GONNA DIE.
HANG IN THERE, YOUR MAJESTY! KING DEDEDE!
KING...
IF I DIED, WHO WOULD RULE THE KINGDOM?

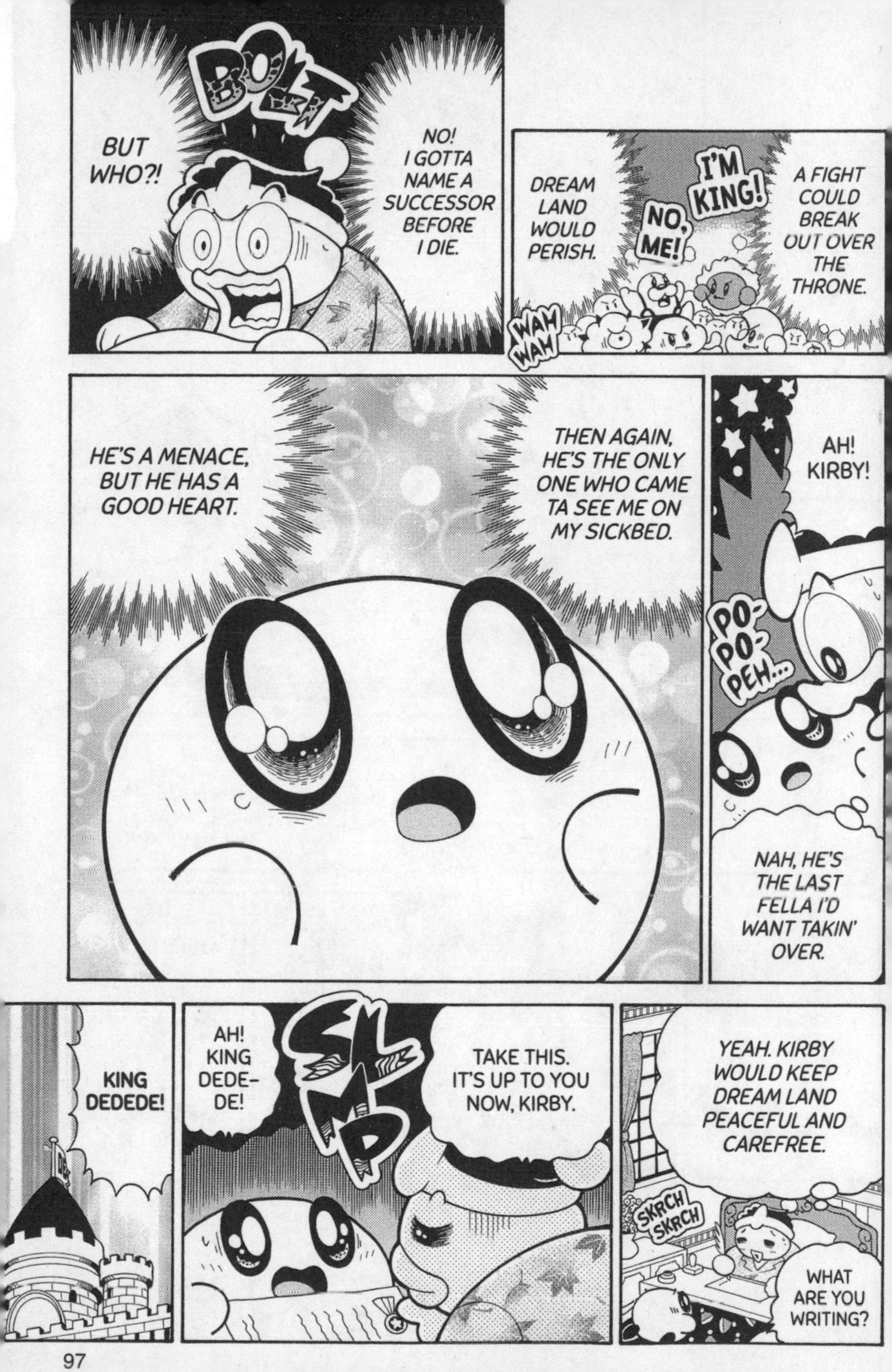
A FIGHT COULD BREAK OUT OVER THE THRONE.
I'M KING!
NO, ME!
DREAM LAND WOULD PERISH.
WAH WAH
BOLT
NO! I GOTTA NAME A SUCCESSOR BEFORE I DIE.
BUT WHO?!
AH! KIRBY!
PO-PO-PEH...
NAH, HE'S THE LAST FELLA I'D WANT TAKIN' OVER.
THEN AGAIN, HE'S THE ONLY ONE WHO CAME TA SEE ME ON MY SICKBED.
HE'S A MENACE, BUT HE HAS A GOOD HEART.
YEAH. KIRBY WOULD KEEP DREAM LAND PEACEFUL AND CAREFREE.
SKRCH SKRCH
WHAT ARE YOU WRITING?
TAKE THIS. IT'S UP TO YOU NOW, KIRBY.
SLMP
AH! KING DEDE-DE!
KING DEDEDE!

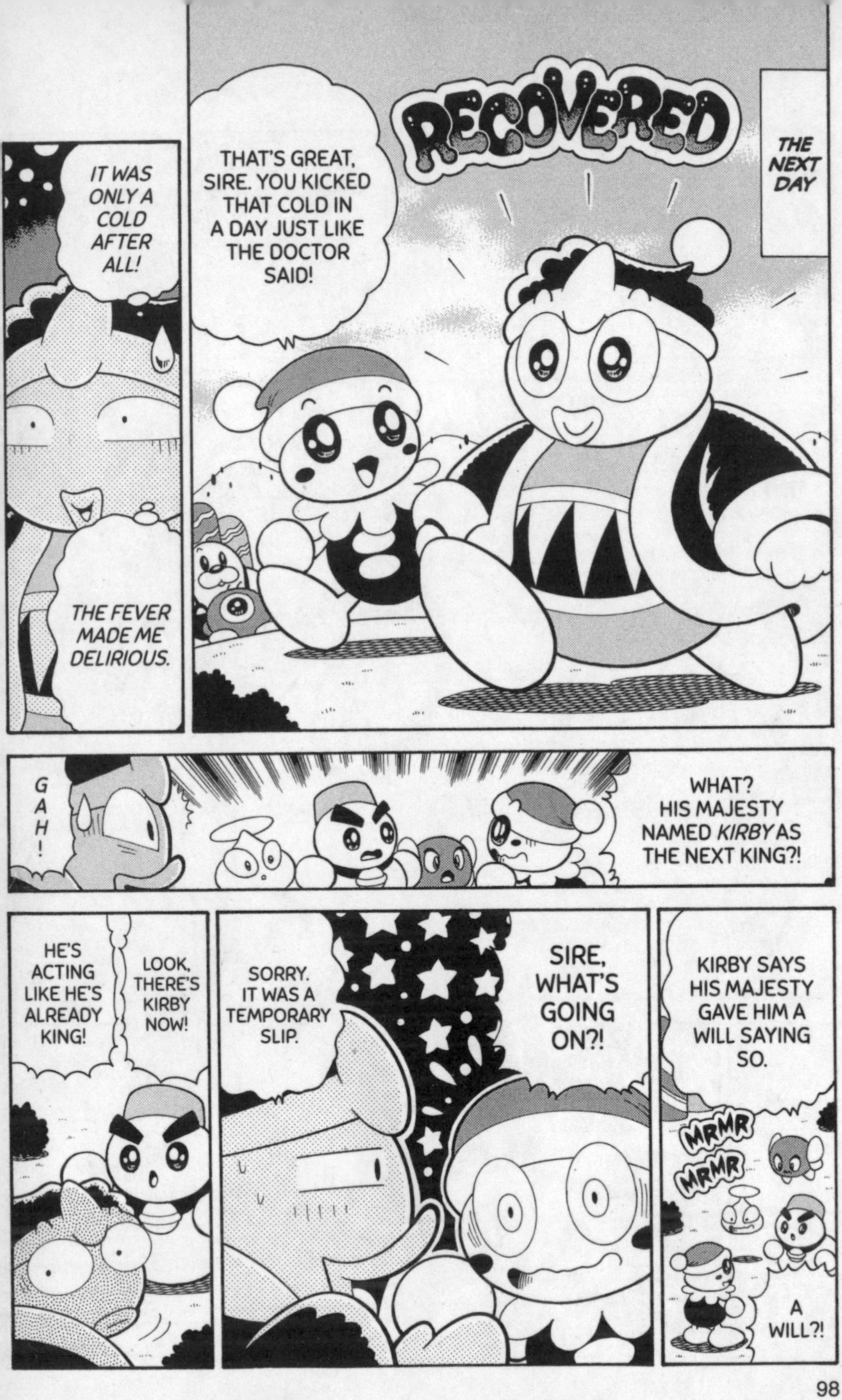
THE NEXT DAY
RECOVERED
THAT'S GREAT, SIRE. YOU KICKED THAT COLD IN A DAY JUST LIKE THE DOCTOR SAID!
IT WAS ONLY A COLD AFTER ALL!
THE FEVER MADE ME DELIRIOUS.
WHAT? HIS MAJESTY NAMED KIRBY AS THE NEXT KING?!
GAH!
KIRBY SAYS HIS MAJESTY GAVE HIM A WILL SAYING SO.
MRMR
MRMR
A WILL?!
SIRE, WHAT'S GOING ON?!
SORRY. IT WAS A TEMPORARY SLIP.
LOOK, THERE'S KIRBY NOW!
HE'S ACTING LIKE HE'S ALREADY KING!

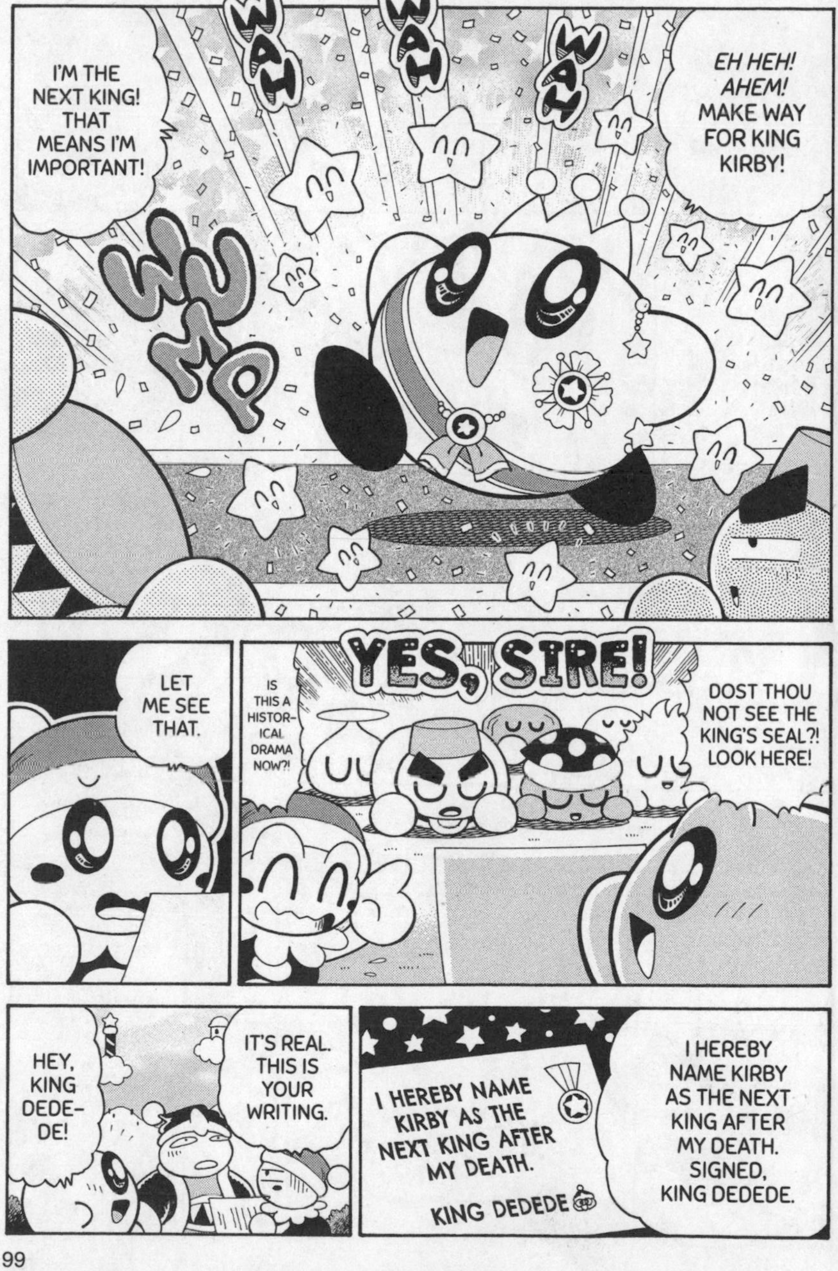
EH HEH! AHEM! MAKE WAY FOR KING KIRBY!
WAH WAH WAH
I'M THE NEXT KING! THAT MEANS I'M IMPORTANT!
WUMP
YES, SIRE!
DOST THOU NOT SEE THE KING'S SEAL?! LOOK HERE!
IS THIS A HISTORICAL DRAMA NOW?!
LET ME SEE THAT.
I HEREBY NAME KIRBY AS THE NEXT KING AFTER MY DEATH. SIGNED, KING DEDEDE.
I HEREBY NAME KIRBY AS THE NEXT KING AFTER MY DEATH.
KING DEDEDE
IT'S REAL. THIS IS YOUR WRITING.
HEY, KING DEDE-DE!

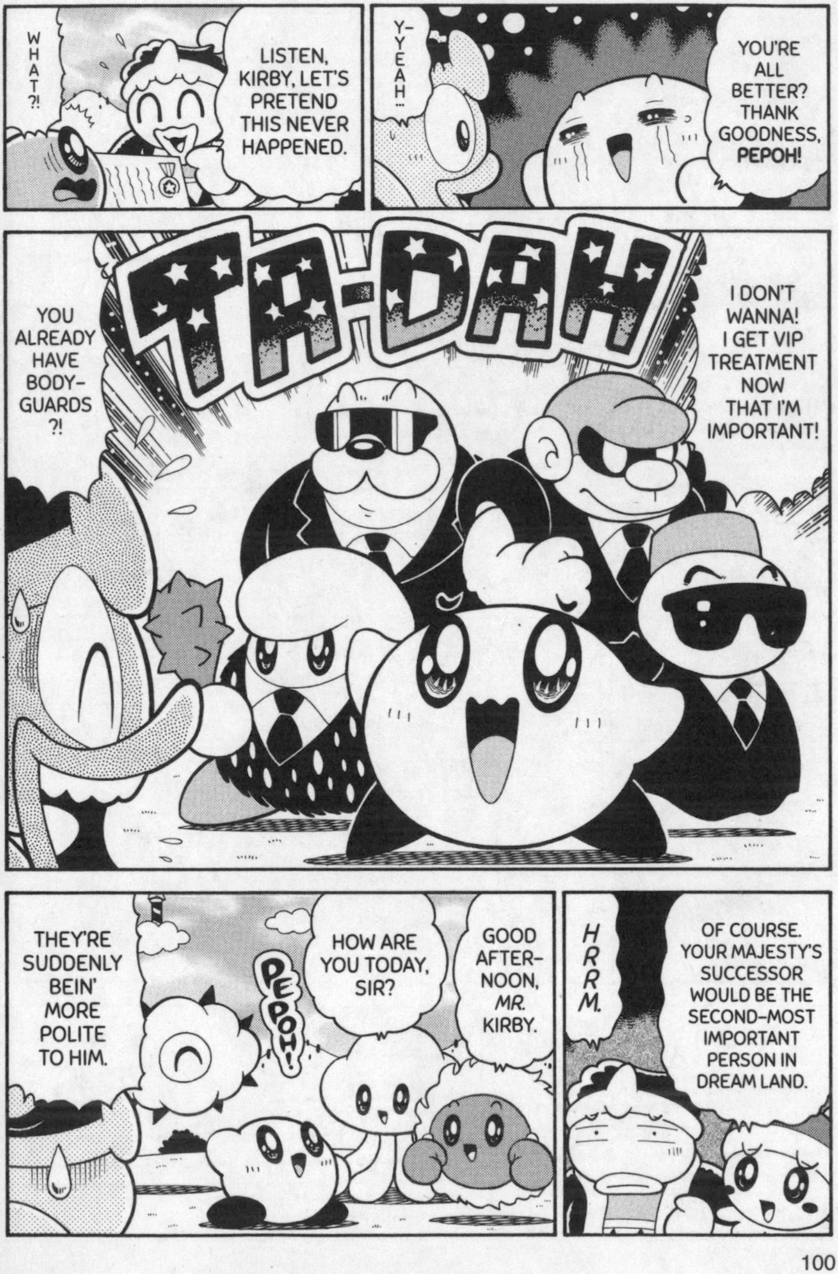
YOU'RE ALL BETTER? THANK GOODNESS, **PEPOH!**
Y-YEAH...
LISTEN, KIRBY, LET'S PRETEND THIS NEVER HAPPENED.
WHAT?!
TA-DAH
I DON'T WANNA! I GET VIP TREATMENT NOW THAT I'M IMPORTANT!
YOU ALREADY HAVE BODY-GUARDS?!
OF COURSE. YOUR MAJESTY'S SUCCESSOR WOULD BE THE SECOND-MOST IMPORTANT PERSON IN DREAM LAND.
HRRM.
GOOD AFTER-NOON, *MR.* KIRBY.
HOW ARE YOU TODAY, SIR?
PEPOH!
THEY'RE SUDDENLY BEIN' MORE POLITE TO HIM.

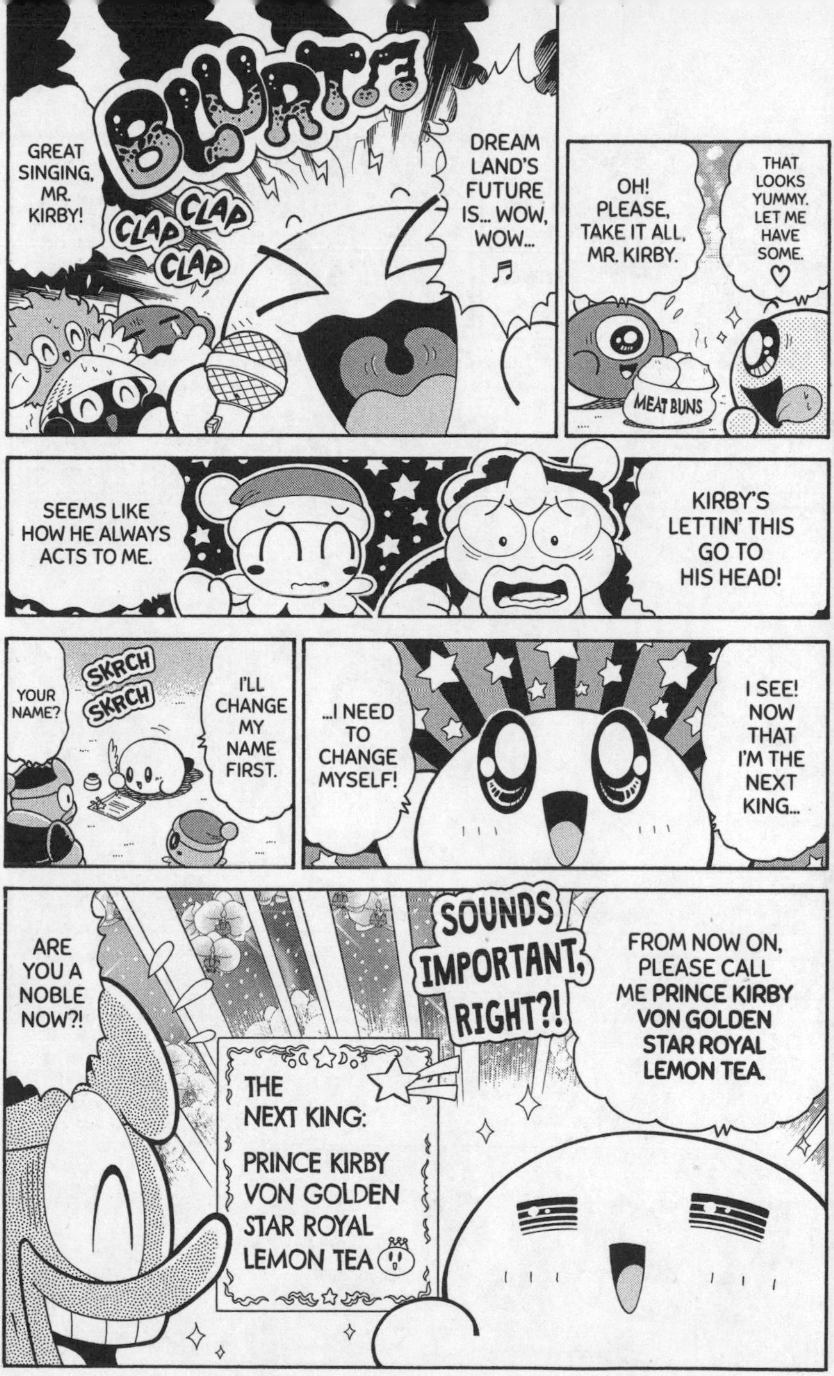
THAT LOOKS YUMMY. LET ME HAVE SOME. ♡
OH! PLEASE, TAKE IT ALL, MR. KIRBY.
MEAT BUNS
DREAM LAND'S FUTURE IS... WOW, WOW... ♬
BLURT
GREAT SINGING, MR. KIRBY!
CLAP CLAP CLAP
KIRBY'S LETTIN' THIS GO TO HIS HEAD!
SEEMS LIKE HOW HE ALWAYS ACTS TO ME.
I SEE! NOW THAT I'M THE NEXT KING...
...I NEED TO CHANGE MYSELF!
I'LL CHANGE MY NAME FIRST.
SKRCH SKRCH
YOUR NAME?
FROM NOW ON, PLEASE CALL ME PRINCE KIRBY VON GOLDEN STAR ROYAL LEMON TEA.
SOUNDS IMPORTANT, RIGHT?!
THE NEXT KING: PRINCE KIRBY VON GOLDEN STAR ROYAL LEMON TEA
ARE YOU A NOBLE NOW?!

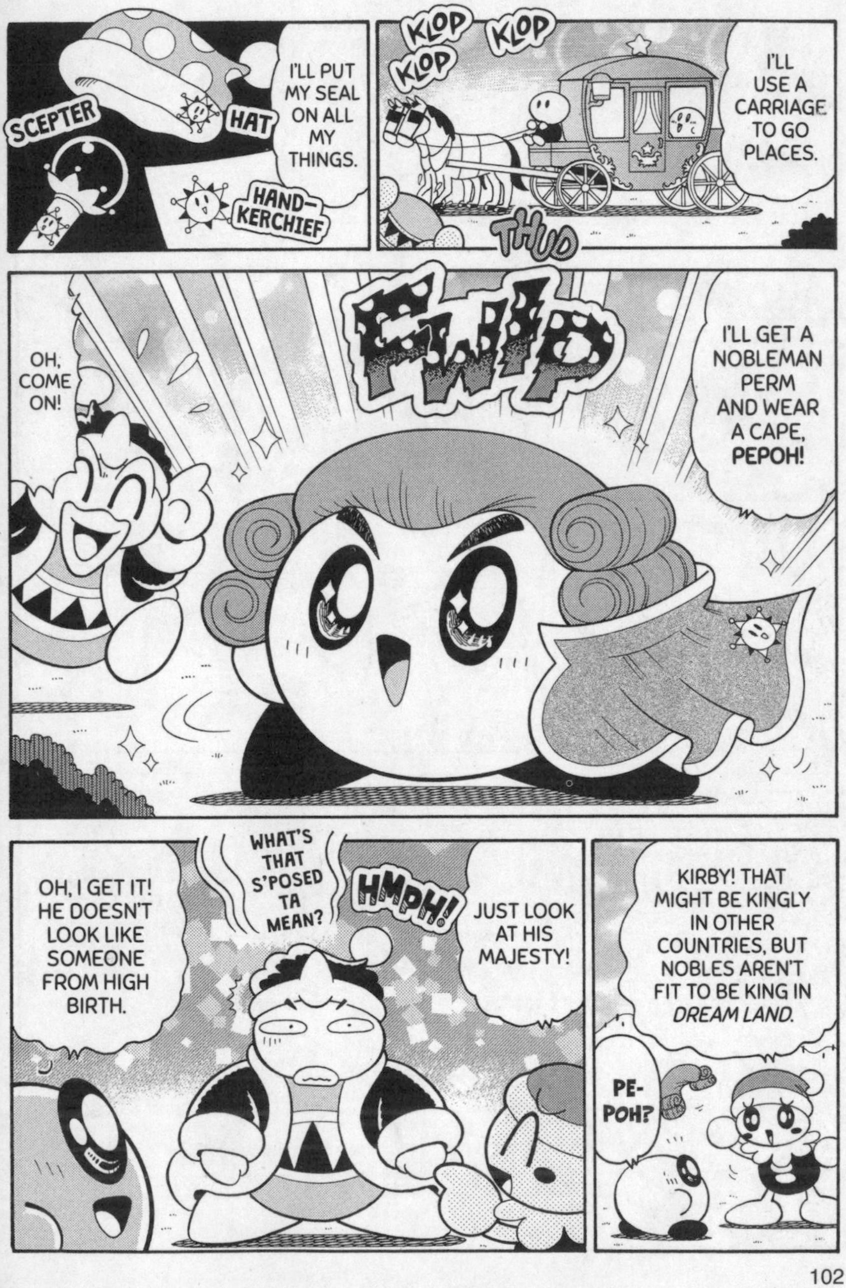
KLOP KLOP
KLOP
I'LL USE A CARRIAGE TO GO PLACES.
THUD
I'LL PUT MY SEAL ON ALL MY THINGS.
HAT
SCEPTER
HAND-KERCHIEF
I'LL GET A NOBLEMAN PERM AND WEAR A CAPE, **PEPOH!**
FWIP
OH, COME ON!
KIRBY! THAT MIGHT BE KINGLY IN OTHER COUNTRIES, BUT NOBLES AREN'T FIT TO BE KING IN *DREAM LAND*.
PE-POH?
JUST LOOK AT HIS MAJESTY!
HMPH!
WHAT'S THAT S'POSED TA MEAN?
OH, I GET IT! HE DOESN'T LOOK LIKE SOMEONE FROM HIGH BIRTH.

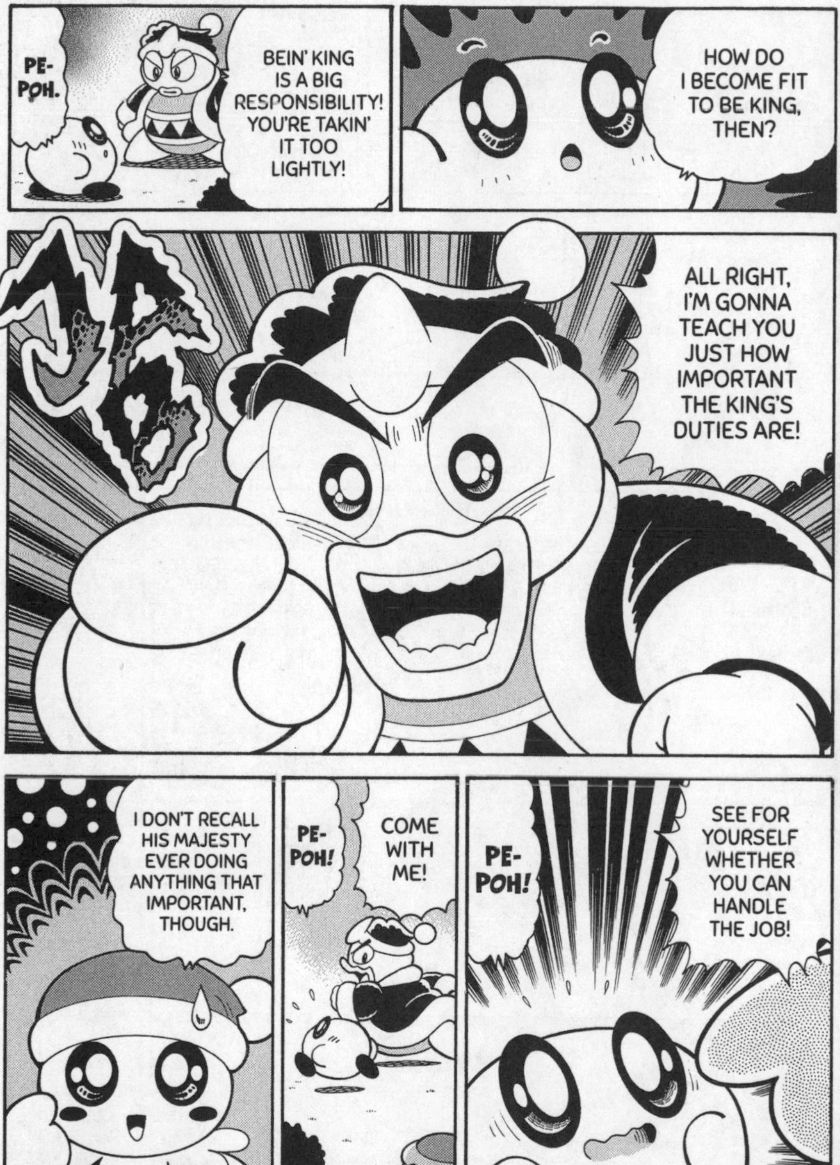
HOW DO I BECOME FIT TO BE KING, THEN?
BEIN' KING IS A BIG RESPONSIBILITY! YOU'RE TAKIN' IT TOO LIGHTLY!
PE-POH.
ALL RIGHT, I'M GONNA TEACH YOU JUST HOW IMPORTANT THE KING'S DUTIES ARE!
SEE FOR YOURSELF WHETHER YOU CAN HANDLE THE JOB!
PE-POH!
COME WITH ME!
PE-POH!
I DON'T RECALL HIS MAJESTY EVER DOING ANYTHING THAT IMPORTANT, THOUGH.

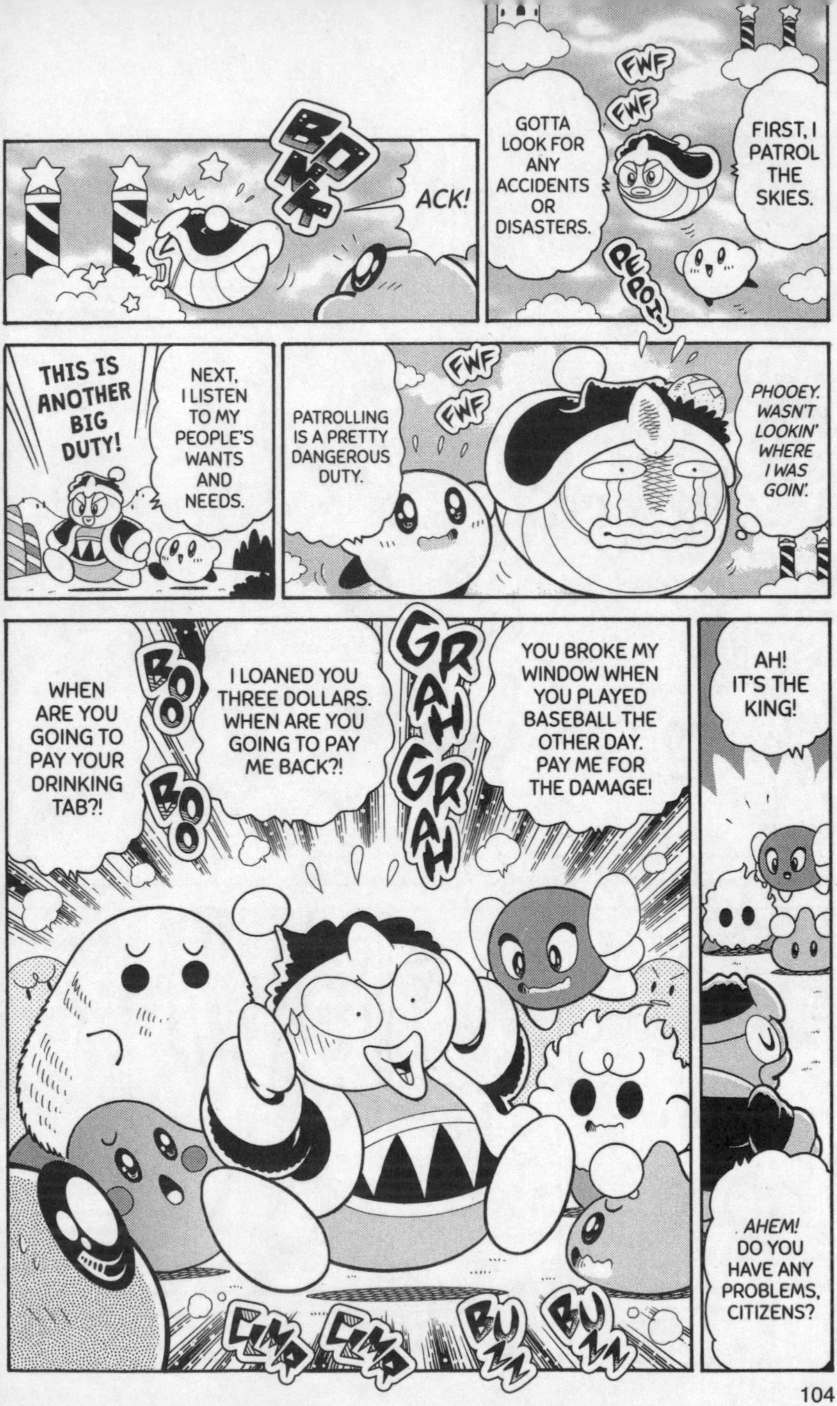
FIRST, I PATROL THE SKIES.
FWF
FWF
GOTTA LOOK FOR ANY ACCIDENTS OR DISASTERS.
PEPOI!
BONK
ACK!
PHOOEY. WASN'T LOOKIN' WHERE I WAS GOIN'.
FWF
FWF
PATROLLING IS A PRETTY DANGEROUS DUTY.
NEXT, I LISTEN TO MY PEOPLE'S WANTS AND NEEDS.
THIS IS ANOTHER BIG DUTY!
AH! IT'S THE KING!
AHEM! DO YOU HAVE ANY PROBLEMS, CITIZENS?
YOU BROKE MY WINDOW WHEN YOU PLAYED BASEBALL THE OTHER DAY. PAY ME FOR THE DAMAGE!
GRAH GRAH
I LOANED YOU THREE DOLLARS. WHEN ARE YOU GOING TO PAY ME BACK?!
BOO BOO
WHEN ARE YOU GOING TO PAY YOUR DRINKING TAB?!

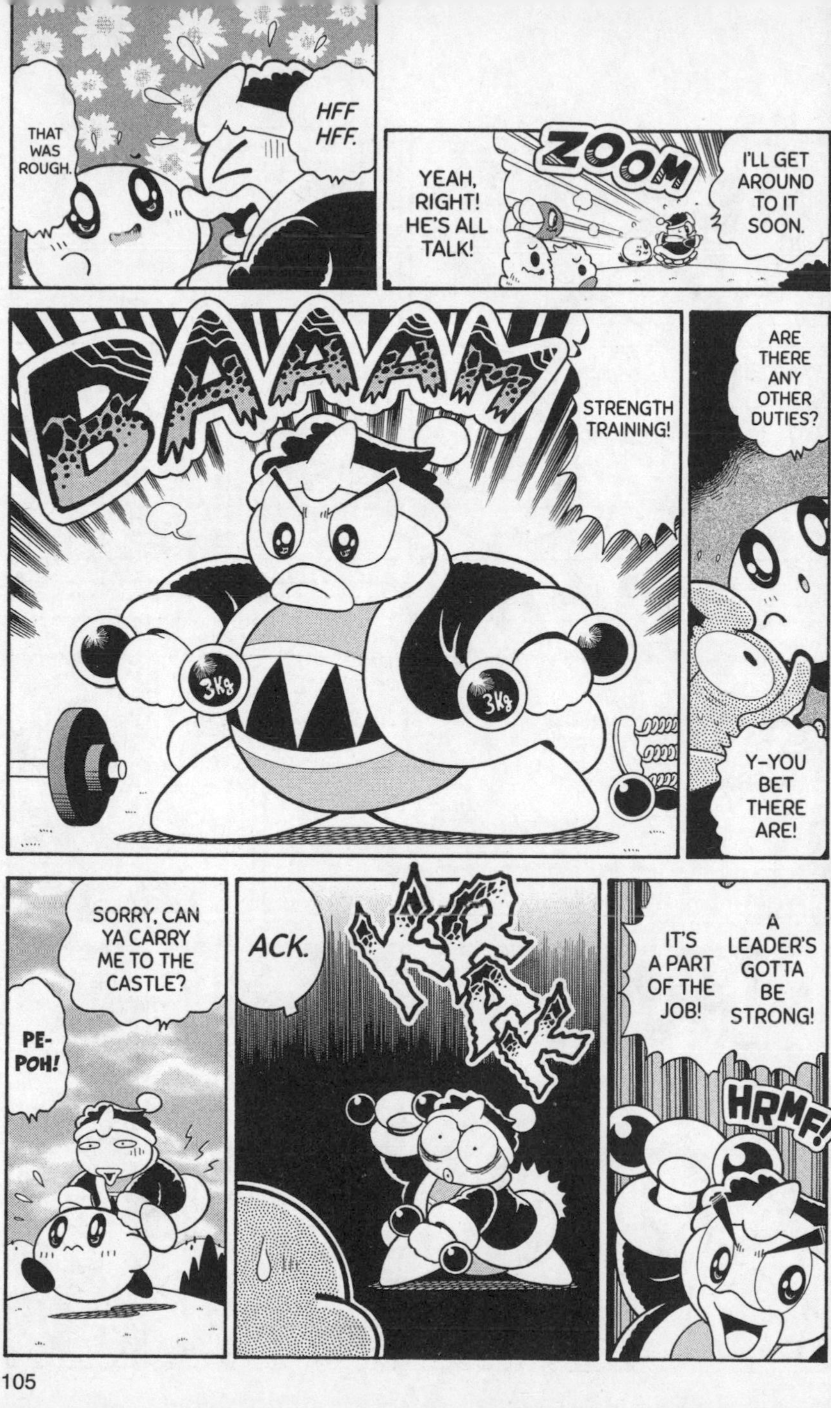
I'LL GET AROUND TO IT SOON.
ZOOM
YEAH, RIGHT! HE'S ALL TALK!
HFF HFF.
THAT WAS ROUGH.
ARE THERE ANY OTHER DUTIES?
Y-YOU BET THERE ARE!
STRENGTH TRAINING!
BAAAM
3Kg
3Kg
A LEADER'S GOTTA BE STRONG!
IT'S A PART OF THE JOB!
HRMF!
ACK.
SORRY, CAN YA CARRY ME TO THE CASTLE?
PE-POH!

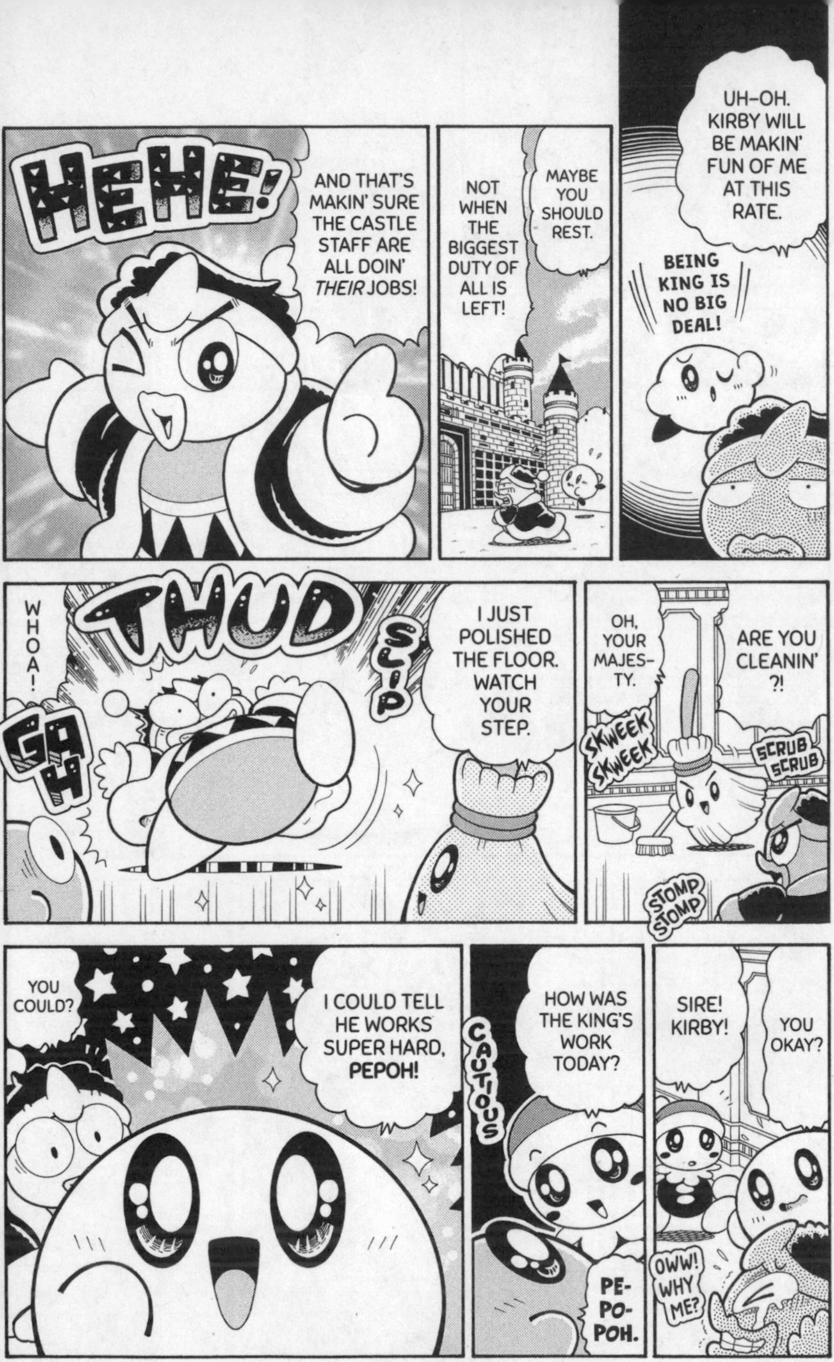
UH-OH. KIRBY WILL BE MAKIN' FUN OF ME AT THIS RATE.
BEING KING IS NO BIG DEAL!
MAYBE YOU SHOULD REST.
NOT WHEN THE BIGGEST DUTY OF ALL IS LEFT!
AND THAT'S MAKIN' SURE THE CASTLE STAFF ARE ALL DOIN' *THEIR* JOBS!
HEHE!
ARE YOU CLEANIN' ?!
OH, YOUR MAJES-TY.
SCRUB SCRUB
SKWEEK SKWEEK
STOMP STOMP
I JUST POLISHED THE FLOOR. WATCH YOUR STEP.
SLIP
THUD
WHOA!
GAH
YOU OKAY?
SIRE! KIRBY!
OWW! WHY ME?
HOW WAS THE KING'S WORK TODAY?
CAUTIOUS
PE-PO-POH.
I COULD TELL HE WORKS SUPER HARD, **PEPOH!**
YOU COULD?

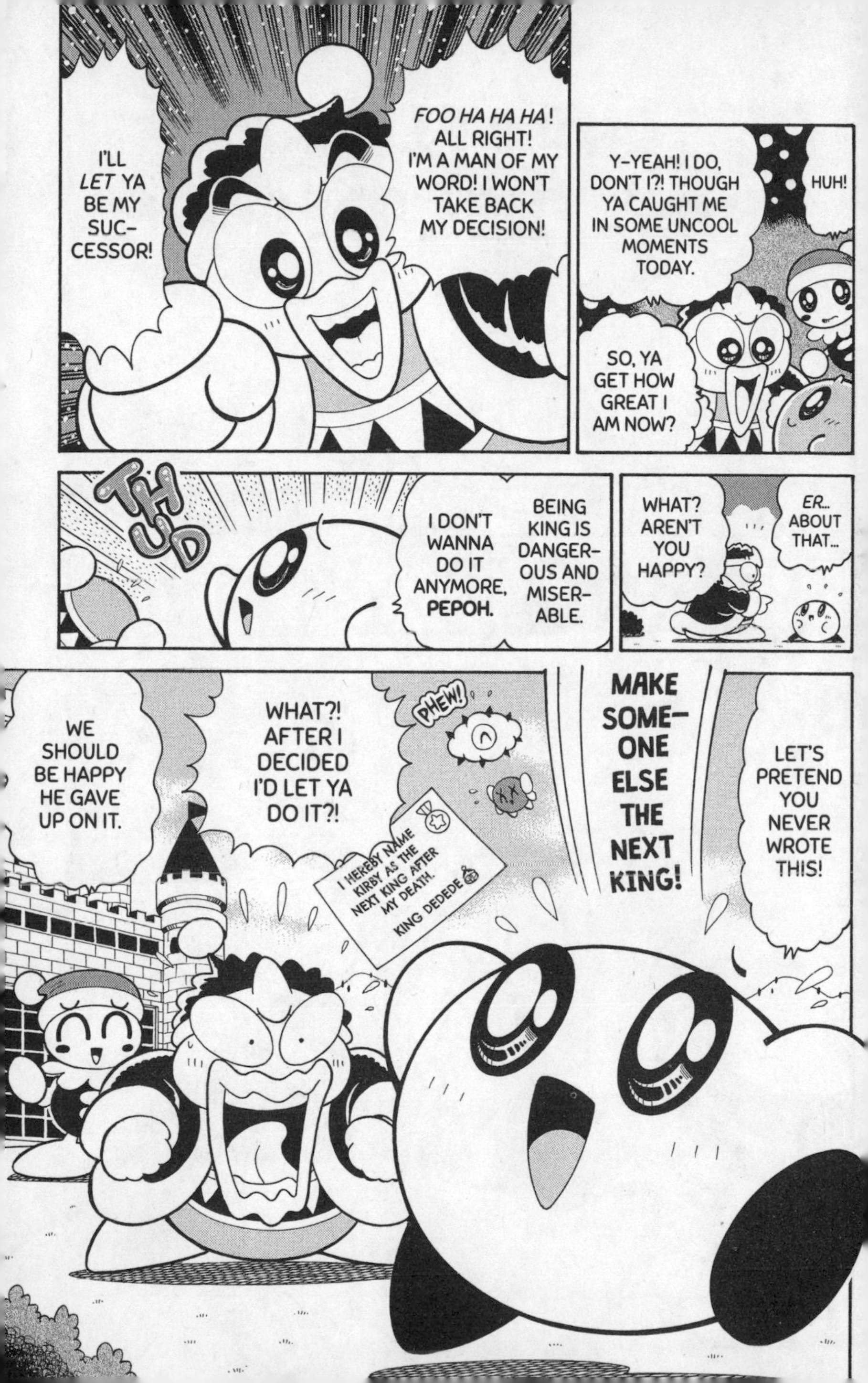
HUH!
Y-YEAH! I DO, DON'T I?! THOUGH YA CAUGHT ME IN SOME UNCOOL MOMENTS TODAY.
SO, YA GET HOW GREAT I AM NOW?
FOO HA HA HA! ALL RIGHT! I'M A MAN OF MY WORD! I WON'T TAKE BACK MY DECISION!
I'LL LET YA BE MY SUC-CESSOR!
ER... ABOUT THAT...
WHAT? AREN'T YOU HAPPY?
BEING KING IS DANGER-OUS AND MISER-ABLE.
I DON'T WANNA DO IT ANYMORE, PEPOH.
THUD
LET'S PRETEND YOU NEVER WROTE THIS!
MAKE SOME-ONE ELSE THE NEXT KING!
PHEW!
I HEREBY NAME KIRBY AS THE NEXT KING AFTER MY DEATH.
KING DEDEDE
WHAT?! AFTER I DECIDED I'D LET YA DO IT?!
WE SHOULD BE HAPPY HE GAVE UP ON IT.

CHAPTER 10: CHASE THE BIG SCOOP!

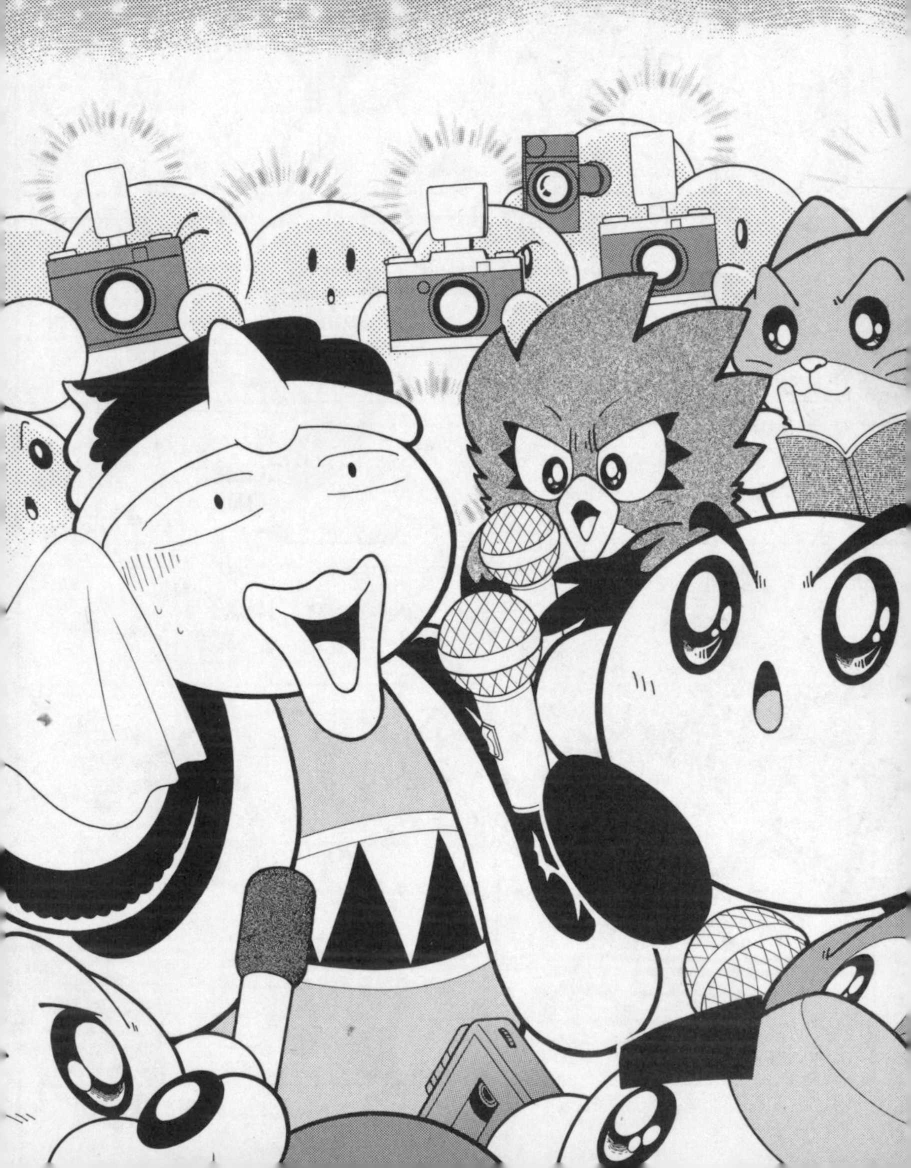

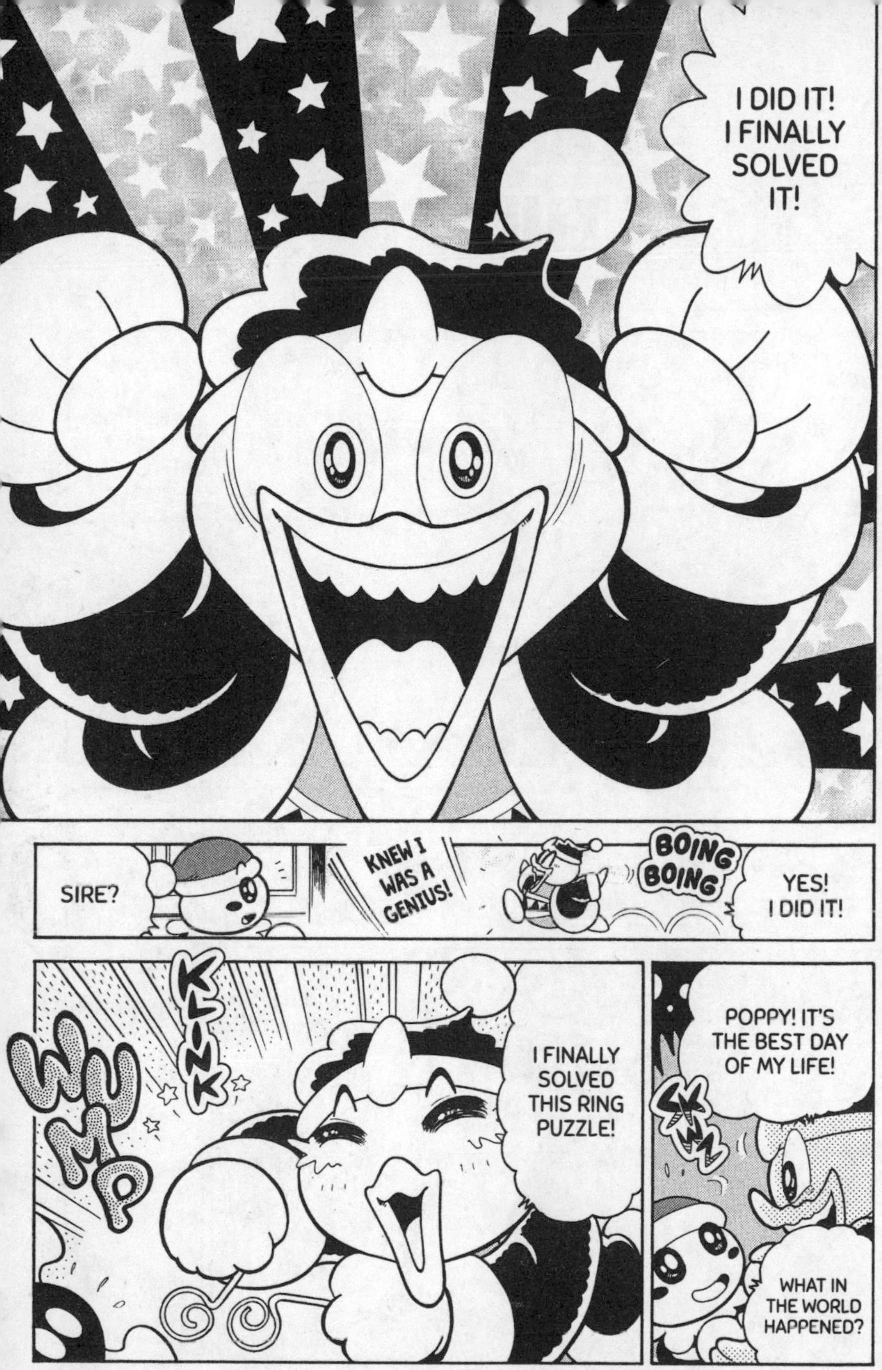
I DID IT! I FINALLY SOLVED IT!
YES! I DID IT!
BOING BOING
KNEW I WAS A GENIUS!
SIRE?
POPPY! IT'S THE BEST DAY OF MY LIFE!
WHAT IN THE WORLD HAPPENED?
I FINALLY SOLVED THIS RING PUZZLE!
KLINK
WUMP

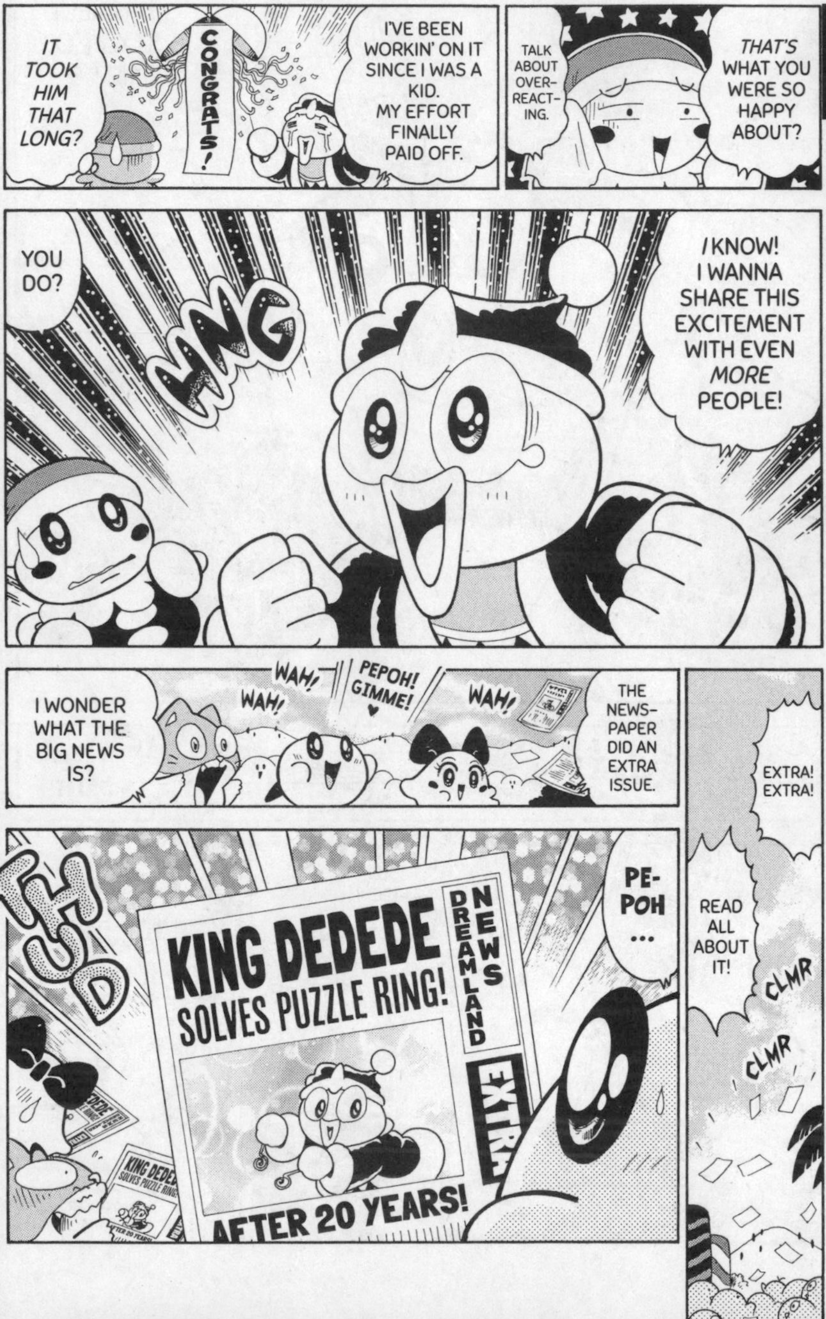
THAT'S WHAT YOU WERE SO HAPPY ABOUT?
TALK ABOUT OVER-REACTING.
I'VE BEEN WORKIN' ON IT SINCE I WAS A KID. MY EFFORT FINALLY PAID OFF.
CONGRATS!
IT TOOK HIM THAT LONG?
I KNOW! I WANNA SHARE THIS EXCITEMENT WITH EVEN MORE PEOPLE!
WNG
YOU DO?
EXTRA! EXTRA!
READ ALL ABOUT IT!
CLMR
CLMR
THE NEWS-PAPER DID AN EXTRA ISSUE.
WAH!
PEPOH! GIMME!
WAH!
WAH!
I WONDER WHAT THE BIG NEWS IS?
PE-POH...
DREAMLAND NEWS
KING DEDEDE SOLVES PUZZLE RING!
EXTRA
AFTER 20 YEARS!
KING DEDEDE SOLVES PUZZLE RING
THUD

AUTHOR'S COMMENT

I WROTE THIS STORY SO I COULD DRAW ITS FINAL PAGE. IT INCLUDES A LOT. WELL, NEWS IS NOT PURE FACT. IT'S SOMETHING SHAPED BY PEOPLE. THAT GOES FOR THE PAST AND THE PRESENT.

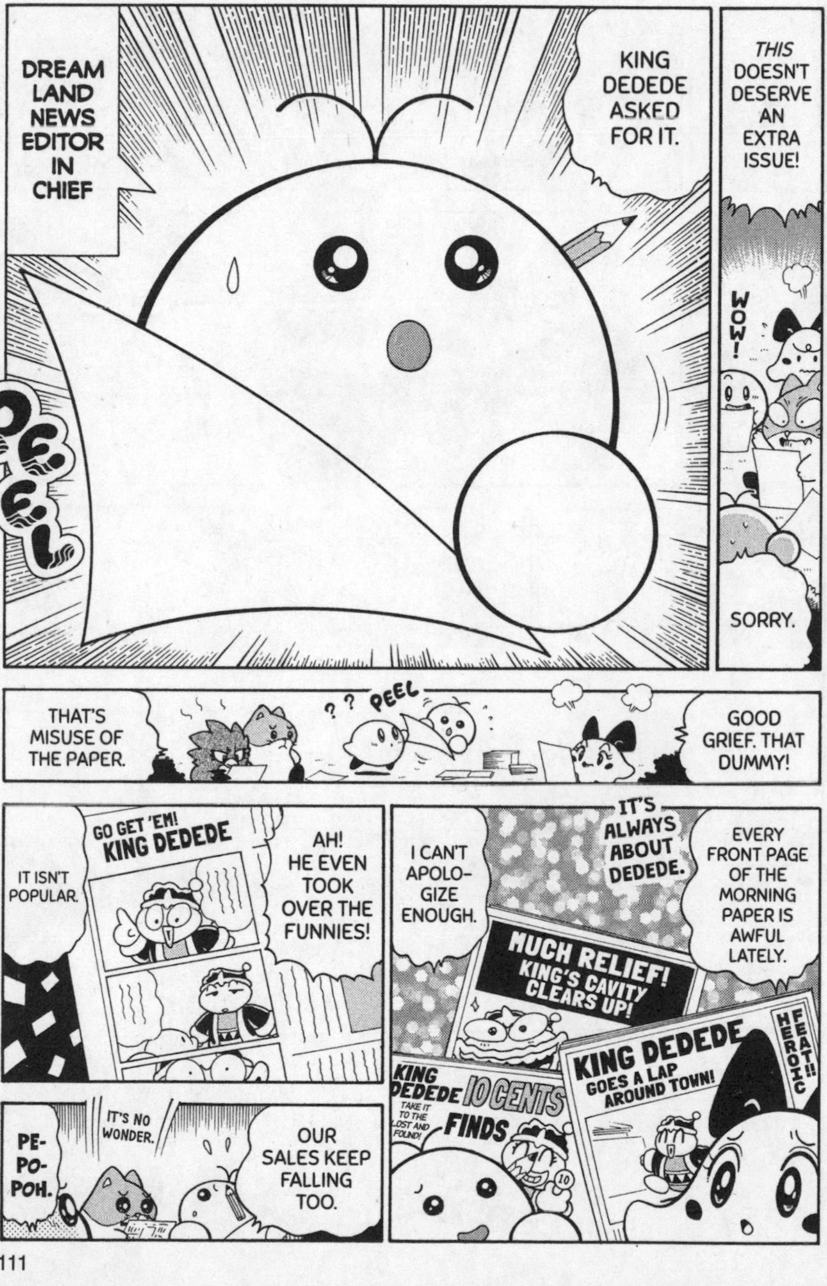
THIS DOESN'T DESERVE AN EXTRA ISSUE!
WOW!
SORRY.
KING DEDEDE ASKED FOR IT.
DREAM LAND NEWS EDITOR IN CHIEF
PEEL
GOOD GRIEF. THAT DUMMY!
PEEL
THAT'S MISUSE OF THE PAPER.
EVERY FRONT PAGE OF THE MORNING PAPER IS AWFUL LATELY.
IT'S ALWAYS ABOUT DEDEDE.
I CAN'T APOLO-GIZE ENOUGH.
MUCH RELIEF! KING'S CAVITY CLEARS UP!
KING DEDEDE GOES A LAP AROUND TOWN!
HEROIC FEAT!!
KING DEDEDE FINDS 10 CENTS
TAKE IT TO THE LOST AND FOUND!
AH! HE EVEN TOOK OVER THE FUNNIES!
GO GET 'EM! KING DEDEDE
IT ISN'T POPULAR.
OUR SALES KEEP FALLING TOO.
IT'S NO WONDER.
PE-PO-POH.

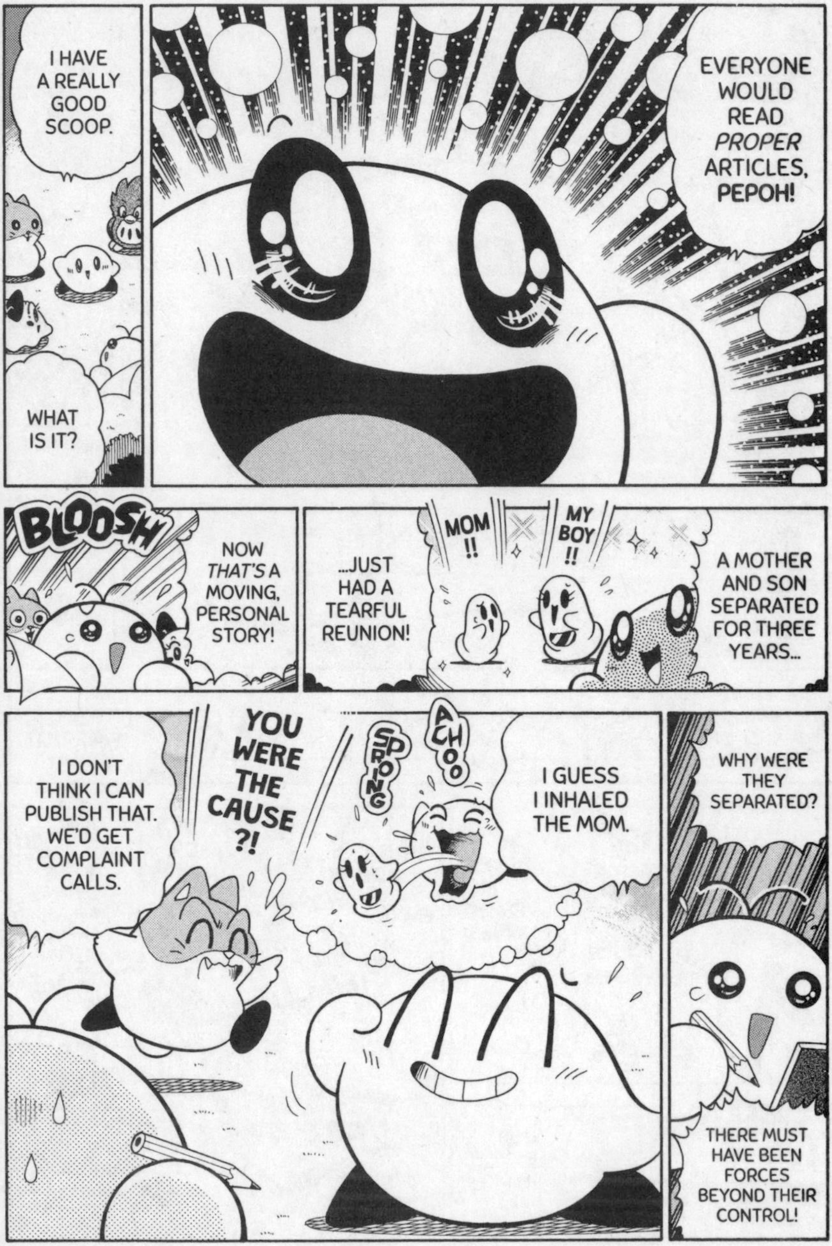
EVERYONE WOULD READ *PROPER* ARTICLES, PEPOH!
I HAVE A REALLY GOOD SCOOP.
WHAT IS IT?
A MOTHER AND SON SEPARATED FOR THREE YEARS...
MY BOY !!
MOM !!
...JUST HAD A TEARFUL REUNION!
BLOOSH
NOW *THAT'S* A MOVING, PERSONAL STORY!
WHY WERE THEY SEPARATED?
THERE MUST HAVE BEEN FORCES BEYOND THEIR CONTROL!
I GUESS I INHALED THE MOM.
ACHOO
SPROING
YOU WERE THE CAUSE ?!
I DON'T THINK I CAN PUBLISH THAT. WE'D GET COMPLAINT CALLS.

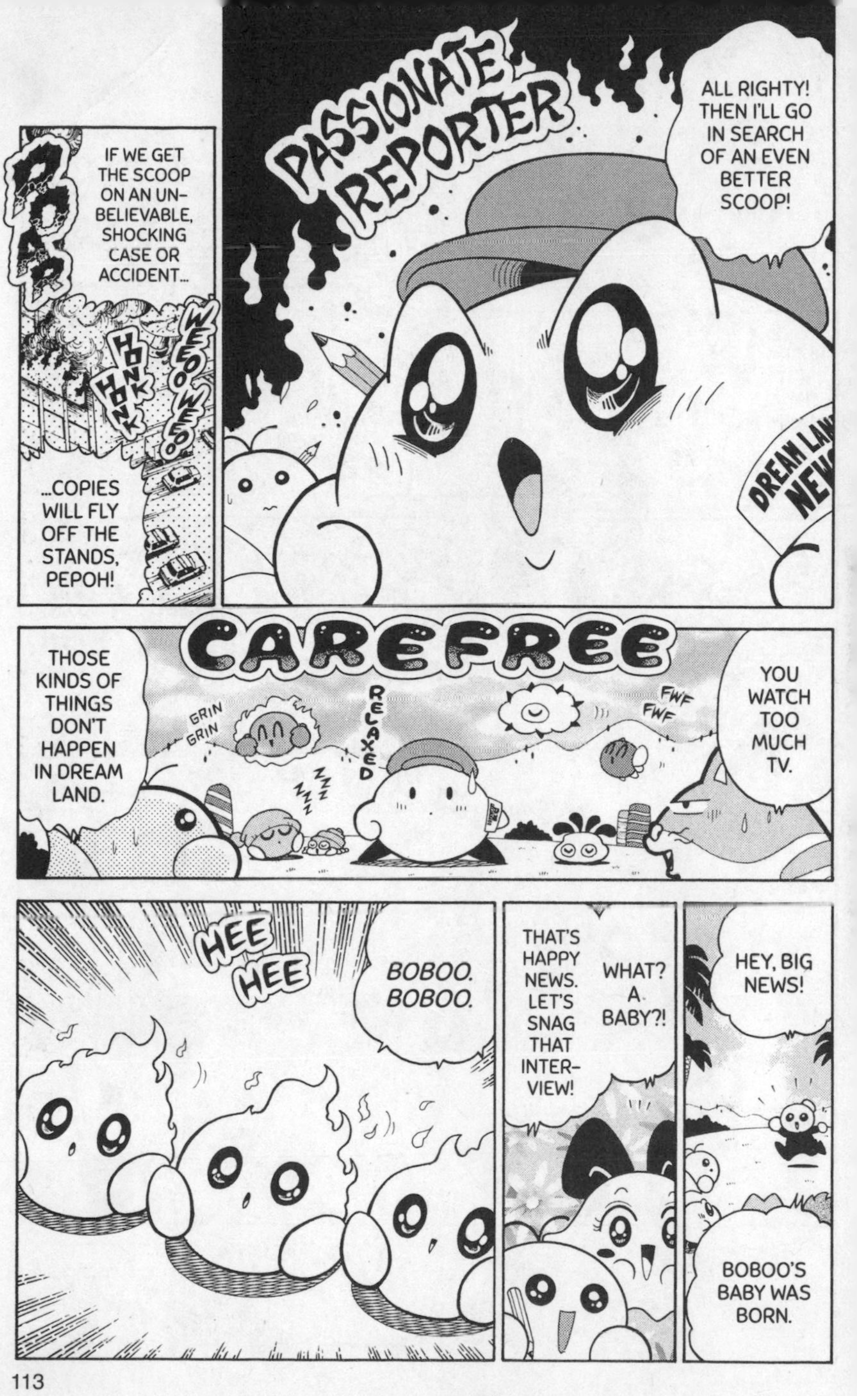
PASSIONATE REPORTER
ALL RIGHTY! THEN I'LL GO IN SEARCH OF AN EVEN BETTER SCOOP!
IF WE GET THE SCOOP ON AN UN-BELIEVABLE, SHOCKING CASE OR ACCIDENT...
ROAR
WEEOO WEEOO
HONK HONK
...COPIES WILL FLY OFF THE STANDS, PEPOH!
CAREFREE
YOU WATCH TOO MUCH TV.
FWF FWF
RELAXED
GRIN GRIN
THOSE KINDS OF THINGS DON'T HAPPEN IN DREAM LAND.
HEY, BIG NEWS!
BOBOO'S BABY WAS BORN.
WHAT? A BABY?!
THAT'S HAPPY NEWS. LET'S SNAG THAT INTERVIEW!
BOBOO. BOBOO.
HEE HEE

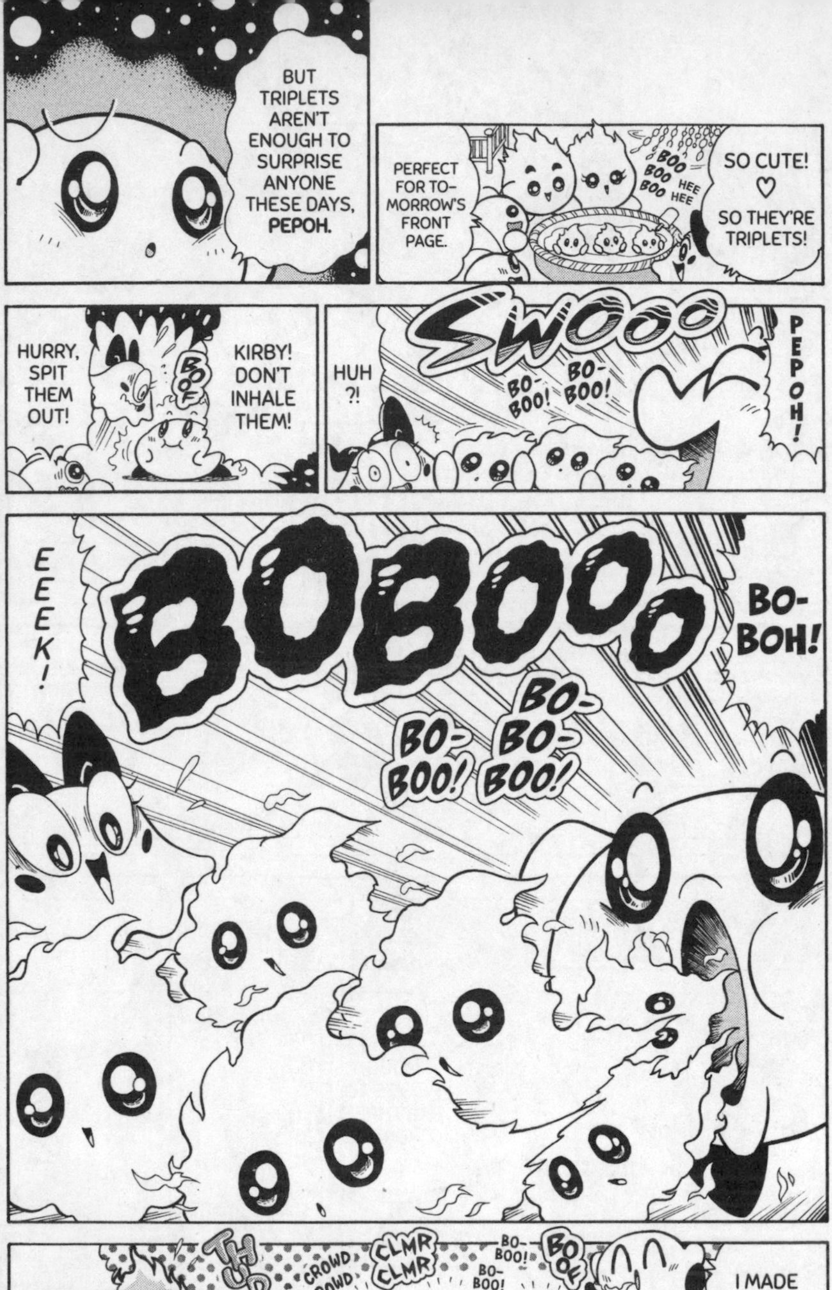
SO CUTE! ♡ SO THEY'RE TRIPLETS!
BOO BOO BOO
HEE HEE
PERFECT FOR TO-MORROW'S FRONT PAGE.
BUT TRIPLETS AREN'T ENOUGH TO SURPRISE ANYONE THESE DAYS, **PEPOH.**
SWOOO
PEPOH!
BO-BOO!
BO-BOO!
HUH ?!
KIRBY! DON'T INHALE THEM!
BOOF
HURRY, SPIT THEM OUT!
BO-BOH!
BOBOOO
EEEK!
BO-BO-BOO!
BO-BOO!
I MADE MORE FOR YOU!
BOOF
BO-BOO!
BO-BOO!
CLMR CLMR
CROWD CROWD
THUD
WAAAH!

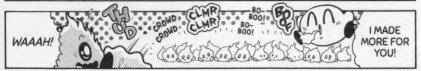

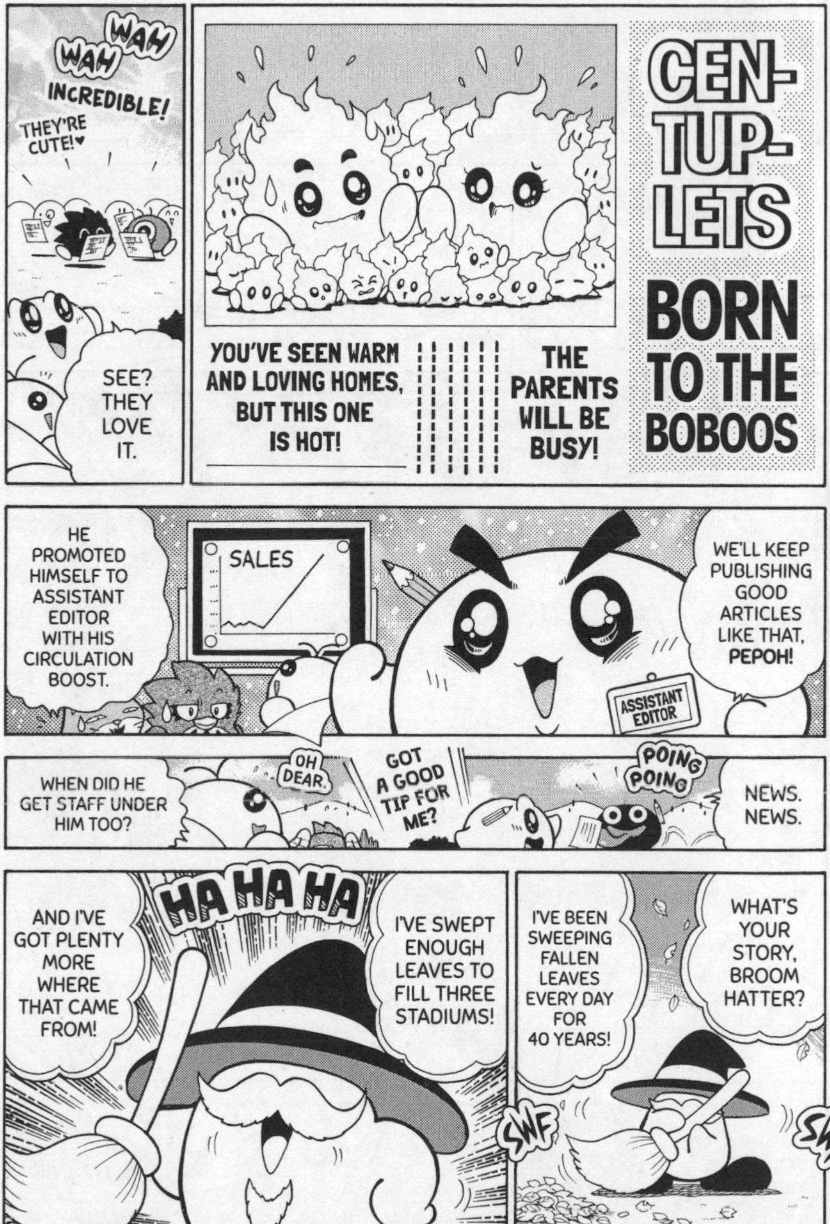
CEN-TUP-LETS BORN TO THE BOBOOS
THE PARENTS WILL BE BUSY!
YOU'VE SEEN WARM AND LOVING HOMES, BUT THIS ONE IS HOT!
WAH WAH
INCREDIBLE!
THEY'RE CUTE!♥
SEE? THEY LOVE IT.
WE'LL KEEP PUBLISHING GOOD ARTICLES LIKE THAT, PEPOH!
ASSISTANT EDITOR
SALES
HE PROMOTED HIMSELF TO ASSISTANT EDITOR WITH HIS CIRCULATION BOOST.
NEWS. NEWS.
POING POING
GOT A GOOD TIP FOR ME?
OH DEAR.
WHEN DID HE GET STAFF UNDER HIM TOO?
WHAT'S YOUR STORY, BROOM HATTER?
I'VE BEEN SWEEPING FALLEN LEAVES EVERY DAY FOR 40 YEARS!
SWF
SWF
I'VE SWEPT ENOUGH LEAVES TO FILL THREE STADIUMS!
HA HA HA
AND I'VE GOT PLENTY MORE WHERE THAT CAME FROM!

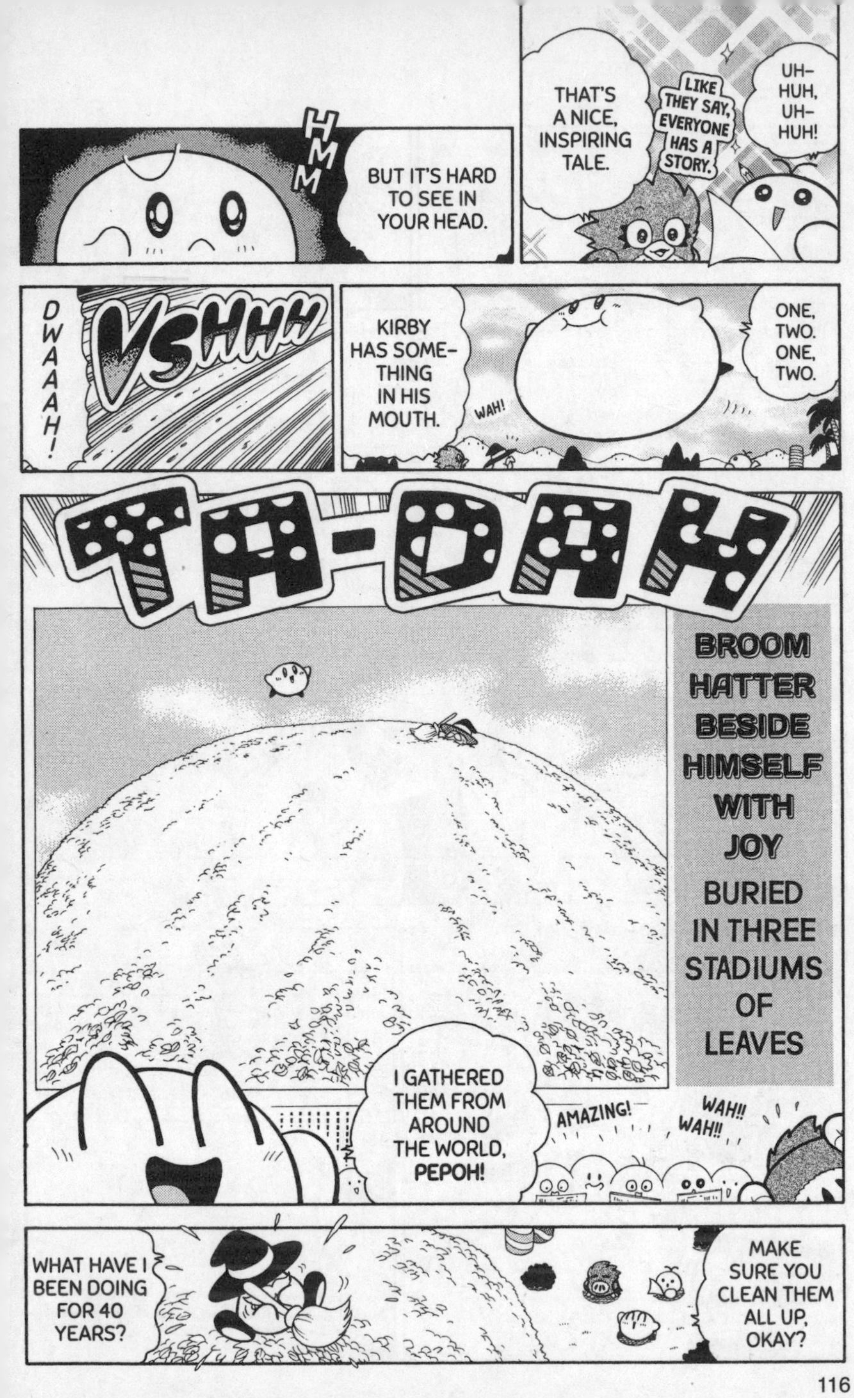
UH-HUH, UH-HUH!
LIKE THEY SAY, EVERYONE HAS A STORY.
THAT'S A NICE, INSPIRING TALE.
HMM
BUT IT'S HARD TO SEE IN YOUR HEAD.
ONE, TWO. ONE, TWO.
KIRBY HAS SOME-THING IN HIS MOUTH.
WAH!
VSHHH
DWAAAAH!
TA-DAH
BROOM HATTER BESIDE HIMSELF WITH JOY
BURIED IN THREE STADIUMS OF LEAVES
WAH!! WAH!!
AMAZING!
I GATHERED THEM FROM AROUND THE WORLD, PEPOH!
MAKE SURE YOU CLEAN THEM ALL UP, OKAY?
WHAT HAVE I BEEN DOING FOR 40 YEARS?

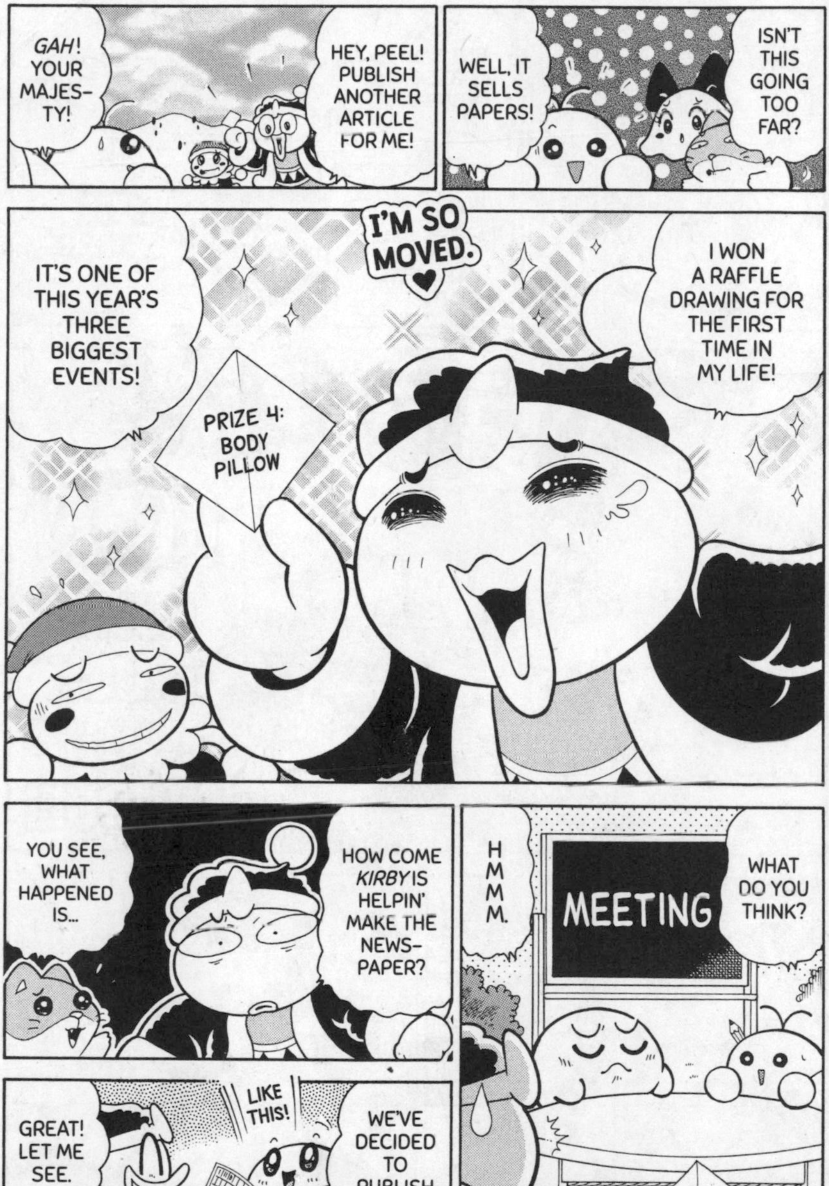
ISN'T THIS GOING TOO FAR?
WELL, IT SELLS PAPERS!
HEY, PEEL! PUBLISH ANOTHER ARTICLE FOR ME!
GAH! YOUR MAJES-TY!
I WON A RAFFLE DRAWING FOR THE FIRST TIME IN MY LIFE!
I'M SO MOVED. ♥
IT'S ONE OF THIS YEAR'S THREE BIGGEST EVENTS!
PRIZE 4: BODY PILLOW
WHAT DO YOU THINK?
MEETING
HMMM.
HOW COME *KIRBY* IS HELPIN' MAKE THE NEWS-PAPER?
YOU SEE, WHAT HAPPENED IS...
WE'VE DECIDED TO PUBLISH IT!
LIKE THIS!
GREAT! LET ME SEE.

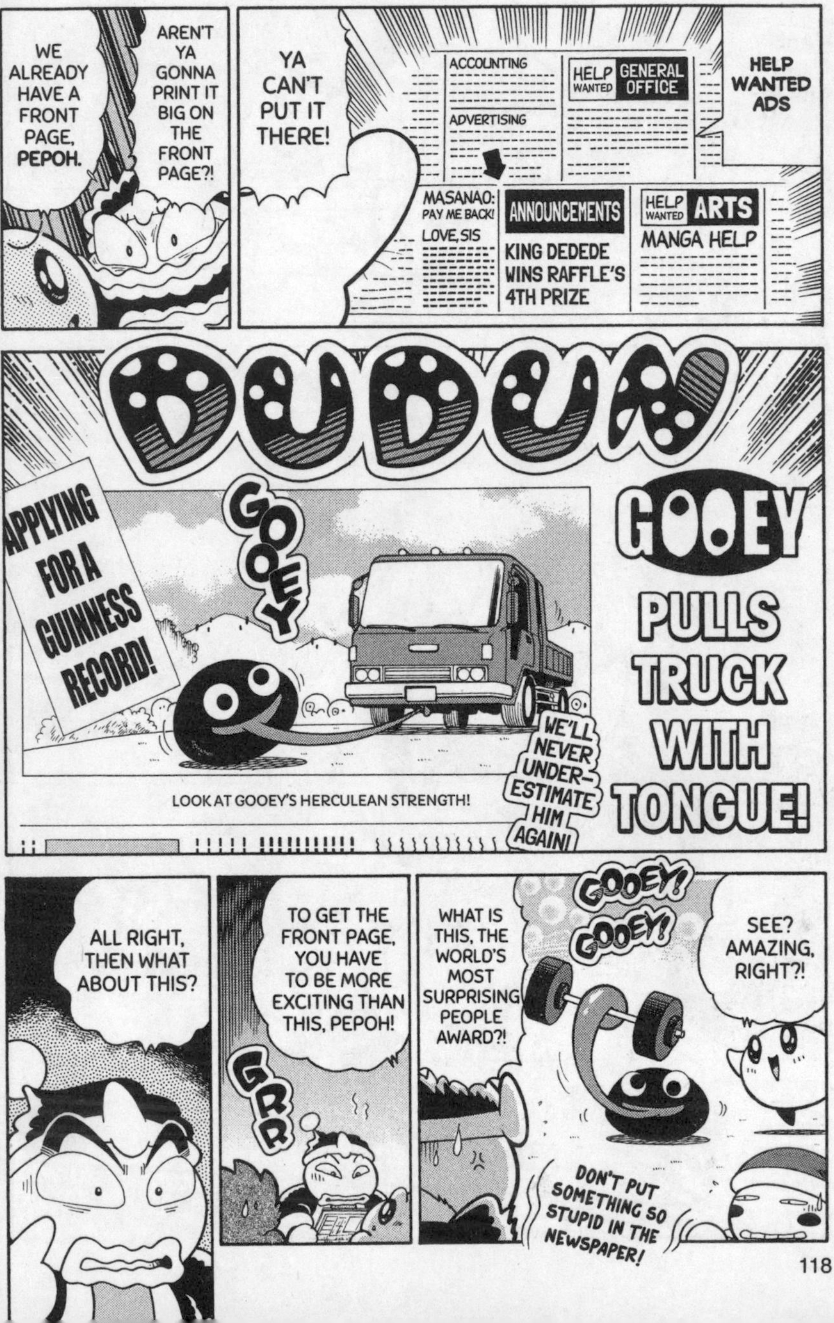
HELP WANTED ADS
ACCOUNTING
ADVERTISING
HELP WANTED GENERAL OFFICE
HELP WANTED ARTS
MANGA HELP
ANNOUNCEMENTS
KING DEDEDE WINS RAFFLE'S 4TH PRIZE
MASANAO: PAY ME BACK! LOVE, SIS
YA CAN'T PUT IT THERE!
AREN'T YA GONNA PRINT IT BIG ON THE FRONT PAGE?!
WE ALREADY HAVE A FRONT PAGE, PEPOH.
DUDUN
GOOEY PULLS TRUCK WITH TONGUE!
WE'LL NEVER UNDER-ESTIMATE HIM AGAIN!
GOOEY
APPLYING FOR A GUINNESS RECORD!
LOOK AT GOOEY'S HERCULEAN STRENGTH!
SEE? AMAZING, RIGHT?!
GOOEY! GOOEY!
WHAT IS THIS, THE WORLD'S MOST SURPRISING PEOPLE AWARD?!
DON'T PUT SOMETHING SO STUPID IN THE NEWSPAPER!
TO GET THE FRONT PAGE, YOU HAVE TO BE MORE EXCITING THAN THIS, PEPOH!
GRR
ALL RIGHT, THEN WHAT ABOUT THIS?

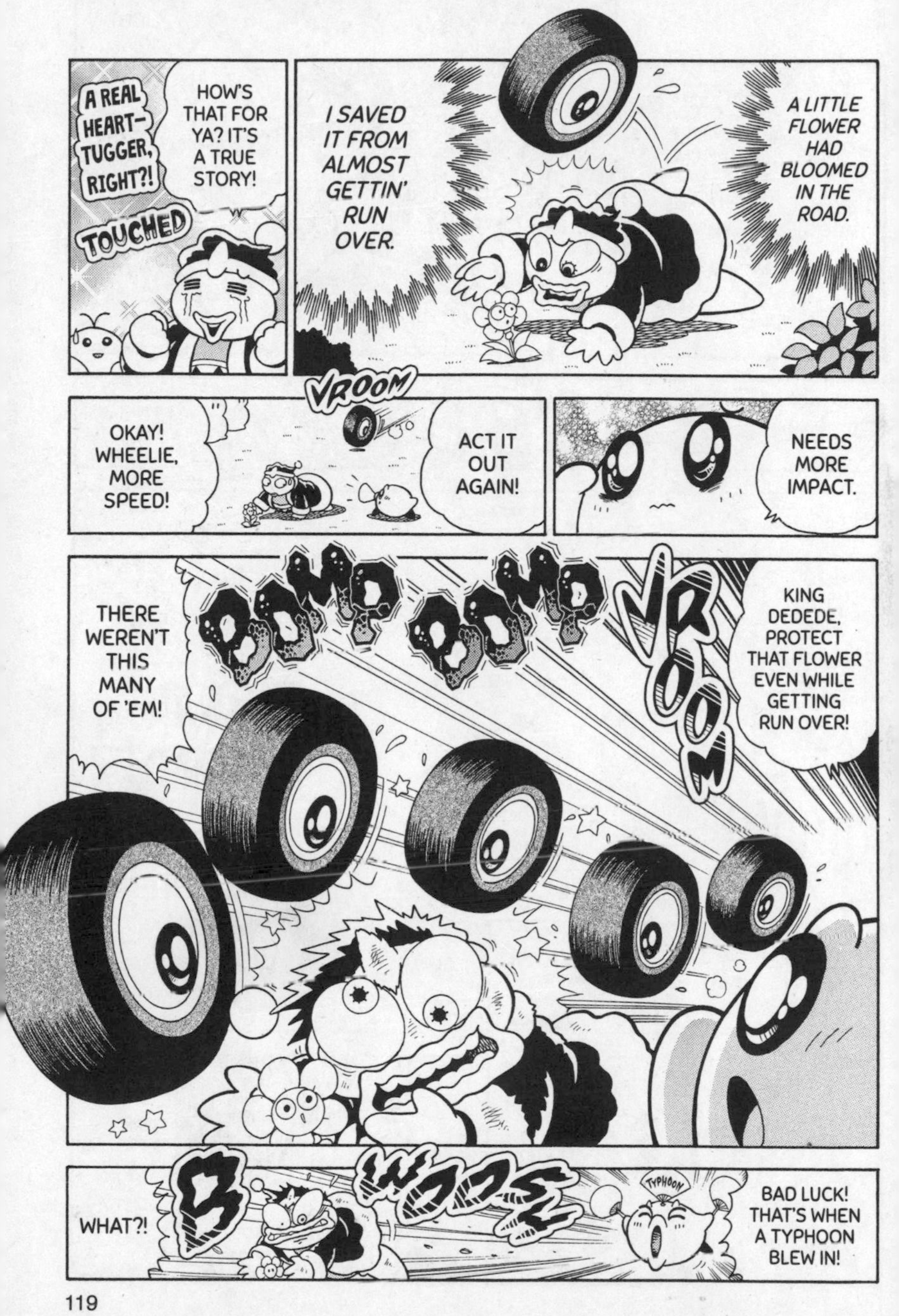
A LITTLE FLOWER HAD BLOOMED IN THE ROAD.
I SAVED IT FROM ALMOST GETTIN' RUN OVER.
HOW'S THAT FOR YA? IT'S A TRUE STORY!
A REAL HEART-TUGGER, RIGHT?!
TOUCHED
NEEDS MORE IMPACT.
ACT IT OUT AGAIN!
VROOM
OKAY! WHEELIE, MORE SPEED!
KING DEDEDE, PROTECT THAT FLOWER EVEN WHILE GETTING RUN OVER!
BOMP BOMP
THERE WEREN'T THIS MANY OF 'EM!
BAD LUCK! THAT'S WHEN A TYPHOON BLEW IN!
TYPHOON
WHAT?!

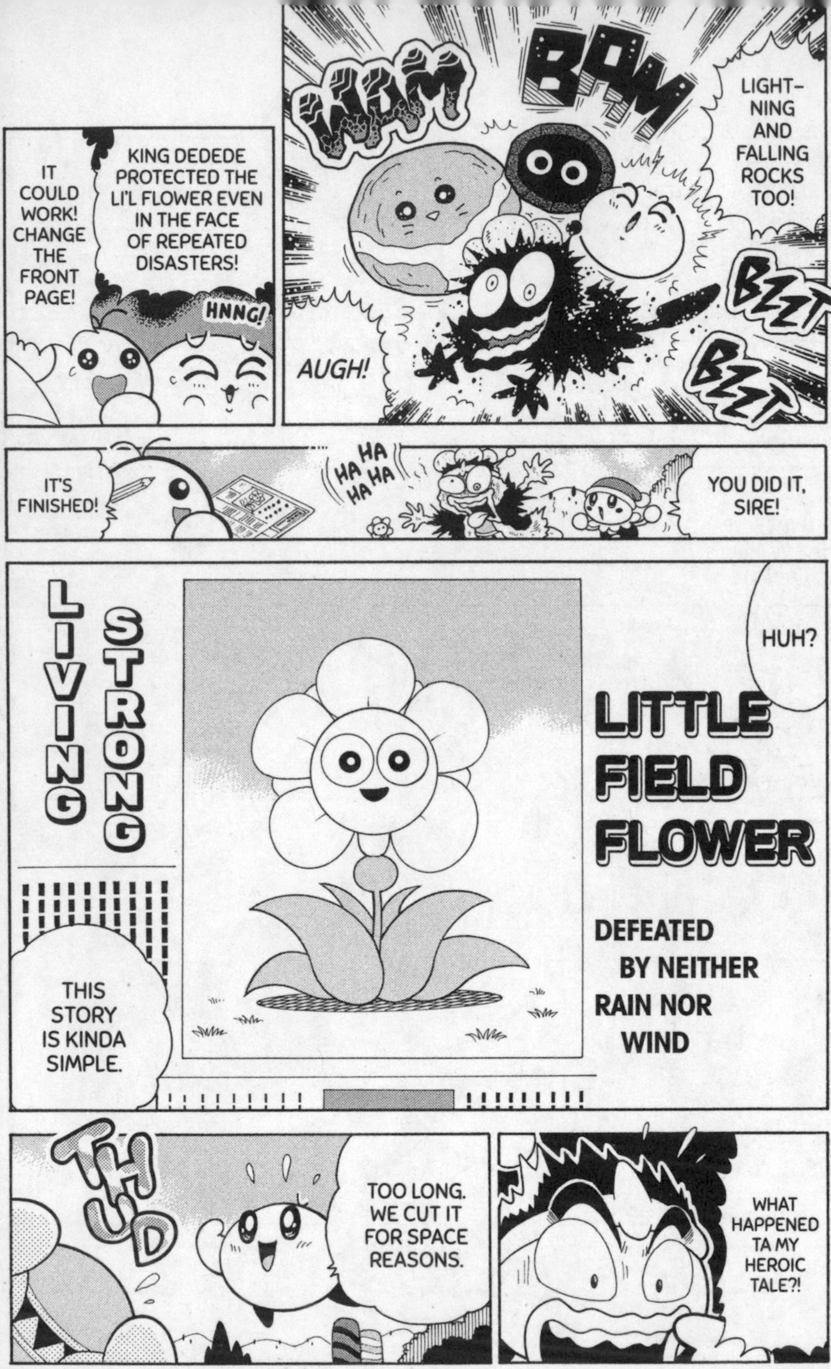
BAM
WHM
LIGHT-NING AND FALLING ROCKS TOO!
BZZT
BZZT
AUGH!
KING DEDEDE PROTECTED THE LI'L FLOWER EVEN IN THE FACE OF REPEATED DISASTERS!
IT COULD WORK! CHANGE THE FRONT PAGE!
HNNG!
YOU DID IT, SIRE!
HA HA HA HA
IT'S FINISHED!
HUH?
LITTLE FIELD FLOWER
DEFEATED BY NEITHER RAIN NOR WIND
LIVING STRONG
THIS STORY IS KINDA SIMPLE.
WHAT HAPPENED TA MY HEROIC TALE?!
TOO LONG. WE CUT IT FOR SPACE REASONS.
THUD

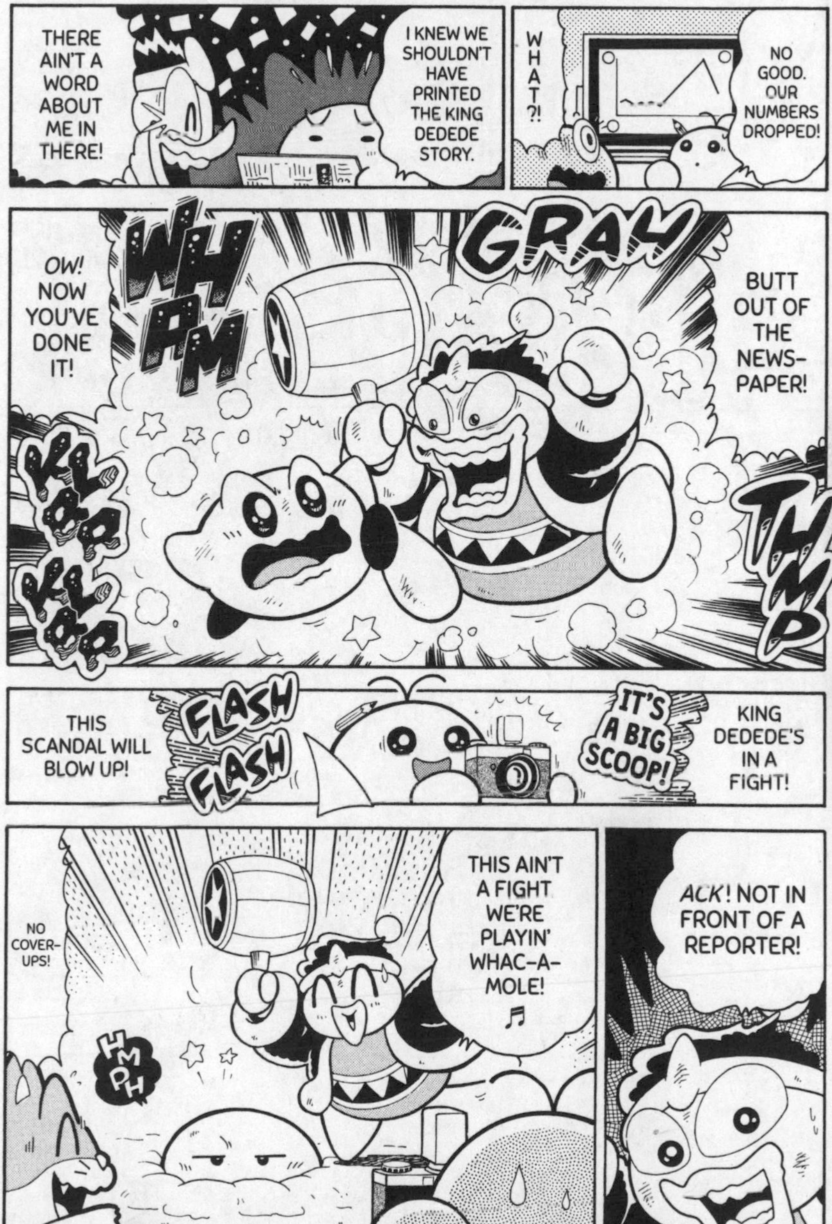
NO GOOD. OUR NUMBERS DROPPED!
WHAT?!
I KNEW WE SHOULDN'T HAVE PRINTED THE KING DEDEDE STORY.
THERE AIN'T A WORD ABOUT ME IN THERE!
GRAW
BUTT OUT OF THE NEWS-PAPER!
WHAM
OW! NOW YOU'VE DONE IT!
THUMP
KLOP KLOP
KING DEDEDE'S IN A FIGHT!
IT'S A BIG SCOOP!
FLASH FLASH
THIS SCANDAL WILL BLOW UP!
ACK! NOT IN FRONT OF A REPORTER!
THIS AIN'T A FIGHT WE'RE PLAYIN' WHAC-A-MOLE! ♪
NO COVER-UPS!
HMPH

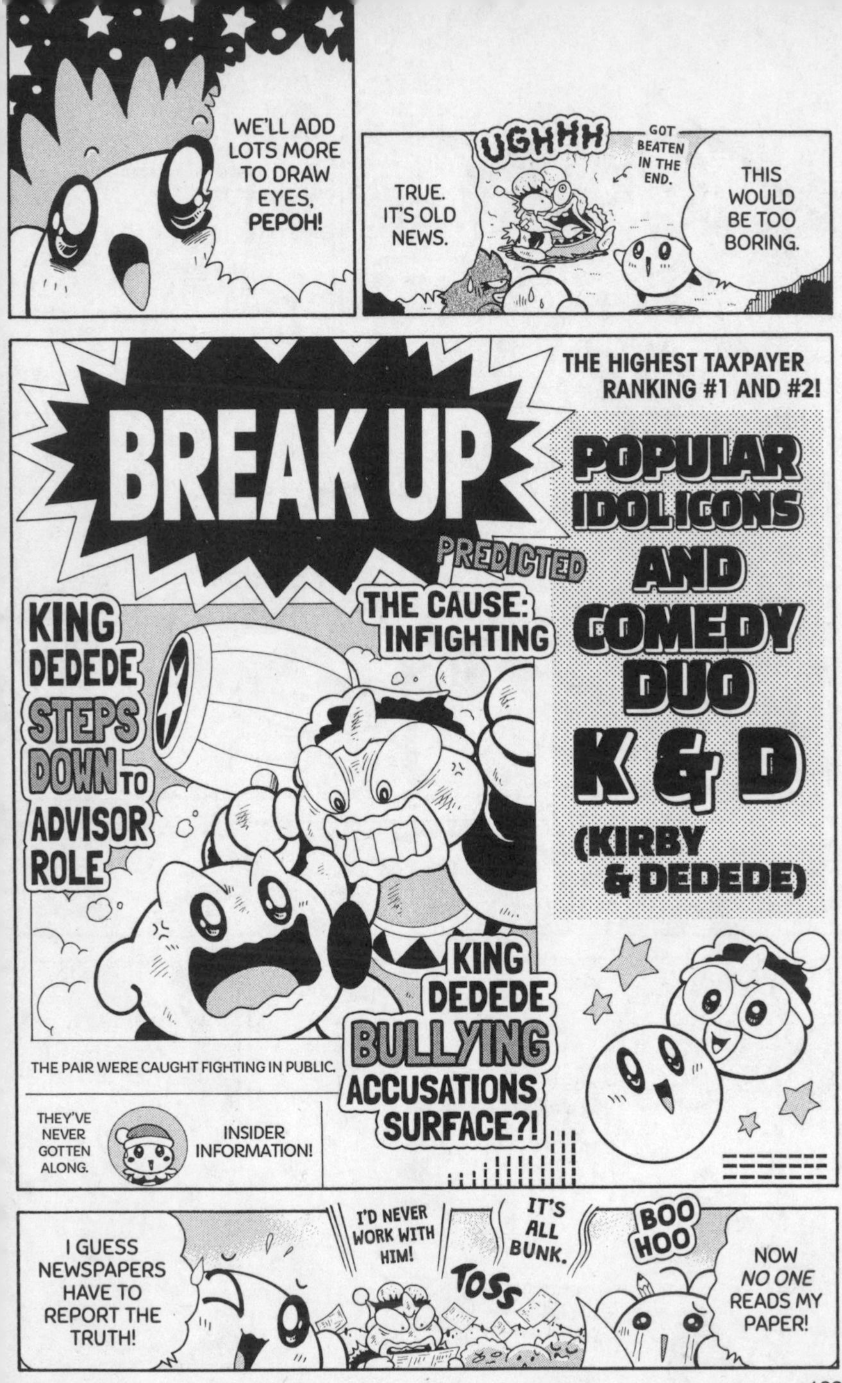
THIS WOULD BE TOO BORING.
GOT BEATEN IN THE END.
UGHHH
TRUE. IT'S OLD NEWS.
WE'LL ADD LOTS MORE TO DRAW EYES, PEPOH!
THE HIGHEST TAXPAYER RANKING #1 AND #2!
POPULAR IDOL ICONS AND COMEDY DUO K & D (KIRBY & DEDEDE)
BREAK UP PREDICTED
THE CAUSE: INFIGHTING
KING DEDEDE STEPS DOWN TO ADVISOR ROLE
KING DEDEDE BULLYING ACCUSATIONS SURFACE?!
THE PAIR WERE CAUGHT FIGHTING IN PUBLIC.
INSIDER INFORMATION!
THEY'VE NEVER GOTTEN ALONG.
NOW NO ONE READS MY PAPER!
BOO HOO
IT'S ALL BUNK.
I'D NEVER WORK WITH HIM!
TOSS
I GUESS NEWSPAPERS HAVE TO REPORT THE TRUTH!

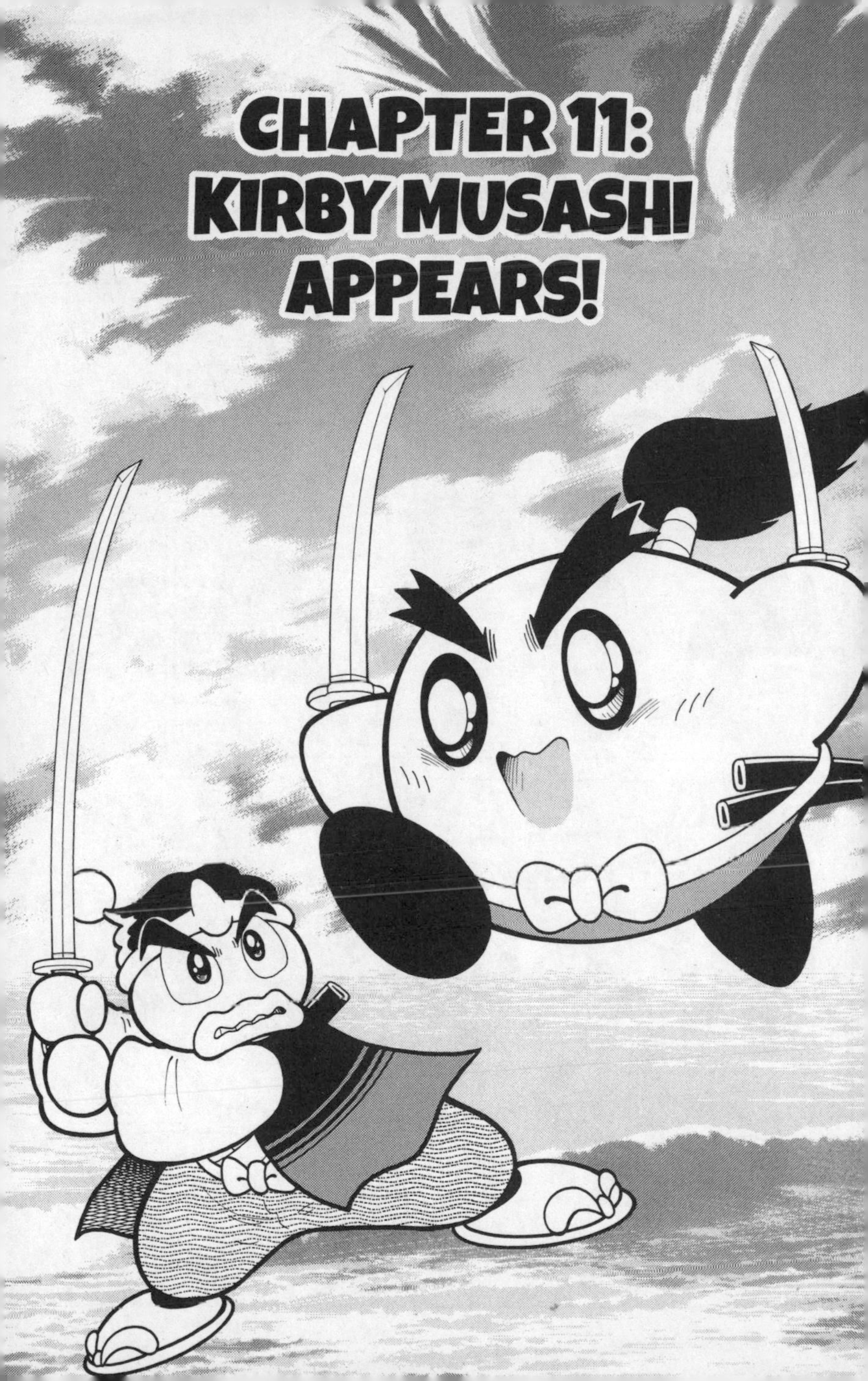
CHAPTER 11:
KIRBY MUSASHI
APPEARS!

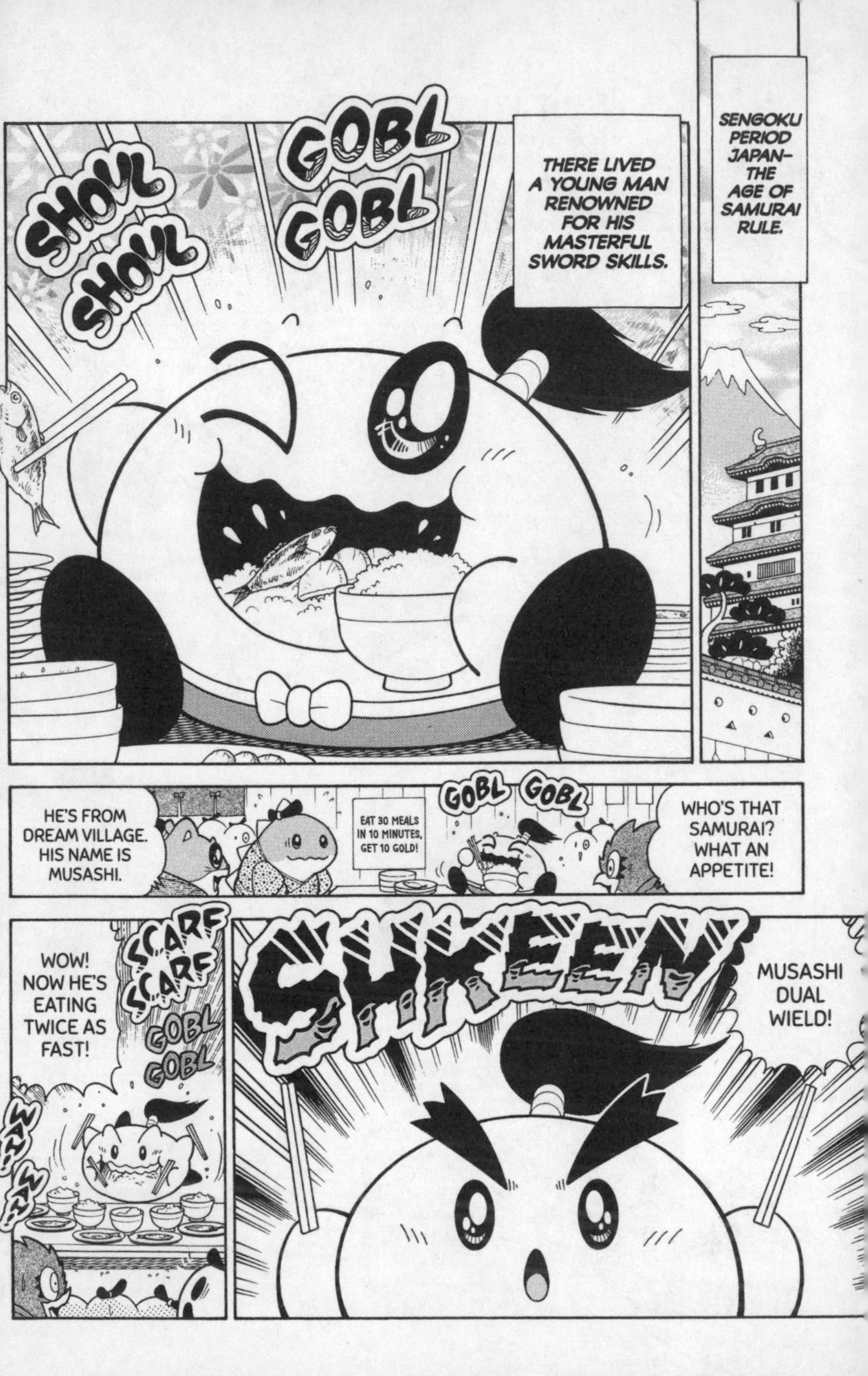
SENGOKU PERIOD JAPAN—THE AGE OF SAMURAI RULE.
THERE LIVED A YOUNG MAN RENOWNED FOR HIS MASTERFUL SWORD SKILLS.
GOBL GOBL
SHOVL SHOVL
WHO'S THAT SAMURAI? WHAT AN APPETITE!
GOBL GOBL
EAT 30 MEALS IN 10 MINUTES, GET 10 GOLD!
HE'S FROM DREAM VILLAGE. HIS NAME IS MUSASHI.
MUSASHI DUAL WIELD!
SHKEEN
SCARF SCARF
WOW! NOW HE'S EATING TWICE AS FAST!
GOBL GOBL
WAH! WAH!

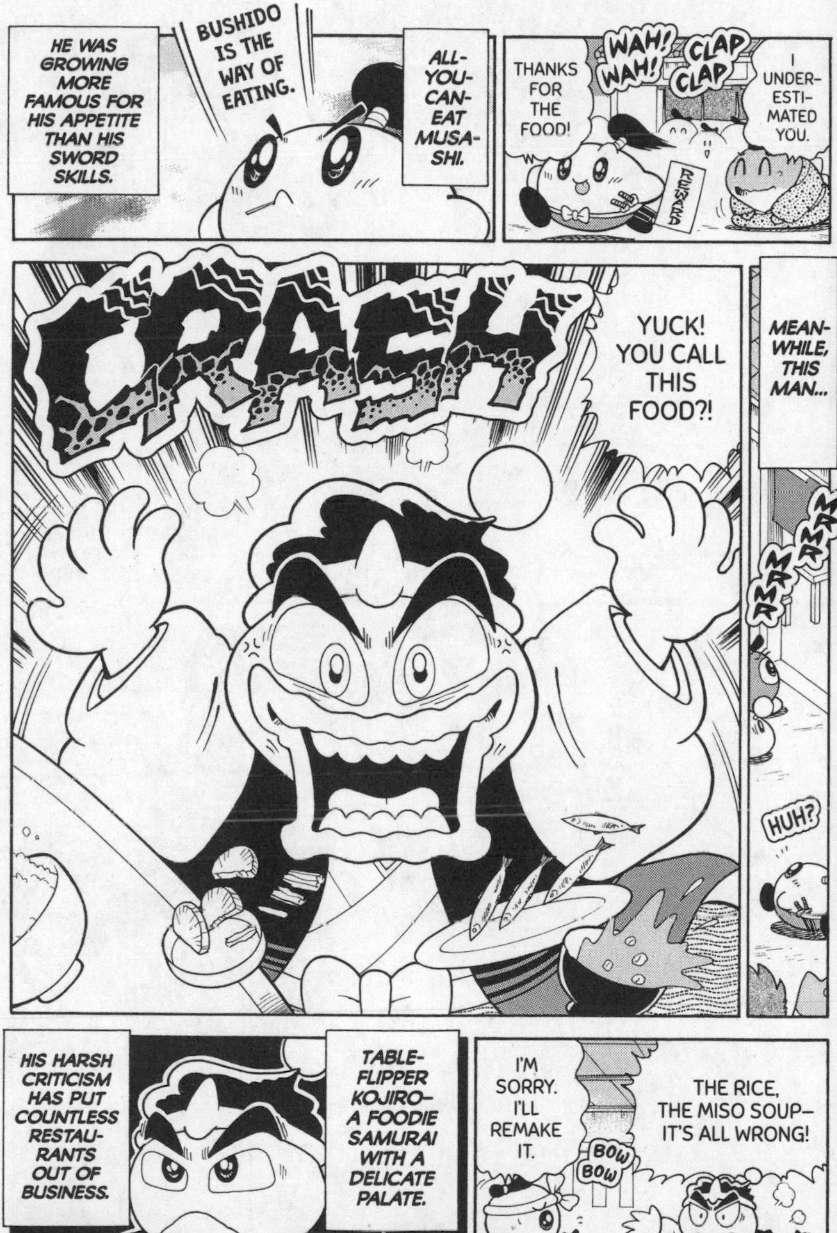
I UNDER-ESTIMATED YOU.
CLAP CLAP
WAH! WAH!
THANKS FOR THE FOOD!
REWARD
ALL-YOU-CAN-EAT MUSASHI.
BUSHIDO IS THE WAY OF EATING.
HE WAS GROWING MORE FAMOUS FOR HIS APPETITE THAN HIS SWORD SKILLS.
MEAN-WHILE, THIS MAN...
MRMR MRMR
HUH?
YUCK! YOU CALL THIS FOOD?!
CRASH
THE RICE, THE MISO SOUP— IT'S ALL WRONG!
I'M SORRY. I'LL REMAKE IT.
BOW BOW
TABLE-FLIPPER KOJIRO— A FOODIE SAMURAI WITH A DELICATE PALATE.
HIS HARSH CRITICISM HAS PUT COUNTLESS RESTAU-RANTS OUT OF BUSINESS.

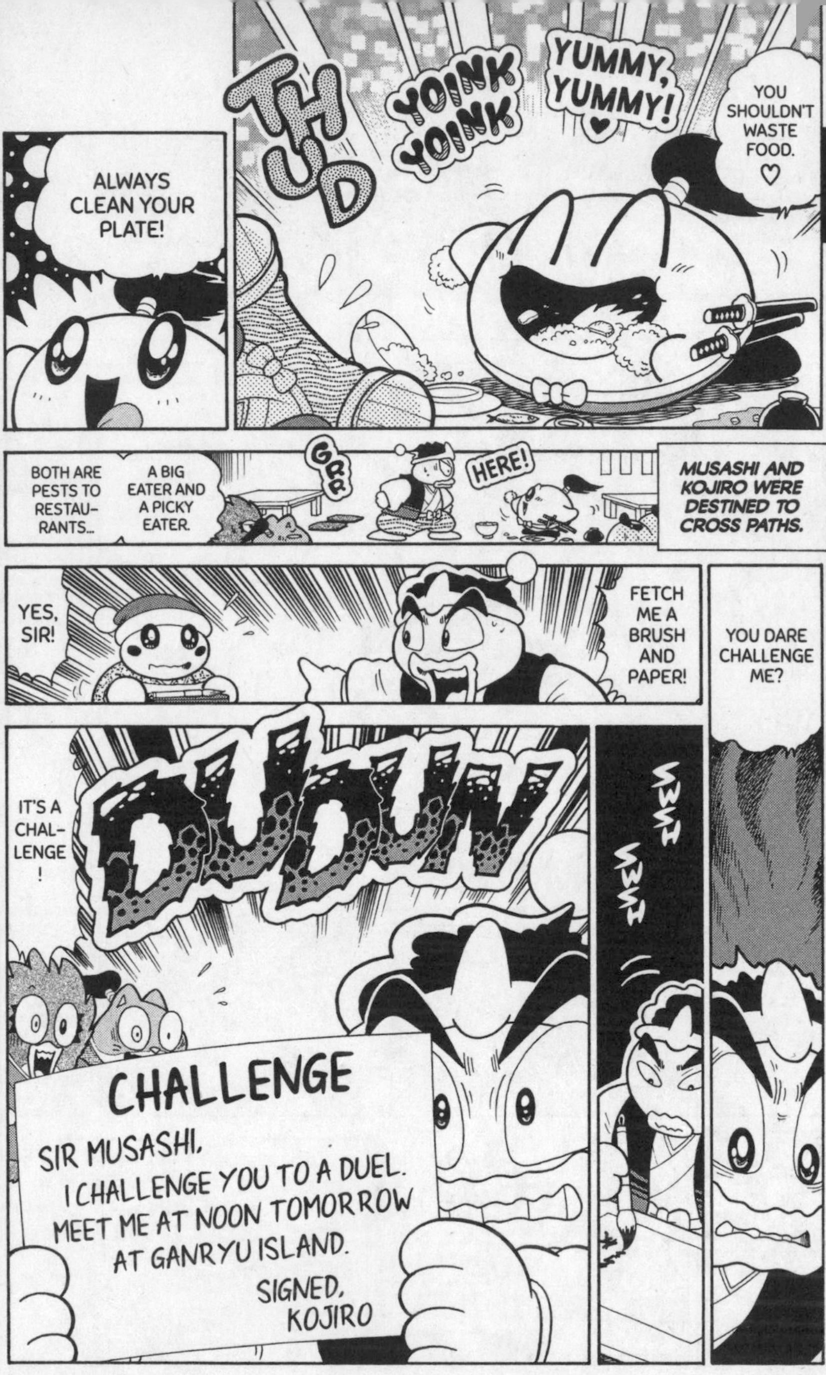
YOU SHOULDN'T WASTE FOOD. ♡
YUMMY, YUMMY! ♥
YOINK YOINK
THUD
ALWAYS CLEAN YOUR PLATE!
MUSASHI AND KOJIRO WERE DESTINED TO CROSS PATHS.
HERE!
GRR
A BIG EATER AND A PICKY EATER.
BOTH ARE PESTS TO RESTAU-RANTS...
YOU DARE CHALLENGE ME?
FETCH ME A BRUSH AND PAPER!
YES, SIR!
SWSH
SWSH
DUDUN
IT'S A CHAL-LENGE!
CHALLENGE
SIR MUSASHI,
I CHALLENGE YOU TO A DUEL.
MEET ME AT NOON TOMORROW
AT GANRYU ISLAND.
SIGNED,
KOJIRO

AUTHOR'S COMMENT

THIS IS ANOTHER HISTORICAL STORY, FROM VOLUME 12. LOOKING AT THAT VOLUME NOW, IT HAD A LOT OF FUN STORIES. THIS ONE IS ONLY EIGHT PAGES YET STILL HAS A LOT PACKED INTO IT.

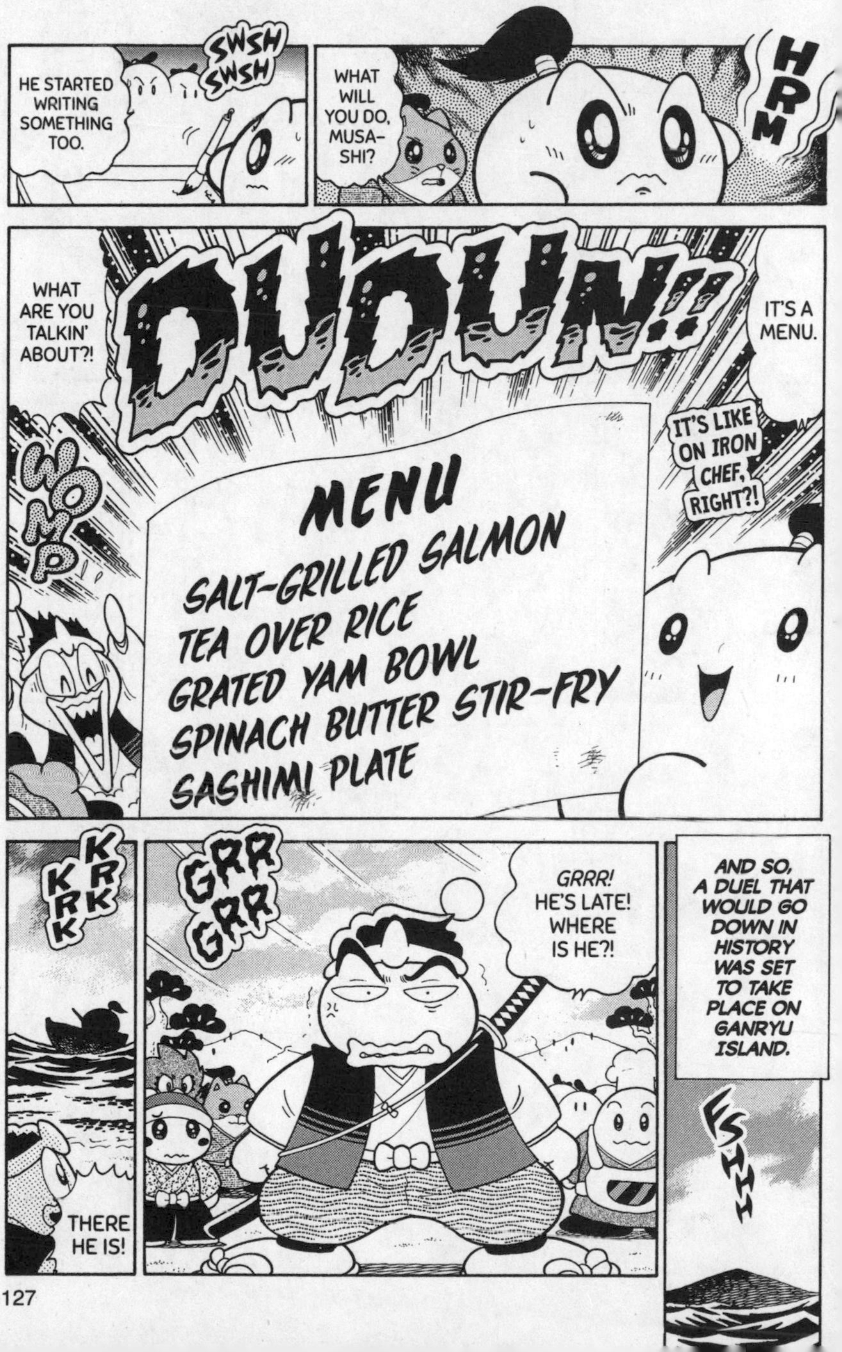
HRM
WHAT WILL YOU DO, MUSASHI?
SWSH SWSH
HE STARTED WRITING SOMETHING TOO.
IT'S A MENU.
IT'S LIKE ON IRON CHEF, RIGHT?!
DUDUN!!
WHAT ARE YOU TALKIN' ABOUT?!
MENU
SALT-GRILLED SALMON
TEA OVER RICE
GRATED YAM BOWL
SPINACH BUTTER STIR-FRY
SASHIMI PLATE
WOMP
AND SO, A DUEL THAT WOULD GO DOWN IN HISTORY WAS SET TO TAKE PLACE ON GANRYU ISLAND.
FSHHH
GRRR! HE'S LATE! WHERE IS HE?!
GRR GRR
KRK KRK
THERE HE IS!

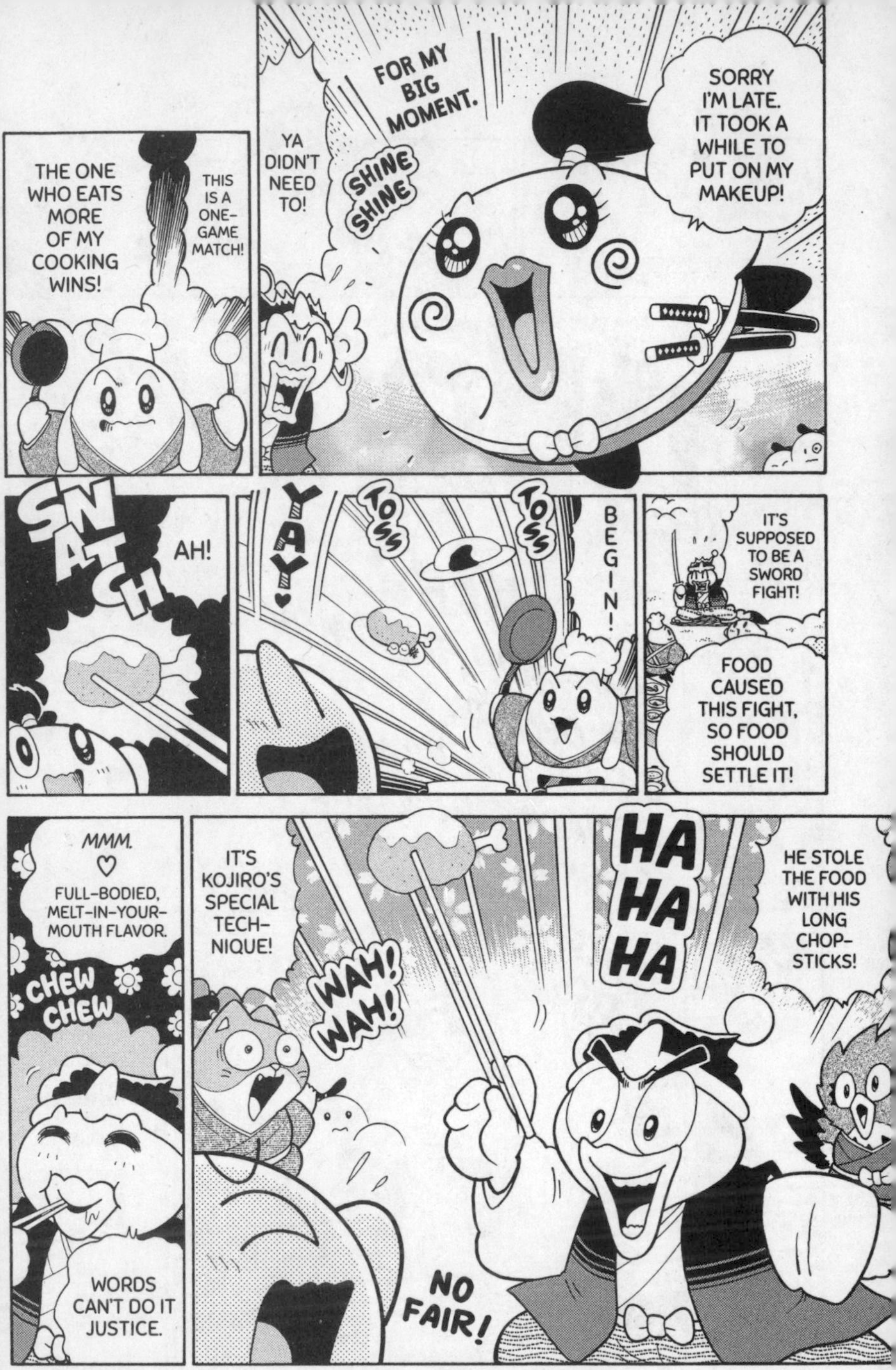
SORRY I'M LATE. IT TOOK A WHILE TO PUT ON MY MAKEUP!
FOR MY BIG MOMENT.
SHINE SHINE
YA DIDN'T NEED TO!
THIS IS A ONE-GAME MATCH!
THE ONE WHO EATS MORE OF MY COOKING WINS!
IT'S SUPPOSED TO BE A SWORD FIGHT!
FOOD CAUSED THIS FIGHT, SO FOOD SHOULD SETTLE IT!
BEGIN!
TOSS
TOSS
YAY!♥
AH!
SNATCH
HE STOLE THE FOOD WITH HIS LONG CHOP-STICKS!
HA HA HA
WAH! WAH!
IT'S KOJIRO'S SPECIAL TECH-NIQUE!
NO FAIR!
MMM. ♡
FULL-BODIED, MELT-IN-YOUR-MOUTH FLAVOR.
CHEW CHEW
WORDS CAN'T DO IT JUSTICE.

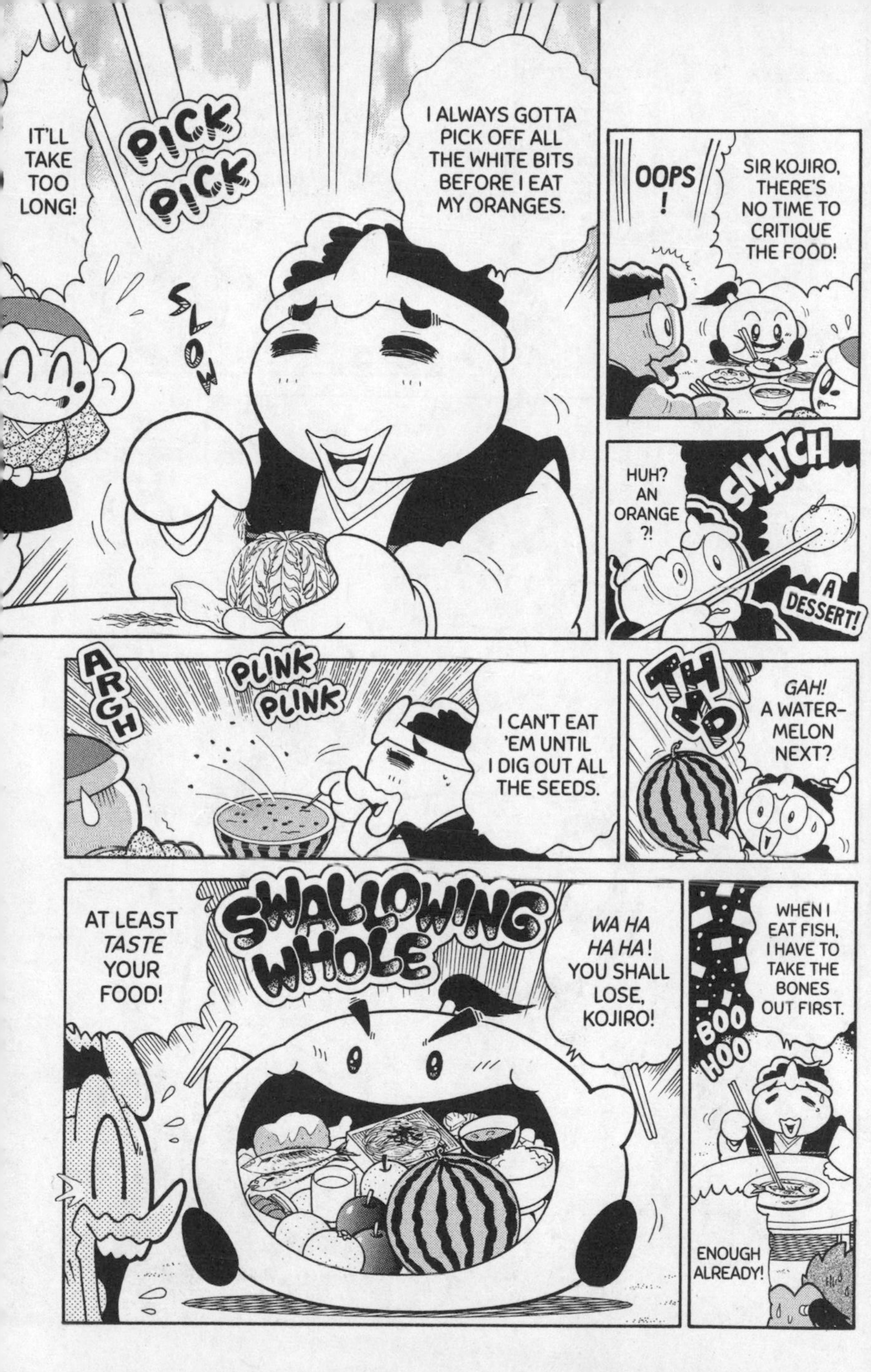
SIR KOJIRO, THERE'S NO TIME TO CRITIQUE THE FOOD!
OOPS !
SNATCH
HUH? AN ORANGE ?!
A DESSERT!
I ALWAYS GOTTA PICK OFF ALL THE WHITE BITS BEFORE I EAT MY ORANGES.
PICK PICK
IT'LL TAKE TOO LONG!
SLOW
GAH! A WATER-MELON NEXT?
THUMP
I CAN'T EAT 'EM UNTIL I DIG OUT ALL THE SEEDS.
PLINK PLINK
ARGH
WHEN I EAT FISH, I HAVE TO TAKE THE BONES OUT FIRST.
BOO HOO
ENOUGH ALREADY!
WA HA HA HA! YOU SHALL LOSE, KOJIRO!
SWALLOWING WHOLE
AT LEAST TASTE YOUR FOOD!

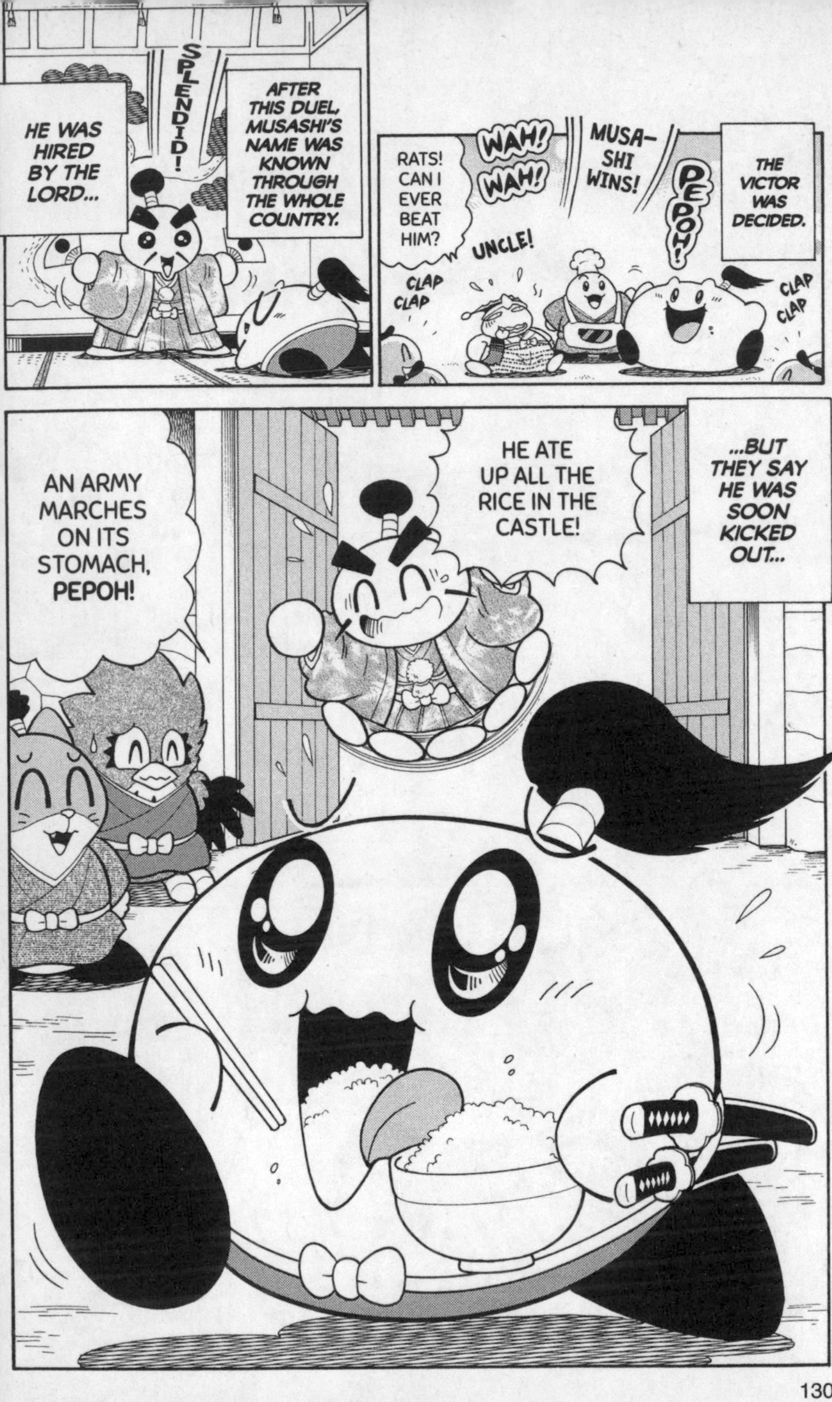
THE VICTOR WAS DECIDED.
CLAP CLAP
PEPOH!
MUSA-SHI WINS!
WAH! WAH!
RATS! CAN I EVER BEAT HIM?
UNCLE!
CLAP CLAP
AFTER THIS DUEL, MUSASHI'S NAME WAS KNOWN THROUGH THE WHOLE COUNTRY.
SPLENDID!
HE WAS HIRED BY THE LORD...
...BUT THEY SAY HE WAS SOON KICKED OUT...
HE ATE UP ALL THE RICE IN THE CASTLE!
AN ARMY MARCHES ON ITS STOMACH, PEPOH!

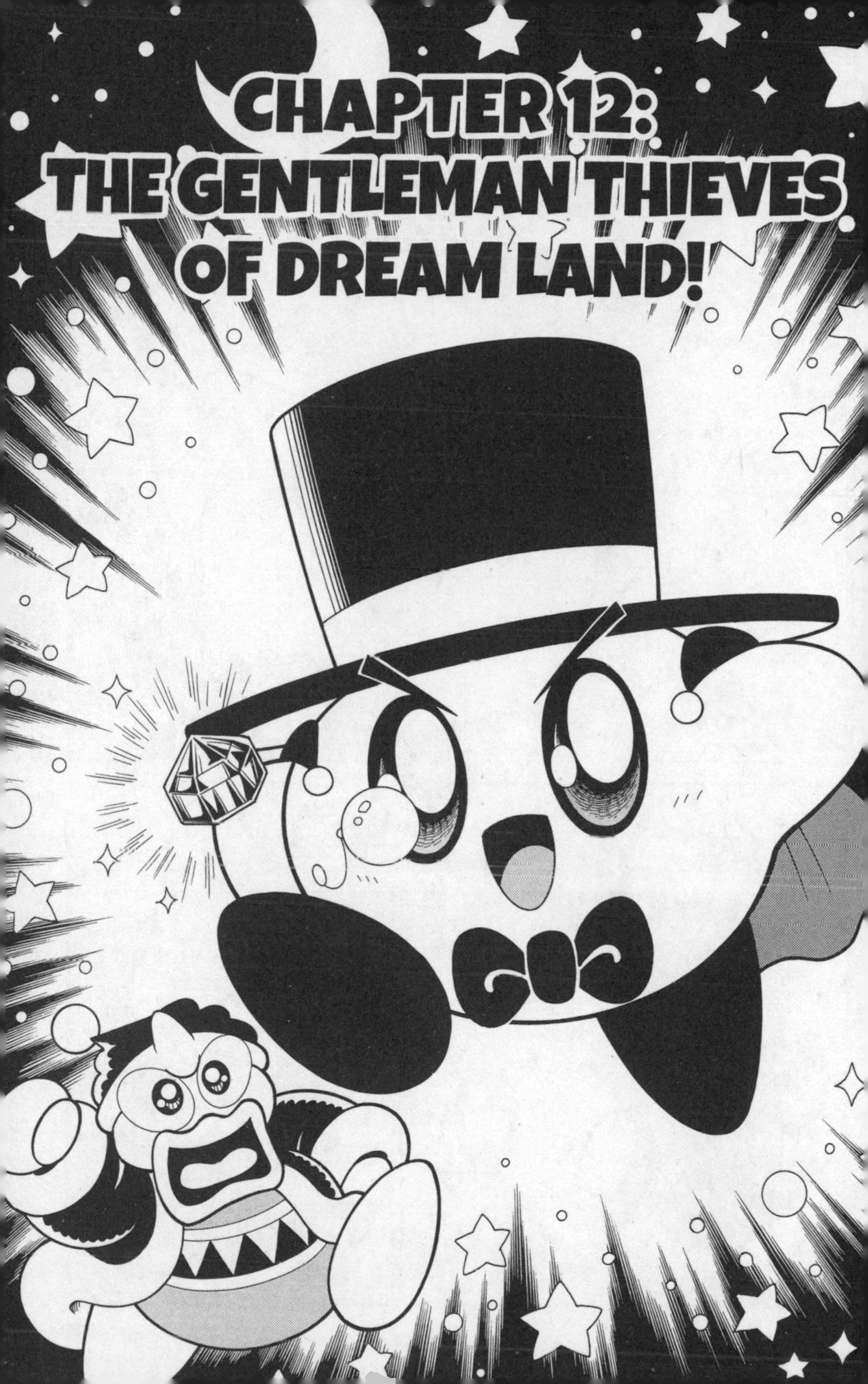
CHAPTER 12:
THE GENTLEMAN THIEVES
OF DREAM LAND!

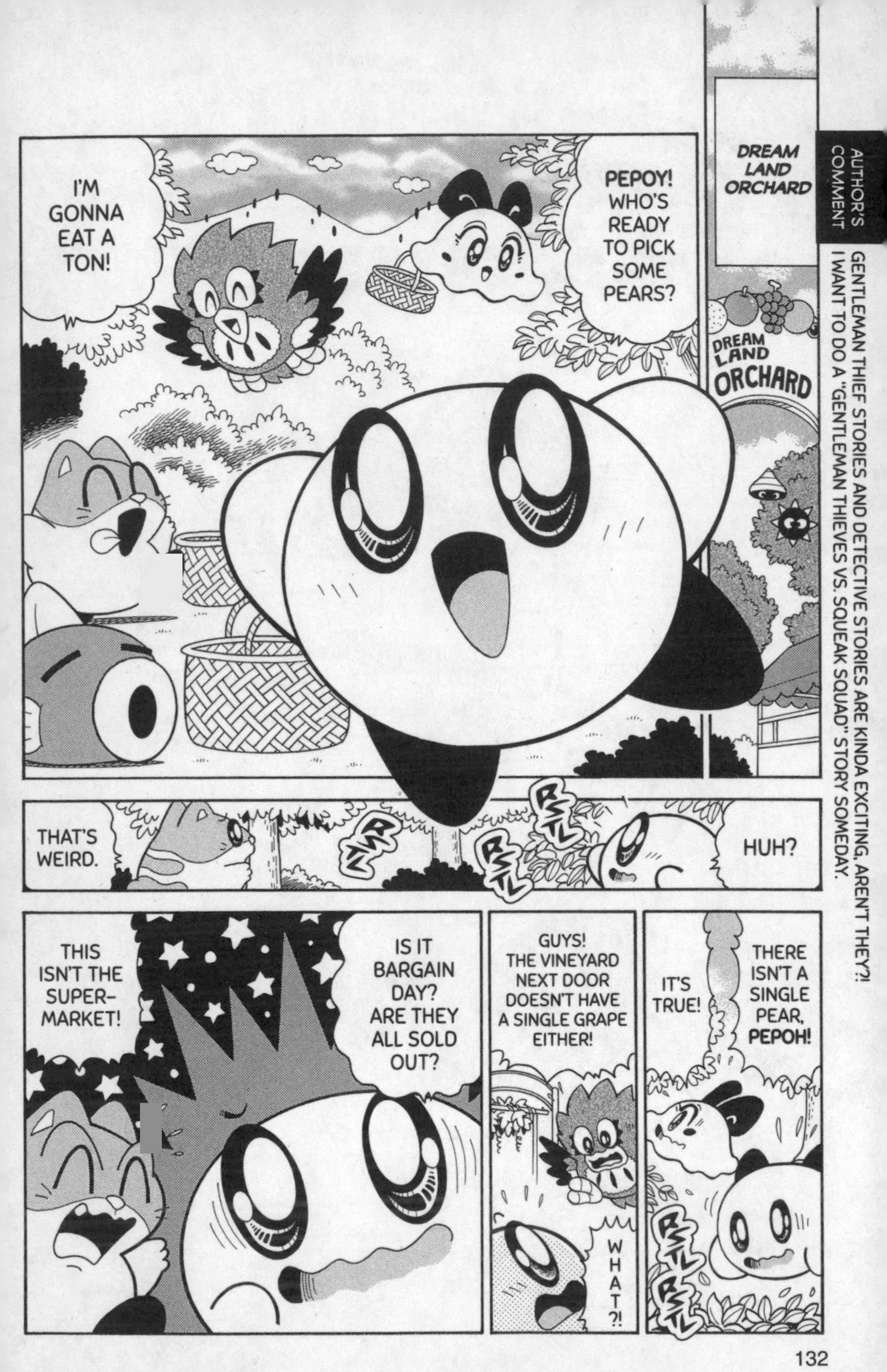
DREAM LAND ORCHARD
DREAM LAND ORCHARD
PEPOY! WHO'S READY TO PICK SOME PEARS?
I'M GONNA EAT A TON!
HUH?
RSTL
RSTL
RSTL
THAT'S WEIRD.
THERE ISN'T A SINGLE PEAR, PEPOH!
RSTL
RSTL
IT'S TRUE!
GUYS! THE VINEYARD NEXT DOOR DOESN'T HAVE A SINGLE GRAPE EITHER!
WHAT?!
IS IT BARGAIN DAY? ARE THEY ALL SOLD OUT?
THIS ISN'T THE SUPER-MARKET!

AUTHOR'S COMMENT

GENTLEMAN THIEF STORIES AND DETECTIVE STORIES ARE KINDA EXCITING, AREN'T THEY?! I WANT TO DO A "GENTLEMAN THIEVES VS. SQUEAK SQUAD" STORY SOMEDAY.

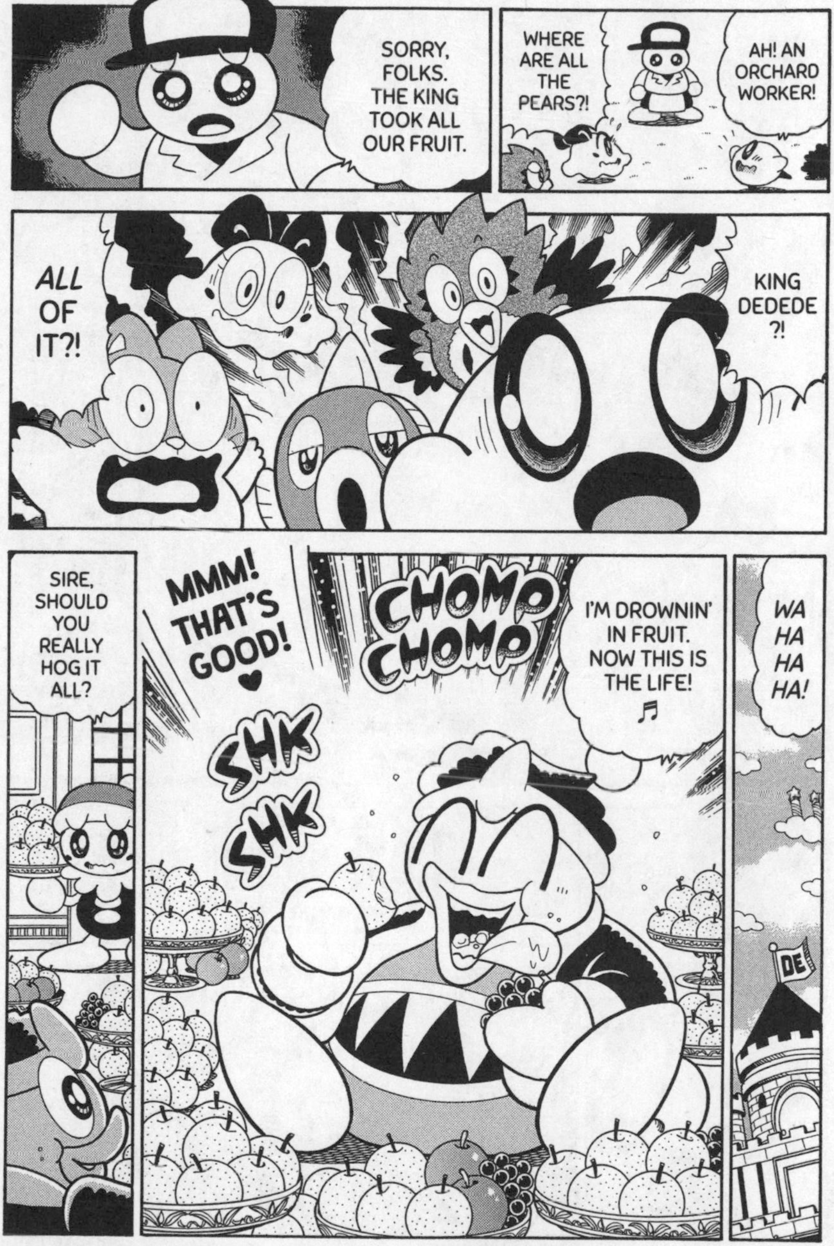
AH! AN ORCHARD WORKER!
WHERE ARE ALL THE PEARS?!
SORRY, FOLKS. THE KING TOOK ALL OUR FRUIT.
KING DEDEDE?!
ALL OF IT?!
WA HA HA HA!
I'M DROWNIN' IN FRUIT. NOW THIS IS THE LIFE! ♬
CHOMP CHOMP
MMM! THAT'S GOOD! ♥
SHK
SHK
SIRE, SHOULD YOU REALLY HOG IT ALL?

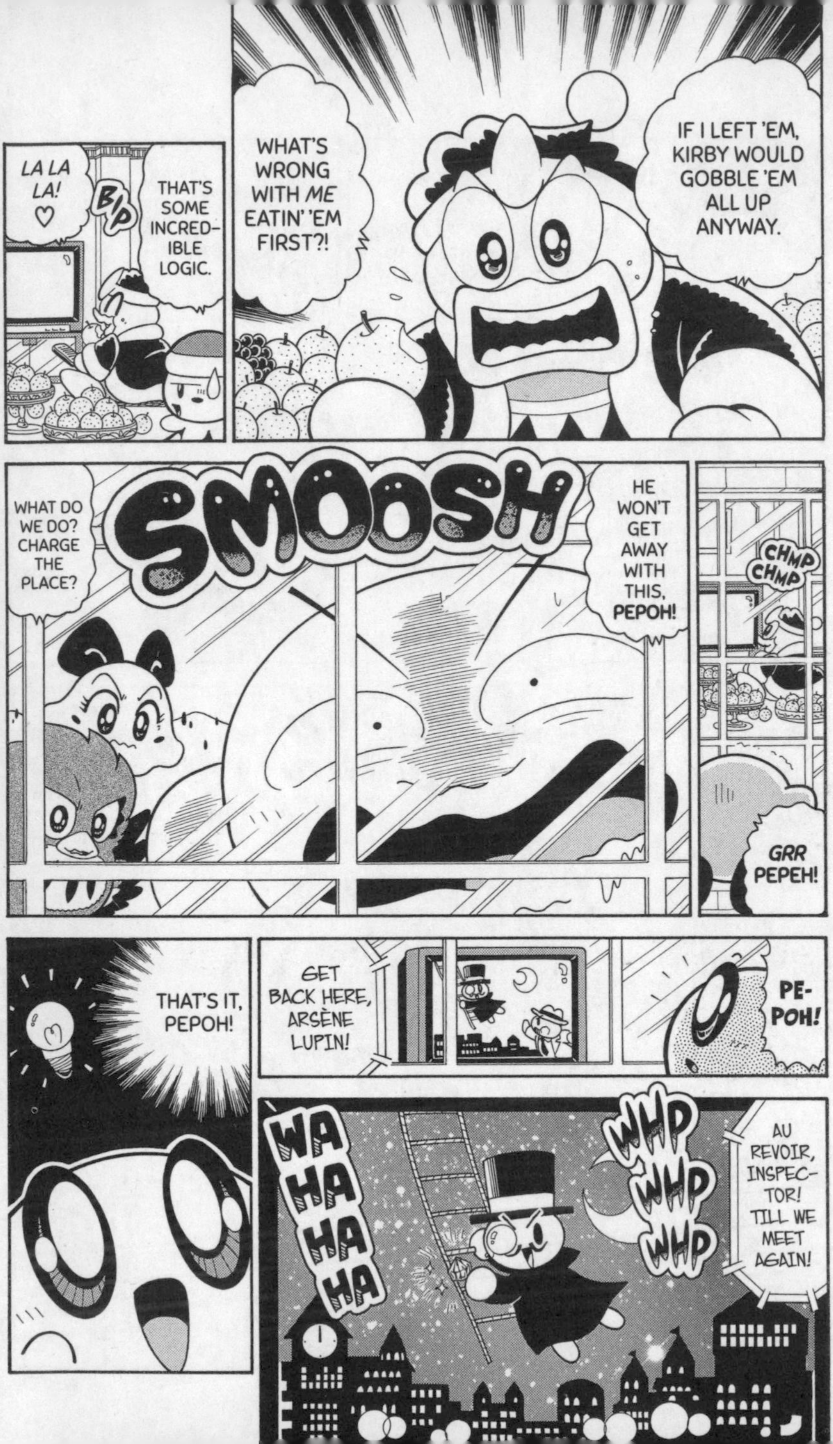
IF I LEFT 'EM, KIRBY WOULD GOBBLE 'EM ALL UP ANYWAY.
WHAT'S WRONG WITH *ME* EATIN' 'EM FIRST?!
THAT'S SOME INCREDIBLE LOGIC.
BIP
LA LA LA! ♡
CHMP CHMP
GRR PEPEH!
HE WON'T GET AWAY WITH THIS, **PEPOH!**
SMOOSH
WHAT DO WE DO? CHARGE THE PLACE?
PE-POH!
GET BACK HERE, ARSÈNE LUPIN!
AU REVOIR, INSPECTOR! TILL WE MEET AGAIN!
WHP WHP WHP
WA HA HA HA HA
THAT'S IT, PEPOH!

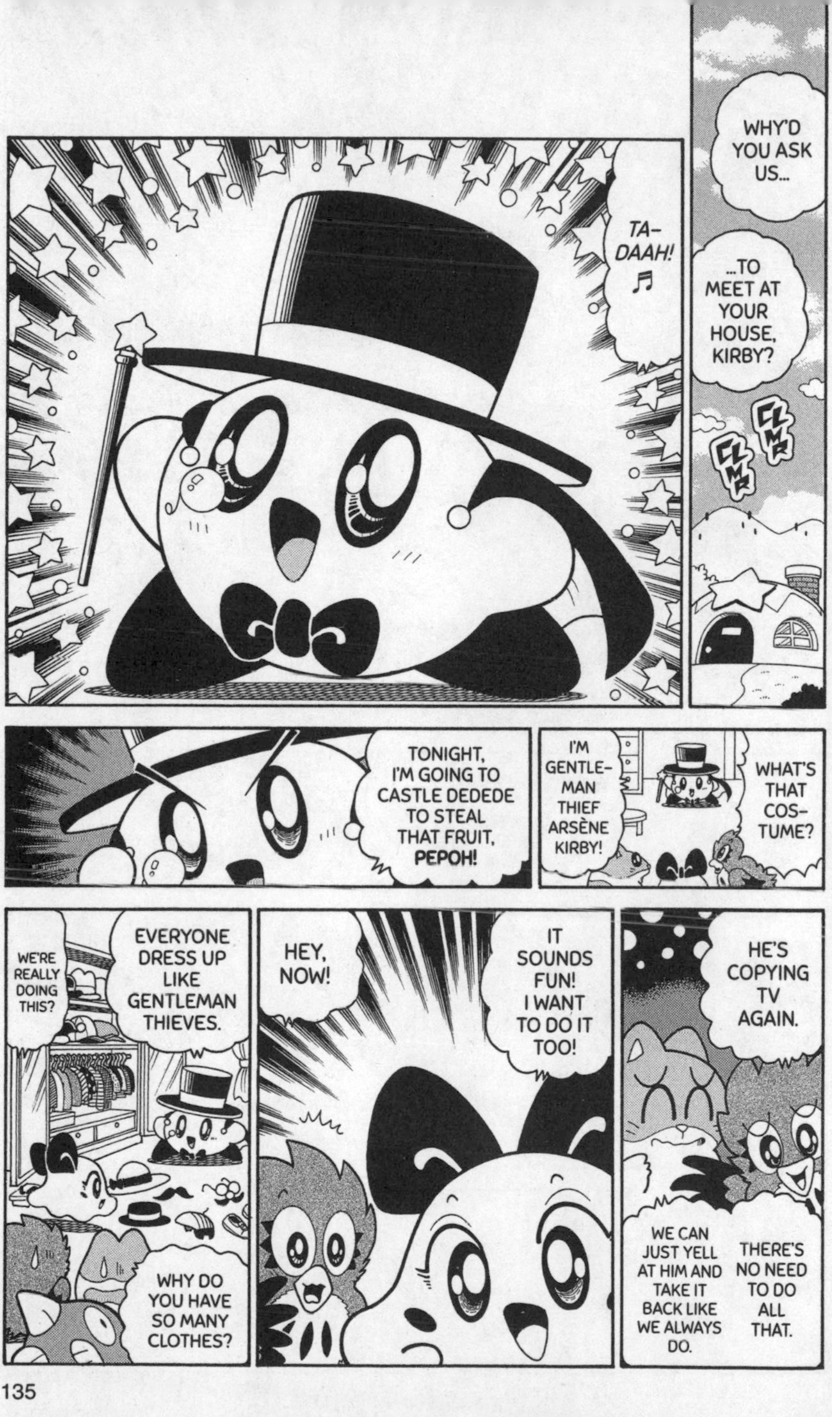
WHY'D YOU ASK US...
...TO MEET AT YOUR HOUSE, KIRBY?
CLMR
CLMR
TA-DAAH! ♬
WHAT'S THAT COS-TUME?
I'M GENTLE-MAN THIEF ARSÈNE KIRBY!
TONIGHT, I'M GOING TO CASTLE DEDEDE TO STEAL THAT FRUIT, **PEPOH!**
HE'S COPYING TV AGAIN.
THERE'S NO NEED TO DO ALL THAT.
WE CAN JUST YELL AT HIM AND TAKE IT BACK LIKE WE ALWAYS DO.
IT SOUNDS FUN! I WANT TO DO IT TOO!
HEY, NOW!
EVERYONE DRESS UP LIKE GENTLEMAN THIEVES.
WE'RE REALLY DOING THIS?
WHY DO YOU HAVE SO MANY CLOTHES?

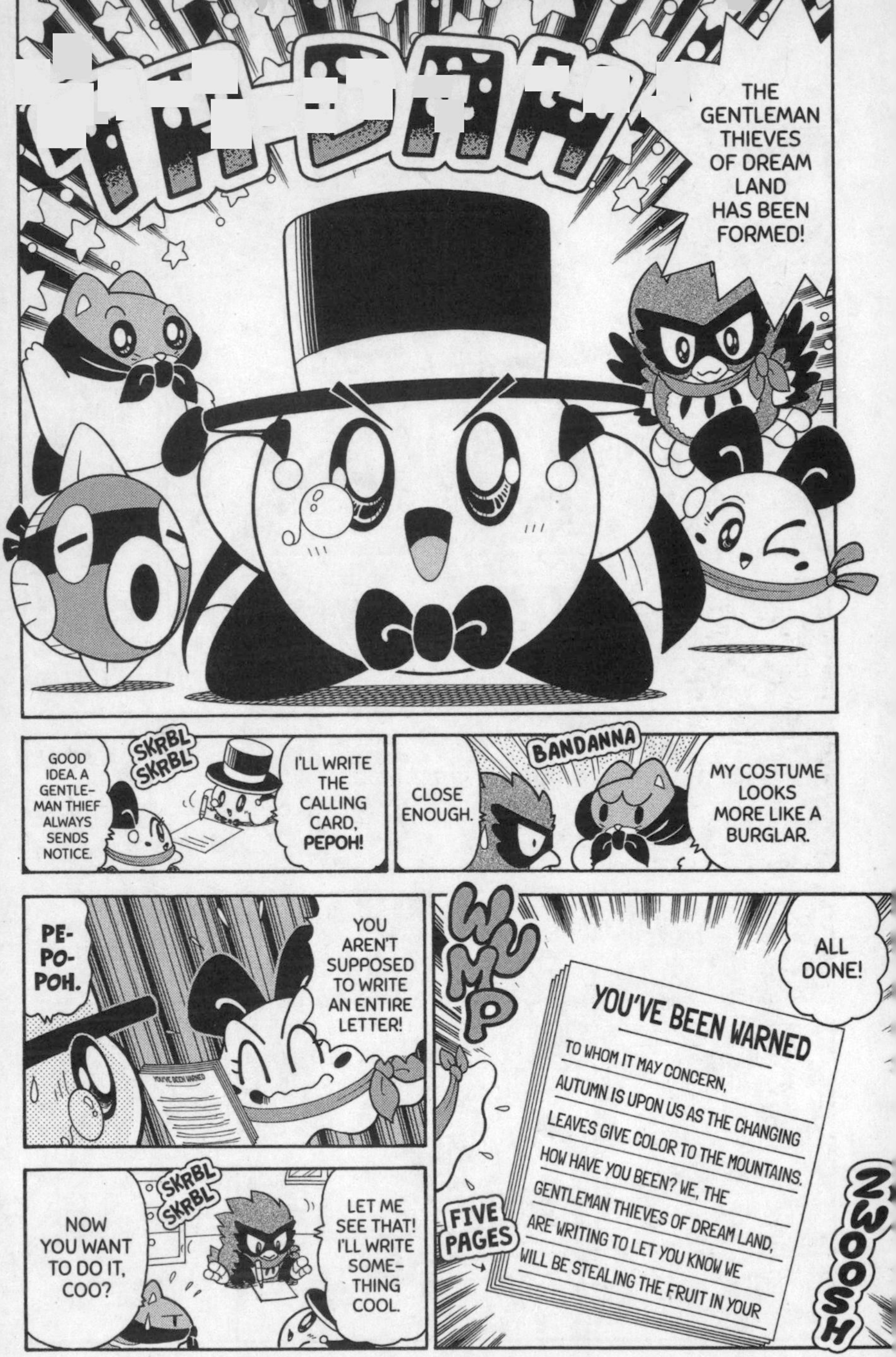
THE GENTLEMAN THIEVES OF DREAM LAND HAS BEEN FORMED!
BANDANNA
MY COSTUME LOOKS MORE LIKE A BURGLAR.
CLOSE ENOUGH.
I'LL WRITE THE CALLING CARD, PEPOH!
SKRBL SKRBL
GOOD IDEA. A GENTLE-MAN THIEF ALWAYS SENDS NOTICE.
ALL DONE!
WUMP
YOU'VE BEEN WARNED
TO WHOM IT MAY CONCERN,
AUTUMN IS UPON US AS THE CHANGING
LEAVES GIVE COLOR TO THE MOUNTAINS.
HOW HAVE YOU BEEN? WE, THE
GENTLEMAN THIEVES OF DREAM LAND,
ARE WRITING TO LET YOU KNOW WE
WILL BE STEALING THE FRUIT IN YOUR
FIVE PAGES
ZWOOSH
YOU AREN'T SUPPOSED TO WRITE AN ENTIRE LETTER!
PE-PO-POH.
LET ME SEE THAT! I'LL WRITE SOME-THING COOL.
SKRBL SKRBL
NOW YOU WANT TO DO IT, COO?

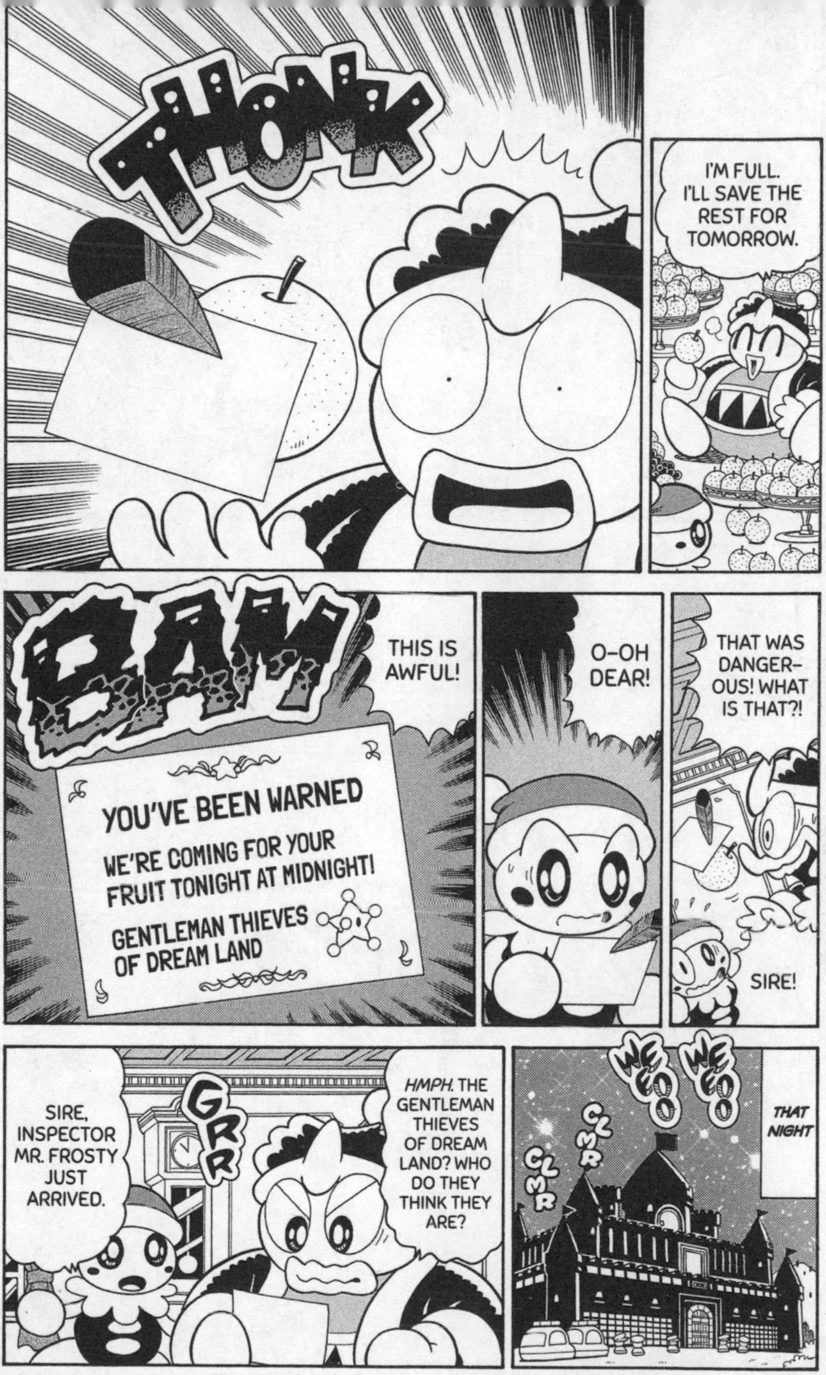
I'M FULL. I'LL SAVE THE REST FOR TOMORROW.
THONK
THAT WAS DANGER-OUS! WHAT IS THAT?!
SIRE!
O-OH DEAR!
THIS IS AWFUL!
BAM
YOU'VE BEEN WARNED
WE'RE COMING FOR YOUR FRUIT TONIGHT AT MIDNIGHT!
GENTLEMAN THIEVES OF DREAM LAND
THAT NIGHT
WEEOO
WEEOO
CLMR
CLMR
HMPH. THE GENTLEMAN THIEVES OF DREAM LAND? WHO DO THEY THINK THEY ARE?
GRR
SIRE, INSPECTOR MR. FROSTY JUST ARRIVED.

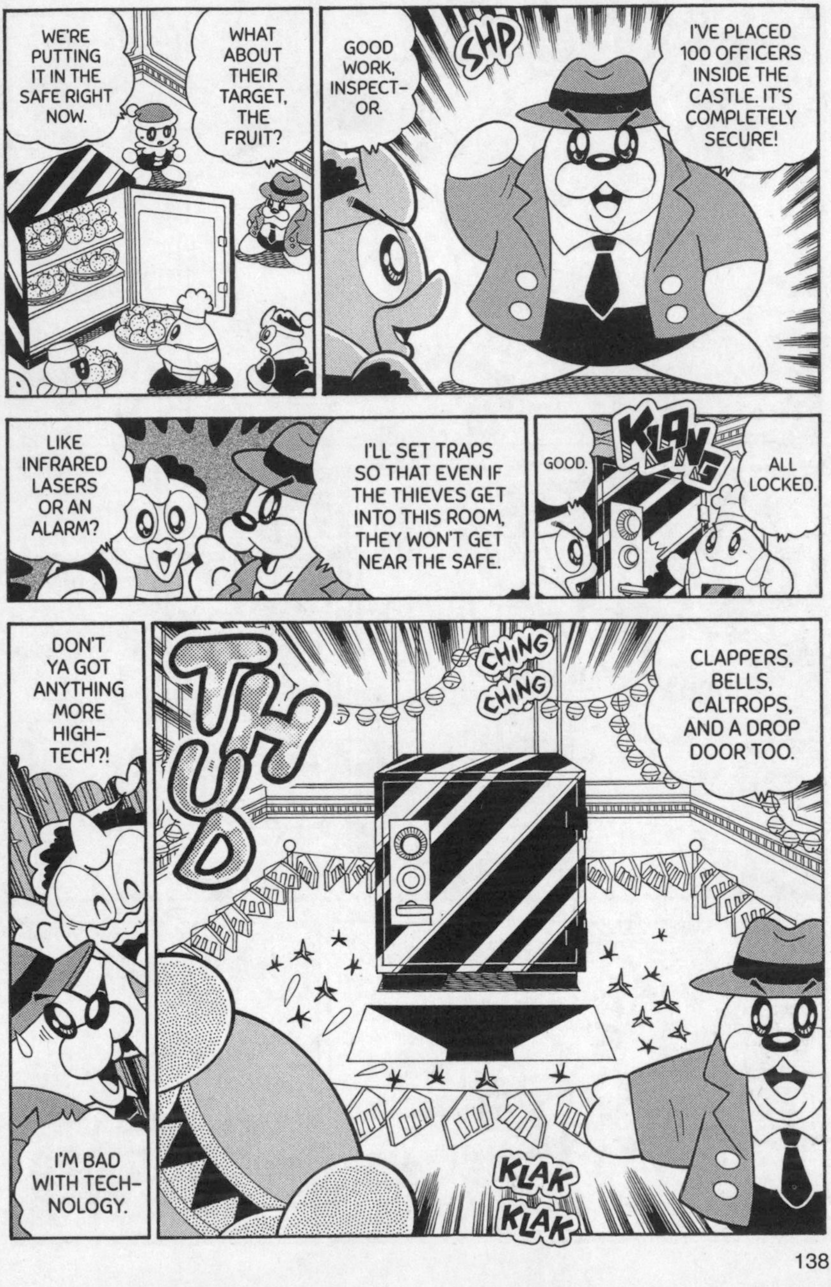
SHP
I'VE PLACED 100 OFFICERS INSIDE THE CASTLE. IT'S COMPLETELY SECURE!
GOOD WORK, INSPECT-OR.
WHAT ABOUT THEIR TARGET, THE FRUIT?
WE'RE PUTTING IT IN THE SAFE RIGHT NOW.
KLANG
ALL LOCKED.
GOOD.
I'LL SET TRAPS SO THAT EVEN IF THE THIEVES GET INTO THIS ROOM, THEY WON'T GET NEAR THE SAFE.
LIKE INFRARED LASERS OR AN ALARM?
CLAPPERS, BELLS, CALTROPS, AND A DROP DOOR TOO.
CHING CHING
THUD
KLAK KLAK
DON'T YA GOT ANYTHING MORE HIGH-TECH?!
I'M BAD WITH TECH-NOLOGY.

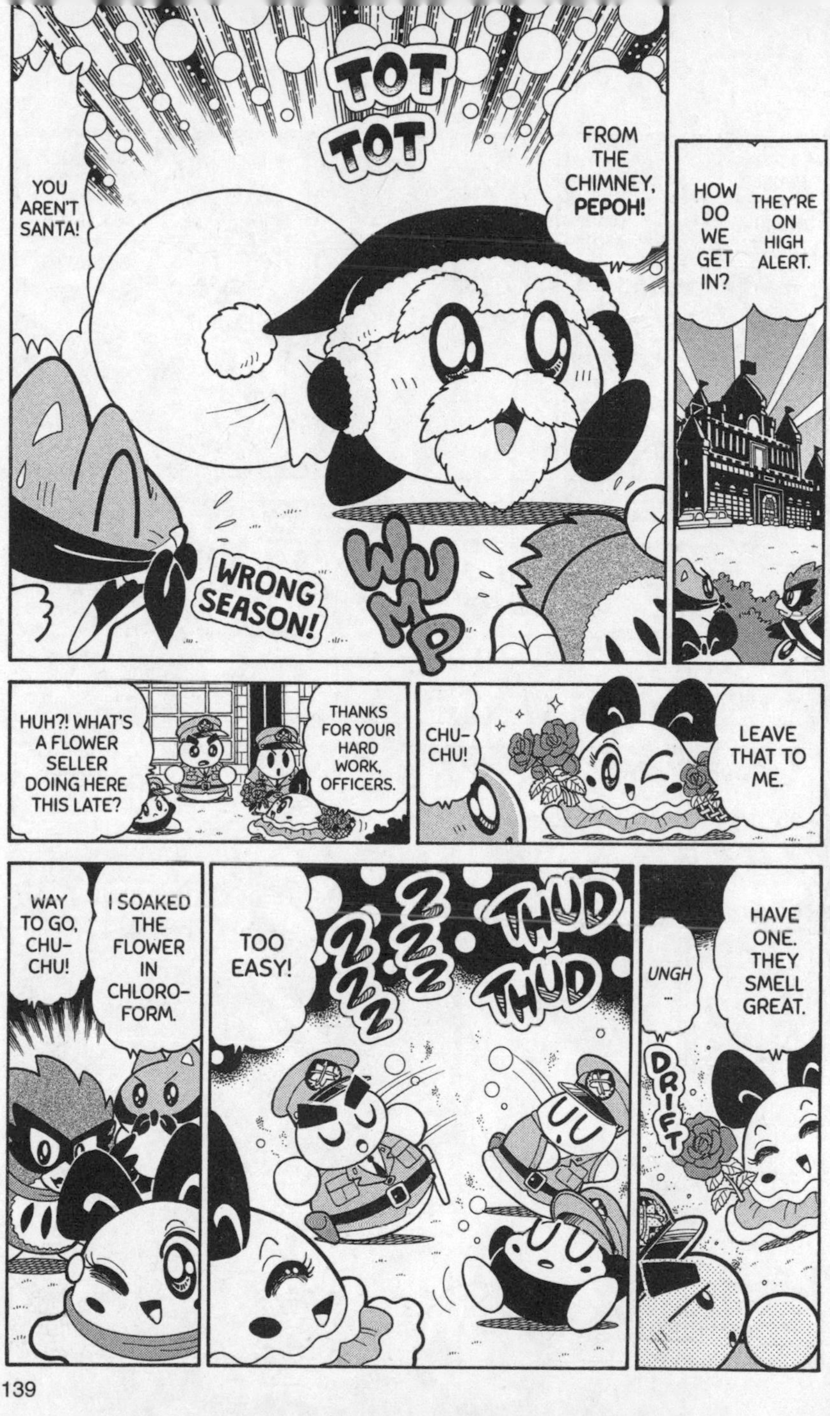
THEY'RE ON HIGH ALERT.
HOW DO WE GET IN?
FROM THE CHIMNEY, **PEPOH!**
TOT TOT
YOU AREN'T SANTA!
WHUMP
WRONG SEASON!
LEAVE THAT TO ME.
CHU-CHU!
THANKS FOR YOUR HARD WORK, OFFICERS.
HUH?! WHAT'S A FLOWER SELLER DOING HERE THIS LATE?
HAVE ONE. THEY SMELL GREAT.
UNGH ...
DRIFT
THUD THUD
ZZZ
ZZZ
TOO EASY!
I SOAKED THE FLOWER IN CHLORO-FORM.
WAY TO GO, CHU-CHU!

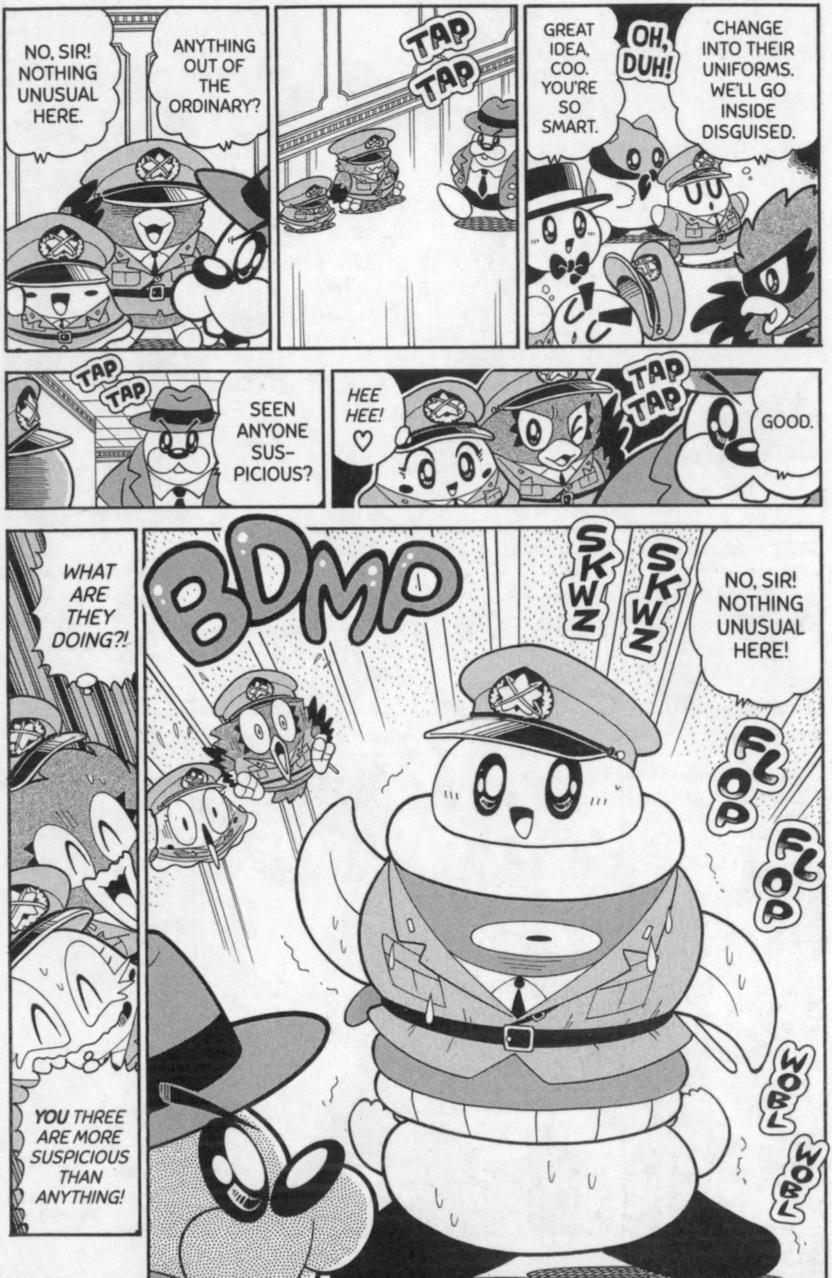
CHANGE INTO THEIR UNIFORMS. WE'LL GO INSIDE DISGUISED.
OH, DUH!
GREAT IDEA, COO. YOU'RE SO SMART.
TAP TAP
ANYTHING OUT OF THE ORDINARY?
NO, SIR! NOTHING UNUSUAL HERE.
GOOD.
TAP TAP
HEE HEE! ♡
TAP TAP
SEEN ANYONE SUS-PICIOUS?
NO, SIR! NOTHING UNUSUAL HERE!
SKWZ SKWZ
BDMP
FLOP FLOP
WOBL WOBL
WHAT ARE THEY DOING?!
YOU THREE ARE MORE SUSPICIOUS THAN ANYTHING!

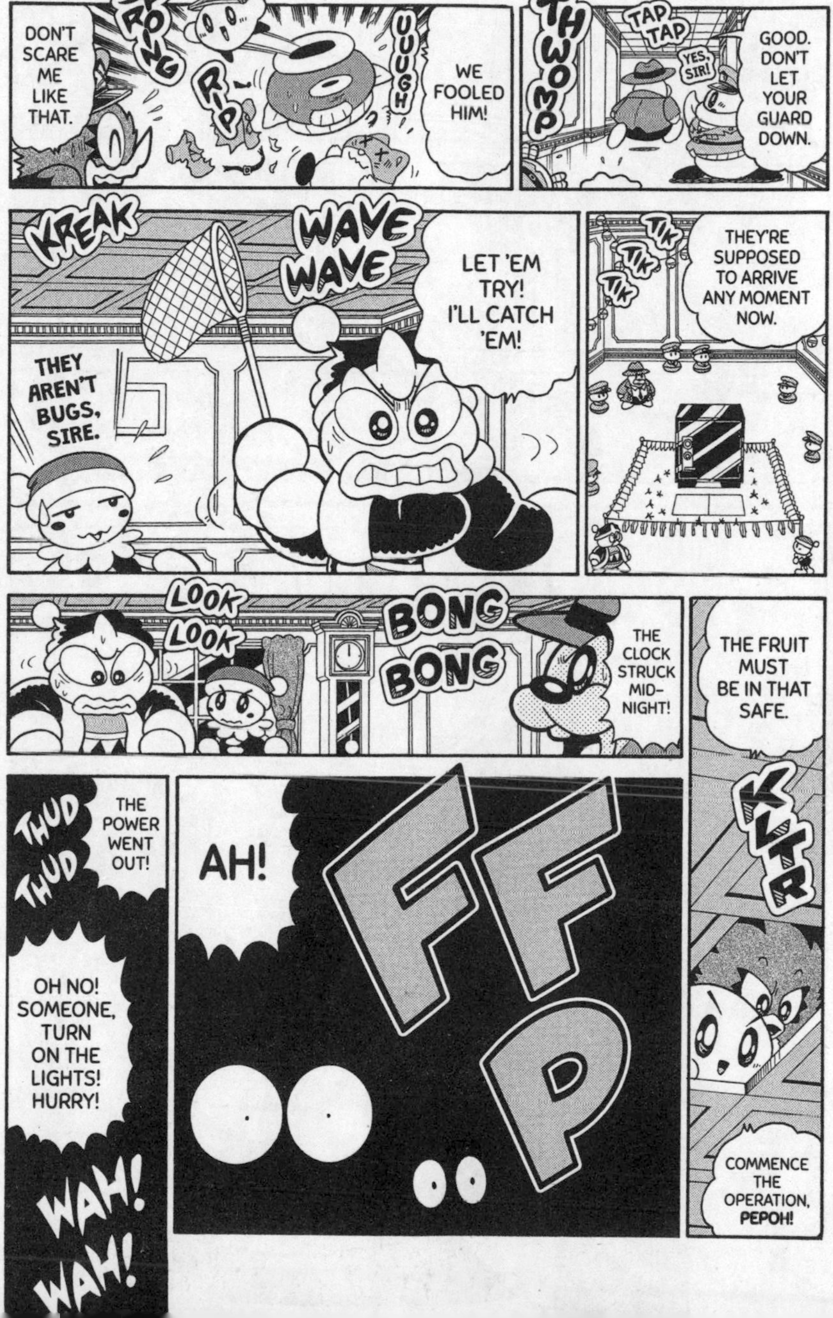
THWOMP
TAP TAP
YES, SIR!
GOOD. DON'T LET YOUR GUARD DOWN.
WE FOOLED HIM!
UUUGH
SPROING
RIP
DON'T SCARE ME LIKE THAT.
THEY'RE SUPPOSED TO ARRIVE ANY MOMENT NOW.
TIK TIK TIK
LET 'EM TRY! I'LL CATCH 'EM!
WAVE WAVE
KREAK
THEY AREN'T BUGS, SIRE.
THE FRUIT MUST BE IN THAT SAFE.
KLTR
COMMENCE THE OPERATION, **PEPOH!**
THE CLOCK STRUCK MID-NIGHT!
BONG BONG
LOOK LOOK
FFP
AH!
THE POWER WENT OUT!
THUD THUD
OH NO! SOMEONE, TURN ON THE LIGHTS! HURRY!
WAH! WAH!

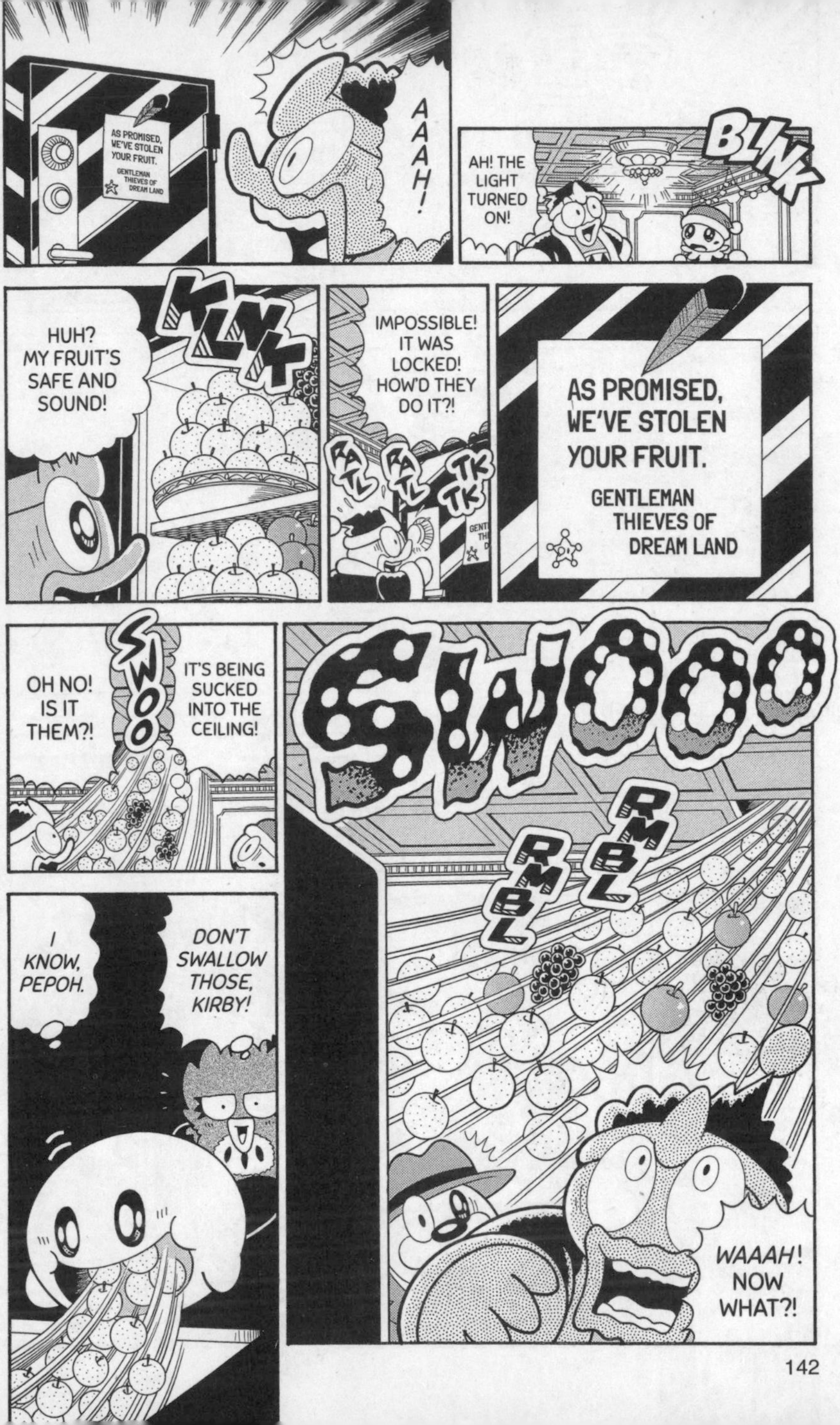
BLINK
AH! THE LIGHT TURNED ON!
AAAAH!
AS PROMISED, WE'VE STOLEN YOUR FRUIT.
GENTLEMAN THIEVES OF DREAM LAND
AS PROMISED, WE'VE STOLEN YOUR FRUIT.
GENTLEMAN THIEVES OF DREAM LAND
IMPOSSIBLE! IT WAS LOCKED! HOW'D THEY DO IT?!
RATL RATL
TK TK
KLNK
HUH? MY FRUIT'S SAFE AND SOUND!
SWOOO
RMBL RMBL
WAAAH! NOW WHAT?!
SWOO
IT'S BEING SUCKED INTO THE CEILING!
OH NO! IS IT THEM?!
DON'T SWALLOW THOSE, KIRBY!
I KNOW, PEPOH.

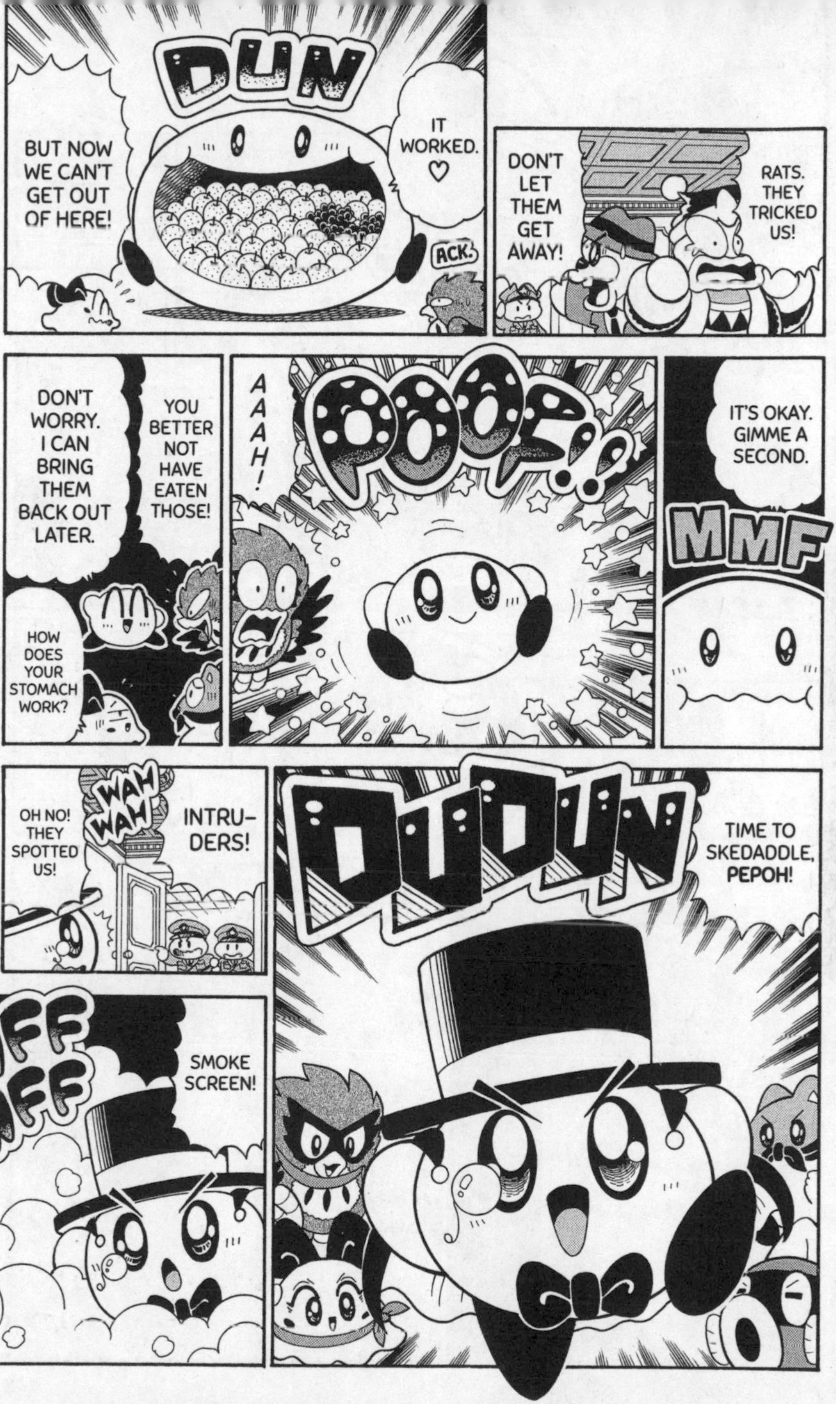
RATS. THEY TRICKED US!
DON'T LET THEM GET AWAY!
DUN
IT WORKED. ♡
BUT NOW WE CAN'T GET OUT OF HERE!
ACK.
IT'S OKAY. GIMME A SECOND.
MMF
POOF!!
AAAAH!
YOU BETTER NOT HAVE EATEN THOSE!
DON'T WORRY. I CAN BRING THEM BACK OUT LATER.
HOW DOES YOUR STOMACH WORK?
DUDUN
TIME TO SKEDADDLE, PEPOH!
INTRU-DERS!
WAH WAH
OH NO! THEY SPOTTED US!
SMOKE SCREEN!
WFF WFF

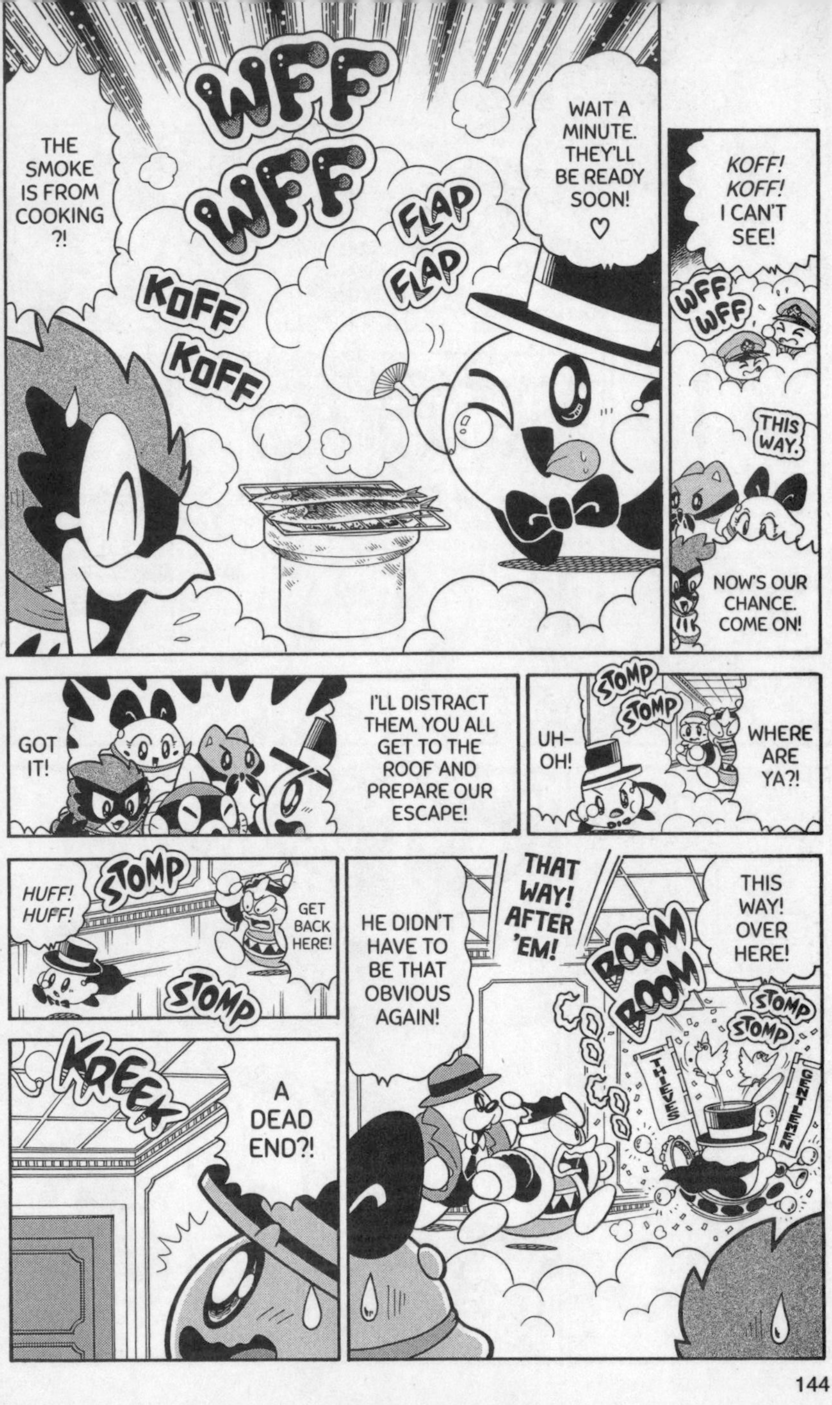
KOFF! KOFF! I CAN'T SEE!
WFF WFF
THIS WAY.
NOW'S OUR CHANCE. COME ON!
WAIT A MINUTE. THEY'LL BE READY SOON! ♡
WFF WFF
FLAP FLAP
THE SMOKE IS FROM COOKING ?!
KOFF KOFF
STOMP STOMP
WHERE ARE YA?!
UH-OH!
I'LL DISTRACT THEM. YOU ALL GET TO THE ROOF AND PREPARE OUR ESCAPE!
GOT IT!
THIS WAY! OVER HERE!
THAT WAY! AFTER 'EM!
BOOM BOOM
STOMP STOMP
THIEVES
GENTLEMEN
HE DIDN'T HAVE TO BE THAT OBVIOUS AGAIN!
STOMP
GET BACK HERE!
HUFF! HUFF!
STOMP
KREEK
A DEAD END?!

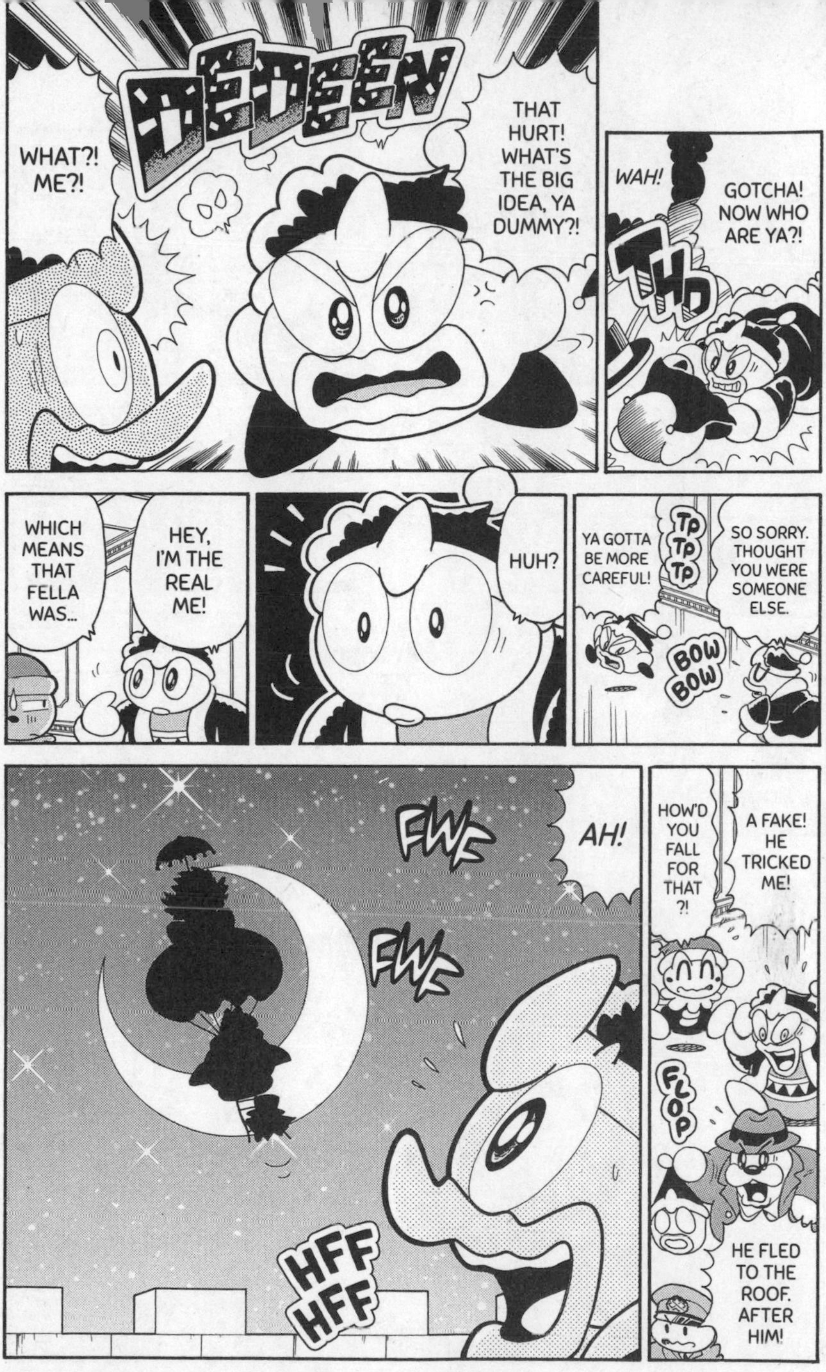
WAH!
GOTCHA! NOW WHO ARE YA?!
THD
DEDEEN
THAT HURT! WHAT'S THE BIG IDEA, YA DUMMY?!
WHAT?! ME?!
SO SORRY. THOUGHT YOU WERE SOMEONE ELSE.
TP TP TP
YA GOTTA BE MORE CAREFUL!
BOW BOW
HUH?
HEY, I'M THE REAL ME!
WHICH MEANS THAT FELLA WAS...
A FAKE! HE TRICKED ME!
HOW'D YOU FALL FOR THAT?!
FLOP
HE FLED TO THE ROOF. AFTER HIM!
AH!
FWE
FWE
HFF HFF

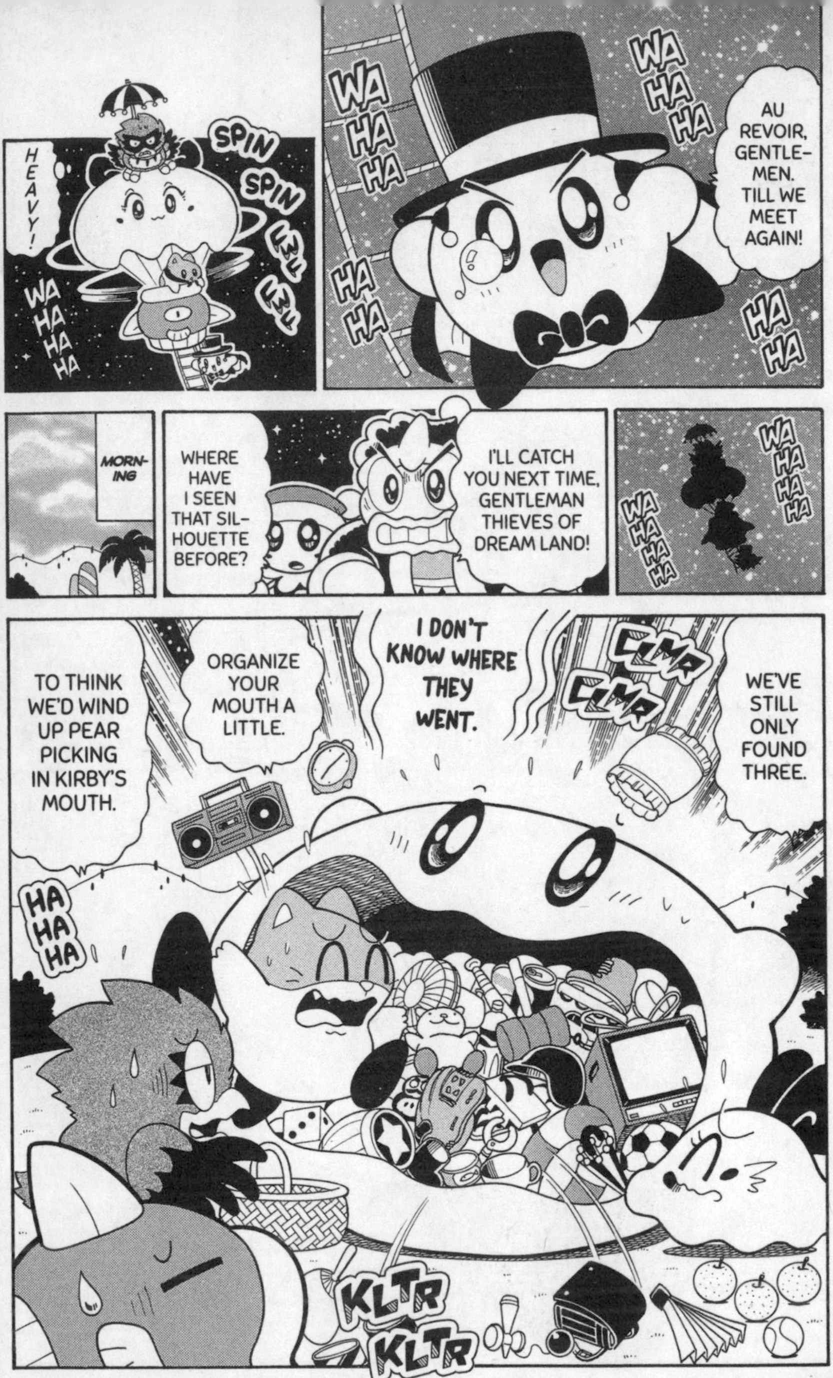
WA HA HA
AU REVOIR, GENTLEMEN. TILL WE MEET AGAIN!
WA HA HA
HA HA
HA HA
SPIN SPIN
FWE FWE
HEAVY!
WA HA HA HA HA
WA HA HA HA HA
WA HA HA HA HA
I'LL CATCH YOU NEXT TIME, GENTLEMAN THIEVES OF DREAM LAND!
WHERE HAVE I SEEN THAT SILHOUETTE BEFORE?
MORNING
WE'VE STILL ONLY FOUND THREE.
CLMR CLMR
I DON'T KNOW WHERE THEY WENT.
ORGANIZE YOUR MOUTH A LITTLE.
TO THINK WE'D WIND UP PEAR PICKING IN KIRBY'S MOUTH.
HA HA HA
KLTR KLTR

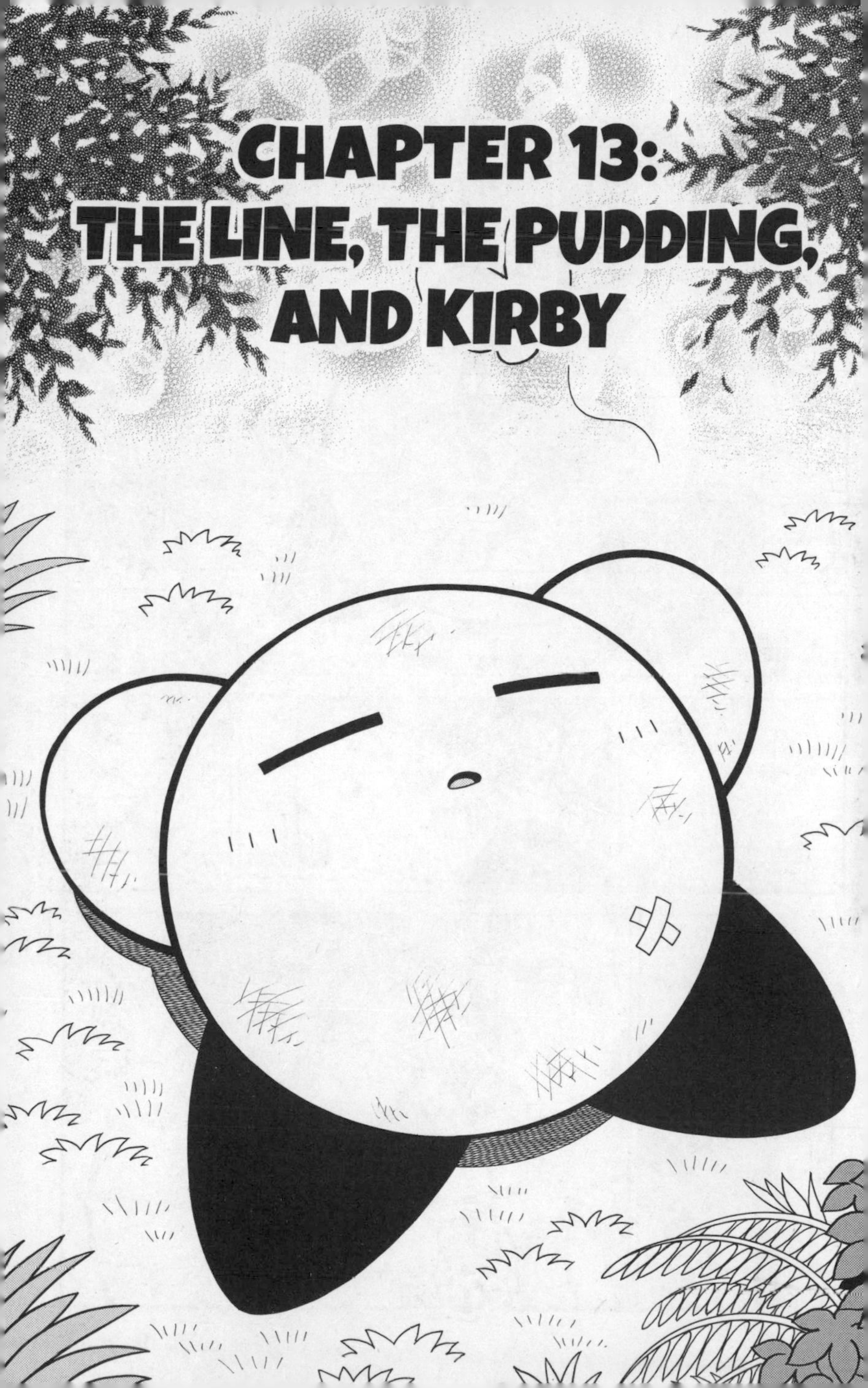
CHAPTER 13:
THE LINE, THE PUDDING, AND KIRBY

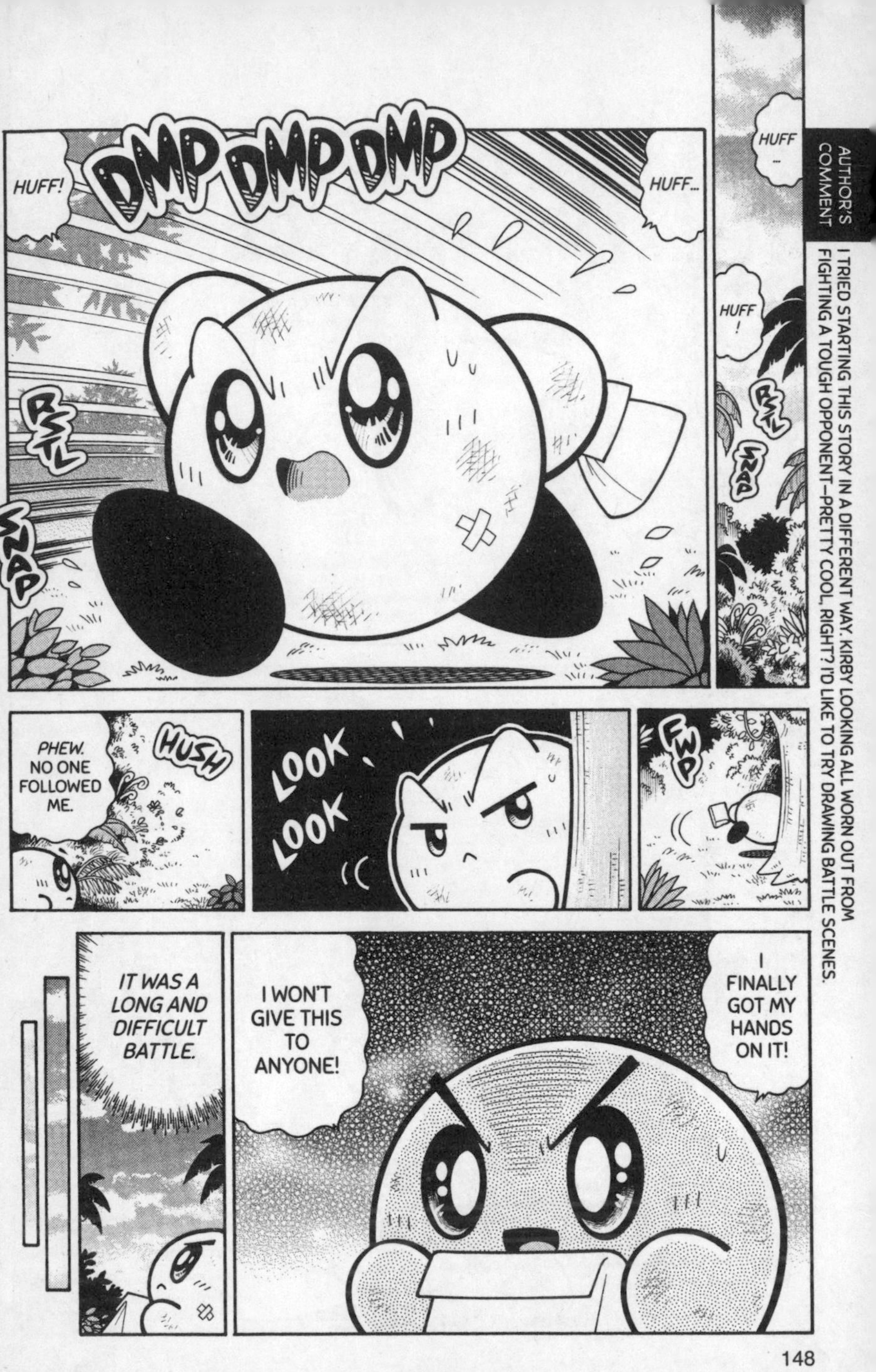
HUFF ...
HUFF !
RSTL
SNAP
HUFF...
DMP DMP DMP DMP
HUFF!
RSTL
SNAP
FWP
LOOK LOOK
HUSH
PHEW. NO ONE FOLLOWED ME.
I FINALLY GOT MY HANDS ON IT!
I WON'T GIVE THIS TO ANYONE!
IT WAS A LONG AND DIFFICULT BATTLE.

AUTHOR'S COMMENT

I TRIED STARTING THIS STORY IN A DIFFERENT WAY. KIRBY LOOKING ALL WORN OUT FROM FIGHTING A TOUGH OPPONENT—PRETTY COOL, RIGHT? I'D LIKE TO TRY DRAWING BATTLE SCENES.

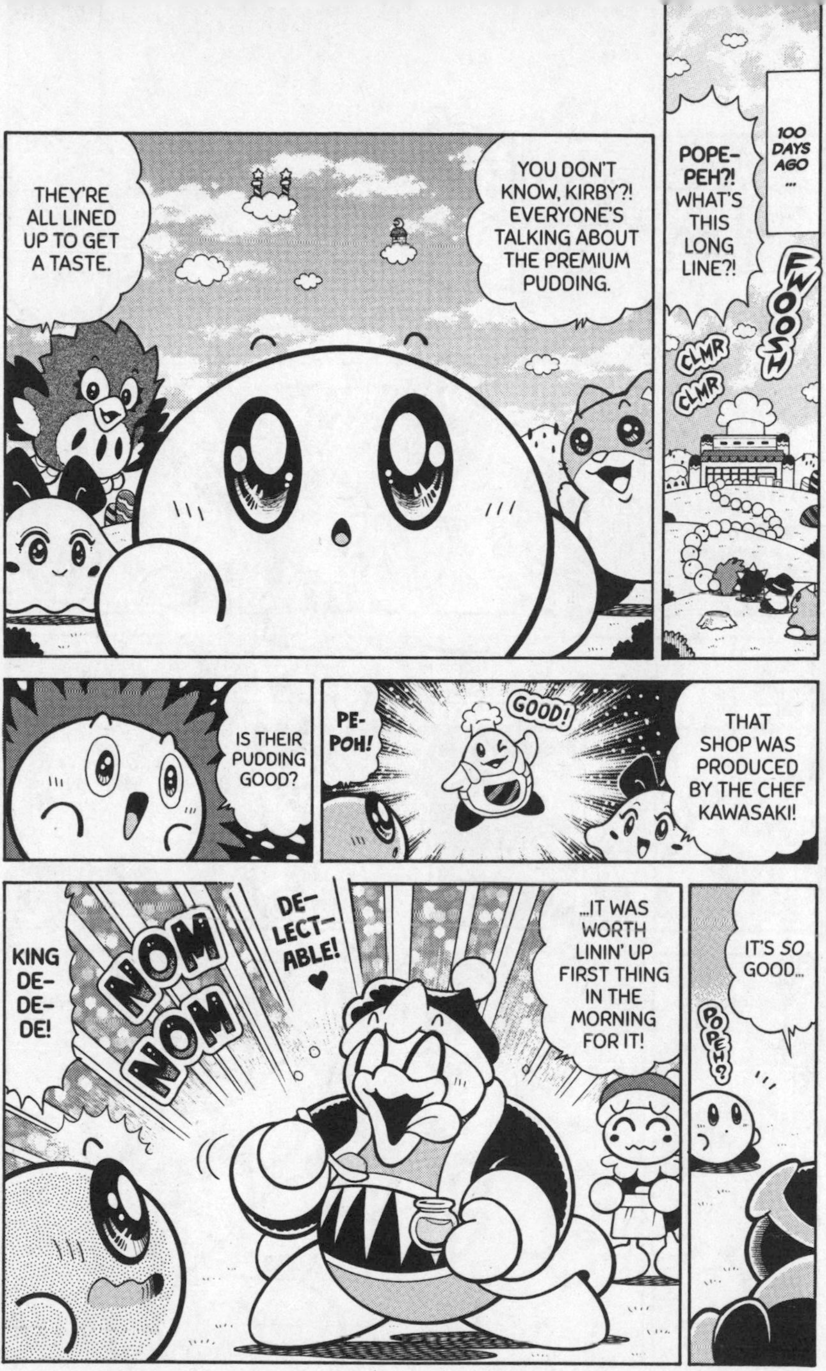
100 DAYS AGO...
POPE-PEH?! WHAT'S THIS LONG LINE?!
FWOOSH
CLMR CLMR
YOU DON'T KNOW, KIRBY?! EVERYONE'S TALKING ABOUT THE PREMIUM PUDDING.
THEY'RE ALL LINED UP TO GET A TASTE.
THAT SHOP WAS PRODUCED BY THE CHEF KAWASAKI!
GOOD!
PE-POH!
IS THEIR PUDDING GOOD?
IT'S *SO* GOOD...
POPEPEH?
...IT WAS WORTH LININ' UP FIRST THING IN THE MORNING FOR IT!
DE-LECT-ABLE! ♥
NOM NOM
KING DE-DE-DE!

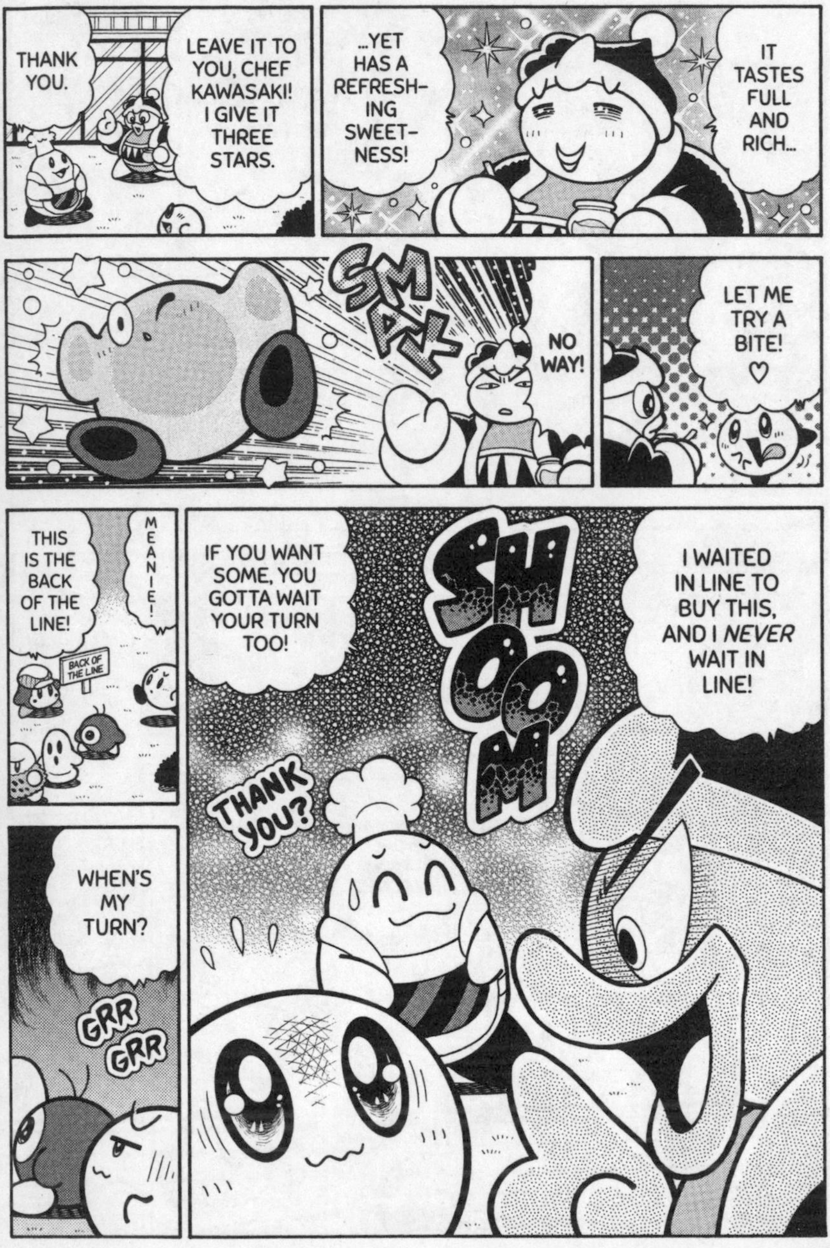
IT TASTES FULL AND RICH...
...YET HAS A REFRESHING SWEETNESS!
LEAVE IT TO YOU, CHEF KAWASAKI! I GIVE IT THREE STARS.
THANK YOU.
LET ME TRY A BITE! ♡
NO WAY!
SMACK
I WAITED IN LINE TO BUY THIS, AND I *NEVER* WAIT IN LINE!
SHOOM
IF YOU WANT SOME, YOU GOTTA WAIT YOUR TURN TOO!
THANK YOU?
MEANIE!
THIS IS THE BACK OF THE LINE!
BACK OF THE LINE
WHEN'S MY TURN?
GRR GRR

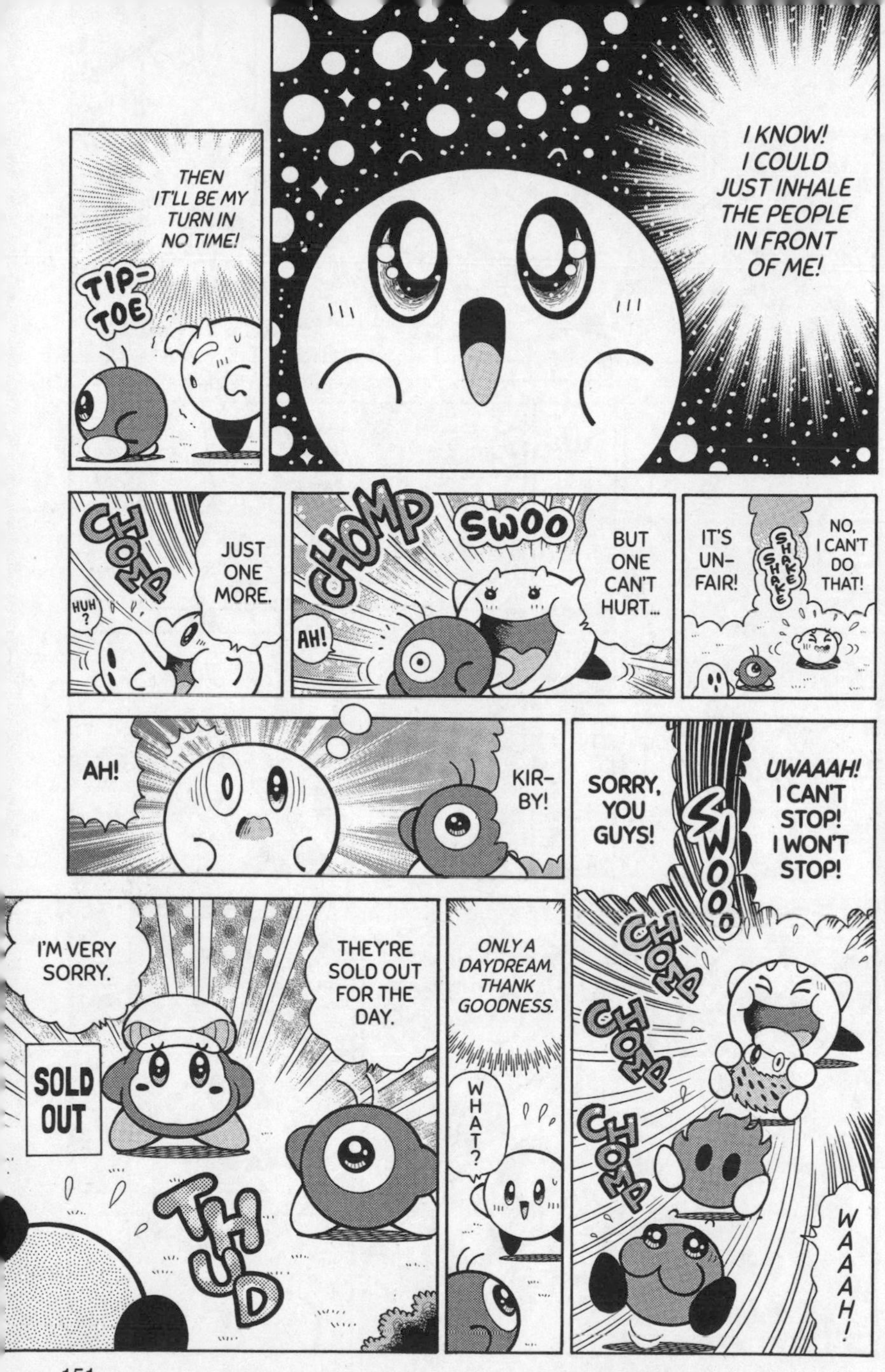
I KNOW! I COULD JUST INHALE THE PEOPLE IN FRONT OF ME!
THEN IT'LL BE MY TURN IN NO TIME!
TIP-TOE
NO, I CAN'T DO THAT!
SHAKE SHAKE
IT'S UN-FAIR!
BUT ONE CAN'T HURT...
SWOO
CHOMP
AH!
JUST ONE MORE.
CHOMP
HUH?
UWAAAH! I CAN'T STOP! I WON'T STOP!
SORRY, YOU GUYS!
SWOOO
CHOMP
CHOMP
CHOMP
WAAAAH!
KIR-BY!
AH!
ONLY A DAYDREAM. THANK GOODNESS.
WHAT?
THEY'RE SOLD OUT FOR THE DAY.
I'M VERY SORRY.
SOLD OUT
THUD

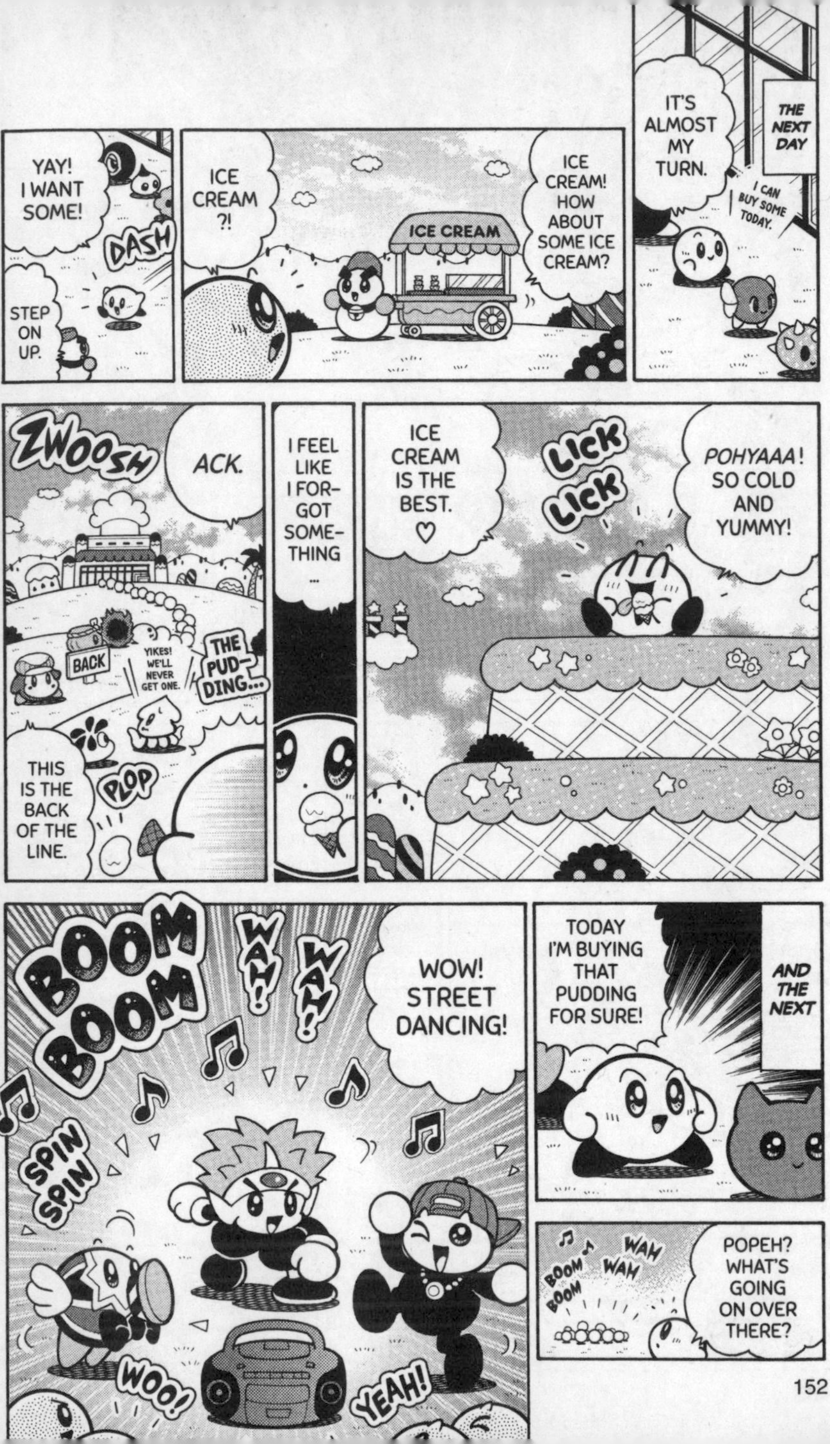
THE NEXT DAY
IT'S ALMOST MY TURN.
I CAN BUY SOME TODAY.
ICE CREAM! HOW ABOUT SOME ICE CREAM?
ICE CREAM
ICE CREAM ?!
YAY! I WANT SOME!
DASH
STEP ON UP.
POHYAAA! SO COLD AND YUMMY!
LICK LICK
ICE CREAM IS THE BEST. ♡
I FEEL LIKE I FORGOT SOMETHING ...
ACK.
ZWOOSH
THE PUDDING...
YIKES! WE'LL NEVER GET ONE.
BACK
THIS IS THE BACK OF THE LINE.
PLOP
AND THE NEXT
TODAY I'M BUYING THAT PUDDING FOR SURE!
POPEH? WHAT'S GOING ON OVER THERE?
WAH WAH
BOOM BOOM
WOW! STREET DANCING!
WAH! WAH!
BOOM BOOM
SPIN SPIN
WOO!
YEAH!

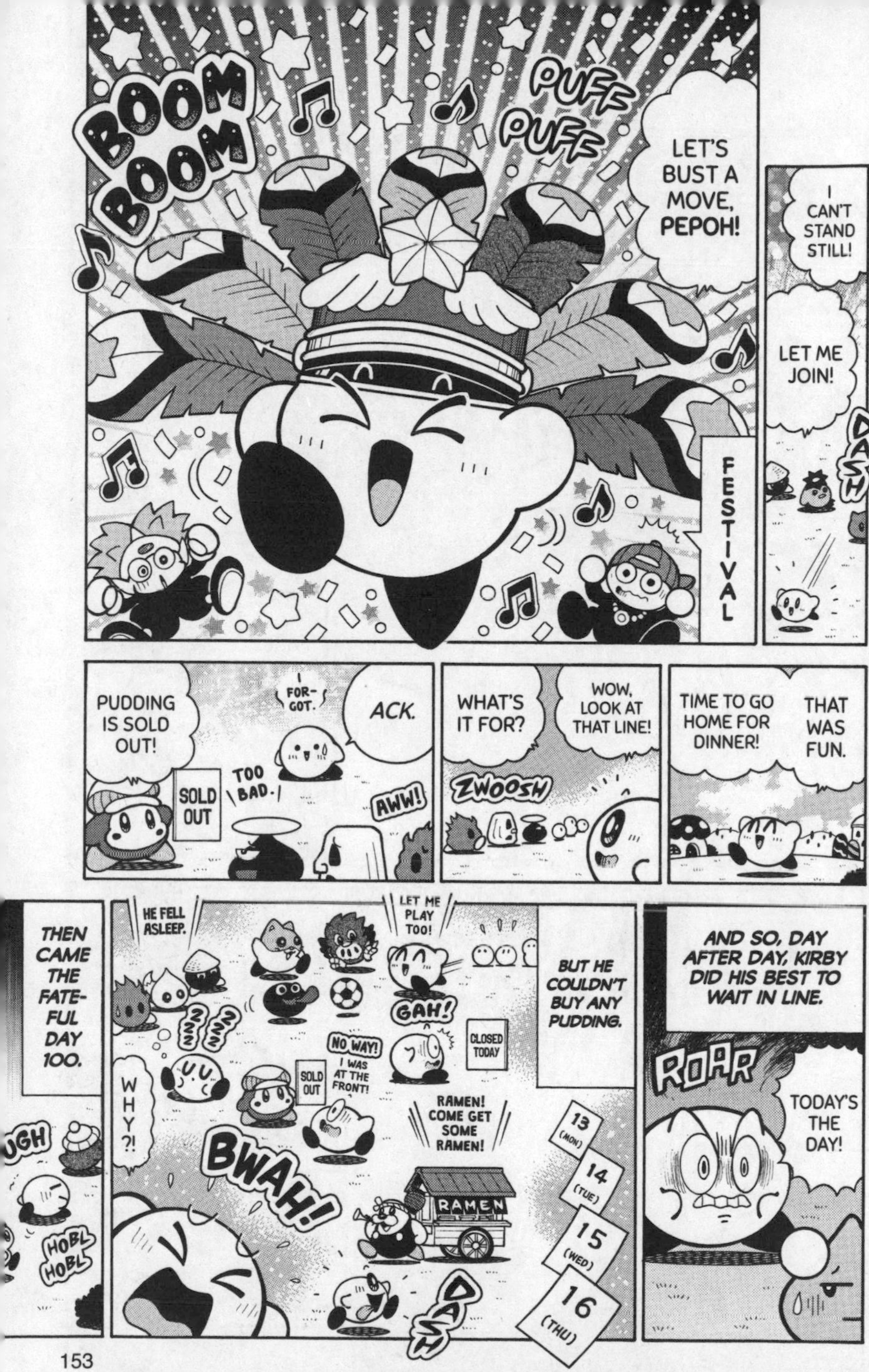
I CAN'T STAND STILL!
LET ME JOIN!
DASH
PUFF PUFF
LET'S BUST A MOVE, PEPOH!
BOOM BOOM
FESTIVAL
THAT WAS FUN.
TIME TO GO HOME FOR DINNER!
WOW, LOOK AT THAT LINE!
WHAT'S IT FOR?
ZWOOSH
ACK.
I FOR-GOT.
PUDDING IS SOLD OUT!
SOLD OUT
TOO BAD.
AWW!
AND SO, DAY AFTER DAY, KIRBY DID HIS BEST TO WAIT IN LINE.
ROAR
TODAY'S THE DAY!
BUT HE COULDN'T BUY ANY PUDDING.
LET ME PLAY TOO!
GAH!
HE FELL ASLEEP.
ZZZ ZZZ
CLOSED TODAY
NO WAY! I WAS AT THE FRONT!
SOLD OUT
WHY?!
RAMEN! COME GET SOME RAMEN!
RAMEN
BWAH!
DASH
13 (MON)
14 (TUE)
15 (WED)
16 (THU)
THEN CAME THE FATE-FUL DAY 100.
UGH
HOBL HOBL

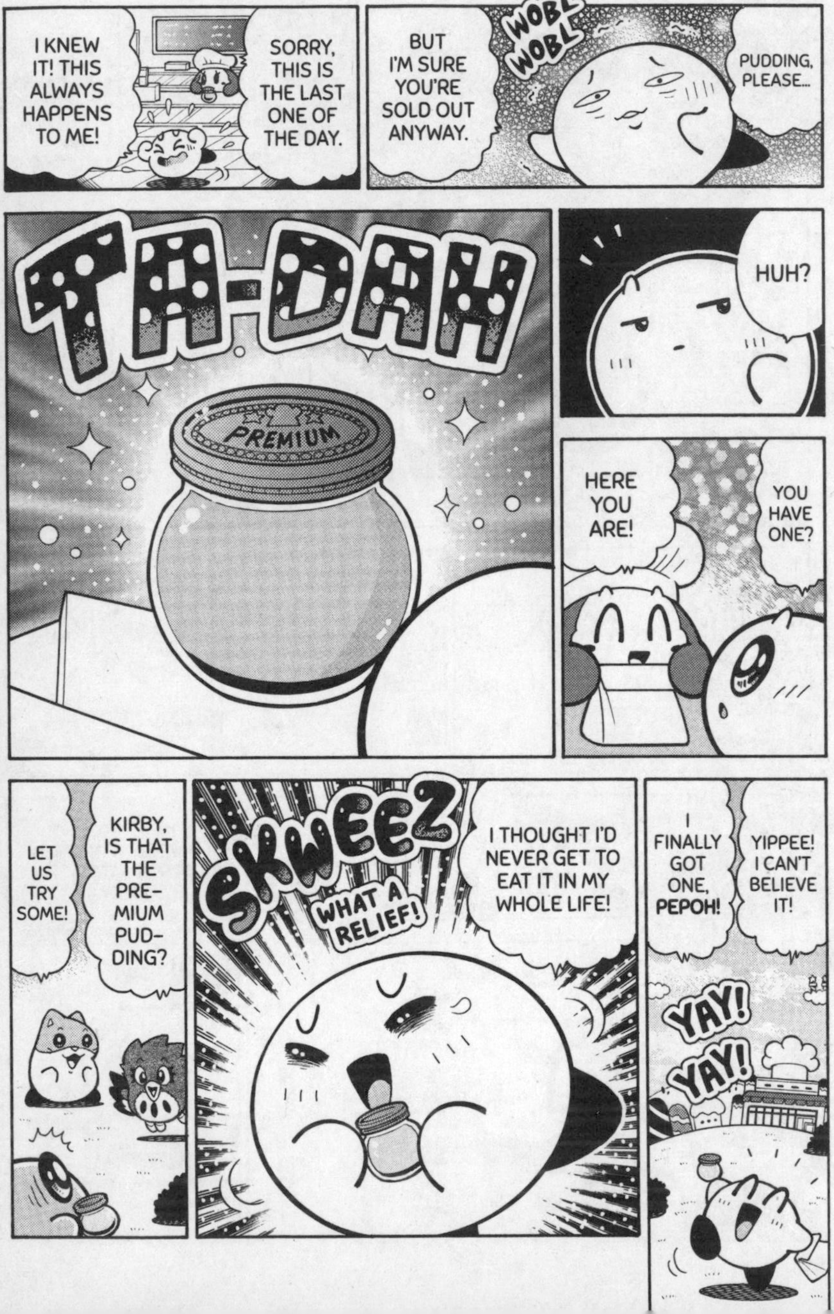
WOBL WOBL
PUDDING, PLEASE...
BUT I'M SURE YOU'RE SOLD OUT ANYWAY.
SORRY, THIS IS THE LAST ONE OF THE DAY.
I KNEW IT! THIS ALWAYS HAPPENS TO ME!
HUH?
YOU HAVE ONE?
HERE YOU ARE!
TA-DAH
PREMIUM
YIPPEE! I CAN'T BELIEVE IT!
I FINALLY GOT ONE, **PEPOH!**
YAY!
YAY!
I THOUGHT I'D NEVER GET TO EAT IT IN MY WHOLE LIFE!
SKWEEZ
WHAT A RELIEF!
KIRBY, IS THAT THE PRE-MIUM PUD-DING?
LET US TRY SOME!

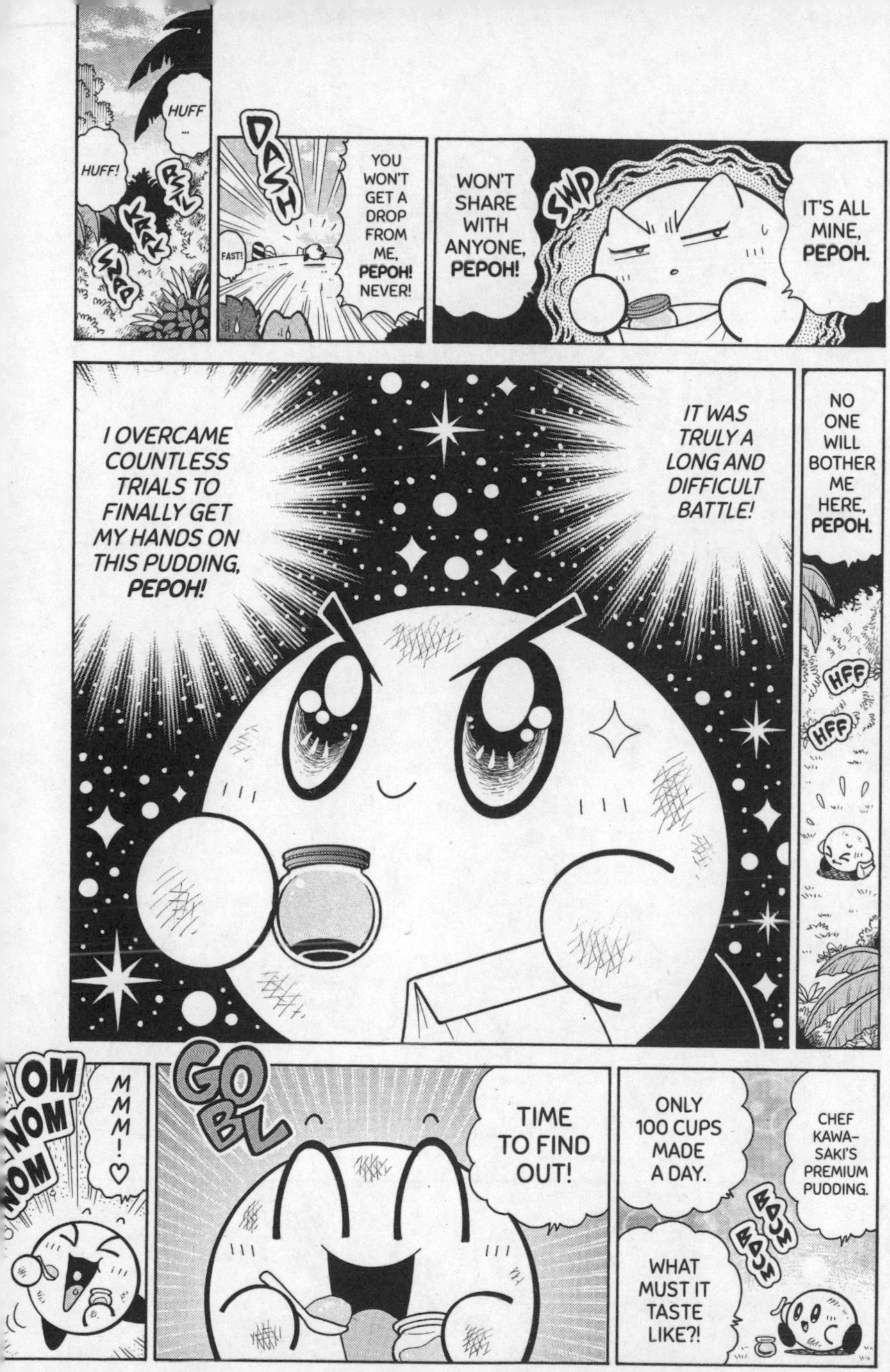
IT'S ALL MINE, **PEPOH.**
SWP
WON'T SHARE WITH ANYONE, **PEPOH!**
DASH
YOU WON'T GET A DROP FROM ME, **PEPOH!** NEVER!
FAST!
HUFF ...
HUFF!
RSTL
KRAK
SNAP
NO ONE WILL BOTHER ME HERE, **PEPOH.**
HFF
HFF
IT WAS TRULY A LONG AND DIFFICULT BATTLE!
I OVERCAME COUNTLESS TRIALS TO FINALLY GET MY HANDS ON THIS PUDDING, **PEPOH!**
CHEF KAWA-SAKI'S PREMIUM PUDDING.
ONLY 100 CUPS MADE A DAY.
BDUM
BDUM
WHAT MUST IT TASTE LIKE?!
TIME TO FIND OUT!
GOBL
MMM!♡
OM NOM NOM

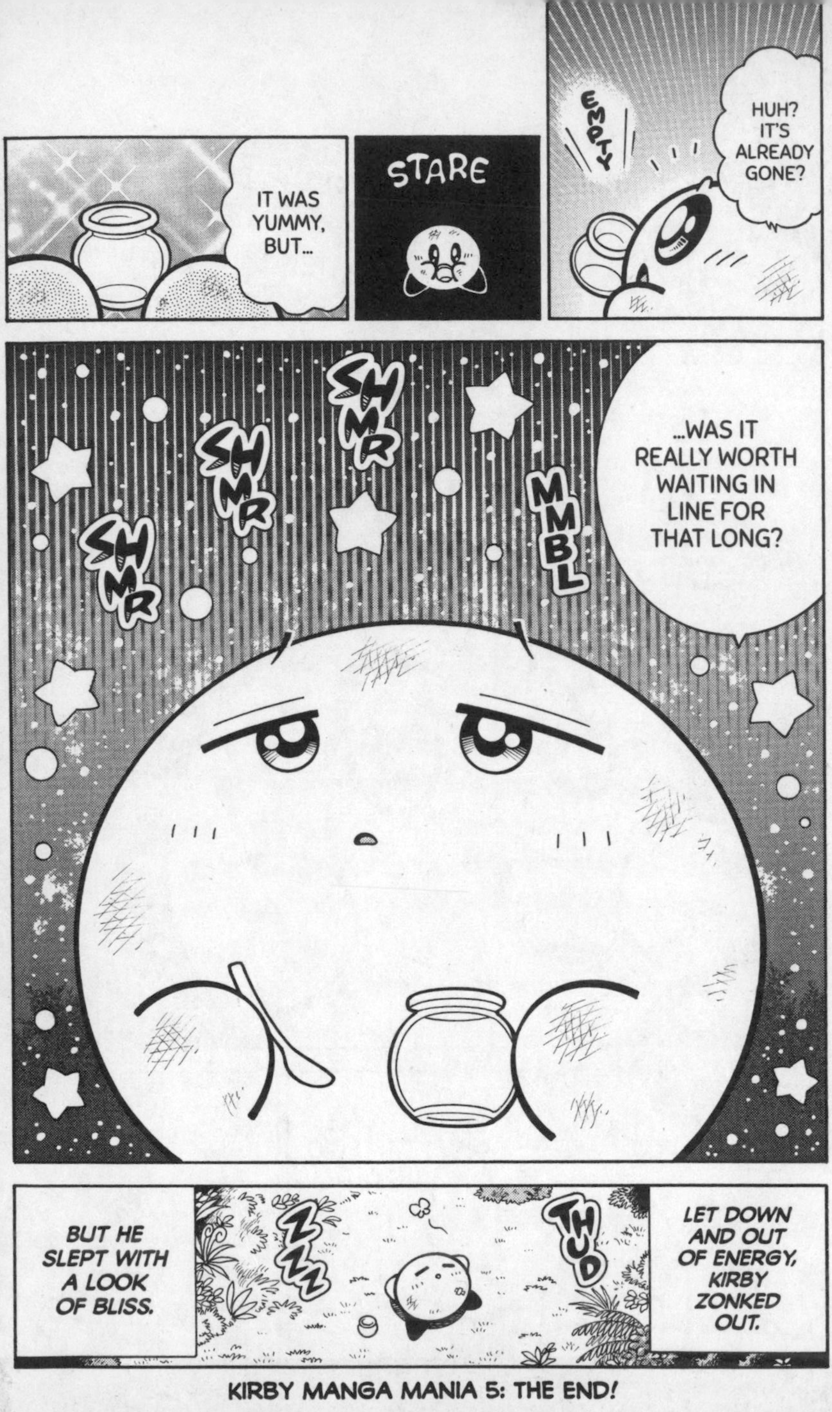
EMPTY
HUH? IT'S ALREADY GONE?
STARE
IT WAS YUMMY, BUT...
...WAS IT REALLY WORTH WAITING IN LINE FOR THAT LONG?
MMBL
SHMR
SHMR
SHMR
LET DOWN AND OUT OF ENERGY, KIRBY ZONKED OUT.
THUD
ZZZ
BUT HE SLEPT WITH A LOOK OF BLISS.

KIRBY MANGA MANIA 5: THE END!

Thank you for reading
Kirby Manga Mania vol. 5.

Gosh, time marches on with no mercy.
I was drawing the brand-new chapters
for a magazine called *Coro Coro Aniki*.
That magazine has now gone digital,
so Kirby has moved from paper to online.
I kinda miss being serialized in a magazine,
but I'll be happy if it gets *Kirby* in
front of even more readers.

The classic chapters in this volume were
once again chosen from across the
original 25-volume run. All chapters, I can
say, receive a passing mark. Even if they
don't leave you doubled over in laughter,
I suspect they'll leave you with fun,
heartwarming, and nostalgic feelings.

See you in the next volume!

HIROKAZU HIKAWA

Kirby Manga Mania Vol. 6 Coming Soon!

I'll steal your heart with laughter.

BWA HA HA HA HA

It's the fifth volume! This one included five new chapters in the front and a bonus chapter at the back. I gave it all I've got to draw them on my own, so please forgive the lousy backgrounds. I hope you enjoyed it!

HIROKAZU HIKAWA

Hirokazu Hikawa was born July 4, 1967, in Aichi Prefecture. He is best known for his manga adaptations of *Bonk* and *Kirby*. In 1987, he won an honorable mention for *Kaisei!! Aozora Kyoushitsu* (Beautiful Day! Outdoor Classroom) at the 14th Fujiko Fujio Awards.

Volume 5
VIZ Media Edition

Story and Art
HIROKAZU HIKAWA

TRANSLATION **Amanda Haley**
ENGLISH ADAPTATION **Jennifer LeBlanc**
TOUCH-UP ART + LETTERING **E.K. Weaver, Jeannie Lee**
DESIGN **Shawn Carrico**
EDITOR **Jennifer LeBlanc**

©Nintendo / HAL Laboratory, Inc.

HOSHINO KIRBY - DEDEDE DE PUPUPU NA MONOGATARI - KESSAKUSEN ZUGOGO HEN
by Hirokazu HIKAWA
© 2021 Hirokazu HIKAWA
All rights reserved.
Original Japanese edition published by SHOGAKUKAN.
English translation rights in the United States of America,
Canada, the United Kingdom, Ireland, Australia
and New Zealand arranged with SHOGAKUKAN.

ORIGINAL COVER DESIGN **SEIKO TSUCHIHASHI [HIVE & CO., LTD.]**

Published by VIZ Media, LLC
P.O. Box 77010
San Francisco, CA 94107

10 9 8 7 6 5 4 3 2 1
First printing, August 2022

viz.com

THIS IS THE LAST PAGE!

Kirby Manga Mania reads from right to left, starting in the upper-right corner. Japanese is read from right to left, meaning that action, sound effects, and word-balloon order are completely reversed from English order.